HOME TEAM

Home Team

*Professional Sports and the
American Metropolis*

Michael N. Danielson

PRINCETON UNIVERSITY PRESS

PRINCETON, NEW JERSEY

Library of Congress Cataloging-in-Publication Data
Danielson, Michael N.
Home team : professional sports and the American
metropolis / Michael N. Danielson.
p.   cm.
Includes bibliographical references (p.   ) and index.
ISBN 0-691-03650-0 (cloth : alk. paper)
1. Sports and state—United States. 2. sports—
United States—Sociological aspects. 3. Sports—
Economic aspects—United States. I. Title
GV706.35.D36   1997
796'.06'9—dc20   96-35200

This book has been composed in Times Roman
Designed by Jan Lilly

Princeton University Press books are printed on
acid-free paper and meet the guidelines for
permanence and durability of the Committee
on Production Guidelines for Book Longevity
of the Council on Library Resources

Printed in the United States of America

2   4   6   8   10   9   7   5   3

For Linda

———

the star of my
home team

Contents

List of Tables

List of Figures

List of Abbreviations

AAFC   All-American Football Conference
ABA   American Basketball Association
ABC   American Broadcasting Company
AFL   American Football League
BAA   Basketball Association of America
CBS   Columbia Broadcasting System
ESPN   Entertainment and Sports Programming Network
FANS   Fight to Advance the Nation's Sports
MLB   Major League Baseball
NBA   National Basketball Association
NBC   National Broadcasting Company
NBL   National Basketball League
NFL   National Football League
NHL   National Hockey League
PCL   Pacific Coast League
USFL   United States Football League
WFL   World Football League
WHA   World Hockey Association

Preface

MUCH AS professional sports combine business and pleasure, this study brings together decades of work on urban development with a lifetime of rooting for various home teams. My teaching, research, and related activities have dealt primarily with the changing fortunes of cities, suburbs, and metropolitan areas, with particular attention to the role of politics and government in an increasingly urban society. The development of professional team sports in the United States and Canada is closely connected with basic urban trends; viable major leagues first emerged in the booming industrial cities of the late nineteenth century; and professional sports spread to cities across the continent as urban growth put more and more places into the big leagues. Professional sports have special connections to urban places, from the names on team jerseys to the close identification of people and places with their home teams. Like other urban businesses, sports teams are affected by changes in the physical setting and accessibility of their locations, by the move of more and more customers to the suburbs, and by shifts in the local political climate. Professional sports have also been strongly influenced by the pervasive competition among places for businesses, a competition in which major league franchises are prized because of the many perceived benefits of having a big league team in town.

The connections between places and professional sports are particularly interesting to a student of urban politics because of expanding public involvement in the sports game. Government provides most of the playing facilities for major league teams and leagues, ever grander arenas and stadiums made available on increasingly favorable terms to teams that constantly ask for more. Professional sports, while insisting that private leagues rather than public laws are the proper means of regulating games, have become a highly political enterprise, seeking public benefits from competing local, state, and provincial jurisdictions and benevolent treatment by national governments. The web of relations between places and major league sports reflect many of the central concerns of urban political analysis: the importance of boosterism and civic pride; competition among jurisdictions; the critical role of higher levels of government in urban politics; the use of special-purpose agencies for major public enterprises like stadiums; the potent influence of economic elites; and the ability of powerful coalitions of business and political leaders to prevail on urban issues involving substantial economic stakes and major land-use changes, issues involving home teams in more and more places in the United States and Canada.

My first home team was the Brooklyn Dodgers, an inherited allegiance from my father, who grew up in Chicago rooting for the White Sox and transferred his loyalties after he moved to New York and settled initially in the large Scandinavian community in the Bay Ridge section of Brooklyn. My dad was a knowledgeable sports fan and an accomplished athlete who pitched success-fully well into his forties in top local softball leagues; and I learned a great deal from him about playing games and following big league sports. During my boyhood on Staten Island, at the time a remote appendage of New York City, team loyalties were a prime form of identification among young males. One did not have to preface "team" with "baseball" in a discussion of sports alle-giances during the 1940s; baseball was the only game in town that forged close emotional ties for most of us. Red Barber brought the games into the living room on the big Zenith radio; trips to Ebbets Field were special events, with an occasional foray into enemy territory at the Polo Grounds and Yankee Sta-dium. Score was kept at the ballpark and old scorecards saved (but not long enough to be valuable); box scores clipped and pasted in scrapbooks (and forgotten); and a few mathematical skills precociously developed so that bat-ting averages could be calculated to three decimal places and the intricacies of the earned-run average mastered.

Other home teams entered the picture after World War II, although none had the same claim on my loyalties as baseball. Interest in basketball began with the placement of a team in New York by the newly organized Basketball Asso-ciation of America in 1946, a season most memorable for sitting courtside at the 69th Street Regiment Armory, where the Knicks played home games when more important events like the circus or dog show were booked into Madison Square Garden. Rangers' hockey games at the Garden were an adventure dur-ing high school, involving an hour-and-a half trip on bus, ferry, and subway to mid-Manhattan, where students could purchase balcony seats for half price, and were afforded a view of only two-thirds of the ice, which gradually faded as the rising smoke of thousands of cigars and cigarettes enveloped the distant players in a blue haze.

Like hundreds of thousands of other fans, I was forsaken by my home team. My last visit to Ebbets Field was during the Dodgers' final season; the neigh-borhood was a bit shabbier, but the grass was as startlingly green as ever. Our usher was a diehard Brooklynite, convinced despite the rumors of possible departure that "they ain't going nowhere 'cause they're the *Brooklyn* Dodgers." But the Brooklyn Dodgers became the Los Angeles Dodgers, following in the footsteps of the Braves, Athletics, and Browns, dragging along the Giants, and changing forever the way we think about the home team. Once the Dodgers were gone, loyalties to place turned out to be stronger than to team; one game in Los Angeles was enough to underscore that these Dodgers were not my home team. So loyalties were transferred to a new home team when the New York Mets took the field in 1962, which also offered the dubious opportunity of rooting for an expansion team, one that lost more games during that inaugural year than any club in major league history

Baseball has remained my prime home team loyalty, although there was a period when the Giants loomed sufficiently large to prompt the purchase of season tickets when the franchise moved to New Jersey, but interest flagged, especially when December winds whistled through Giants Stadium. Knicks games were more fun when tickets were cheaper and easier to get; and the Rangers, like hockey more generally for most sports fans in the United States, have never been a major rooting interest. Rival leagues and relocated teams also have been part of the New York picture, but the Jets and the American Football League, the Nets and the American Basketball Association, and the NHL's Devils from Denver were never serious contestants for affection in a metropolis that already offered the Giants, Knicks, and Rangers as the real home teams.

Thoughts of combining these urban and sports interests into something more than an occasional example in a course or seminar took a more serious turn about a decade ago. Initially, these interests focused on college sports, a product of my involvement for a number of years as the faculty advisor to Princeton's basketball team, and collaborative research was discussed with my friend and former colleague, Henry Bienen, who is now the president of Northwestern University, where he has more than intellectual interest in the complex problems of big-time intercollegiate athletics. The project that led to this book finally advanced beyond the interesting possibility category five years ago, when a decision was made to offer an undergraduate policy task force on cities and professional sports at Princeton University

The task force on cities and major league sports examined a wide range of topics during the spring of 1992, including existing leagues, new leagues, expansion, franchise moves, ownership policies, stadium development, marketing, labor relations, antitrust, Congress, and television. We discussed these issues in Princeton with Herbert Belgrade, chairman of the Maryland Stadium Authority; the late Howard Cosell of ABC Sports; Arthur T. Johnson, professor of public administration at the University of Maryland-Baltimore County; Bowie Kuhn, the former commissioner of baseball; and Robert Mulcahy, executive director of the New Jersey Sports and Exposition Authority. At the end of the semester, the task force was the guest of the Maryland Stadium Authority for a game at the newly opened Camden Yards, at which time the members had an opportunity to discuss their findings with Larry Luchino, president of the Baltimore Orioles. I enjoyed immensely working with the group of eleven students: seniors Michael Goldberg and Daniel Mach, who prepared the findings and recommendations, and the juniors who did most of the work: Katherine T. Doyle, Eben Garnett, Paul L. McDonald, David Menschel, Derek Sean Milan, Mary Catherine Saidla, Marc Sole, Clinton R. Uhlir, and Damon Watson. Their enthusiasm, energy, intelligence, and good sense underscored the pleasures of teaching in the Woodrow Wilson School's undergraduate program, as well as why directing this program has been a most enjoyable assignment over the past six years.

The book that grew out of these beginnings is aimed at the general reader, as well as those interested in urban development, the political economy of sports, and public policy. It is informed by the work of specialists in a number of fields, including my areas of political science and urban studies, as well as economics, geography, history, law, political science, sociology, and urban studies. Extensive use is made of the writings of the legion of journalists who have covered professional teams since the organization of the first leagues in the 1870s, work which increasingly has focused on the business of professional sports, the connections of teams to places, and the enlarging role of government in supporting big league teams in the United States and Canada. Although illustrative material is drawn from the four major professional team sports and many of the places where big league teams play, the analysis is broadly based rather than focused on a few case studies. The goal is to understand the complex connections between places and major league sports, and to assess the implications of growing public investments in home teams.

Many people have helped with this project. Leigh Bienen, a good friend and administrative director of the School's undergraduate program, was enthusiastic about the sports task force and insured that various support mechanisms were in place. Ingrid Reed, at the time assistant dean of the Woodrow Wilson School, put her formidable energies and contacts to work in organizing the arrangements for the task force guests. Laird Klingler, the librarian at the Woodrow Wilson School, was, as always, extremely helpful; particularly appreciated was his wizardry with electronic information retrieval and his cheerful handling of the substantial amount of material that was borrowed on interlibrary loan. Ellen Kemp, the computer manager at the Woodrow Wilson School, was supportive throughout, providing needed software, computer upgrades, and help with the inevitable glitches and crashes. Various staff members at the Woodrow Wilson School copied all sorts of materials, which was a life saver during months my mobility was limited following back surgeries.

Patricia Trinity, valued friend and colleague, shepherded the production of this manuscript from its beginnings, oversaw the research assistants who have worked on the project, tracked down various pieces of information, and otherwise was as indispensable in helping with this project as she is in managing the Center of Domestic and Comparative Policy Studies at the Woodrow Wilson School, which I direct.

Research support came from the Woodrow Wilson School during the tenures of Deans Henry Bienen and Michael Rothschild; and from Princeton's Center for Domestic and Comparative Policy Studies, with funds for urban policy studies made available through the generosity of the Garfield Foundation. The ready availability of Lexis/Nexis at the Woodrow Wilson School was enormously helpful in this research, as were other electronic data bases accessible through the University's computer facilities. Newspaper references throughout, with the exception of the *New York Times, Newark Star-Ledger*, and *Trenton Times*, are from material retrieved electronically, and page numbers are not used for any newspaper references.

Over the duration of the project, I was helped with the research by a number of graduate and undergraduate assistants who combined a love of sports with a readiness to search data bases and card catalogs, and to dig into mountains of materials. Much of the final preparation of the data, tables, and figures was undertaken by Adam Shrager, a graduate student in politics who combines an interest in urban politics with work in demography. Detailed case studies on Detroit, Tampa-St. Petersburg, and Washington were skillfully pulled together by Gregory Stankiewicz, a Ph.D. candidate in public policy who is working on the impact of tax revolts on cities and social programs. Kevin D. Skillin was my undergraduate research assistant for the past three years; Kevin did extensive bibliographic work and reviewed a formidable set of congressional hearings for information relevant to the connections between cities and the major leagues. Other undergraduate research assistants who worked on the project at various stages of development were James Govert, Kevin Hudson, Jeffrey Kreisler, Robert G. Marks, and Clinton Uhlir.

A number of friends and colleagues at Princeton were helpful in one way or another. Julian Wolpert pointed me in the right direction in tracking down the contribution of geography to the study of sport. Jameson W. Doig suggested the parallels between professional sports and ports in terms of cooperation among cities within a competitive framework. Conversations with Gene Grossman have helped sharpen my thinking about the economic dimensions of professional sports. And Hal Feiveson always helps me adjust my New Yorker's view of the sporting world with the perspective that only a Cubs' fan can bring to those wonderful bonds we forge with the home team, even if home has been somewhere else for a long time.

Walter Lippincott, editor and director of Princeton University Press, has been enthusiastic about the project since our initial discussion in the summer of 1993, and it has been a pleasure to work with Walter and his associates from start to finish. Margaret Case at the Press edited the manuscript with skill and sympathy during a hectic couple of weeks in the summer of 1996. Among the various comments on the manuscript, particularly helpful were the suggestions of Steven A. Riess, professor of history at Northern Illinois University, whose work covers similar ground from a more historical perspective.

Responsibility for what is between the covers is mine, which is daunting considering the amount of information about four sports, a dozen leagues, forty-odd metropolitan areas, and over a hundred teams that will be subject to the scrutiny of those eagle-eyed sports fans who read on.

HOME TEAM

1

Places to Play

ON November 6, 1995, Arthur Modell, the owner of the Cleveland Browns, announced that he was moving his football team to Baltimore. The Browns had played in Cleveland for fifty seasons, initially in the All-American Football Conference, a new league organized after World War II, and in the National Football League following the merger of the two leagues in 1949. The Browns were immensely popular in Cleveland and its environs, filling Municipal Stadium with over seventy thousand fans game after game. Modell had owned the Browns for more than thirty years, was a staunch defender of franchise stability, and had become a pillar of civic life in Cleveland since buying the team. Cleveland reacted with shock and anger. Modell was vilified in the press, on talk radio, and at rallies; fans hanged Modell in effigy and a few even threatened his life. Advertisers removed their messages from Municipal Stadium and otherwise distanced themselves from the pariah owner and his team. Politicians went to court to force the Browns to honor their stadium lease, demanded that the National Football League keep the Browns in Cleveland, and beseeched Congress for help in preventing footloose teams from jilting their fans and cities.

Flanking Modell on the podium when the move was announced in Baltimore was Governor Parris Glendening of Maryland, basking in the glory of victory in the long quest to replace the beloved Baltimore Colts, a team that had been moved to Indianapolis in 1984. In the years following the departure of the Colts, city and state officials had wooed seven NFL teams, and vigorously competed for one of the expansion franchises that took the field in 1995. Maryland had created a state stadium agency, dedicated lottery funds for sports facilities, built the Baltimore Orioles a dazzling new ballpark, and promised a state-of-the art football stadium under terms that grew more favorable with each setback. Finally, the Maryland Stadium Authority made an offer that Modell could not resist—$65 million up front, a new stadium rent free, and bountiful revenues from luxury seating, concessions, and advertising.

What began in November in Baltimore ended three months later when the National Football League negotiated a settlement that permitted Modell to move his team, but promised Cleveland a replacement team by 1999, provided the city built a new sports palace to replace its obsolete Municipal Stadium. Cleveland would retain the Browns' name and colors for its new team, along with a $12 million indemnification and league help in financing the new stadium. Maryland dropped its $36 million antitrust lawsuit against the NFL, filed after the league delayed action on the relocation of the team, and Cleveland shelved its legal campaign to prevent the Browns from leaving. Modell looked to a bright financial future in Baltimore, with anticipated revenues in his new home town far exceeding the team's income in Cleveland.

Relocating the Browns was an especially dramatic episode in a continuing saga of change in the places where major league teams play in the United States and Canada. Shortly after Modell dropped his bombshell, the owner of the Houston Oilers was in Nashville, side by side with a beaming mayor, to declare that he was moving his team to the Tennessee city after thirty-five years in Houston. A year before these announced moves, both the Rams and Raiders had departed from the Los Angeles area. The Rams, who had come to Los Angeles from Cleveland in 1946 and then moved within Southern California to Anaheim, were transferred to St. Louis, which in 1988 had lost to Phoenix its NFL Cardinals, a team that had relocated to St. Louis from Chicago in 1960. The Raiders, who had moved from Oakland to replace the Rams in the Los Angeles Coliseum, went back to Oakland. The flight of the Rams and Raiders left the NFL without a franchise in the second largest metropolitan area, a situation that tempted a number of teams who were attracted by the size of the Los Angeles market and dissatisfied with their current stadiums, leases, and revenues. While the NFL was wrestling with the Browns' move, the owner of the Seattle Seahawks decided to break his lease at the King Dome and shift his team to Los Angeles. Seattle, which had already lost one baseball team and barely managed to keep the Mariners, responded with legal action, political threats, demands that the NFL not abandon the Pacific Northwest, and a frenzied search for a buyer who would keep the team in town.

This ongoing game of musical chairs is part of the complicated relationship between professional team sports and the cities and metropolitan areas where all the big league teams in the United States and Canada are located. Connections between places and the major leagues have multiplied in the wake of the explosive growth of professional sports over the past half century. The number of teams has increased dramatically, from 46 in 1950 to 113 in 1996. More teams has meant that more places are represented in the big leagues: 43 metropolitan areas had teams in 1996, compared with 22 in 1950. Underlying this expansion has been the popularity of professional team sports. Attendance at major league sporting events has risen sharply since 1960, from fewer than 28 million to 120 million in 1994.[1] Television audiences have grown even faster, with national networks, local stations, and cable outlets broadcasting an ever richer menu of games. Revenues of professional teams and leagues have expanded rapidly, as has demand and prices for major league franchises. In the process, teams have become more valuable assets to localities, which have invested growing amounts of public funds in sports facilities in order to secure a place in the big leagues.

Professional team sports also have a special connection with places. More than most forms of entertainment, sports teams engage loyalty. For professional sports, these attachments usually are communally based; most people root for the home team. As a result, professional team sports are an important connection between people and the places where they live. These bonds are collective, since large numbers of people in a city or metropolitan area or region root for the same team. They are reinforced by the preoccupation of local sports pages, television news, and talk radio with the home team. Because of the close identification between people, places, and teams, professional sports is a distinctive business, one that is valued for more than its entertainment value or place in the local economy. Threats by a sports team to depart are different from those of a sausage factory or insurance company; and efforts to retain or attract a big league team typically involve public subsidies far greater than would be lavished on an ordinary business of the same size.

This study examines the connections between major league sports and the places where professional teams play, the cities and other urban locales that attach their names, their hearts, and increasing amounts of their tax revenues to big league teams. Urban settings have been essential to professional sports since the organization of the first baseball leagues in the 1870s. Cities, later metropolitan areas, and today broader urban regions aggregate the people and wealth necessary to sustain professional sports. Just as important, these places provide the primary attachment to teams, the locus of most of a team's fans, customers, viewers, and listeners. Teams in turn offer a common cause for diverse and increasingly far-flung urban dwellers, as well as confirmation that a place belongs in the ranks of big league metropolises.

Professional teams are located in particular places, and leagues seek to have franchises in the most attractive locales. "Sport," argues John Bale, a geographer, "is a world of hierarchy and territoriality."[2] Hierarchy in this context refers to the size of places, a critical factor in determining the location of major league teams. Territoriality deals with the area in which a team operates, usually with exclusive rights conferred by a league. A team's location sets the size of its market for paying customers and local broadcast revenues, and the locations of teams strongly influence a league's appeal to national broadcasters and advertisers.

The concern here is with the major professional team sports—baseball, basketball, football, and hockey—played in the United States and Canada. These enterprises share a number of important characteristics. Each sport is based on privately owned teams organized into leagues that are collective enterprises of the member franchises.[3] Teams and leagues have generally similar arrangements with players, broadcasters, and governments that provide arenas and stadiums; and all major league teams are based in particular places.

Considerable variations also exist among the four sports. Baseball plays ten times as many regular season games as football—162 compared with 16—and twice as many as basketball and hockey, which have 82-game schedules. Differences in the number of games, size of arenas and stadiums, and proportion of seats filled produce substantial variations in attendance among the four sports. Labor requirements range from NFL squads that numbered forty-five active players in 1996, to twenty-five in baseball, twenty-two in hockey, and thirteen in basketball. The NFL has the most lucrative television contracts and shares these revenues equally among its teams; the NHL earns the least from television and shares the fewest revenues. Largely because of the league's national television contracts, NFL franchises were estimated in 1996 to be worth considerably more than the other sports, with an average value of $174 million compared to $127 million for basketball teams, $115 million for baseball franchises, and $74 million for hockey clubs.[4]

Baseball, basketball, football, and hockey have different histories and places in popular culture. Baseball was the first professional team sport to win wide popular appeal: the precursors of major league baseball were organized in the 1870s. During its first half century, baseball, as one its historians notes, was "in the enviable position of having no serious competition from other commercialized sports."[5] Professional football and hockey leagues did not achieve relative stability until the 1930s, and basketball reached the same stage only after World War II. Baseball's dominant position has steadily eroded in the second half of the twentieth century. From 1960 to 1993, its share of major league attendance dropped from 73 percent to 58 percent. Professional football surpassed baseball as the nation's premier professional sport in the 1970s, at least as measured by broadcast audiences and polls. Professional basketball has been on a fast track for more than a decade. More than baseball or football, professional basketball appeals to young people; its pace and intensity are in tune with popular culture at the end of the twentieth century. Hockey is clearly the least popular of the major professional team sports; it is a Canadian game with limited appeal in the United States.

In examining connections between places and professional team sports, the concern is with places where teams play or want to play, as well as places that seek big league teams. The focus here is with places where major league teams are located for championship play. Places where teams prepare for the major league season are beyond the scope of this study, as are places that host minor league teams. Professional team sports outside the United States and Canada are not examined, nor is Canada's version of professional football.

Home Teams

Major league teams are based in particular places. Most of these places are in the United States, which in 1996 had 103 of the 113 teams in the four major leagues.[6] The other ten franchises were in Canada: Montreal and Toronto in baseball, Toronto and Vancouver in basketball, and six Canadian teams in the National Hockey League. All places with teams are within metropolitan areas, in either the central city or the suburbs.[7] With few exceptions, teams are based in one place, as were all major league clubs in 1996. Three regional franchises have in the past operated in the American Basketball Association: the Carolina Cougars divided home games among Greensboro, Raleigh, and Charlotte; the Virginia Squires played in Hampton, Norfolk, Richmond, and Roanoke; and a team played in Jacksonville, Tampa, and West Palm Beach as well as at its principal base in Miami. For the 1972 and 1973 seasons, the National Basketball Association had a franchise that divided its games between Kansas City and Omaha and was known as the Kansas City-Omaha Kings.

Most teams play all their home games in one place during the regular season. A notable exception was football's Green Bay Packers, which regularly scheduled some home games in Milwaukee from 1933 to 1994. A few NBA teams also have staged home games in other cities. The Boston Celtics usually play a few games in Hartford, and the NBA's most stellar individual performance, Wilt Chamberlain's 100-point game, occurred in Hershey, Pennsylvania, where the Philadelphia Warriors scheduled an occasional game. Teams considering relocation have played elsewhere to test the waters or enhance their bargaining position with their home town. The Chicago White Sox scheduled games in Milwaukee, which was eager to get back in the big leagues following the departure of the Braves to Atlanta. The Brooklyn Dodgers played a few games across the Hudson River in Jersey City as part of the complicated maneuvering that preceded the team's move to Los Angeles. And the Minneapolis Lakers auditioned in Los Angeles during the season before the team relocated to the west coast.

In the early 1990s, the National Hockey League scheduled regular season games in cities that did not have a team in the league. The NHL hoped to demonstrate to broadcasters hockey's widening appeal, as well as gauge interest in places where the league might expand. The venture was not particularly successful. The Toronto Maple Leafs and Ottawa Senators played to a half-empty arena in Hamilton, Ontario, where fans were not thrilled to watch a game involving Ottawa, which had recently beat out Hamilton for an expansion franchise. A game scheduled for Birmingham, Alabama, was canceled after only 1,400 tickets were sold in an arena seating 17,000. The NHL's experience underscores why professional teams play the overwhelming majority of their home games in one place. Home is where the home team's fans are; representing a particular place provides teams with a base of support.

From the start, professional sports teams identified closely with the places were they played. William A. Hulbert, a Chicago businessman whose White Stockings were charter members of the National League in 1876, "never spoke of what *he* would do, or what his *club* would do, but it was always what *Chicago* would do."[8] Capitalizing on community pride and loyalty has always been good business for professional teams. Civic spirit was demonstrated by supporting the home team, especially by buying tickets. Cities, for their part, embraced sports teams as a means of promoting place interests. Having a team marked a city as being in the big leagues, while not having one meant a place was minor league or bush league.

Professional teams not only represented cities, they became symbols of the places where they played—what Gregory P. Stone terms "collective representations," the "objectification and representation of the community, sustained in communication to which communities owe their persistence beyond the lifetime of their members."[9] One manifestation is in team names derived from the community. The name of the Dodgers came from the tag of "trolley dodgers" for Brooklyn's inhabitants in a city crisscrossed by streetcar lines. The Boston Celtics celebrated the city's Irish heritage, and the Minnesota Vikings the Scandinavians of the upper midwest. The 76ers of Philadelphia and 49ers of San Francisco capture critical dates in the history of their cities, whereas Montreal's Canadiens and Toronto's Maple Leafs signify the essence of French and English Canada. And the Steelers and Brewers proclaim the products that made Pittsburgh and Milwaukee famous.

The symbolic role of professional teams distinguishes them from most other enterprises that bear a city's name. People connect with places through their identification with teams. As Bale notes, "sport is one of the few things that binds people to place simply through ascription."[10] Perhaps nowhere was this bond stronger than in Brooklyn, whose municipal status was lost in 1898 through merger with New York City. The baseball team sustained Brooklyn's identity despite the loss of its municipal autonomy; the Dodgers meant Brooklyn was in the big leagues. The intensity of the feelings fostered by these connections between places and teams makes professional sports special; like other teams, "the Dodgers were more than a business. They represented a cultural totem, a tangible symbol of the community and its values."[11]

Teams also represent places in competition with other localities; they personify, intensify, and create rivalries between cities. Rivalries among places are rooted in the pervasive competition for economic development and political favor; they are fueled by boosterism, the civic religion of being bigger and thus better than rival places. Professional sports capitalized on these rivalries, regularizing them with fixed schedules, pennant races, and championship games. Teams both took advantage of existing rivalries and fostered new ones as they sought more customers for the home team. "Determining urban supremacy in terms of population growth, community leadership, or quality of life might be difficult," Benjamin Rader points out, "but baseball games offered an unambiguous test of urban supremacy in the form of a symbolic contest."[12] A glance at the standings on the sports page indicated where the home town placed in this surrogate competition for first place among America's cities.

Hometown Fans

Fans are the most committed followers of professional sports; they provide the essential customer base, both for attendance at games and broadcasts. Most fans live or have lived in the area where their team is located. They root for teams that bear the hometown's name, and for players that play for the home team. In the early days of team sports, these loyalties were reinforced by players who were hometown boys. Professionalization, however, quickly led to recruitment of the best players without regard to where they lived; and critics questioned the loyalties of places to teams manned by mercenaries who were paid to play for the home team. "Local patriotism, as manifested in baseball," the *New York Times* argued in 1907, "is a strange, irrational pastime. The crowd of local patriots have no hesitation in violently applauding this season as a native the same player whom last year they violently hissed as an alien enemy."[13] What the *Times'* argument underscores is the reality that the locality of teams rather than players is what matters for most people who follow professional sports. As a result, loyalties to teams are not significantly affected by players coming and going in trades, by free-agent signings and departures, or by rookies making the team and veterans retiring.

Rooting for the home team is both an individual and collective experience. The individual fan is part of a group with similar interests; Allen Guttmann terms this shared experience "representational sport" in which "individual identification with the athletes and collective membership in the community combine."[14] Because supporting the local team is a collective experience shared by substantial numbers of people, professional team sports are an instrument of social and political integration. Sport, as Janet Lever notes, provides people with "common symbols, a collective identity, and a reason for solidarity,"[15] not to mention something to talk about. Successful home teams enhance civic pride; fans who chant "we're number one" are trumpeting the superiority of both their team and their town. In rallying around the home team, people identify more closely with a broader civic framework in the spatially, socially, and politically fragmented metropolis.

Collective experiences are complicated when more than one team represents the same city or metropolitan area. In such situations, loyalties often are divided along geographical lines. The three baseball teams in New York before 1957 were located in different boroughs, as were many of their fans. In Chicago, the Cubs' primary base of support has been on the north side of the city and its hinterland, whereas the White Sox have drawn their fans largely from the southern half of the metropolitan area. The New York area's three hockey teams are spread among Long Island, New York City, and northern New Jersey. San Francisco Bay separates the San Francisco Giants and Oakland Athletics and their fans, as well as the 49ers and Raiders and their backers. In other places, fan and civic support has tended to gravitate toward the stronger club. In Philadelphia, notes Bruce Kuklick, "the Phillies, a persistently poor club, were a distinctly secondary consideration for Philadelphia rooters. The A's were the city's team."[16] And when the Phillies won a pennant in 1950, they displaced the Athletics as the city's team; soon they were the city's only team, when the A's departed for Kansas City in 1955.

Shared experiences in rooting for the home team vary among sports. Baseball, it is frequently claimed, fosters closer communal ties than other sports. Rader suggests that "professional football had never engendered quite the same sense of community as baseball, and television further undermined its capacity to encourage rootedness. . . . Television quickly transformed football games into national spectacles."[17] Rootedness, collective experiences, and community loyalty are difficult to assess. Certainly professional baseball has had more time to sink roots and develop attachments than football, basketball, or hockey. Baseball took root during a period of rapid urban growth and change, a time when cities were seeking means of identification and integration. Baseball also has the longest season; teams play almost every day from April to October, so there are more games to attend and watch and read about and thus more opportunities to connect teams and the places where they play. Still, the notion that baseball has a unique impact on places is dubious. Washington's two failed baseball teams never brought the nation's capital together in the way that the Washington Redskins have for decades. Winning, of course, helps explains the stronger attachments to the often successful Redskins compared with the usually hapless Senators. But in Pittsburgh, where both the Pirates and Steelers frequently fielded winners since 1970, the football team has fostered considerably more communal loyalty than the baseball franchise.

Emotional attachment to home teams underlies the intensity of many issues involving major league sports and place, particularly the question of franchise movement. Losing the home team is a wrenching experience for fans in a particular locale; and critics argue that franchise moves have undermined home-team loyalties more generally. John F. Rooney, Jr., contends that franchise movements caused "extreme dislocation of fan-team relationships"; William Baker thinks baseball's "franchise shifts . . . severed the ties of local loyalty, a traditional strength of the game"; and David A. Karp and William C. Yoels question whether "sport is today as potent a basis for community identification as during earlier decades" before franchise shifts, expansion, and the organization of new leagues.[18]

Hometown loyalties, of course, do not disappear when teams move; instead connections are established between a relocated team and its new hometown. Similarly, expansion and new leagues increase the number of places that have teams and thus the number of communities that benefit from loyalties inspired by professional sports teams. Traditionalists, however, contend that loyalties in new places are different from the connections engendered by sixteen baseball teams playing in ten cities for a half century or more. Those who root for teams that began elsewhere supposedly are not the same as the fans left behind; and the horde of expansion teams does not generate the same kind of community feeling as "real" fans in the "real" major leagues. According to Rader, "casual spectators replaced fierce partisans . . . in the stands of many sporting events" in places like Anaheim and Kansas City.[19]

Again, intensity and loyalty are difficult to measure, especially when the present is being compared to a past often seen through rose-colored glasses. One measure of fan support is attendance, and there is no significant difference in attendance in recent years between older and newer locales; in 1991, the ten baseball teams that have been in the same city since 1903 averaged 2.13 million fans, compared to 2.10 million for the sixteen teams that arrived in their present location after 1953. Smaller proportions of intensely partisan fans result in part from basic changes in the marketing of professional sports in old and new venues, as teams have sought to expand their customer base by attracting businesses, families, and females. Less intense attachments to home teams also reflects changes in the mobility and interests of the population more generally rather than whether a place had a team before or after the explosion of professional leagues. Everything changes, not just the name of the city attached to the Athletics or Colts or Lakers. Most sports fan adapt to change, like supporters of the departed Dodgers and Giants who switched their loyalty to the expansion Mets; and large numbers of people have welcomed changes that have given them home teams in Atlanta, Charlotte, Houston, Phoenix, Seattle, and all the other places that were outside the pale of major league sports in 1950.

Home Team Advantage

Place also affects the outcomes of professional sporting events. More games are won at home than on the road by good, average, and bad teams. Barry Schwartz and Stephen F. Barsky found that home teams won 53 percent of baseball games, 55 percent in football, and 64 percent of hockey games during the 1971 season.[20] Home team advantage is relatively consistent over time; and home teams enjoy an even greater advantage in postseason play. For the most successful teams in basketball, football, and hockey, the regular season is primarily a quest for home court, field, or ice advantage during the playoffs, which goes to the team with the best record.[21]

That teams play better at home is not surprising. Home games provide a familiar place in terms of playing surface, lights, weather, and other peculiarities of a particular stadium or arena. Players presumably are more comfortable when they play at home than when on the road; they live in familiar surroundings and are less fatigued by travel and time differences. Home games are played in front of a team's supporters, whose vocal support encourages the home team and creates an unfriendly, even hostile, environment for opponents and officials. Electronic scoreboards in many arenas and stadiums urge hometown fans to make more noise when the opposing team is on the foul line or in the huddle or when an official has ruled against the home team. Crowd effects are most intense in the confined spaces of indoor arenas; "NBA crowds," notes a sportswriter, have "the effect of mob intimidation on visitors and officials alike."[22]

Schwartz and Barsky argue that fan support is the principal source of the home team's advantage. In their analysis, "home advantage is largely traceable to superior offensive performances," which "are precisely the kind of activities most likely to elicit the approval of a friendly audience."[23] Community support is also identified as the critical factor in home-team advantage by Mark S. Mizruchi in a study of the 1981–1982 NBA season. Mizruchi concludes that differences among teams result primarily from the intensity of local commitment and identification, with the most successful home teams operating in smaller metropolitan areas (where they are more highly valued), playing in older and smaller arenas, and having a long association with the community.[24] Professional sports figures agree that fans make the difference; "the home field advantage," NFL Commissioner Pete Rozelle told a congressional committee in 1972, "is essentially no more than . . . the crowd."[25]

The fact that teams do better at home raises the question of whether some locations are better places to play than others. A good deal of folklore exists about good sports towns and bad ones, baseball or football cities, lively and dead hometown crowds. Merlin Olsen, a sportscaster who played for the Rams, calls Los Angeles "a city of spectators, not fans."[26] The NFL's Cardinals failed to develop the same kind of support in St. Louis as the baseball Cardinals, a player explained, because "we're a football team in a baseball town."[27] Moving beyond folklore is difficult. Two commonly used measures of local support, attendance and television audiences, are affected by the size of the market area and by the performance of the team, and attendance is also influenced by the capacity of arenas and stadiums. Another way to shed light on good and bad places to play is hometown advantage. To the degree that home advantage results from local support, teams with higher than average home advantage presumably are located in better places to play. And good sports towns should have higher than average home team advantages for each of their major league teams. As indicated in Table 1.1, home team advantage varies substantially around league norms, but only Denver was a markedly

*Table 1.1   Hometown Advantage Index by Sport in Metropolitan Areas
with Two or More Teams: 1990–1993*

Metropolitan Area	MLB	NBA	NFL	NHL	Mean
Denver	119	112	114	–	115
Atlanta	98	100	127	–	108
Tampa	–	–	117	91	104
Pittsburgh	101	–	111	99	104
St. Louis	106	–	–	101	103
Houston	107	95	106	–	103
Seattle	104	97	103	–	101
Philadelphia	104	101	97	103	101
Cleveland	104	103	96	–	101
Detroit	101	101	103	98	101
Phoenix	–	96	105	–	101
San Francisco-Oakland-San Jose	102	95	93	110	100
New York	104	97	94	102	99
Toronto	92	–	–	106	99
Minneapolis	100	104	90	101	99
Washington-Baltimore	98	105	99	91	98
Dallas	105	98	94	96	98
Boston	105	98	93	97	98
Los Angeles	101	99	96	96	98
Chicago	100	90	100	95	96
Miami	99	108	97	80	96

INDEX = 100 for average league home team advantage; home team advantage is calculated by
dividing home wins by total wins.

better place to play across the board during the early 1990s. This suggests that
good places to play are sport-specific, or that a better measurement is needed,
or perhaps that altitude has a disproportionate adverse affect on the performance of visiting teams in the Mile High City.

Expanding the Realm

Connections between professional teams and places have to be considered in
the context of the rapidly expanding reach of most teams. Before World War
II, ballparks and arenas were located in cities and almost all of the customers
were city dwellers. With the accelerating diffusion of urban growth, teams'
turf expanded beyond the city limits; thus, the Chicago of the Bears encompassed the city and its spreading suburbs. Radio, television, and interstate
highways further extended these spatial networks; the Red Sox, for example,
drew listeners, viewers, and customers from all of New England. Network
television broadcasts broadened the followings of teams; the Dallas Cowboys
became America's team, and the Miami Dolphins, Pittsburgh Steelers, and
Oakland Raiders developed national followings. National cable networks did
the same for the Atlanta Braves and Chicago Cubs. Sports advertising, once

primarily local and aimed at hometown fans, became dominated by major corporations seeking national markets for their beer, automobiles, and sneakers. Increasingly aggressive marketing has spread team apparel across the country and beyond, with the home team often abandoned in favor of teams with attractive clothing, fashionable colors, and jazzy logos.

None of these developments, however, has severed the connections between professional teams and the places where they play. Despite their extensive national television following, the Braves and the Cubs draw most of their paying customers from Atlanta and Chicago and adjacent areas. Spatial rather than electronic connections continue to frame what Rooney terms the "fan region . . . the geographical area which identifies with a given team."[28] Fan regions remain the base of fan support, ticket buyers, listeners, and viewers for all professional teams. But these regions are both more extensive than ever before and generate a declining share of team revenues as national television and marketing income increases.

Games, Places, and Politics

Another critical change in the relationship between places and professional sports has been increased government involvement. Historically, as Steven A. Riess points out, professional sports had "three main elements: spectators, owners, and players."[29] Governments got into the game primarily because places began building arenas and stadiums for big league teams. Professional sports, which for decades had fended off government interference, found that places were willing to assume an increasing share of the costs of facilities that once had been borne wholly by teams. Almost every stadium and most arenas built over the past half century have been financed with public funds; and these facilities have been offered to teams under ever more favorable terms.

Franchise shifts, expansion, and conflicts between leagues have further entangled government in professional sports. Public officials have been involved in efforts to lure teams and block their departure, to persuade leagues to expand to a particular city, and to insure that league mergers protected the interests of this or that place. Rapid urban growth in the south and west generated political pressures from a lengthening list of places for relocation of franchises and expansion of leagues. The spread of metropolitan areas spurred suburban interest in housing major league teams. Members of Congress have introduced legislation to undo franchise shifts, regulate team movement, and insure league control over relocation. Federal and state courts have grappled with efforts to block teams from moving and to prevent leagues from abandoning places with teams.

These public actions and political conflicts are shaped by the intensity of the connections between places and professional sports, by the identification of places with their teams, and by bonding of fans to the home team. Politicians recognize that attachments to teams are emotional, visible, and usually intense. Public officials and business leaders value major league teams as instruments of economic development and affirmations of the importance of their city or metropolitan area. The possible move of a professional team is bigger news, attracts more political attention, causes more public concern than the moves of far larger businesses that leave town, and prompts greater readiness to spend tax dollars to prevent the move. Public provision of sports facilities has further broadened the scope and increased the stakes of sports issues. With public arenas and stadiums have come conflicts over the desirability, location, and financing of sports projects, as well as wrangles among and within governments over control of sports agencies and their lucrative contracts and jobs.

Connections between Places and Teams

The remaining chapters analyze the relationships between places and professional team sports, seeking to understand why teams and leagues are where they are, why places invest so much in teams, and who wins and loses in the politics of professional sports. Urbanization is a key factor in the analysis. The forces of urban growth and change have largely determined the location of teams, spatial structure of leagues, franchise shifts, and league expansion. Professional teams are where the people are—in big cities, larger metropolitan areas, and major television markets. Teams have moved and leagues have expanded primarily in order to encompass newer urban areas following urban dwellers and business westward, southward, and outward toward the suburbs.

Urban analysis, however, provides only part of the answer to understanding the location of teams and the spatial structure of leagues. Anomalies exist in each sport; teams are not in some places where they should be in terms of market size, and are located in other areas that are smaller than major league norms. Fewer franchises are located in large metropolitan areas than might be expected in terms of market size. Professional teams also have been less likely to relocate to the suburbs than most other businesses in metropolitan areas. And urban variations do not explain differences in the willingness of places to invest in professional sports.

Among the key factors that interact with urbanization to shape the relationship between teams and places is the organization of professional sports. Private ownership of teams is a fundamental reality, as is organization of sports leagues as cartels that control the supply of franchises. Places, no matter how attractive in general urban terms, are represented in a league only if someone has the means and interest to own a team. Prospective owners have to be acceptable to the members of a league. And owners operating as leagues exercise considerable control over franchise locations.

Competition among places is another critical element in the relationship of cities, suburbs, states, and provinces with professional sports. Demand for big league teams exceeds the supply of franchises made available by leagues. Competition is particularly fierce because major league teams are highly valued by places, and the number of competitors has been steadily increasing. The mismatch between supply and demand greatly enhances the power of teams and leagues in their dealings with places. Bidding for teams escalates public subsidies for professional sports, while the uncertainty created by mounting competition bolsters the local influence of those who promote public investments in major league sports. Competition for teams, a zero-sum political game in which one place's gain is another's loss, severely limits collective action in dealing with professional sports and undermines national legislative efforts to regulate relocation and expansion.

Competition, too, only partially explains the relationships between professional sports and places. Teams and leagues do not have complete freedom of movement. Leagues have to be represented in larger markets if they are to command top dollars from national broadcasters; they also run the risk that a new league will be organized to take advantage of open markets. As a result, leagues have to be in some places even if there are better deals elsewhere, and teams cannot go just anywhere to get a better deal. Places, for their part, vary in their willingness and ability to compete for teams; some vigorously bid up prices while others are unwilling to pay to attract or keep a major league team, which helps explain why teams move, as well as why some places make better offers than others.

Differences in competitive behavior reflect the fact that the places involved with professional sports are distinctive entities. Political and economic variations affect how professional sports are valued locally, as well as the competition for resources that might be used for sports facilities and the outcome of conflicts over sports. Place interests in professional sports are further structured by the diversity of urban governmental jurisdictions in the United States, as well as by the growing role of state governments in sports issues and the representation of local and state interests in Congress; and are further complicated by the distinctive practices of Canadian cities and provinces.

The connections between professional sports and places are also powerfully shaped by the political power of economic elites operating within the friendly confines of the capitalist political economies of the United States and Canada. A market political economy legitimates private ownership of professional sports, promotes public investments in playing facilities that benefit private sports businesses and other powerful economic interests, and fosters aggregations of economic influence that often dominate the politics of professional sports. Team owners frequently get what they want from cities, suburbs, states, and provinces—new and improved stadiums, more attractive leases, tax breaks, and other subsidies. Professional sports increasingly are connected to a growing web of powerful business interests; more and more teams have ownership ties to big business, and leagues have forged alliances with broad-casters and other corporate empires. The sports industry also is closely linked with major business interests in most of the cities that have or want major league teams, particularly the powerful firms that cluster in downtown areas where sports facilities increasingly are located.

For many who study sport and society, capitalism is the key to understanding professional sports. Commercialization, professionalization, corporatization, and capitalist consolidation are seen as making professional sports an integral part of the process of capitalist accumulation, control over the economy, and dominance of the state.[30] Urban politics often is viewed through the same prism, with public interests seen as subordinated to those of dominant capitalists who control the primary instruments of state power.[31] Capitalism and economic elites are viewed here in less deterministic terms. Capitalism frames the political economy but does not predetermine specific outcomes; business power is formidable but not omnipotent. Teams, leagues, and their business allies often triumph in political contests with localities, publics, and governments, but not always and not in the same way in different places. As a result, teams and their business supporters typically bargain rather than dictate, usually settle for less than their initial demands in negotiations with cities and states, and sometimes come away empty handed. In sports as in much else in the United States and Canada, capital is powerful and privileged, but is neither the only important contestant nor the sure winner in places that play in the big leagues.

Government is also a critical element in the connections between places and professional sports. Governments determine the national rules under which professional sports and associated businesses operate, including antitrust regulation, broadcasting practices, and tax policies. Local, state, and provincial governments make the authoritative decisions about building sports facilities and providing other subsidies for the home team. Public agencies plan, build, finance, and operate arenas and stadiums. It is true that teams, leagues, and allied business interests strongly influence many of these decisions, producing outcomes that generally are very favorable to professional sports. Local political leaders often are allied with business elites on issues like professional sports, forming what has been termed "urban regimes" that are particularly influential in promoting economic development and urban revitalization.[32] But politicians and public agencies bring their own interests and objectives to these relationships. Variations in the skill, resources, and priorities of political leaders often play a critical role in determining what team plays where, under what conditions.

None of these factors unilaterally explains the relationships between places and professional team sports, any more than a single factor like defense or offense or wealth always explains which team will win a particular game or pennant. Outcomes result from the interplay of a number of elements—demographics, private ownership of teams, league cartels, competition for teams, variations among places, economic influence, and political differences. This interplay, as shown in the pages that follow, usually produces outcomes heavily skewed in favor of teams and leagues and their business and political allies, leaving the rest of us to pay the rising public costs of having a home team.

2

Urban Games

PROFESSIONAL team sports are a product of urbanization. "The city," Steven A. Riess emphasizes, "was the place where sport became rationalized, specialized, organized, commercialized, and professionalized."[1] Before the accelerated growth of cities in the second half of the nineteenth century, organized sports were insignificant. As cities grew, they aggregated markets for sports, an expanding urban economy provided substantial numbers of people with the means to pay for entertainment, and spectator sports provided a welcome diversion in the strange new world of the industrial city.[2] Industrial growth multiplied the number of major cities, creating a network of large urban centers that provided the base for organizing professional sports into leagues composed of teams representing cities. Transportation within cities improved access to professional sporting events, while development of the railroad web fostered intercity competition and formation of leagues. The telegraph, telephone, and mass production of newspapers provided city dwellers with more information about local teams and games in other places.[3]

Professional sports were also a product of the business ethos of the late nineteenth-century city. In cities dominated by private enterprise, sports offered another opportunity for profit seeking. Teams were privately owned; they were organized into private leagues; and they played in private ballparks. They were part of what Sam B. Warner calls the "private city," places where private objectives were paramount, where what he terms "privatism" was the civic creed.[4]

Baseball and Industrial Cities

Although baseball celebrates its pastoral origins—enshrined in the myth that the game was invented in rural New York, a myth perpetuated in the location of the Baseball Hall of Fame in Cooperstown, a town from yesterday—the pastime that became professional baseball was a city game; the first teams were organized in cities and their players were city dwellers. Relatively well-off sportsmen developed the game in northeastern cities in the middle of the nineteenth century. The Knickerbocker Base Ball Club of New York, which began playing ball in 1842, set down the first rules of baseball. Additional amateur clubs were formed in New York and other cities; these clubs organized as the National Association of Base Ball Players in 1858. Baseball quickly outgrew its class and amateur origins, as players were recruited on the basis of ability rather than social standing.[5] Amateur clubs gave way to teams that paid some players and charged spectators for admission to their games. Spectators as well as teams changed as baseball flourished in the cities, and the well-mannered audiences for games between social clubs were replaced by raucous urban crowds.

Initially, teams played other clubs in the same city; with the improvement of rail links came intercity competition. As the level of competition increased, teams sought better players, which hastened professionalization. The best players went to teams whose backers offered the most attractive deals, and most of these teams were in larger cities. Cincinnati fielded the first admittedly all-professional team in 1869; and the Red Stockings convincingly demonstrated the superiority of professional baseball, running up fifty-seven victories and a tie on a triumphant exhibition tour. The step from intercity competition and exhibition tours to organized league play was taken in 1871 with the organization of the National Association of Professional Base Ball Players. The National Association began with six of its nine teams in major cities—New York, Philadelphia, Boston, Chicago, Cleveland, and Washington. Like most fledgling professional sports leagues, the National Association was an unstable organization. Three of the original nine teams dropped out after the first season. During the league's five years, teams played in seventeen cities, and the size of the league fluctuated from eight to thirteen teams. Only Boston and New York were represented for all five seasons.

In 1876, the National Association was supplanted by the National League. The new league marked another major step in the development of professional team sports, as the team owners who organized the new league took control of the game away from the players and their clubs, who had formed the National Association. The National League placed teams in six of the largest cities—Boston, Chicago, Cincinnati, New York, Philadelphia, and St. Louis—along with Hartford and Louisville. Over the next decade, teams came and went in cities large and small, as the organization experienced the instability common to all new sports leagues. Fourteen other cities joined the league between 1878 and 1887—Baltimore, Brooklyn, Buffalo, Cleveland, Detroit, Indianapolis, Kansas City, Milwaukee, Pittsburgh, Providence, Syracuse, Troy, Washington, and Worcester. Financial problems were endemic in the early years, and only Boston and Chicago were continuously represented between 1876 and 1900.

Among the places that came and went, larger cities usually returned, since the league needed teams in the major urban centers and entrepreneurs were most likely to be successful in larger cities with their greater number of potential customers. Teams in the nation's first and second cities, New York and Philadelphia, did not survive the initial season, but both returned to stay in 1883. Cincinnati, Cleveland, Detroit, St. Louis, and Washington lost their initial franchises, but all had teams when the map of major league baseball was set at the turn of the century. Smaller cities, on the other hand, were gone for good when they lost their teams; places like Hartford, Louisville, Providence, Syracuse, Troy, and Worcester were unable to provide sufficient markets to sustain teams or get back in the big leagues.

Like most successful professional sports leagues, the National League was challenged by rival organizations. New leagues faced the same demographic opportunities and constraints as the National. The American Association sought to capitalize on the opportunities presented by the absence of the National League in a number of larger cities, opening in 1882 with teams in Baltimore, Cincinnati, Louisville, Philadelphia, Pittsburgh, and St. Louis. Over the next decade, the Association granted franchises that competed directly with National League teams in New York and Boston, in other larger cities without a major league team, and in a number of smaller cities. Four of the league's six charter members stayed the course until the Association merged with the National League in 1892, but other locales were highly unstable. Altogether nineteen cities had teams in the American Association; ten lasted for only one or two seasons. Two other rival leagues, the Union Association in 1884 and the Players League in 1890, perished after a single season of ruinous competition with the National League and American Association in the most attractive markets.

From 1892 until the end of the decade, the National League was the only major league, with teams in the nation's eight largest cities—New York, Chicago, Philadelphia, Brooklyn, St. Louis, Boston, Baltimore, and Cleveland—as well as Cincinnati, Pittsburgh, Washington, and Louisville. The modern National League took form in 1899 as Baltimore, Cleveland, Louisville, and Washington were dropped, leaving an eight-team league firmly rooted in major urban centers. Six of the teams were in the five biggest cities—New York (with two teams after Brooklyn was consolidated into New York City in 1898), Chicago, Philadelphia, St. Louis, and Boston—and the other two, Cincinnati and Pittsburgh, were the tenth and eleventh largest in 1900.

No sooner had the National League settled on an eight-team format than the league faced a new challenge. Beginning in 1894, the Western League, one of the strongest minor leagues, commenced a series of franchise moves from smaller to larger cities. Renamed the American League in 1900, it put teams in Chicago and Cleveland, and located in Baltimore, Boston, Philadelphia, and

Washington the following year. The appeal of the largest urban centers led the league to move from Milwaukee to St. Louis in 1902 and to relocate the Baltimore franchise to New York in 1903.[6] Completion of the franchise shifts that established the American League as a second major league were the final moves in a complex game of musical cities; twenty-eight cities had big-league baseball teams between 1876 and 1903, but when the teams finally were in place in 1903, eleven of the sixteen franchises were in the five largest cities.

Major league baseball now claimed the major industrial cities in the northeastern quarter of the nation, along with the nation's capital. Big league baseball was where the people were. The ten baseball cities had 9.2 million inhabitants in 1900, who formed 84 percent of the population in cities with 250,000 or more residents. Baseball's cities dominated the industrial heartland; they were the urban dynamo of the rapidly expanding American economy. Baseball flourished as its cities grew; between 1900 and 1930, the population of the ten cities almost doubled, and attendance grew even more rapidly than population during these years.

New Games for the Cities

Other professional team sports followed in baseball's urban footsteps. Each had an early period of instability to sort out places, owners, and leagues. Smaller cities were abandoned and by mid-century, professional football, hockey, and basketball had gravitated toward the biggest cities, producing maps for each sport that overlapped considerably with baseball's spatial blueprint.

Football was first played by college teams at the same time that professional baseball was getting organized, and the college game overshadowed professional football until well into the twentieth century. Athletic clubs took up the game in the 1880s, and as in the case of baseball a generation earlier, "winning became important" and "athletic clubs went after the best players, using financial inducements to secure their services."[7] Unlike baseball, where the professional game flourished in larger cities, pro football first took root in working-class towns in Pennsylvania and the industrial midwest. What would become the National Football League was organized as the American Professional Football Association in 1919, with five teams.[8] Not until 1921 was the league able to establish a fixed schedule with teams in eleven midwestern cities, of which only four—Chicago, Cincinnati, Cleveland, and Detroit—were large enough to support major league baseball. The new league struggled for more than a decade to find places that would sustain professional football. Teams came and went, playing out of more than thirty cities during the 1920s. Most of these places were too small to underwrite big league sports, but large cities were no guarantee of success. In both Cleveland and Detroit three separate franchises failed in the league's initial decade, victims of too little money, too many losing games, and unpredictable weather. By the Depression, teams in all the smaller cities were gone except for the one in Green Bay, which remained to remind the NFL of its origins in places like Canton, Hammond, and Massillon.

As smaller cities were squeezed out, the National Football League regrouped around teams in larger markets, expanding from its midwestern base to the east coast. Franchises were added in the mid-1920s in New York and Philadelphia, and in Boston in 1932.[9] Teams finally took root in Detroit (1934) and Cleveland (1937), as well as in Pittsburgh (1932). After 1937, when the Boston team was relocated to Washington, the league had a relatively stable set of franchises, all in major cities except for Green Bay; there were teams in five of the largest markets, and seven were in cities with major league baseball.

Professional ice hockey, like football, first took root in working-class towns; the game, notes Richard Gruneau, "was stripped of its amateur trappings, and was reconstituted as violent spectator sport in the mining towns of Cobalt, Haileybury, Timmins, Sault Ste. Marie, and Houghton, Michigan."[10] Leagues were organized after the turn of the century, and in the early years followed the familiar pattern of short-lived teams and unstable leagues. Two leagues organized in 1910 merged seven years later to form the National Hockey League, with two teams in Montreal and franchises in Ottawa and Toronto.[11]

During the next quarter century, expansion, contraction, and franchise shifts were as frequent as in baseball and football, as the NHL searched for the right places to play. In 1924, the NHL expanded to Boston, the first step in a process that would shift the league's locus from Canada to the United States. The Hamilton club moved to New York in 1925, and an expansion franchise went to Pittsburgh. The following year, the league added teams from Chicago and Detroit and a second franchise in New York. The league now had ten teams, but it had overexpanded and shed four teams between 1931 and 1942. Pittsburgh and Ottawa, the league's smallest markets, were unable to survive the Depression, despite shifts to larger cities in search of more customers—Pittsburgh to Philadelphia and Ottawa to St. Louis. The other failures were the weaker teams in the NHL's two shared markets; Montreal's Maroons hung up their skates in 1938 and the New York Americans failed to face off for the 1942–1943 season. What was left for the next quarter century was six teams in major markets—the two biggest Canadian cities, Montreal and Toronto, and three of the four largest cities in the United States, New York, Chicago, and Detroit, as well as Boston, which ranked ninth in population in 1940.

Basketball was the last of the four sports to develop a stable league structure based in large cities. Early leagues were limited to nearby locales, mostly in the northeast, and were loosely structured. Mushrooming interest in sports during the 1920s prompted the creation of a more broadly based professional league. The American Basketball League opened in 1925 with teams in New York, Chicago, and four other large cities in the east and midwest. In its six years, the league demonstrated that good demographics do not guarantee success. Teams failed to last more than a season or two in Boston, Detroit, Philadelphia, and Baltimore. Large cities were replaced by smaller ones; by 1930 four of the seven teams were located in Fort Wayne, Paterson, Rochester, and Toledo. And all the teams were losing money as the Depression deepened, leading to the league's collapse following the 1930–1931 season.

After the failure of the American Basketball League, the professional game was kept alive by local and regional leagues, of which the strongest was the National Basketball League, organized in 1937. Most NBL teams were based in small midwestern cities, and some were sponsored by industrial corporations. As with other leagues in their early years, the NBL was in considerable flux; twenty-seven cities had teams in the league over its thirteen seasons. Unlike the successful leagues that emerged in baseball, football, and hockey, the National Basketball League was unable to establish a presence in major urban centers; its most durable franchises were in Oshkosh and Sheboygan. Nor did the league look like the big time; teams played in a mélange of old arenas and drafty gyms, where they attracted little attention.

Professional basketball reemerged from the bush leagues with the formation of the Basketball Association of America in 1946. The BAA was organized by arena owners in large eastern and midwestern cities who wanted another attraction to fill empty seats on nights between hockey games, college basketball, prize fights, rodeos, and circuses. From the start the BAA resembled a major league, with charter teams in Boston, Chicago, Cleveland, Detroit, New York, Philadelphia, Pittsburgh, Providence, St. Louis, Toronto, and Washington. But the new league did not establish itself immediately, notwithstanding its favorable demographics and big league arenas. Four of the eleven franchises folded in the first year; and many of the best players never left the NBL, which survived despite smaller markets, inferior playing facilities, and shaky finances. The older league also had strong ties to some of its cities; Riess emphasizes that "its owners were civic minded and less profit oriented. Loyal fans appreciated management's efforts to provide high-quality sport with small-town informality that encouraged community pride."[12]

Despite the appeal of the National Basketball League to fans in smaller cities, the Basketball Association of America, with its base in large urban centers, was where professional basketball was going. Four of the strongest franchises in the NBL—Fort Wayne, Indianapolis, Minneapolis, and Rochester—jumped to the BAA in 1948; and the following year what was left of the NBL merged with the BAA to form the National Basketball Association. At the outset, the NBA was a curious amalgam of large and small cities; some of the former and almost all of the latter would depart during the league's first decade. Six of the seventeen teams did not return for the 1950–1951 season, including Anderson, Sheboygan, and Waterloo. The following year, the Rock Island franchise was shifted to Milwaukee, the Fort Wayne team was moved to Detroit, and the Rochester team to Cincinnati in 1957. After these changes, seven of the eight surviving teams were in major cities. In 1963, the last remnant of the NBL, the Syracuse Nationals, was sold and moved to Philadelphia, completing the transition of professional basketball from its small-city roots to a major league with teams in the same places as other professional team sports.

Go West—and South

Locating successful teams in larger cities was only part of the challenge that urbanization posed for professional sports; equally important was the necessity for sports leagues to adapt to the changing distribution of the urban population. At mid-century, all but one professional team in the United States was located in the northeast and midwest areas, which had a declining share of the nation's population. Differential rates of population growth eroded the logic of baseball's ten-city network based on the old industrial heartland. In 1900, baseball had two or more teams in the five largest cities; half a century later, when metropolitan areas were the appropriate market area for professional sports, the third-largest metropolitan area, Los Angeles, had no teams, while the second- and fourth-ranked areas had two each. More than half a million more people lived in the San Francisco metropolitan area, which was without major league baseball, than in the St. Louis area, which had a team in each league. For the mayor of Los Angeles, it seemed "absurd to envision a population center of this size without Major League Baseball."[13]

Leagues had to move westward and southward or risk being regional rather than the national leagues promised by their names. And the prime target was bound to be California, the largest and fastest growing state in the west. California offered prime locations for major league teams in Los Angeles and San Francisco, the third- and seventh-ranked metropolitan areas in 1950, and among the most rapidly growing large urban areas during the previous decade. Urbanization and demographic change, however, did not produce automatic responses from professional sports. Nor did population and economic shifts determine the methods or the timing of efforts to place teams in new markets.

Response to these changes was delayed by a set of formidable external constraints. The Depression was not a time for bold new ventures as professional sports struggled to survive. World War II then kept professional sports in place by severely reducing personnel and travel. Dependence on trains limited the range of leagues, particularly for baseball, whose teams played almost every day. Internal considerations also shaped the response of leagues to market change. Baseball, the dominant sport, was a conservative industry. The national pastime had been in the same places since the turn of the century; most owners were wary of change and reluctant to admit new members to their exclusive club. Hockey, with only six teams, was even more hidebound than baseball. Most NHL teams were successful and their owners saw no need for change; they feared a repeat of the ill-fated expansion in the 1920s, with subsequent instability and contraction. Owners in professional football were reluctant to expand after a long struggle to build viable franchises in the very industrial cities that were now losing ground to newer centers in the west and south. And professional basketball had not even established itself in the major eastern and midwestern cities at the time when other sports began to ponder whether there really was gold in those western cities.

Professional football proved to be the most venturesome in moving west and south, largely because rival leagues placed teams in open markets. Football was the first sport to strike out for California as a new league, the All-American Football Conference, located teams in Los Angeles and San Francisco in 1946. The AAFC also put a team in Cleveland, which persuaded the NFL's Rams to move to Los Angeles. The NFL's absorption of the AAFC in 1949 added San Francisco to its roster, giving the league teams in California almost a decade before baseball moved west. Football also led the way to the growing markets in Texas; the NFL initially placed a team in Dallas in 1952, with a spectacular lack of success, and returned to stay in 1960 in head-to-head competition with the new American Football League, which located teams in Houston and Dallas. Professional football expanded into the south with franchises in Atlanta, Miami, and New Orleans in the 1960s. The most recent expansions added metropolitan areas in the west and south, Seattle and Tampa-St. Petersburg in 1976, and Charlotte and Jacksonville in 1995.

Baseball might have beaten football to California had not the United States gone to war at the end of 1941. Preparations were underway to move the St. Louis Browns to Los Angeles after the team convinced the American League that the rapid development of commercial air service put the west coast within baseball's reach; and formal approval was to be given in late December. Before action could be taken, the attack on Pearl Harbor foreclosed the proposed move, stranding the Browns in St. Louis until 1954. After the war, booming California was more attractive to baseball than ever, which led to conflict between the major leagues and the Pacific Coast League, which fielded teams in Los Angeles and San Francisco. PCL owners feared, with good reason, that their league would be seriously damaged if its biggest markets were invaded by the American or National League; they argued that creation of a third major league based on the PCL was the best way to bring big league baseball to the west coast. Neither the American or National League, however, was interested in forfeiting California to a third league. Moreover, those who wanted major league baseball in Los Angeles desired the real thing, rather than the PCL gussied up as a big league; as an influential sportswriter insisted, "Los Angeles shouldn't be shackled to little cities like Sacramento, San Diego, and Portland."[14]

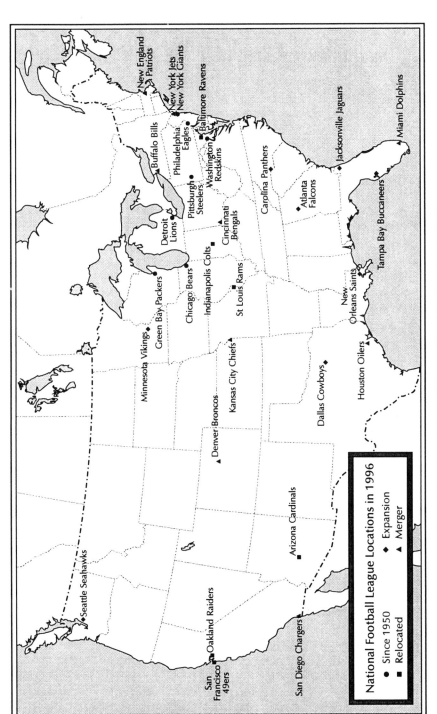

Figure 2.1 National Football League Franchise Locations in 1996

National Football League Locations in 1996

● Since 1950   ◆ Expansion
■ Relocated   ▲ Merger

New England Patriots

New York Jets
New York Giants

Baltimore Ravens

Buffalo Bills

Philadelphia Eagles

Washington Redskins

Pittsburgh Steelers

Carolina Panthers

Jacksonville Jaguars

Miami Dolphins

Atlanta Falcons

Detroit Lions

Cincinnati Bengals

Tampa Bay Buccaneers

Chicago Bears

Indianapolis Colts

St Louis Rams

New Orleans Saints

Green Bay Packers

Minnesota Vikings

Kansas City Chiefs

Houston Oilers

Denver Broncos

Dallas Cowboys

Arizona Cardinals

Seattle Seahawks

Oakland Raiders

San Francisco 49ers

San Diego Chargers

With a third league unacceptable, various questions arose: when major league baseball would come to California, and whether through expansion or relocation, and if the latter, which team or teams. Another effort was made to move the Browns to Los Angeles, but the shift was blocked by team owners who were not about to let Bill Veeck, the Brown's maverick owner, reap the riches in California. Instead of the woeful Browns, Los Angeles wound up with the National League's most successful team when the Dodgers moved west in 1957, accompanied by the Giants, who went to San Francisco. Los Angeles got a second team when the American League expanded in 1961, and the Bay Area another in 1966 when the Kansas City Athletics were relocated to Oakland.

Expansion and relocation further extended baseball's territorial realm. The southern and northern ends of the west coast were added through expansion to San Diego and Seattle in 1969, and to Seattle again in 1976 after the first attempt failed. Texas' two largest metropolitan areas obtained teams through expansion to Houston in 1962 and the move of the Washington Senators to the Dallas-Fort Worth area in 1971. Baseball also moved into the southeast, with the Milwaukee Braves moving to Atlanta in 1966 and Miami winning an expansion franchise in 1993, and Tampa-St. Petersburg for 1998. Baseball filled out its western roster by expanding to Denver in 1993 and Phoenix for 1998, as well as north to Canada's two largest metropolitan areas, Montreal in 1969 and Toronto in 1976.

Professional basketball followed football and baseball to the west coast; and like football and baseball extended its spatial network through a mixture of relocation and expansion. What has been different about the growth of the NBA has been the league's emphasis on growing population centers in the west and south. Expansion teams went to Seattle, Phoenix, Portland, Charlotte, and Orlando, all places with no other major league sports teams at the time; and the NBA was the first to tap San Antonio (added when the NBA absorbed the American Basketball Association in 1976) and Salt Lake City and Sacramento (through relocation). The NBA also followed football and baseball into major western and southern metropolitan areas—moving teams to Los Angeles in 1960, San Francisco in 1962, Atlanta in 1968, and Houston in 1971, and expanding to Dallas in 1980 and Miami in 1988. As a result of these moves, the NBA entered the 1990s with more teams in the Sunbelt and fewer in the Rustbelt than major league baseball, football, or hockey.

Hockey, with the fewest teams at the dawn of the expansion era, was the last professional sport to break away from a traditional base in the northeast and midwest. The reluctance of the NHL to expand stemmed from the conservatism of team owners who were reaping big profits in their six large markets; there were no franchises that wanted or needed to move, and there were a lot of uncertainties about the appeal of hockey in the west and south. The NHL finally made its move in 1967, doubling the size of the league with six expansion

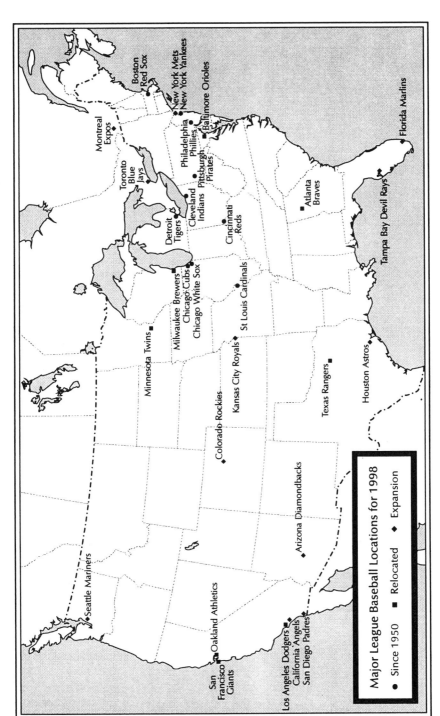

Figure 2.2   Major League Baseball Franchise Locations for 1998

Major League Baseball Locations for 1998

● Since 1950   ■ Relocated   ◆ Expansion

Boston Red Sox
New York Mets
New York Yankees
Baltimore Orioles
Florida Marlins
Montreal Expos
Philadelphia Phillies
Pittsburgh Pirates
Toronto Blue Jays
Cleveland Indians
Cincinnati Reds
Atlanta Braves
Tampa Bay Devil Rays
Detroit Tigers
Milwaukee Brewers
Chicago Cubs
Chicago White Sox
St Louis Cardinals
Minnesota Twins
Kansas City Royals
Houston Astros
Colorado Rockies
Texas Rangers
Seattle Mariners
Arizona Diamondbacks
Oakland Athletics
San Francisco Giants
Los Angeles Dodgers
California Angels
San Diego Padres

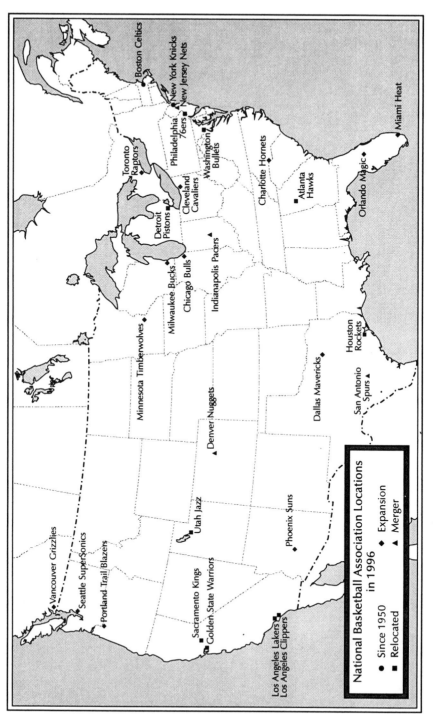

Figure 2.3 National Basketball League Franchise Locations in 1996

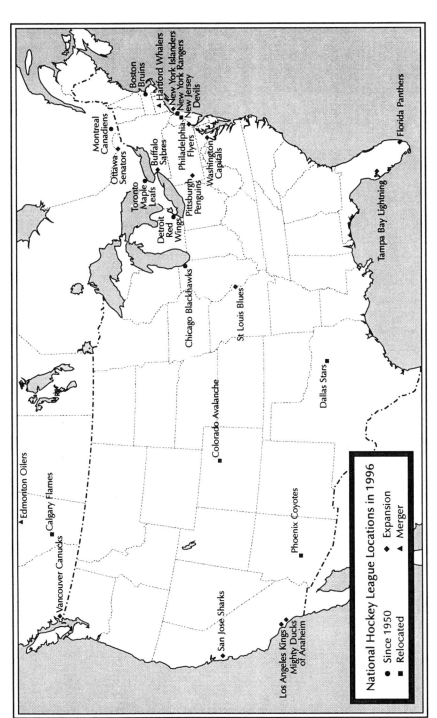

Figure 2.4   National Hockey League Franchise Locations in 1996

National Hockey League Locations in 1996

- Since 1950
◆ Expansion
■ Relocated
▲ Merger

Boston Bruins
Hartford Whalers
New York Islanders
New York Rangers
New Jersey Devils
Montreal Canadiens
Ottawa Senators
Buffalo Sabres
Philadelphia Flyers
Washington Capitals
Toronto Maple Leafs
Pittsburgh Penguins
Detroit Red Wings
Florida Panthers
Chicago Blackhawks
St Louis Blues
Tampa Bay Lightning
Dallas Stars
Colorado Avalanche
Edmonton Oilers
Calgary Flames
Vancouver Canucks
Phoenix Coyotes
San Jose Sharks
Los Angeles Kings
Mighty Ducks of Anaheim

franchises—all in the United States to the dismay of Canadians. But only Los Angeles and San Francisco represented radical changes in the league's spatial framework.[15] Over the next decade, the NHL ventured into the American west and south with an expansion team in Atlanta and a relocated franchise in Denver; but both of these teams failed, as did the San Francisco expansion franchise, leaving Los Angeles as the only NHL team in the United States outside the northeast and midwest until the 1990s. Beginning with expansion to San Jose in 1991, the NHL embarked on an effort to become a truly national hockey league in the United States. Additional expansion teams were located in Tampa-St. Petersburg, Anaheim, and Miami, while the Minneapolis franchise was moved to Dallas, the Quebec Nordiques relocated to Denver, and the Winnipeg Jets to Phoenix.

Even with these new moves, the NHL operates in fewer metropolitan areas in the United States than baseball, basketball, or football, and has a higher proportion of its American teams in the northeast and midwest. Three NHL teams play in the New York metropolitan area, and another in nearby Hartford. This locational pattern is explained by hockey's regional appeal rather than demographics, as of course is the presence of the National Hockey League in six Canadian metropolitan areas. Three of the Canadian areas—Calgary, Edmonton, and Ottawa—have no other major league teams and are smaller than any other urban area in the big leagues except Green Bay.

From City to Metropolis and Beyond

Professional team sports were city games until well into the twentieth century. Professional sports were part of the complex of entertainment facilities concentrated in cities—theaters, movie houses, night clubs, concert halls, and museums. City limits encompassed most of the urban population, and city dwellers composed the primary clientele for professional sports. By mid-century, urban growth had extended the market for professional sports to metropolitan areas, as people and jobs spread to the suburbs at an accelerating rate. Among those moving outward were professional sports' most attractive customers, relatively affluent white males and their families.

Concomitant with metropolitan growth were economic and social changes in cities that steadily eroded their appeal for professional sports. Ballparks were often in decaying areas undergoing racial transition, and a number of arenas were at the increasingly seedy fringes of the central business district. Sports customers saw these areas as undesirable and dangerous; and even when safe, sports facilities in older cities offered insufficient parking for a metropolitan population addicted to automobiles.

The growing black population of most older cities adversely affected professional sports on both sides of America's racial divide. Whites were reluctant to come to ballparks and arenas in black areas, or in cities with large black populations. African Americans, for their part, were less likely than whites to attend professional sporting events. Many blacks had less money to spend on professional sports than the whites they replaced in cities. Blacks also had an understandable lack of enthusiasm for major league sports: black players had been systematically excluded until the racial barriers were slowly breached after World War II; black spectators were banned in a few places, segregated in some ballparks and arenas, and made to feel unwelcome at most.

With their customers moving outward, and concerned over deteriorating city conditions, thousands of businesses relocated to the suburbs in the decades following World War II, among them a number of major league teams. Four of the New York area's nine teams now play in East Rutherford, New Jersey, and another is located in Uniondale on Long Island. Four of the six teams in the Los Angeles area are based in the suburbs, as are two of the four major league clubs in the Detroit and Miami areas. Still, professional sports remains more city-bound than most activities in the dispersing metropolis. Only six of the forty-five arenas and nine of the forty-six stadiums used by professional sports teams in 1995 were located in suburbs. To a considerable degree, the heavy proportion of professional sports facilities located in central cities results from strenuous public efforts to make arenas and stadiums in cities available on terms that teams could not resist, efforts that are discussed in later chapters.

Regardless of whether they play in cities or suburbs, teams draw their customers, viewers, and listeners from ever-larger geographic areas; a growing number have adopted state or regional names designed to attract fans from a broader market base, including three Minnesotas, two New Jerseys, and all of baseball's expansion teams in the 1990s—the Arizona Diamondbacks, Colorado Rockies, Florida Marlins, and Tampa Bay Devil Rays. Benjamin Rader sees these new names as indicative of a loss of place connections on the part of professional sports, noting that "several teams did not even represent clearly definable communities."[16] Metropolitan areas, to be sure, are more diffuse than they used to be, which is why many of the teams that play in the suburbs have regional or state names; but whether fans are less connected to the Minnesota Twins or the Texas Rangers than they were when these teams were the Washington Senators is not easily determined. What is clear is that baseball's new teams in 1993, the Colorado Rockies and Florida Marlins—neither of which represented "clearly definable communities,"—drew the largest home crowds ever to watch expansion clubs.

The Right Places

Adaptation of professional sports to urban change has produced a remarkably rational map of professional sports in the United States and Canada. Teams and leagues have moved to bigger cities, relocated and expanded to tap growing markets, and adjusted to the far-flung diffusion of urban populations. As the chapters that follow indicate, much of what has happened has been unplanned,

Table 2.1   Metropolitan Areas with Major League Teams Ranked by 1990 Population
(Includes MLB Expansion through 1998)

Rank	Metropolitan area	MLB	NBA	NFL	NHL	Total	1990 Population[a]
1	New York	2	2	2	3	9	19,342,013
2	Los Angeles	2	2	0	2	6	14,531,529
3	Chicago	2	1	1	1	5	8,239,820
4	Washington-Baltimore	1	1	1	1	4	6,727,050
5	San Fran.-Oakland-San Jose	2	1	2	1	6	6,253,311
6	Philadelphia	1	1	1	1	4	5,892,937
7	Boston	1	1	1	1	4	5,455,403
8	Detroit	1	1	1	1	4	5,187,171
9	Dallas	1	1	1	1	4	4,037,282
10	Toronto	1	1	0	1	3	3,893,046
11	Houston	1	1	1	0	3	3,731,131
12	Miami	1	1	1	1	4	3,192,582
13	Montreal	1	0	0	1	2	3,127,242
14	Seattle	1	1	1	0	3	2,970,328
15	Atlanta	1	1	1	0	3	2,959,950
16	Cleveland	1	1	1	0	3	2,859,644
17	Minneapolis	1	1	1	0	3	2,538,834
18	San Diego	1	0	1	0	2	2,498,016
19	St. Louis	1	0	1	1	3	2,492,525
20	Pittsburgh	1	0	1	1	3	2,394,811
21	Phoenix	1	1	1	1	4	2,238,840
22	Tampa	1	0	1	1	3	2,067,959
23	Denver	1	1	1	1	4	1,980,140
24	Cincinnati	1	0	1	0	2	1,817,571
25	Portland	0	1	0	0	1	1,793,476
26	Milwaukee	1	1	0	0	2	1,607,183
27	Vancouver	0	1	0	1	2	1,602,502
28	Kansas City	1	0	1	0	2	1,582,875
29	Sacramento	0	1	0	0	1	1,481,102
32	Indianapolis	0	1	1	0	2	1,380,491
33	San Antonio	0	1	0	0	1	1,324,749
34	New Orleans	0	0	1	0	1	1,285,270
35	Orlando	0	1	0	0	1	1,224,852
36	Buffalo	0	0	1	1	2	1,189,288
37	Charlotte	0	1	1	0	2	1,162,093
38	Hartford	0	0	0	1	1	1,157,585
40	Salt Lake City	0	1	0	0	1	1,072,227
61	Ottawa	0	0	0	1	1	920,857
63	Jacksonville	0	0	1	0	1	906,727
72	Edmonton	0	0	0	1	1	839,924
76	Calgary	0	0	0	1	1	754,033
201	Green Bay	0	0	1	0	1	194,594
	Total	30	29	30	26	115	

[a] Canadian populations are for 1991.

franchise shifts and expansion have not always been successful, and many places have been treated badly by teams and leagues. Still, professional sports has wound up in locations that offer more people in more places access to major league sports than ever before. In 1996, as Table 2.1 indicates, almost every team was in a metropolitan area with a population over one million; the exceptions were the Green Bay Packers, Jacksonville Jaguars, and the three hockey teams in smaller Canadian markets. The vast majority of teams were in metropolitan areas with populations of 1.5 million or more, including all 30 in major league baseball. The twelve largest metropolitan areas had 56 of the 113 major league clubs, almost half of all franchises.

Professional sports have also been highly attentive to developing markets in the rapidly growing metropolitan areas of the Sunbelt. Almost all new major league locations in recent years have involved these areas, particularly smaller ones whose robust growth has caught the attention of professional sports. Orlando grew more than 50 percent in the 1980s, which helped the area land a NBA team despite the smallest total population in the league. A pair of small Sunbelt areas, Charlotte and Jacksonville, were the fastest growing finalists for 1995 NFL expansion teams, and the ultimate winners over larger and less dynamic metropolitan areas.

In the process of growing, moving, and assimilating rivals, professional team sports have become national in reality as well as name. Writing in 1974, John F. Rooney Jr. welcomed the spread of big league baseball across the nation: "the geographical structure of major league baseball is now more representative of the national population distribution than at anytime before. Major league baseball is finally becoming a truly national game, at least from a geographical standpoint."[17] Even David Q. Voigt, a sharp critic of "the mercenary carpetbagging and the blundering that blighted its expansion" concedes that "major league baseball managed to plant thriving outposts in every section of the mainland, and even reached into Canada. Such outward growth fortified the game."[18] The number of such outposts has steadily increased, as baseball has been planted in the Rocky Mountains and Florida, basketball and football in rapidly growing Sunbelt metropolises, and hockey across the southern tier of the United States.

3

Market Tests

ARKET SIZE is a fundamental factor in the relationship between places and major league team sports; it shapes the behavior of teams, leagues, local interests, places with and without teams, and their advocates at all levels of government. Since some teams inevitably play in bigger urban areas than others, there have been substantial differences in the markets served by leagues since their beginnings. The biggest National League city in 1876, New York, was twenty-five times larger than Hartford, the smallest. Between 1900 and 1940, when city boundaries generally defined the market for major league sports, the largest baseball market was at least ten times the size of the smallest, and the disparity was greater in 1940 than at the beginning of the century.

Expansion of sports leagues has widened the range of markets, since leagues have grown primarily by adding smaller metropolitan areas to their roster. Between 1960 and 1990, the ratio of the largest to smallest metropolitan area in baseball increased from 10.5 to 12.2; over the same period, the range almost doubled in the National Football League (omitting Green Bay), from 8.3 to 16.3; while the ratio in the National Hockey League increased more than fourfold, from 7.0 to 31.1, as the league expanded from six teams in relatively large markets to twenty-five, including a number of small Canadian metropolitan areas. In the National Basketball Association, the 1960 range was higher than in later years because Syracuse, the last of the smaller city teams, was still in the league; between 1970 and 1990, however, the ratio of the largest to smallest market increased from 15.1 to 18.0 as the NBA expanded to smaller metropolitan areas.

Differences in market size have a pervasive impact on professional team sports, affecting everything from performance of teams to the value of franchises. The importance of market size is reinforced by the ability of leagues to control locations of teams. Sports teams generally have not been able to move freely because of exclusive territorial rights that leagues confer on their franchises. As a result, fewer teams share large markets than might otherwise be the case: New York and Los Angeles could accommodate as many as four teams in a league and still have more metropolitan population per team than most franchises. Thus, territorial rights both enhance the demographic advantages of large markets and increase the differences in size between the largest and smallest markets.

Discussions of market size in professional sports are complicated by lack of agreement on definitions. Large and small markets are flexible concepts with no firm criteria for classifying teams. A 1991 newspaper article on the views of baseball executives on market size indicated that small markets were "teams outside of New York, Chicago and California."[1] The following year, an article in the *Sporting News* included Philadelphia, Boston, and Toronto, as well as New York, Los Angeles, and Chicago in a list of baseball's large markets.[2] Terming Toronto a large market while omitting Detroit and Dallas, which are substantially larger metropolitan areas, is puzzling. Similar problems arise with designating smaller markets. Gerald W. Scully, in an analysis of baseball economics, identifies seven small-market "cities"—Cincinnati, Cleveland, Kansas City, Milwaukee, Oakland, San Francisco, and Seattle—a curious list since Pittsburgh, St. Louis, San Diego, and Minneapolis-St. Paul are all smaller metropolitan areas than Cleveland, and Atlanta is smaller than Seattle.[3] To some degree, these problems in defining large and small markets result from using other criteria in addition to population. Teams in large metropolitan areas are lumped together with rich teams, while clubs in small markets are combined with those with low revenues. Montreal is usually listed among baseball's endangered smaller-market teams because of its attendance and revenue problems, even though it is located in the thirteenth largest metropolitan area in Canada and the United States.

Bigger Is Better

In general, the larger the market, the better a team does, both as a business and in competition with other teams. Areas with large populations have greater revenue potential; they provide more prospective customers, listeners, and viewers. Greater attendance, larger audiences, and higher ticket prices in big metropolitan areas mean more income, and more money generally buys a more successful team.[4] The built-in advantage of teams in large markets is underscored when per-capita attendance is examined; teams in smaller markets substantially outdraw franchises in larger areas on a per-capita basis, but teams in larger areas generally attract more customers. In 1991, the Kansas City Royals, playing in the smallest metropolitan area in baseball, attracted 1.37 customers for each area resident, while the New York Mets drew fewer than one-tenth of this per capita, only .12 per resident, but still outdrew Kansas City 2.28 million to 2.16 million. The relationship between market size and attendance is less important when demand for tickets exceeds capacity. In the NFL, where two-thirds of the teams are usually sold out, stadium size has more impact on attendance than metropolitan population. But NFL teams, like those in other leagues, rely increasingly on luxury seating revenues; and large metropolitan markets contain far more corporate customers for luxury boxes than smaller urban centers.

Broadcasting has reinforced the advantages of teams based in big markets in all professional sports except football, where all regular season games are covered by national television contracts, with income shared equally by the league's teams. Revenues from local television and radio are directly related to market size, and variations in broadcast income tend to be substantially larger than differences in gate revenues. In 1991, twelve baseball teams in the eight metropolitan areas with populations of more than five million averaged $15.9 million in broadcasting revenues, with the New York Yankees receiving $45.4 million. The teams playing in the ten metropolitan areas with fewer than three million residents received an average of $6.6 million in broadcasting revenues, with the Seattle Mariners the lowest at $3 million. Similar variations, depending on market size, exist among local broadcasting revenues for basketball and hockey teams. Cable and pay-per-view television increase the attractions of large metropolitan areas because the biggest markets connect many more households than smaller areas. Despite poor teams and dwindling attendance, the New York Islanders commanded the NHL's best cable deal in 1990s because of the size of the team's television market.

Historically, playing as well as revenue has been influenced by market differences, and the two forms of success are mutually reinforcing. As David S. Davenport emphasizes, "a large market area provides a revenue base that supplies the means to attract the talent for a strong club that can then attract even more customers and more revenue."[5] And more customers and revenues provide resources for additional quality players and coaches, and so on. Empirical studies have produced considerable agreement that "variations in market strengths among major league baseball clubs have exerted a significant influence on relative team quality" and that "for most sports . . . big cities have winning teams and small cities have losing teams."[6] In the NBA during 1987–1988, Roger G. Noll found that "fans in the largest cities were about twice as likely to have a home team in contention for the championship than fans in smaller cities."[7] Market size has been less critical to success in the NFL, although "the four largest cities in the league accounted for thirty-three out of seventy-two divisional titles" between 1933 and 1968.[8]

In larger markets, winning tends to have a higher business payoff than in smaller ones. Successful teams are likely to generate a greater number of additional customers, viewers, and listeners from a large metropolitan population. As a result, concludes Scully, "the marginal revenue of a win is greater in the big city market than in the market of the small city."[9] Because winning has been worth more in larger than smaller markets, star players have had more value to teams in major urban centers. In baseball, the greater value of stars to big-city clubs produced a steady flow of talented ballplayers sold by teams in smaller markets to the New York Yankees. Player sales from poorer to richer teams and bidding for free agents further skews competitive outcomes in the direction of large-market teams.

All of these factors come together to make teams in the largest metropolitan areas the most attractive businesses in professional sports. They draw more fans, sell more season tickets and luxury boxes, and collect the lion's share of local broadcast revenues in baseball, basketball, and hockey. Higher revenues mean more resources to spend on players—for bigger salaries, better scouting and minor league operations, and to acquire players from other teams. Winning more games means getting in the playoffs more often, and further increasing revenues, as well as being able to charge more for broadcasting rights because more people watch winning than losing teams. "If you're interested in making big operating profits in professional sports," emphasizes Jack Kent Cooke, who owned the Kings and Lakers in Los Angeles, "you've got to be in New York, Los Angeles, or Chicago. In that kind of market, you'd have to be a cipher not to make money."[10]

Leagues as well as teams desire to be in the largest markets. The more teams a league has in big metropolitan centers, the more successful teams it is likely to have. Not being represented in a major metropolitan area increases the likelihood that a rival league will attempt to capture the market. Television has reinforced this incentive. Professional sports' basic appeal to broadcasters is the size of the audience that can be delivered to the sponsors who are buying time for their commercials. Since the primary audience for most games are fans in a team's market area, broadcasters are attracted by teams in the largest metropolitan areas and by leagues that have successful franchises in major markets.

Size, of course, is not the only desirable market characteristic for teams, leagues, broadcasters, and advertisers. Rapidly growing metropolitan areas are more attractive than stagnant ones, as are locales that do not impinge on markets of existing teams. Affluent markets offer more potential customers than less well-off urban areas. Luxury boxes are easier to sell in metropolitan areas that house corporate headquarters and other major businesses. And lucrative arena and stadium deals can modify the basic calculus that makes large markets more attractive than smaller ones for professional team sports.

Markets and Revenues

Market differences pose fundamental problems for professional team sports and the places where major league teams play. The advantages of teams in large markets constantly threaten to undermine competitive balance to the detriment of the collective interests of teams in a league. "How good a game are we going to have," asks an official of a small-market team in the NFL, "if the Cincinnatis can't be competitive with the New Yorks? New York and Los

Angeles need somebody to play every year. If we can't be competitive, who are they going to play?"[11] Sports leagues have grappled with the economic and competitive imbalances rooted in market differences from the earliest days of professional baseball. From the start, the impact of market size on a team's business and playing fortunes has depended on revenue sharing within a league. "The smaller the visitor's share of gate revenues," concludes Henry G. Demmert, "the greater the effect of intermarket variations on the revenue functions of the individual clubs."[12]

A small-market team that depends heavily on its own revenues must, as Noll points out, "work especially hard on developing its home market."[13] Developing the home market for these teams primarily involves increasing attendance, since broadcast revenues are largely set by the size of the market rather than the efforts of the team. "The first thing you have to understand about teams in cities such as ours, with a limited population base," emphasizes the owner of the Milwaukee Brewers, is that "we depend more on attendance, on gate receipts, to survive than teams from the bigger markets."[14] Greater dependence on gate receipts increases the vulnerability of small-market teams. If a team like baseball's Brewers or the NBA's Indiana Pacers does not play well, its revenues can drop substantially, jeopardizing the future of the franchise. Absence of any sharing of gate revenues hastened the demise of professional basketball in the smaller cities that survived the merger of the BAA and NBL. In football, the most extensive revenue sharing in professional sports has been a critical factor in maintaining a franchise in Green Bay, by far the smallest metropolitan area with a big league team; "we're only here because Pete Rozelle convinced the owners to share that money," emphasizes the Packers' president.[15]

Sharing is the most obvious solution to the problem posed by the differences in revenues that result from variations in market size. The more extensively revenues are shared, the less likely should be the economic and competitive dominance of teams in the largest cities and metropolitan areas. Revenue sharing is almost as old as professional sports; and its basic rationale has changed little since the early days of major league baseball, when sharing was embraced as a means of insuring economic health and stability. What has changed over time are the revenues that are available for sharing and the arrangements for distributing revenues among teams.

Gate receipts are shared with the visiting team in baseball and football, but not in basketball or hockey. The NFL has the most generous arrangement, providing for a sixty-forty split between the home and visiting team.[16] Baseball shares gate revenues under different formulas in the American and National League, with the visiting team getting 20 percent of ticket receipts in the American League and approximately fifty cents per paying customer in the National League. Revenues from luxury boxes and other special seating arrangements are generally not shared; income from stadium concessions and parking also belong to the home team or its landlord. Not having to share luxury and concessions revenues tends to reinforce the advantages of teams in big markets, since the market for luxury seating typically is more robust in larger than smaller metropolitan areas, and because attendance usually is greater and concession sales higher in the major markets.

Revenues derived from contracts between individual teams and local broadcasters for coverage on radio, free television, cable TV, and pay-per-view are not shared in any league. Local broadcasting revenues are most important in baseball, where 2,268 regular season games are scheduled, relatively few of which are nationally televised. Revenues from local broadcast rights vary in baseball, basketball, and hockey, with teams in larger markets capturing the lion's share of this income. Seven of the twenty-six teams accounted for more than half the local broadcasting revenues in 1991, with franchises in New York, Philadelphia, Boston, and Los Angeles topping the list. Because of these disparities, local broadcast revenues magnify market differences. In the past, notes the owner of the Philadelphia Phillies, market disparities were "not nearly as great, because income was almost entirely from attendance. A club such as Baltimore or Cincinnati can draw almost as many paying fans as the Yankees if they have winning teams. But no matter how well their teams play, there's a limit to the amount of income that they can derive from television."[17]

National broadcasting revenues are shared equally in all leagues. These revenues are the most important in the National Football League, where they constituted 64 percent of team revenues in 1994, and have been steadily growing since the NFL's first network contract in 1962. Baseball's national broadcasting revenues have also been substantial, providing $12 million to each team in 1996. The NBA's national broadcasting revenues rose to $10.7 million per team for 1993, and composed 28 percent of the revenues. NHL teams receive substantially less in national broadcasting revenues, leaving the league with the least amount of shared revenue, approximately 15 percent compared to almost two-thirds in the NFL. Income from merchandising is also shared equally by teams in each league. Once a minor sideshow for major league sports, merchandising has become an increasingly important source of revenue. Gross sales of clothing and other items licensed by major leagues reached $6.5 billion in 1992, producing over $500 million for the four leagues.

The distinction between national and local telecasts, and thus between shared and unshared revenues, has been complicated by the development of national cable networks based on stations with local television rights to major league baseball and basketball games. Teams without such deals wanted a piece of the action, while those with lucrative cable connections insisted these were revenues from local telecasts. The issue has been particularly contentious in baseball, where the stakes have grown with the creation of extensive networks to distribute telecasts of teams based in Atlanta, Chicago, and New York. Over time, the have-nots were able to use their superior numbers to force

Table 3.1   Best and Worst Cumulative Records of Teams
by League: 1984–1987

	Best	Worst	Spread
NFL	.794	.222	.572
NBA	.765	.280	.485
NHL	.698	.339	.359
MLB	.599	.427	.172

the haves to pay a portion of their cable network revenues into a shared pool, with the figure reaching 25 percent in the mid-1990s.

Increased competitiveness is a principal objective of revenue sharing; reducing economic disparities among teams is supposed to lessen the advantages of large-market teams on the field, court, and ice. The more revenues a league shares, presumably the more competitive the teams in the league. James Quirk and Mohamed El Hodiri, however, found that differences in sharing gate receipts among leagues had little effect on competitiveness measured by the range between the best and worst team records over long periods of time. Football, with the most sharing of gate receipts, had a wider spread between its best and worst team than basketball or hockey, neither of which shared gate receipts. Quirk and El Hodiri conclude that "while the peculiarities of each sport might affect the relationship between the distribution of skills and percentage of games won, the data do not indicate that gate-sharing arrangements have any inherent equalizing effect."[18] Similar findings emerge from an examination of cumulative team records for the mid 1980s, a time when shared revenues from national television contracts were more important than during the years before 1969 analyzed by Quirk and El-Hodiri.[19] Here too, as indicated in Table 3.1, the spread between the best and worst records was greatest in the NFL and least in baseball, suggesting that revenue sharing has little direct relationship to the overall competitiveness of leagues.

Whatever its effects on competitiveness, revenue sharing clearly tends to equalize franchise values. Estimates of team values in 1996 found the least variation in the National Football League, as indicated in Table 3.2. The NFL's small ratio of highest to lowest value results primarily from the high values of NFL teams in smaller markets whose income potential has been substantially enhanced by revenue sharing. High average franchise values in the NFL also reflect the cushion provided by extensive revenue sharing to potential buyers of teams; "football is the safest bet," advises an expert on sports investing, "because the NFL relies heavily on revenue sharing."[20]

Revenue differences based on market size are widely seen as prompting the movement of teams. Noll believes that "the importance of home gate receipts explains why basketball franchises are substantially more prone than teams in other sports to move from city to city."[21] Scully thinks "the increased socialization of revenues has greatly reduced, but not eliminated, the threat of fran-

Table 3.2   Variations in the Estimated Value of Major League Franchises: 1996

	Highest Five	Average	Lowest Five	Ratio Highest-Lowest
NFL	$215,200,000	$174,000,000	$145,200,000	1.48
NBA	$186,200,000	$127,000,000	$72,000,000	2.02
MLB	$167,800,000	$115,000,000	$68,400,000	2.45
NHL	$115,00,000	$74,000,000	$41,600,000	2.78

SOURCE: Tustar Atre et al., "The High-Stakes Game of Team Ownership," *Financial World*, May 20, 1996, 53–65.

chise relocation" in baseball.[22] And Senator John C. Danforth has termed "the wide disparity in revenues available to teams in large and small cities . . . the underlying cause of franchise instability."[23] Yet extensive revenue sharing in the National Football League has not been associated with franchise stability. More teams moved in the 1980s and 1990s in the NFL than in the other league—seven compared with five in the NHL, two in the NBA, and none in baseball. Indeed sharing may increase the attractions to NFL owners of new locales with the potential of enhancing revenues that do not have to be shared. In making their ill-fated move to Los Angeles, the Raiders had visions of unshared riches from luxury boxes and television deals in a huge market with enormous potential for cable and pay-for-view revenues. Securing better stadium deals in Indianapolis, Phoenix, St. Louis, Nashville, and Baltimore increased revenues that the Colts, Cardinals, Rams, Oilers, and Browns did not have to share with other teams.

Advocates portray revenue sharing as benefiting teams in large as well as small markets. Sharing that "strengthens some of the clubs financially without hurting others," contends Ira Horowitz, "will presumably tend to . . . enhance the profits of all clubs."[24] Failing to share, contends Lance Davis, hurts strong as well as weak teams, resulting in "not only unprofitable franchises but also noncompetitive teams, and such teams must be a drag on the long-run profits of even the most profitable franchises."[25] The most persuasive argument for revenue sharing is the success of the NFL; the league that shares the most has the highest franchise values, the biggest national television contracts, and the most fans. Why, then, have other leagues not emulated the NFL? The answer lies primarily in market differences; larger-market teams in the other leagues are reluctant to lose their economic and competitive advantages. Sharing as much revenue as the NFL does would reduce the income and value of the most successful baseball, basketball, and hockey teams. Revenue sharing is a zero-sum game; more for the Kansas City Royals and Pittsburgh Pirates means less for the New York Yankees and Los Angeles Dodgers.

By their nature, zero-sum games are conflictual; in professional sports the struggle between large and small, rich and poor, dates back to the first baseball leagues. Baseball teams in the strongest markets fended off periodic efforts to share more revenues, often with the help of league requirements that major policy changes be approved by extraordinary majorities. During the Depression, baseball's "'have-not' franchises promoted a profit-sharing scheme, but it was voted down by the wealthier clubs."[26] In 1953, Bill Veeck, the maverick owner of the St. Louis Browns, proposed an equal split of gate receipts and a share of television money for visiting teams. Veeck won support of five of the American League's eight teams, but the opposition of the richest teams with the strongest interest in the status quo—the New York Yankees, the Detroit Tigers, and Boston Red Sox—left the pro-sharing faction short of the six votes needed to change league rules. In 1979, the NBA teams in New York, Los Angeles, Chicago, Philadelphia, and Boston joined forces to block efforts by franchises in smaller markets to share gate revenues.

Prosperous teams have generally stood fast for individual enterprise. After the big-market teams scotched revenue sharing during the Depression, the owner of the Yankees opined that "there is no charity in baseball," and that "every owner must make his own fight for existence."[27] Asked in 1995 about the prospects of sharing more hockey revenues with troubled franchises in smaller markets, the president of the Boston Bruins emphasized "that communism died" and "you won't see it revived in the NHL."[28] George Steinbrenner reminded those who wanted a share of the Yankees' television money that "nobody forces anybody to buy a franchise in Cleveland or Milwaukee . . . Everything costs more in New York."[29]

Baseball grappled continuously with revenue-sharing proposals as labor costs escalated in the late 1980s. More and more teams in smaller metropolitan areas, squeezed by rising costs and worried about the growth prospects of national television revenues, favored some kind of sharing of local television money. Teams in lesser markets pressured the big-market clubs by threatening to terminate the reciprocal arrangements that assign all revenues from local telecasts to the home team. Agreement finally was reached among owners on a revenue-sharing plan, but implementation was conditioned on imposition of a salary cap on player salaries, which was unacceptable to the players, precipitating a season-ending strike in 1994 before compromises by both sides produced an agreement in 1996 on a modified revenue-sharing scheme and a tax on high-salary teams rather than a cap.

Markets and Labor Costs

That revenue sharing became entertwined with salary limitations in a dispute rooted in market differences is not surprising. From the beginning, leagues have argued that labor restrictions were necessary to prevent dominance by the richest teams in the biggest markets. Baseball adopted the reserve clause that bound players to a team in 1879, and similar provisions were embraced by other professional team sports as they developed. Pro football began drafting college players in 1936, a system that provided one team with exclusive bargaining rights; the draft subsequently was adopted by other sports. More recent labor restrictions include limitations on free agency, requirements for compensation when free agents switch teams, and caps on team payrolls. No convincing evidence exists, however, to bolster claims that labor restrictions have leveled the playing field for small-market clubs or restrained owners who sought to buy success at the expense of the competitive prospects of other teams. The reserve clause and other restrictive labor practices did not prevent teams in larger markets from using their superior resources to acquire players from teams in smaller markets. Noll finds that labor arrangements have had no effect on competitive balance in the NBA; and he points to the dominance of the Boston Celtics and Los Angeles Lakers in the NBA "decade after decade, regardless of the state of the player market . . . their ability to dominate the league was unaffected by whether the NBA's teams were safe, secure monopolies (as was the case from about 1950 until the mid-1960s) or whether they were involved in some form of competition for players, either within the league or with teams from another league."[30]

Nonetheless, free agency and other changes have significantly increased labor costs for professional sports, which has heightened concern that teams in big markets will use their superior economic power to acquire the best players. With fewer restrictions on players, salaries increasingly are determined by the workings of a national labor market, while teams, except in the NFL, derive most of their revenues from local markets. Cincinnati or Kansas City has to pay the same for a top left-handed relief pitcher as the Yankees or Dodgers; free-agent power forwards command the same salary in Sacramento as in Chicago. As a result, emphasizes the owner of the Minnesota Twins, "we have exactly the same salary structure as a big market like New York or Los Angeles. But our revenues are only half, sometimes less."[31]

Compounding the problems of small-market baseball teams is an arbitration system for resolving salary disputes in which decisions are based on the existing salary structure for players of similar ability and are not supposed to take into account the financial resources of the particular team.[32] As a result, salaries for players eligible for arbitration are beyond the control of their team; "we have a system that doesn't permit owners to level off salaries of their own accord," emphasizes a baseball official, "an owner can't just simply say, 'Well, I'm tapped out, I'm not paying you more.' If a player made a million last year and hit .270, you know he's going to make a million-five next year."[33] "The judgment of one owner," notes a team executive, "now affects everyone"; and these typically are the judgments of the owners of the richest teams in the larger markets.[34] The combined effect of free agency and arbitration, argued Commissioner Fay Vincent in 1991, meant ""small-market clubs simply have no choice but to arrange their payrolls on an entirely different scale [than] larger market teams."[35]

Rising labor costs and concerns about market differences have led the sports establishment to embrace salary caps as a means of limiting the economic advantages of teams in large metropolitan areas. Faced with a crisis that threatened to decimate four or five weak franchises in small markets, the NBA adopted a salary cap in 1983. Ten years later, the NFL capped salaries, and baseball owners precipitated a devastating strike in 1994 by insisting that the national pastime could not survive unless limitations were placed on team payrolls. Appraisals differ on the impact of salary caps on disparities between the richest and poorest teams in the NBA. Paul D. Staudohar thinks "salary caps protect teams in the smaller market from having their free-agent players gobbled up by clubs in the big cities."[36] Noll, on the other hand, concludes that caps have not had much effect on strengthening weaker teams because "a player's current team is permitted to match any external salary offer, and most players would rather stay with a good team than switch to a weak one."[37]

Salary caps appear no more likely to resolve the dilemma posed by market differences than other schemes that sports leagues have used to protect owners from each other. Short of a system that combines rigid salary caps with complete revenue sharing, large-market teams will retain substantial advantages. Teams in major urban centers have more resources; they are in a better position to bid for the most attractive free agents; and they insure that caps are porous, or find loopholes that permit them to collect superstars. Clubs in smaller areas, on the other hand, cluster around the salary minimum in the NBA; "owners in Indianapolis, San Antonio, and Seattle try to pay as little as the league allows."[38] Prosperous teams, moreover, reap the largest financial rewards from limits on labor costs, especially in a league like the NBA, which shares relatively little income; "for many large market teams in professional basketball," a sportswriter emphasizes, "the salary cap serves as a license to print money."[39]

Beating the Market

Markets create probabilities rather than determine outcomes, both on the field and the balance sheet. Being in the largest metropolitan area does not guarantee that a team will either win games or make lots of money; teams have to organize and market an appealing product in attractive surroundings in order to attract customers, advertisers, and favorable media attention. During the eighteen years between 1947 and 1964, when the Yankees were winning fifteen pennants, the New York Knicks won nothing despite the advantages of being in the nation's largest market with the most lucrative broadcasting possibilities. As Benjamin Rader points out, the Yankees' success was a product of "superior resources arising from larger attendance, more broadcast revenues, and skilled management," while the Knicks' failure resulted from an ineffective management that "repeatedly made ill-advised trades and drafted players for their immediate publicity value rather than future potential for the team."[40]

Although assuring nothing, market size does set the basic parameters in which each professional sports team operates. Market size is a given; the forces that affect the population and economic fortunes of a city, metropolitan area, or larger urban region are beyond the influence of a team. In the end, the only way for a team to alter significantly the nature of its market is to relocate to another metropolitan area. Short of moving, which rarely puts a team in a larger market, teams have to play with the hands they are dealt in a particular place. And everything else being equal, teams are more likely to succeed economically and competitively in larger than smaller markets, which is why owners prefer large markets to small ones, and why teams in small markets are most likely to move or fail.

Market constraints are surmounted in a variety of ways. Being in the right league certainly helps. Success depends in part on the appeal of the particular sport and league in a team's market, on the competitiveness of a league, its structure and schedule (which determine the attractiveness of a team's opponents), and on the number of stars in a league, like Michael Jordan or Wayne Gretsky, who can bolster attendance and television audiences. Leagues provide more or less shared revenue, which can significantly affect the dependence of a team on its home base; and league policies such as salary caps can provide clubs in lesser markets with some protection against runaway labor costs (although salary arbitration in baseball increases the vulnerability of franchises in smaller metropolitan areas).

Teams are also businesses that can be managed well (as were the Yankees) or poorly (like the Knicks), as well as political actors that can be more or less effective in securing favorable arrangements for playing facilities and other government benefits. Personnel management has always been a critical element in a business so heavily dependent on the skills of its labor force. The handicaps of a small market can be lessened by adroit scouting, drafting, developing, and acquiring the right players, as well as putting able people in charge in the front office and on the bench. Adroit personnel management brought Wayne Gretsky to the Edmonton Oilers and provided a supporting cast that made the Oilers, playing in one of the smallest major league markets in North America, into the best team in the NHL in the 1980s. Creative leadership also can offset market handicaps. Branch Rickey built an extensive network of minor league affiliates that transformed the St. Louis Cardinals from a weak team sharing a stagnant market into a powerhouse that won nine pennants between 1926 and 1946; and the rich harvest of Rickey's farm system made the Cardinals the most profitable team in the National League as surplus players were peddled to less productive clubs.

Marketing has become an increasingly important part of the business of professional sports. Skillful marketing can overcome some of the drawbacks of smaller markets through advertising campaigns, direct mailings, special promotions, and corporate sponsorships. Bowie Kuhn notes that the Kansas City Royals "brilliantly marketed baseball, with attendance consistently over two million in one of our smallest franchise areas."[41] Particularly impressive has been the marketing of the Charlotte Hornets, an expansion franchise in the second smallest metropolitan area in the NBA, which has used every trick of the trade to mobilize businesses, customers, and advertisers from an area far more extensive than its metropolitan base, and in the process continuously sell out one of the largest arenas in the league.

Market Minimums

Although the handicaps of small markets can be mitigated, size inevitably limits the number of metropolitan areas that have teams. Minimum market sizes vary from sport to sport, depending on the frequency of games, operating costs, and revenue sources. These minimums are flexible and dynamic, changing over time with shifting urban patterns, increasing revenues, and league arrangements for sharing revenues. Sharing of broadcast revenues has a particularly strong effect on minimum market size; the greater the revenue sharing and the more lucrative the broadcasting contracts, the smaller the metropolitan area that can support a team, providing the league has teams in big markets with the largest concentrations of viewers.

Baseball requires larger markets than other team sports. The number and frequency of games means that most of the market for ticket sales is metropolitan. Lack of sharing of a significant portion of broadcast revenues makes the size of the local broadcast market a critical factor in the viability of baseball franchises. Baseball also has high operating costs, with average salaries of over $1 million in 1993, lots of players under contract, and minor league teams to support. Major league baseball in 1996 operated in twenty-four of the twenty-seven largest metropolitan areas; the smallest, Kansas City, had a population of 1.58 million in 1990. And for its 1998 expansion, baseball tapped two of the three areas larger than Kansas City that did not have teams, Phoenix with 2.24 million and Tampa-St. Petersburg with 2.07 million.

Professional football can operate successfully in smaller markets than baseball. NFL teams play once a week, usually on Sunday afternoon, with each of the eight home games an "event" able to attract customers from substantial distances. Most games are sold out, with large numbers of season ticket holders insuring a solid revenue base. Football squads are large, but average salaries have been substantially lower than in baseball. And revenues are extensively shared; each team's share of the NFL's national broadcasting revenues was greater than the maximum outlays permitted under the league's salary cap in 1995. Before its latest expansion, the NFL was operating in three metropolitan areas—Indianapolis (1.38 million), New Orleans (1.29 million), and Buffalo (1.19 million)—that were smaller than baseball's least populous market, as well as in Green Bay, the testament to how small a metropolitan area can support professional football when there are generous shared revenues. Both expansion teams that began play in 1995 were located in areas smaller than Buffalo—Charlotte (1.16 million) and Jacksonville (938,000).[42]

Professional basketball combines smaller payrolls than baseball or football, with limited but growing shared revenues. Most paying customers for the forty-one home games come from the metropolitan area since basketball, like baseball, schedules most games at night during weekdays. Noll concluded in 1974 that "unless more even gate-sharing arrangements are made, it appears that most professional basketball teams are located in cities too small to allow a team to show an operating profit."[43] Bigger national television revenues to share, combined with salary caps, better marketing (particularly in smaller markets like Charlotte), and a more attractive product featuring stars like Magic Johnson and Michael Jordan, have given a number of NBA franchises a second life since Noll's appraisal. Recent expansion teams have been successful in Orlando (1.22 million) and Charlotte (1.16 million); and more established teams have done well in San Antonio (1.32 million) and Salt Lake City (1.07 million), in part because the NBA did not share any of these small areas with another major league franchise until the NFL expanded to Charlotte in 1995.

Hockey—with the lowest average salaries, the least revenue sharing, and a schedule that is similar to that of professional basketball—has had two sets of market minimums, both of which are in flux. In Canada, the NHL has operated in smaller metropolitan areas than any other league, with teams in five areas until 1995 that ranged in population from Edmonton (828,000) down to Winnipeg (652,000) and Quebec City (622,000). Even with the departure of Quebec and Winnipeg in 1995–1996, the NHL continues to play in Calgary (754,000), which is only 70 percent the size of Salt Lake City, the smallest market in the NBA. In the United States, the NHL operates in two small northeastern areas, Buffalo (1.19 million) and Hartford (1.16 million), but its emphasis in recent years has been on larger markets such as Los Angeles, San Francisco, Dallas, and Miami.

Markets set boundaries for professional team sports, boundaries that are constantly in flux as metropolitan areas grow and change. Understanding what happens within these boundaries is the concern of the remainder of this study. Metropolitan markets only secure and retain teams if private owners wish to operate in a particular place. Being competitive means insuring that teams have new arenas and stadiums, or new deals on existing or renovated facilities, all designed to maximize team revenues from ticket sales, luxury suites, other premium seating, concessions, and advertising. Dramatic boosts in revenues from new facilities, some analysts argue, means "we have a situation developing in sports where market size isn't the most important factor in determining a team's ability to make a profit."[44] Certainly the accelerating rush by places to bestow lavish facilities and bountiful deals on sports teams has lessened the connection between market size and revenues. But big markets will continue to have inherent advantages; they offer more customers for all the things that generate higher revenues; they provide most of the audiences that want to follow the home team on television; and their governments also can build new arenas and stadiums that permit their teams to secure more of the riches of the biggest and wealthiest places in North America.

4

Private Businesses

FOLLOWING the victory of the Chicago Bears in the Super Bowl in 1986, Senator John C. Danforth emphasized that the victory was Chicago's. "Never mind that the Bears are a business, privately owned and operated for profit. They are, more importantly, the *Chicago* Bears, the 'monsters of the Midway,' *Chicago's* team."[1] Understanding the connections between Chicago and its Bears, and other places and their teams, requires that we "mind" that the Bears, like almost every other major league sports team in the United States and Canada, are a private business. Private ownership fundamentally shapes the relationship between teams and the places where they play. Places do not have major league teams unless someone wants to own a franchise in a particular location; their interests are critically affected by who owns a team and the owner's commitment to a city. Decisions about where teams will play are made by owners and leagues that are private organizations serving the interests of their member teams.

Private Games

Professional sports were a logical product of the age of enterprise. Baseball was an activity that people were willing to pay to see; and entrepreneurs came forward to produce games for profit. Following the creation of the National League of Professional Base Ball Clubs in 1876, capitalists took control of baseball from players and their clubs. Teams in the new league were controlled by owners who brought entrepreneurial skills to the game, along with private capital to invest in bigger and better ballparks; the league played regular schedules, established minimum population size for teams, and granted exclusive territorial rights for franchises. Under the new regime of private ownership, baseball mirrored the rampant capitalism of late nineteenth-century America as owners sought monopoly control over their industry and its labor force. Baseball's capitalists combined the National League and rival American Association into a single cartel, extended their realm over minor leagues, and then merged the National and American Leagues to maintain their monopoly. Agreements among leagues and exclusive territorial rights provided control over the supply of the owners' product, thus limiting competition for customers in cities with professional teams. Introduction of the reserve clause in 1879 ended the free market in labor, reducing players to hired hands bound to the team that held their contract. Baseball provided the model for other professional sports. Teams would be privately owned and organized into private leagues; capital would control labor; owners would seek local monopolies through exclusive territorial franchises; and leagues would operate as cartels that eliminated or absorbed rival leagues.

Relationships among teams and places evolved in the context of the dominant business ethos that proclaimed the desirability and superiority of private enterprise. Professional sports reinforced its private realm by claiming to be a game rather than a business, insisting that organizing games and satisfying fans by private teams and leagues was the American way. The private nature of professional sports was bolstered by private ownership of almost all ballparks and arenas until the middle of the twentieth century. In this private world, public and community ownership were alien ideas stoutly resisted by team owners and their leagues. Despite four decades of mounting public investment in the arenas and stadiums used by most professional teams, no teams in 1996 were owned by local, state, or provincial governments; and only the Packers were owned by a community, through a private nonprofit corporation created as a means of keeping the team in Green Bay.[2]

Owners in professional sports own player contracts, equipment, advertising and broadcasting contracts, a lease for a stadium or arena (except for the few teams that own their playing facility), and, usually a team's most valuable asset, a franchise to play in a league with exclusive rights to a particular territory. Arenas and stadiums, the principal capital asset in professional sports, belong in most places to the governments that build them. Of particular importance for places is the fact that owners can sell what they own. Sports franchises are properties that can be bought or sold by particular individuals or corporations. Transactions involving teams, regardless of their implications for places, are essentially private matters, subject to approval by leagues but rarely by public agencies.

Owners and Places

Most professional sports teams once had local owners who depended on sports for their livelihood. Today, relatively few owners are primarily in the sports business, and a fair number are outsiders whose principal residence or place of business is not located in the same place as their team. All teams, however, remain locally based with a franchise to operate in a particular urban area. The horizontal consolidation of local firms common to most industries never occurred in professional sports; ownership of more than one team in a league has been widely viewed as detrimental to the integrity of the game.

Changing patterns of ownership in professional sports mirror general developments in the economy, most significantly the decline of locally owned firms and the rise of national and international corporate conglomerates. Ownership changes also reflect the transformation of professional sports from small businesses into substantial industries. Teams have become increasingly expensive to own and operate. Wealthy owners have always been desirable in professional sports; today they are indispensable because only the rich can afford to buy teams. Professional sports typically have attracted new money; as a sportswriter notes, "sports money is new money, out for some fun."[3] The 1960s brought oil money, most notably to the professional football franchises in Texas. More recently have come real estate developers, fast-food tycoons, communications empires, electronic wizards, and entertainment conglomerates. Wayne Huizenga, who acquired baseball, hockey, and football teams in the early 1990s, made his multimillions in two characteristic late twentieth-century industries, waste disposal and video rentals. Corporate and absentee owners, as well as more teams operated as subsidiaries of larger enterprises, some observers argue, reduce the commitment of teams to particular places; "the new owners, whether corporate or individual," argue Randy Roberts and James Olson, "often had less loyalty to particular cities and communities than the earlier generation."[4]

Local owners of the earlier generation typically had strong place connections. The Philadelphia Athletics of the new American League in 1901 were owned by Ben Shibe and Al Reach, who manufactured sporting goods in Philadelphia. George Halas got into professional football with the Bears of the Staley Starch Company, moved the team to his native Chicago, and spent the rest of his life as Poppa Bear. Professional basketball was brought to Minneapolis after World War II by three local businessmen who bought the moribund Detroit franchise in the National Basketball League for $15,000. Most of the people who owned teams before the 1950s were rooted in the places where their team played; neither they nor their teams were likely to move. Art Rooney, founder of the Pittsburgh Steelers, "never thought of moving the club, or selling the club. . . . Pittsburgh is my home. The Pittsburgh Steelers are my team."[5]

Rising prices and increased demand for teams has reduced the ranks of local owners. What was once primarily a local market has become regional, national, and international. Increasingly, potential owners have been unable to acquire a team in their own locale, or have found more attractive opportunities elsewhere. Art Modell admits he had "never been to Cleveland" before buying the Browns in 1961, but "that was the team that was for sale."[6] Ray Kroc, a Chicago native who built McDonald's into a megabusiness, was unable to buy his beloved Cubs so he settled for the San Diego Padres. Owners from elsewhere like Modell and Kroc are not new to major league sports—the St. Louis Browns were owned in the early days of the American League by Robert Lee Hedges, a manufacturer from Cincinnati, and another Cincinnatian, John T. Brush, bought the New York Giants in 1902. What is new is the number of outsiders who own teams, the mobility of franchises over the past forty years, and the concern that outsiders are more likely to move a team. Local owners are believed to care more about the community, and therefore to be more committed to a place and less likely to move their team. When the Washington Senators were acquired by Robert Short, a Minneapolis businessman, the fact that "Short had no real ties to Washington," in Commissioner Bowie Kuhn's view, was "an ominous sign that augured badly for the struggling expansion franchise."[7] Home town ties, however, had not prevented Short from moving the Lakers from Minneapolis to Los Angeles a few years earlier.

Evidence concerning the relationship between the locality of ownership and mobility of teams is mixed. Local owners have usually kept teams in town, but not always. The most notorious relocation, the shift of the Dodgers to Los Angeles, was engineered by Walter O'Malley, who was born and bred in Brooklyn; and the Giant's owner, Horace Stoneham, who moved the team to San Francisco, was a native New Yorker whose family had acquired the team in 1918. Other local owners who moved were Short, who took the Lakers west; the Bidwells, who relocated the Cardinals from their native Chicago to St. Louis; and Louis Perini, a Boston contractor who started the game of musical chairs in baseball by shifting the Braves to Milwaukee in 1953. Outsiders sometimes have moved teams, but more often have kept their franchise in place. Ralph Wilson has owned the Buffalo Bills from the beginning of the American Football League in 1960, commuting to games from his home in the Detroit area. Purchase of the San Diego Padres in 1974 by Kroc, an outsider, foreclosed a move to Washington. During the two decades that Larry Weinberg was an absentee owner of the Portland Trail Blazers, there never was "a serious threat that the city would wake up and find itself the former home of the Honolulu Trail Blazers. Weinberg . . . hired good people, provided competitive basketball and made the Trail Blazers an important part of the community."[8]

Everything considered, places are understandably less secure when the home team has an absentee owner. Some outside owners never make any pretense about their intention to move their team. Arnold Johnson, a Chicago businessman, bought the Philadelphia Athletics in 1954 so that he could move the team to Kansas City, where he had interests in the city's minor league franchise. Similarly, Bud Selig and his partners acquired the moribund Seattle Pilots in 1970 for the express purpose of bringing major league baseball back to Milwaukee. More common are outsiders like the Chicago-based syndicate that acquired the Milwaukee Braves in 1962, assuring the locals that they were there to stay, and then moving on to a better deal in Atlanta in 1966. Having the home team owned by Charles O. Finley was like riding an endless roller coaster. Finley, who controlled the Athletics from his home near Chicago, moved his team from Kansas City to Oakland after seven years of promises and threats, and then played the same game in Oakland before finally selling to local buyers. Another Chicago-based owner, Robert Irsay, outdid Finley in terms of melodrama, alternating negotiations in Baltimore with threats to move the Colts to Jacksonville, Memphis, and Phoenix before he finally shipped his team off to Indianapolis.

Absentee owners of smaller-market teams cause the most anxiety. When the Seattle Seahawks, which had been locally owned, were acquired in 1988 by two Californians, "the comfort level dropped dramatically."[9] For good reason, as the new ownership proved to have little commitment to Seattle and sought to move the team to Los Angeles in the wake of the departure of the Raiders and Rams in 1995. Seattle also had persistent worries with absentee owners of its baseball team. The Mariners were purchased in 1981 by a California real estate tycoon who made no secret of his lack of commitment to Seattle. In 1989, the team was sold again to outsiders led by Jeff Smulyan, president of Emmis Broadcasting in Indianapolis. Three years later Smulyan and his partners were on the verge of selling the team to buyers who intended to relocate the franchise to St. Petersburg, when the Mariners were rescued by a local syndicate. Purchase of the Baltimore Orioles in 1979 by Edward Bennett Williams raised fears that the team would be moved to Washington, where Williams lived and worked. Williams added to Baltimore's anxiety by talking about playing some games in Washington, or moving to a new stadium between the two cities, or relocating the team to Washington. Whether Williams was serious or simply using his options as bargaining chips in his quest for a new stadium is unclear; there was probably some of both. What is clear is that being an absentee owner with options strengthened Williams' hand in negotiations that secured a new stadium for the Orioles in Baltimore on very favorable terms.

Big Business

The same forces that brought more absentee owners changed professional sports from a world of individual entrepreneurs, often running shoestring operations, into big businesses. Owner George Halas "played end for the Bears, coached the club, handled the administrative details, collected tickets, wrote publicity releases, and booked the games."[10] Professional hockey in the early years was in the hands of "hard-bitten, up-from-nowhere, bred-in-the-game owners . . . who struggled for years to keep their businesses alive."[11] Their teams were the principal business of Halas and the hockey owners, as it was for many of their contemporaries in professional sports; success or failure depended on selling tickets to their games.

As professional sports became bigger and teams more expensive, the number of owners whose primary business was sports steadily declined. Bill Veeck sold the Chicago White Sox in 1980, convinced that "there's no longer room for someone who just happens to like baseball and makes his living this way."[12] A few years later, Calvin Griffith, whose family had been in the baseball business for decades in Washington and Minneapolis, came to conclusion that "poor little guys like me, who had no business but baseball, had to get out of it. We only had one pocket to get into."[13] The declining ranks of sports entrepreneurs is often depicted as bad for sports, fans, and places. Bowie Kuhn bemoans the "new breed" of owners who lack "any real sense of the game or appreciation of its verities rooted in the nineteenth century."[14] Perhaps, but fondness for the good old days needs to be tempered with the realization that the old breed of owners were not always good for the game or the home team. Consider the Philadelphia Phillies, "notorious during the twenties and thirties as a club teetering on the brink of ruin, saved only by selling players to other clubs. The owners of the Phillies had no independent sources of wealth, and finally the club went bankrupt and was taken over by the league in the early forties."[15] As for loyalties to the places where the sports entrepreneurs did business, some like the Rooneys never considered leaving, whereas others like Horace Stoneham and Calvin Griffith picked up stakes and moved the family business.

Along with sports entrepreneurs, another disappearing breed of team owners is sportsmen, described by Kuhn as "persons who loved and cared about the game and who would support what was best for the game overall, even if that was adverse to their club's interests."[16] Sportsmen, like entrepreneurs, have largely been priced out of big league sports; modern teams are too expensive to be operated without much concern for business matters in the style of Philip Wrigley in Chicago or Tom Yawkey in Boston. The passing from the scene of sportsmen is widely seen as another adverse development for places in their relations with professional sports. Sportsmen typically had strong place loyalties; Wrigley and Yawkey were committed to their cities, cared about their fans, and lavished attention on their intimate ballparks; and they never talked about moving. Sportsmen owners are often contrasted with businessmen or promoters or hustlers, interested primarily in profits, tax write-offs, broadcasting income, and the resale value of the franchise, and ready to move a team if the next pasture seemed greener.[17] Dedicated sportsmen certainly were a blessing to places in terms of franchise stability, but there never were more than a handful in any sport. And whatever their virtues in terms of caring about cities and fans, teams owned by sportsmen were not particularly successful on the field. Wrigley's Cubs, for example won no pennants or division crowns during the quarter century preceding the team's sale to the Chicago Tribune Company in 1981.

With the changing scale of the sports business have come new kinds of owners, most with their primary economic interests in other businesses. Some teams have been acquired by corporations, where they became parts of large organizations rather than the principal business of their owners. Corporate ownership of professional sports teams has been seen by a number of observers as having adverse effects on places. Ralph Andreano viewed acquisition of the New York Yankees by CBS as potentially increasing the disparities between teams in large and small markets: "the already uneven wealth and income base of the teams in the American League can only be distorted further by this transaction."[18] There is little evidence, however, that corporations with deep pockets have further tilted the playing field in favor of large markets. Certainly CBS did not enhance the Yankees' competitive advantage; the nine seasons that CBS owned the team were spectacularly unsuccessful compared with the Bronx Bombers' previous performance.

Corporations are also suspected of having less commitment to places and sports businesses than individual owners. Corporate loyalty to places has been steadily diminishing, as evidenced by thousands of closed factories and relocated corporate offices across the United States and Canada. As part of a large conglomerate, a sports team is likely to be subject to the same calculations that lead corporations to terminate locations for their other operations. "If and when corporations see that other vehicles of investment are more advantageous," argues Rob Beamish, "there is little to prevent them from withdrawing financial support from professional sport."[19] Many of the corporate barons that acquire sports franchises, however, have strong connections to the place where a team plays. Local considerations were a substantial part of the attraction of the St. Louis Cardinals to Anheuser-Busch, the Cubs to the Chicago Tribune Company, and the Braves and Hawks to Ted Turner and his Atlanta-based broadcasting empire. And because these corporations are closely identified with the places where their teams play, corporate locational and financial commitment is likely to be strong.

Commitment is also the key factor in other forms of ownership that are seen as weakening ties between teams and places. Syndicate arrangements, usually in the form of a limited partnership with a lead investor serving as managing partner, are alleged to produce detached ownership. Noting that "some clubs, like the Reds, Indians, Astros, and White Sox, came under syndicate ownership," David Q. Voigt concludes that "more often than not, their investors were preoccupied by outside business interests."[20] Such preoccupations are sometimes accompanied by weak ties to the team's home area; but partnership arrangements seem less critical than the owners' ties to place, and especially the commitment of the lead partner. Acquisition of the Jets in 1963 by a syndicate with strong roots in the New York area and led by Sonny Werblin, a skillful showman who headed the Music Corporation of America, saved the franchise and helped force the merger of the American Football League with the NFL.

Whether owned by corporations or rich individuals, sports teams increasingly are acquired to serve an owner's principal business—beer, television, pizza, blue jeans, or whatever. Teams advance primary business interests by attracting publicity for an owner's firm or product. Owning the Cardinals helped make Anheuser-Busch a dominant presence in sports advertising, sponsoring games and affixing its brand names at telegenic locations for all but three major league baseball teams by 1992. Across the border, Canada's leading brewers have gobbled up sports teams as a means of promoting their products. Molson Breweries owns the Montreal Canadiens and Labatt Brewing Company the Toronto Blue Jays. As a Labatt executive explains, the reasons for buying the Blue Jays had a great deal to do with selling beer and very little to do with the baseball: "Our investment in the Blue Jays gives us broadcast and sponsorship rights for television and radio. If we didn't own the team, we would have to have a long-term contract for those rights, and we feel ownership is cheaper in the long run."[21]

In recent years, professional sports teams have been particularly attractive to the communications industry. Broadcasting rather than baseball or basketball was the appeal of the Braves and Hawks to Ted Turner and his television superstation. Primary business considerations led the Chicago Tribune Company to purchase the Chicago Cubs, which are the principal attraction of the Tribune's superstation network. "We own the Nuggets because we're an entertainment company," emphasizes Comsat Video Enterprises. "We distribute entertainment. We package entertainment. We create entertainment."[22] And to have more entertainment to distribute, package, and create, Comsat added a hockey team to its portfolio in 1995, buying the Quebec Nordiques and moving the franchise to Denver. Similar business objectives led Comcast, the fourth largest cable television operator in the United States, to acquire a majority interest in Philadelphia's Flyers and 76ers in 1996. Other components of the entertainment industry have been drawn to professional sports teams as a means of enhancing their primary business. For the Walt Disney Company, a hockey team playing at its home base in Anaheim was another weapon in its arsenal of selling a good time. Named after a Disney movie about a kid's hockey team, the Mighty Ducks were replete with opportunities for merchandising, promoting other Disney products, and packaging hockey tickets with visits to Disneyland and stays at Disney's hotel. "Hockey," emphasizes a financial analyst, "is just another avenue to market the Disney product stream."[23]

The multiple business interests of a growing number of team owners is seen as another factor weakening connections between major league teams and places. This concern is closely related to worries about corporate ownership: teams become instrumental properties, valuable as long as they are useful to an owner's primary business, and likely to be discarded when the team no longer serves the main business, or the owner's interests change, or the enterprise is sold or merged or taken over by someone with different business priorities. As with corporations, these are legitimate concerns, underscoring the reality that a growing number of teams are subsidiary operations whose basic value is functional rather than locational. But the weakening of ties to place inherent in the use of teams to advance other business interests tends to be offset by the strong ties of most of these owners to the places where their teams play. Such owners are not likely to move their teams, and have strong incentives to sell to purchasers committed to keeping a team in town, as was the case when Anheuser-Busch sold the Cardinals in 1995.

More than a Business

For most owners, professional sports is more than a business proposition, whatever the appeals of the sports business itself or a team's contribution to a primary economic interest. Owners are attracted by love of the game, glamor, publicity, ego gratification, civic duty, and other considerations that make professional sports a special kind of business. Games themselves are a powerful allure to people who have played sports or are avid fans. The fan as owner is a dream come true, a chance to live the fantasy of being in charge of the home team. Owning a sports team provides public attention and recognition that few other businesses attract; more people read the sports pages than the business pages, and television rarely bothers with George Steinbrenner's shipbuilding business. Peter Pocklington, owner of the Edmonton Oilers, calls "hockey . . . a ticket to an almost crazy place in the sun" that "allows me to talk on things I like to speak out about and to be recognized."[24] And the ultimate satisfaction for an owner is to be a winner, standing on a box in a sweaty dressing room amid geysers of cheap champagne to accept the Super Bowl or Stanley Cup.

Place considerations are an important part of the special appeal of owning professional sports teams. Owners sometimes become involved to get their city into the big leagues or to keep the home team from moving, often at the urging of civic leaders and public officials. Walter Haas of Levi, Strauss agreed to rescue the Oakland Athletics in 1979 out of "a sense of civic duty."[25] Gerald and Allan Phipps put up the money to keep the Broncos in Denver because "it's our contribution to making Denver a complete city . . . as necessary to a community as libraries, museums, and a symphony orchestra."[26] Voigt questions whether civic pride counts for much with baseball owners, arguing "most were wealthy businessmen, set on enhancing their outside interests and upgrading their social status through baseball affiliations."[27] To be sure, claims of civic pride often mask business interests; or, perhaps more accurately, civic considerations are entertwined with economic considerations. August A. Busch Jr. maintained that he bought his baseball team "to save the Cardinals for St. Louis."[28] Certainly the Cardinals' tenure in St. Louis was at risk in 1953 following the conviction of the team's owner for tax violations, since a buyer might have moved the team. That Anheuser-Busch profited handsomely from the acquisition of the team does not nullify the civic element in the equation, nor reduce the importance of civic considerations in protecting the interests of places in keeping teams.

The rising appeal of owning professional sports teams increases the number of people and corporations interested in buying franchises. For places, this is a coin with two sides. More individuals and companies wanting to own major league teams generates pressures for more teams, and thus more opportunities for places to have teams. On the other hand, increased demand for teams also means more potential buyers for existing teams and greater insecurity for places, since ownership changes usually mean a new ball game in the relationship between places and teams. Owning a team has also become more attractive with the rapidly rising economic stakes, especially the advent of lucrative broadcasting contracts. Greater demand drives up franchise prices, which can reduce the number of prospective buyers committed to keeping a franchise in a particular city.

Adding to the attraction of owning professional sports teams is the tax shelter offered by player contracts, which have been treated as depreciable assets in the United States.[29] Tax advantages have been criticized as detrimental to place interests because they encourage turnovers in ownership, reduce commitment to place, and increase the likelihood that teams will be sold to someone that wants to relocate a franchise. Turnover is encouraged because tax benefits are limited to a fixed period of time, at the end of which the purchaser has a strong incentive to sell the team to a buyer who can then recycle the depreciation process. Tax benefits also make teams attractive commodities for reasons having little to do with sport or place; owners who have little commitment to the places where their tax shelters are located are likely to be less interested in building a stable base for a team in a particular place, and more frequently are absentee owners. "If a team is resold every few years," Roger G. Noll points out, "it is likely that occasionally the highest bidder will be someone from another geographical area who wishes to acquire the team."[30] This kind of turnover, Benjamin A. Okner argues, encourages relocation, since buyers are "primarily interested only in short-term attendance," and may wish to move a team to a new market that will provide "more fan support for a few years than the team's old hometown would."[31] Evidence to support or reject these hypotheses is not easily assessed. James Quirk and Rodney D. Fort show that turnover increased somewhat during the heyday of tax shelters.[32] How much of the higher incidence of turnover is attributable to tax considerations, however, is difficult to determine; as Robert C. Berry and Glenn M. Wong point out, "fast profits, tax advantages, cooling of ardor for being an owner, financial miscalculations, legal problems, personality conflicts—all these and more contribute to the turnover."[33]

Increased turnover, whatever its cause, increases uncertainty for places with teams; new owners usually mean new management, new relationships, and new demands with respect to facilities. Each sale raises the possibility of new owners with less commitment to a particular place or owners who want to move a team somewhere else. Unraveling the connections between ownership changes and relocation of teams is complicated. Relatively few teams have been moved immediately by new owners. In baseball, only three of the ten moves since 1953 involved ownership changes: the St. Louis Browns to Baltimore in 1954, the Philadelphia Athletics to Kansas City in 1955, and Seattle Pilots to Milwaukee in 1970.[34] None of the relocations involving established NFL franchises—the Cardinals to St. Louis and then Phoenix, the Raiders to Los Angeles and back to Oakland, the Colts to Indianapolis, the Rams to St. Louis, the Browns to Baltimore, and the Oilers to Nashville—was undertaken by new owners.

Private ownership is uncertain by its nature, putting places at the mercy of owners who make decisions about staying or moving, and demand more or less with respect to facilities. An owner may want to get out of the sports business, or desire to reap the appreciated value of a team. Owners even trade franchises, as occurred in 1972 when the Los Angeles Rams and Baltimore Colts changed hands in a complicated deal in which Robert Irsay bought the Rams from the estate of its previous owner and immediately swapped the team to Carroll Rosenbloom in return for Rosenbloom's Colt franchise. Rosenbloom was the big winner, exchanging Baltimore for the second biggest market without increasing his equity; both Los Angeles and Baltimore were big losers, since each wound up with an owner with little commitment to remain in place. Rosenbloom subsequently shifted the Rams to Anaheim and Irsay took the Colts to Indianapolis.

Death is the biggest uncertainty, raising the question of what happens to a team after its owner dies. The sequence of events that led to the swapping of the Colts and Rams franchises was triggered by the death of Dan Reeves, the long-time owner of the Rams. Once he had committed the Orioles to Baltimore, Edward Bennett Williams noted the concern was no longer whether he would move the team but that "I might die and my estate might sell the franchise."[35] After Williams' death the team was sold, but the new owner kept the team in Baltimore. As with the Orioles, death usually has led to the sale of teams, and thus increased uncertainty for places about the future of a franchise, but has not been a significant factor in team movement, aside from the ownership changes following the death of Reeves.

Profits and Places

Professional sports are more than a business to most team owners, but they still are a business. Noll, summarizing the findings of a 1974 study of professional sports undertaken by the Brookings Institution, emphasizes that the authors "find no evidence that the prime motivation of the vast majority is any consideration other than profits."[36] Profits have been a principal attraction for owners from the start of professional sports; those whose principal business was sports had to be profitable to survive, while others with money to invest were attracted by the prospect of making more. If Wayne Huizinga, enormously successful in waste disposal, video rental, and real estate, "couldn't make a profit in baseball," he "wouldn't be in it. . . . We're not in this business just for the love of sport and wanting to do something for South Florida."[37]

Profits are also important to places. Expansion is more likely when prospective owners anticipate substantial profits, as is formation of new leagues. Profitable franchises generally are more stable; unprofitable teams are prime candidates for relocation. Claims that a team is losing money in its present location are the most common rationale for relocation, and pressures on places for better deals for playing facilities and other subsidies often are based on team assertions about losses or inadequate profits. Owners and league officials insist that higher costs threaten to reduce the number of places with teams, with small markets the most vulnerable to losses resulting from players' rising salaries.

For places, the difficulty is that outsiders have a hard time in determining whether teams are making or losing money. Claims that teams have operating losses, or will be in the red, or that profits are decreasing are a constant refrain of teams and leagues that are negotiating with places. Verifying these claims is almost impossible because of the lack of reliable data on team finances. Most teams are privately held enterprises that do not have to report their finances. A variety of creative accounting methods makes claims of losses or falling profits by teams and leagues largely meaningless. Profits are hidden through tax-sheltered income, excessive administrative expenses, undervaluing assets, and complicated transactions with other businesses controlled by team owners.

Despite insistent talk of mounting losses and plummeting profits, there have been neither bankruptcies nor a reduction in the number of teams over the past two decades. Instead, more teams play in more places, are watched by ever larger crowds and television audiences, and generate growing revenues for team owners. Established teams and expansion franchises are sold for ever higher prices to buyers who are not in short supply. The robust market for teams is the best indicator of the financial health of the sports business. Gerald W. Scully's 1989 analysis of baseball economics concludes that the "historical appreciation of franchise values is the most convincing testament of the economic returns to ownership."[38] Consider the plight of George Argyros, who complained incessantly about losing money while he owned the Mariners, talked about leaving Seattle for greener pastures, used his financial problems to press for more subsidies, and sold a team he had purchased for $13 million for $76 million eight years later, clearing $25 million after expenses and interest.

Players and Places

Professional sports began with players; and the very few people with big league skills remain indispensable to the professional sports business. Although players are a constant, their role in the sports business and in the connection between professional sports and places has changed considerably. Players began by forming teams in places where they lived; then moved to places where teams would pay for their services; then entered a long period in which teams effectively owned players; and finally emerged in the last third of the twentieth century as increasingly in control of their destinies. Easing of restrictive labor practices has enabled players to claim a greater share of the revenues of professional sports, exercise more influence on the sports business, and have more freedom of choice over where they play.

All of these developments have important implications for places. Rising labor costs have intensified pressures on places to provide more support or face the loss of their teams. "All small-market owners are facing massive financial disorientation," argued the owner of the Milwaukee Brewers in 1991, in calling for "help from our communities in so many ways."[39] The growing power of players and their organizations has reduced the autonomy of owners and leagues over expansion, merger, and subdivision of leagues. Basketball players delayed merger of the NBA and the American Basketball Association until an agreement was reached that was acceptable to players. Baseball's realignment into three divisions in each league with another round of playoffs was restructured from the owners' original proposal to meet the demands of the Major League Players Association, whose approval was required by baseball's collective bargaining agreement.

Players also have much more control over where they work under contemporary labor arrangements. With greater freedom to decide where to play, place interests of professional athletes have become increasingly important. For many, to be sure, the best place to play is the team that offers the most money. But players are influenced by opportunities to play regularly, as well as by a team's style of play, coaching staff, playing facilities, and prospects of winning championships. Places are also attractive or unattractive on their own terms. Increased freedom of choice has permitted professional athletes to work close to home or in a place where they prefer to live. When he signed with the Houston Astros as a free agent, Doug Drabek emphasized that "it's not often you get a chance to play where you live, and most players like to take advantage of that."[40] Professional athletes are also influenced by living costs, weather, life style, taxes, quality of schools, and all the other things that affect individual and family locational choices. Despite fears that free agents would flock to New York and its wealthy big market teams, many players have avoided New York with its high housing costs, long commutes to the pleasanter residential suburbs, and sensation-seeking tabloids.

For many connected with professional sports, freedom of movement for players dilutes the connection between teams and places and fans. The reserve clause was essential, baseball argued, to maintain continuity and fan loyalty. Players play where they want, contemporary critics argue, at the cost of continuity and the identification of players with teams. "Players change teams now as casually as they change jockstraps," complains sportscaster Dick Schaap.[41] "There aren't any real teams anymore, teams that grow old together anymore," laments Pete Rose, "everybody's always changing . . . everybody'll play out their options all the time."[42] Teams in the past, of course, changed personnel; what was different was that teams controlled player movement. Fans have always been bothered by departures of favorite players, unless the home team wound up doing better with a new cast of characters. For most fans, however, the primal connection in professional teams sports is with the home team rather than a particular set of players.

Fans and the Sports Business

Fans are customers for the products produced by the private sports business; they buy tickets, refreshments, team and league merchandise, cable sports programming, and products that advertisers peddle on sports broadcasts. Emotional attachments to teams make fans a particular kind of customer; fans love their team, they are loyal and devoted, sticking with their team through bad seasons and losing streaks. Fans, however, are only part of the spectator or viewer base of professional sports, and generally a declining part. Much of the intensive marketing by teams is designed to attract customers who are not particularly interested in the game being played. Giveaways, animated scoreboards, and laser light shows are designed to enlarge the customer base beyond fans who come because of the game. So are better food, clean restrooms, blaring music, and other diversions such as the Tampa Bay Lightning's Fan Land with games and giant television screens. "A ball club isn't just a team," explains an official of the Oakland Athletics, "it's an entertainment entity or a lifestyle medium, much like Disneyland. Our market research showed us we had to pour a lot of resources into making the stadium more pleasant and into making the game appeal to more people."[43]

The most important customers of professional teams are not fans, but businesses that constitute the primary market for luxury seating and season tickets. Jerry Gorman and Kirk Calhoun estimate that the corporate community buys 90 percent of all luxury seating.[44] In 1985, business and corporate sales accounted for approximately half of the gate revenues in baseball, basketball, and hockey, and the proportion has steadily risen since.[45] Season tickets are extremely attractive to teams, providing revenue up front while guaranteeing that a certain number of seats will be sold regardless of the fortunes of the team or the vagaries of the weather. Purchasers of season tickets get the best seats, and in the case of some NFL and NHL teams, all the seats. With rising prices, season tickets have become increasingly expensive, especially for eighty-one baseball games or forty-one basketball or hockey contests. Increasingly, average fans are priced out of good seats or any seats, especially working- and lower-middle-class males who historically provided the fan base for professional team sports. By and large, teams have shed few tears for the fans they have lost. When the Dallas Cowboys required season ticket holders to buy bonds that helped finance the construction of a new stadium, the Cowboys' owner acknowledged that the team "lost a whole group . . . who couldn't afford to buy the bonds," but insisted that "we discriminated against them . . . no more than all America discriminates against people who don't have enough money to buy everything they want."[46]

Fans also have little influence on the sports business. They tend to articulate their interests weakly, seeing themselves as devotees rather than customers. Few fans have organized to press their collective interests in access to professional sporting events, in part because their interests are fragmented by place and by sport, as well as by whether they attend games or watch on television. FANS—Fight to Advance the Nation's Sports—was organized in 1977 by Ralph Nader to protect consumer rights in sports; another group, the National Sports Fan Association, was dedicated to making "professional sports accessible and affordable to the average American family."[47] These and other organizations have failed to attract much attention or many fans.

Loyal, unorganized, and a declining part of the customer base, fans are a minor consideration in the calculations of professional sports most of the time. Fan interests in affordable tickets and a team worthy of their loyalty are typically invoked by teams and leagues to advance their own objectives, usually in connection with disputes with players. Higher salaries and free agency, owners and league officials warn fans, mean more expensive tickets and fewer players loyal to the home team. When concern is professed by the sports establishment, fan interests turn out to be the same as the interests of owners and leagues. Commissioner Peter Ueberroth, for example, talked about protecting fans by intervening to prevent a baseball strike because "the fan cannot go unrepresented."[48] Little is heard about loyalty to fans, however, when teams and league pursue their business interests in higher prices, affluent customers, and more profitable locations.

Privatism in Perspective

The bottom line in understanding the relationship between professional sports and places is that teams belong to their owners—not to places where they play or fans who root for the home team or governments that pour millions into arenas and stadiums. This fundamental reality often gets lost in discussions about teams, places, and fans. For example, in an editorial entitled "Stopping

Sports Terrorism" prompted by the threatened departure of the Raiders in 1987, the *Los Angeles Times* suggested that "Congress could order the NFL and major league baseball to grant a franchise to any city that wanted one."[49] Franchises, of course, are not granted to cities, they are issued to private owners by private leagues. Places have no formal role in determining who owns teams that play in their cities, wear their names on their uniforms, and usually perform in public facilities. Sometimes places can influence the prospective ownership of an expansion team, but final decisions about owners and location of expansion teams are made by leagues rather than public officials.

Confusion over the ownership of professional sports is understandable. Teams are both private businesses and collective goods; teams belong to their owners, but are also community symbols and representatives of the places where they play. The sports business encourages fans and places to think of home teams as theirs; teams count on civic loyalty and emotional attachments to bolster attendance, fatten broadcast audiences, and provide support for new playing facilities and other public subsidies. Calling baseball "a community asset," an owner describes himself as "just the caretaker of the major-league franchise in town, and that franchise really belongs to the town."[50] Being a community asset implies public responsibilities, but professional sports insists that teams and leagues rather than government are the appropriate arbiters of these communal responsibilities. Bowie Kuhn argues that most owners "had a deep sense of dedication to the game and to the public," and that "it was important that the clubs retain control of the game."[51] Community assets but privately owned, increasingly publicly funded but resolutely private businesses, professional sports have secured the best of both worlds, winning public investments while maintaining private control.

Further complicating the business reality are persistent efforts to portray professional sports as games rather than business, with the business part a necessary nuisance in order to get on with the games, to enjoy the competition, and to root for the home team. People are attracted to professional sports by the games rather than the businesses that produce the show; places are connected to teams primarily by communal and emotional ties to the team playing the game rather than the team as a business enterprise. Professional sports understandably seek to emphasize sports rather than business. Baseball sells itself as the national pastime, not as the national sports business.

Notions of sport as more than business, of teams belonging to their communities, and of games that are collectively owned lead to visions of paradise lost, of an idyllic past when professional sport was not primarily a business. A journalist wrote in 1980 that "the national pastime—for decades played by larger-then-life heroes in a romantic atmosphere—now is a business people by entrepreneurs and often-wealthy employees."[52] The National Sports Fan Association rues transformation of the "sacred institution" of professional sports into "the business of sports entertainment."[53] Those who hearken to the good old days need a reality check; professional sports became a business once people owned teams and made their living from games. A decade after the organization of the National League, John Montgomery Ward, who played major league ball and later organized the Players League, wrote: "What was formerly a pastime has now become a business, capital is invested from business motives, and the officers and stockholders of the different clubs include men of social standing and established business capacity."[54]

For places, the bottom line in the privately controlled world of professional sports is that places only have teams when a private owner is willing to operate a team in a particular city or metropolitan area. Business and civic leaders, local media, elected officials, and sports agencies are not going to keep their team or get a new one, unless there is an owner committed to the place. When a franchise is for sale or about to be moved, the owner must be willing to accommodate a buyer who will stay put. After Robert Short decided to move the Senators to Texas, Bill Veeck put together a group that sought to buy the team for $9 million and keep the franchise in Washington, but Short was not interested and moved his team to Arlington. Owners decide when they will sell, and how much time will be given to local interests to buy the team or find a buyer committed to staying in town. Sellers also set the price for their team, which may be more than a home town buyer is willing to pay. If an owner decides to move, and is not blocked by the league, the private nature of professional sports is underlined for the community that loses what turned out not to be its team. As the essence of privatism was put by Robert Irsay when he moved the Colts from Baltimore to Indianapolis: "This is my team. I own it, and I'll do whatever I want with it."[55] And just in case the jubilant denizens of Indianapolis missed his point about who owned their new home team which would be playing in a stadium built with their tax dollars, Irsay bluntly reminded them that "it's not your ball team. Its mine . . . I paid for it."[56]

5

Business Partners

PROFESSIONAL sports are closely connected to other private businesses. Concessionaires and advertisers have been partners of professional teams since the early days of baseball, along with suppliers of sporting goods and transportation services. Newspapers spread the word about the home team, in return adding readers who turn first to the sports pages. Radio and television provide teams and their leagues with another product to sell—broadcast rights—and in the process have transformed every aspect of professional sports, including the relationship between teams and the places where they play. Most business partners of professional sports were local firms until well into the twentieth century, reflecting the localized markets of teams and the decentralized organization of many businesses that dealt with teams, such as newspapers, transit companies, and suppliers of beverages, hot dogs, and other products consumed at ballparks and arenas. Increasingly, professional teams and leagues deal with national firms—a great deal of broadcast money comes from national networks, the biggest advertisers are national and multinational firms, and concessionaires typically are national rather than local companies. These business developments reduce economic connections between a team and the place where it plays, while network broadcasts of games and nationwide marketing of major league apparel loosens the emotional bonds between fans and home teams.

Selling and Sports

Concessions are an industry that grew out of the opportunity provided by professional sporting events to sell food, drink, scorecards, and souvenirs to spectators. One of the first concessionaires was Harry M. Stevens, who began selling scorecards in Columbus in 1887 and moved on to New York, where he is reputed to have sold the first ballpark hot dog at the Polo Grounds in 1901. A century after Stevens began peddling scorecards, Harry M. Stevens Inc. had grown from a local enterprise to a national business, selling everything from hot dogs to hors d'oeuvres in luxury boxes in arenas and stadiums across the country. Concessions expanded into other businesses serving the sports indus-try, such as custodial services, security, and stadium management. With the expanding reach of sports concessionaires have come closer partnerships with professional sports. Delaware North, a major rival of Stevens, has participated in the financing of Busch Stadium in St. Louis, the Ballpark in Arlington, and Crossroads Arena in Buffalo in return for long-term concessions contracts.

Advertising has been the principal attraction of professional sports for most businesses. Because athletic contests draw audiences that other businesses want for customers, advertising has been an integral part of the professional sports scene from the start. Businesses have peddled their wares in game pro-grams, trading cards, signs on outfield fences, animated displays on electronic message boards, and the barrage of commercials that interrupt every sports broadcast. The most important advertisers are the big buyers of television time, who value the appeal of professional sports to particular groups, most notably younger males who buy beer, sneakers, and fast food. Brewers have forged the closest links, investing heavily in television advertising and even owning teams to maximize exposure to their brews.

Modern marketing has multiplied connections between professional sports and its business partners. Promotions attach company names to balls, caps, tote bags, and all sorts of other giveaways at arenas and stadiums. Corporate spon-sors pay substantial sums for exclusive arrangements with teams or leagues; advertisers pay for not having competitors hawk their product at the ballpark, while companies become the official rental car or airline of a league. Teams and broadcasters have sold off a growing list of parts of games to particular sponsors, such as time-outs, pitching changes, and out-of-town scores. More and more teams bundle advertising, sponsorship, and marketing; "we'll put together packages to build traffic in your stores," emphasizes a NBA owner, "including team appearances and displays."[1]

Increasingly popular and expensive is the practice of having a corporate name attached to an arena or stadium. Once a company or individual had to own a team to get its name (and product) on the front of the building, as with Wrigley Field in Chicago or Busch Stadium in St. Louis. Now airlines, banks, and other companies can buy naming rights without having to purchase a team. Buying the name of arenas and stadiums usually confers exclusive product rights; Pepsi Cola's $68-million twenty-year deal to put its brand on Denver's new arena included sole "pouring rights" for soft drinks as well as "exclusive exposure on all television and radio broadcasts, signs, ticket promotions and marketing campaigns" for all events at the Pepsi Center.[2]

Given the practices in other sports and countries, opportunities for expand-ing advertising and marketing relationships seem unlimited. Professional golf-ers and race-car drivers have become living advertisements for their sponsors' products; leagues or teams could sell the most photogenic parts of their uni-forms to Budweiser, Coca-Cola, McDonald's, and other heavy hitters from the corporate sports world. Tennis and golf tournaments are named for their sponsors, as are most college bowl games. Major league baseball teams in Japan and basketball clubs in Europe are named for the companies that sponsor them; baseball owners might follow suit and field Turner's Braves and Little Caesar's Tigers, and in the process lose another connection with the places where major league teams play.

National firms increasingly are the most attractive business partners for professional teams and leagues. Only companies with a national or international base have the resources to underwrite major broadcast sponsorships. Such firms also have the means and marketing skills to undertake similar operations in numerous locales, whether the company is bidding for a concessions contract or seeking to be the exclusive soft drink sold at the stadium and advertised in local broadcasts. Expansion of league business activities has reinforced substitution of national for local services, stadium advertisers, and broadcast sponsors. League marketing efforts typically involve agreements that give license holders exclusive rights throughout the league. In addition to weakening the place connections of major league teams, the growing web of business relationships with national firms increases the importance of market size and a league's market coverage. National advertisers want their products peddled in the markets where most beer drinkers, pizza eaters, and buyers of athletic shoes live. They are also more interested in sponsoring broadcasts or becoming a league's official widget if a league reaches important markets in all parts of the country.

Locally based business partners, however, continue to be very significant to teams. Business, as noted in Chapter Four, has become the most important customer of most major league teams, accounting for a growing proportion of season ticket sales and the bulk of the income from luxury boxes. Almost all of these purchases are made by local firms or the local offices of larger enterprises. Support from local businesses in the form of ticket purchases, luxury seating, advertising, and other commitments has become an essential element in the financing of arenas and stadiums, and the economic and political clout of these interests often determines whether new facilities are built. Among the vast array of firms based in a metropolitan area, the most important partners for professional sports tend to be the largest local firms and major corporations based in a particular place, such as Coca-Cola in Atlanta. Without such rich and powerful business connections, a team will be severely handicapped in the quest for more revenues, modern playing facilities, and favorable deals with local, state, and provincial governments.

Sports and the Mass Media

Newspapers have played an important part in the success of professional sports in American cities. Sports teams and newspapers had a mutual interest in the home town, which led papers to provide extensive and sympathetic coverage to local teams; as David Q. Voigt notes, "this coverage helped sell papers, which pleased publishers, and since it provided free advertising and whetted appetites for baseball, owners were pleased."[3] Sportswriters identified closely with the home team, championing the locals and fostering rivalries with teams from competing cities. Newspapers folded the home team into the general boosterism by which metropolitan dailies promoted their city, and in the process reinforced the connections between teams and places where they played. As professional sports expanded and attracted more interest, so did press coverage, making room for football, hockey, and basketball as they joined baseball in carrying the home town's banners.

Radio extended the reach of sports reporting, providing the listener with a more timely account of the game than the story that would appear in tomorrow's paper. But broadcasting went beyond the newspaper—which increased awareness of the product of professional sport but did not change its nature—by creating a new product, the rights to broadcast games. Broadcast rights were valuable because stations and networks could sell time to advertisers. Teams and leagues are able to sell these rights because broadcasts were judged to be the property of the team originating the game. In ruling for the Pittsburgh Pirates, which sued a radio station that broadcast games without the team's consent, a federal district court ruled in 1938 that the team "by reason of its creation of the game, its control of the park, and its restriction of the dissemination of news therefrom, has a property right in such news, and the right to control the use thereof for a reasonable time following the games."[4] Now the game was not the only product or, in time, the prime product; instead professional sports increasingly were used to sell products by those who advertised on broadcasts of sporting events.

Broadcasting also changed the nature of the sports business by extending the market for professional teams. Radio and then television brought major league games to more people, since broadcast networks often reached beyond the area covered by hometown newspapers. Some of those connected to teams by broadcasting became part of the primary customer base of people who went to games. Far more were added to the broadcast audience that constituted the growing secondary customer base of professional sports, particularly with the advent of television. "By 1951," notes Benjamin Rader, "some fifty million fans watched the Series on television—far more fans than had seen the Series live over its entire forty-eight-year history."[5]

Broadcasting represented both opportunity and threat to professional sports; the opportunity of more business, the threat of lost business. Some saw radio as another promotional instrument; like the sports pages, broadcasts would increase interest in the game, thus attracting more fans to the ballpark. Announcers were hired by the team rather than the station; most were home-team boosters whose job was to sell the team to listeners. Others in professional sports feared that people would be content to listen to a game on their radio rather than buy tickets, concerns that led New York's three baseball teams in 1934 to agree to ban radio broadcasts of their games. Television posed this dilemma even more sharply because video offered an increasingly attractive alternative to the live event. Initially, television was more promise than performance; one or two cameras with fixed lenses produced tiny figures on small black and white screens. But the technology improved rapidly, soon providing a better view than most seats in the stadium or arena.

At the outset of the television age, few in professional sports realized that the new medium fundamentally altered the connection between the spectator and the event, creating a new and far larger audience than customers who paid their way into the ballpark or arena. Instead, the sports establishment viewed television with alarm. In 1951, the president of the National Hockey League called television "the greatest menace in the entertainment world."[6] Commissioner Ford Frick felt that "baseball has to keep television from making the show too good. . . . The view a fan gets at home should not be any better than that of the fan in the worst seat in the ball park."[7] Professional sports' initial experiences with television seemed to confirm these fears. Home games of the Los Angeles Rams were televised in 1950, and attendance was almost halved; when home games were blacked out the following year, attendance rebounded. Both the Boston Braves and Cleveland Indians drew record crowds in winning pennants in 1948, and both experienced sharp drops in attendance over the next few years during which most of their home games were televised.[8]

Television, like radio, however, quickly proved irresistible to professional sports. The attraction, of course, was money; the ability of teams to sell radio and then television rights overcame fears that broadcasts would drain off paying spectators. Broadcasting revenues proved particularly attractive; they involved no additional direct costs and were "less subject to the changing whims of fan allegiance than is typically the case with attendance."[9] By 1939, major league baseball teams were receiving over $800,000 for radio rights, with the largest amounts going to teams in the biggest market, the New York Giants and New York Yankees, whose agreement not to broadcast games was abandoned as the monetary stakes grew. Today, broadcast money accounts for approximately half of the revenues of professional team sports. The National Football League forged the most lucrative partnership with broadcasters, who provided 58 percent of the league's revenues in 1995; the NBA was next with 41 percent, then baseball with 37 percent; the NHL lagged far behind, with less than 20 percent.[10]

Broadcasters inevitably sought control over the product they were selling to advertisers. Games were scheduled to fit the needs of television, often at the expense of those who bought tickets to watch the home team. Commercials were accommodated in basketball and football with television time-outs, which altered the flow of games and coaching strategies. As broadcast rights became increasingly expensive, more commercial time was scheduled, interrupting play more often and lengthening games. All of baseball's major attractions—the all-star game, league championship games, and World Series—

were scheduled at night to reach larger audiences, as was the Super Bowl. Longer seasons provided more games to broadcast and advertising time to sell. And league structures were altered to provide for additional playoff games to be televised.

As rewards from television grew, major league sports increasingly thought in the same terms as broadcasters, worrying about audience shares, advertising rates, and time slots, and seeking new ways to package their games to make them more attractive to broadcasters and advertisers. Inevitably, accommodating the needs of broadcasters reduced the control of teams and leagues over their business, and led them to consult closely with their broadcast partners on a wide range of issues. According to William O. Johnson, "no sensible entrepreneur buys a team, stages a major event, builds a stadium or even sets the starting hour of a game without first clearing it with a man from Mass.Com."[11] Perhaps a bit hyperbolic, but only a bit; when the NFL prepared to contest the move of the Raiders to Los Angeles, the league, according to Commissioner Pete Rozelle, was careful to "ascertain the views of the three television networks."[12]

Packaging professional sports for television viewers clearly has adverse effects on those who buy tickets to games. Some observers predict that the logic of televised sports will obviate the need for spectators. "Stadiums," suggest Peter R. Shergold, "will become little more than studios; . . . and the contests an arrangement between sports owners, players, and media entrepreneurs."[13] Ron Powers argues that paying spectators were incidental to the United States Football League; because the league derived most of its revenues from television, "the live fans were not directly necessary to the financial survival of the league. . . . The fans were necessary as *props*—as a kind of extended studio audience, to strengthen the illusion of the television viewer at home that he was watching a credible sporting event."[14] The USFL, however, was an extreme case, and a very unsuccessful league in part because of its failure to attract fans to its games. Television has not obviated the need for spectators. Even in the National Football League, which derived 58 percent of its revenue from television, gate and other stadium income was almost S29 million for the average team in 1995. NFL teams, like those in the other leagues, seek to maximize their revenues from paying customers through bigger and better facilities, higher-priced seating, control over concessions, and favorable stadium deals. And teams and leagues, along with broadcasters and advertisers, need crowded arenas and stadiums, since seas of empty seats undermine the credibility of a major league and the value of its product.

Local fans and home teams were not made obsolete by television, but they were no longer the whole show, as in the past. Television has attenuated the connections between teams and places; the greater the flow of national television revenues, the less dependent were teams on their local markets. Inevitably, games played in places before hometown crowds, the essence of professional team sports, became less central. And professional sports increasingly would be judged as businesses in terms of the size and demographic characteristics of the television audiences commanded by a league.

Television and Markets

Broadcasting, like professional team sports, is highly sensitive to geographically defined markets. Also similar to sports with its teams and leagues is the two-level organization of broadcasting into stations and networks. Until fairly recently, teams dealt primarily with stations that broadcast their games locally, and leagues contracted with networks for national coverage. Local broadcasting of professional sports builds on traditional connections among people, places, and teams. Local radio coverage and telecasts draw listeners and viewers primarily from those who support the home team. Revenues from local broadcasting depend heavily on the size of the local market, with teams in the largest markets selling their broadcast rights for anywhere from three to twenty times as much as the smallest markets.

Stations are linked into networks for both local and national sports broadcasts. Radio coverage of games on ad hoc networks significantly increased the reach of the Boston Red Sox, Chicago Cubs, St. Louis Cardinals, and other baseball teams. In 1951, Chicago Bears' games were televised to eleven cities through a network put together by the team. National networks initially broadcast games that would attract a broader audience, beginning with radio coverage of baseball's all-star game and World Series. The first national telecasts of regular season games were arranged by networks in deals with individual teams rather than leagues, when the Dumont network televised five NFL games in 1951 and ABC began the baseball "Game of the Week" two years later. Not until the 1960s did leagues rather than teams deal with national networks for broadcasts of regular season games. The shift from a local to national broadcasting base has been most advanced in the case of football, where league contracts with national networks provide for exclusive telecasts of regular season and playoff games. Other sports have mixed national network and local broadcasts, usually with some means of restricting local telecasts that compete with network games.

The partners of professional sports in the quest for national broadcasting audiences and dollars were the three networks that dominated television in the United States until recently. Leagues were paired with a single network until the football merger led the NFL to deal with CBS and NBC; and the NFL soon added ABC to its stable with a nationally televised game on Monday night. Opportunities for more connections and revenues multiplied as networks proliferated in the 1980s, primarily in response to the spread of cable television. The NFL brought ESPN, the all-sports cable network, into its fold in 1987, and three years later included another cable outfit, the Turner Broadcasting System, in a five-network television package. Baseball signed a $400 million deal with ESPN for 1990 to 1993, along with its $1.06 billion contract with CBS for the same period, while the NBA had broadcast agreements with Turner Broadcasting and NBC. For the new networks, these sports contracts represented a readiness to play in the big leagues of broadcasting. And in 1993, Fox, another newcomer eager to establish its place as a major network, outbid CBS for the largest piece of the NFL's television pie, agreeing to spend $1.58 billion over four years, and then added baseball and hockey to its product line. Joining Fox Sports in the 1995 baseball deal along with NBC and ESPN was an additional new player, Liberty Media-Fox Cable.

National television coverage of regular season games did not draw on a natural reservoir of interest, which is why networks initially were interested in all-star contests, the World Series, and other games likely to attract national audiences. Of the four sports, football has been the most successful in moving from local to national markets for regular season games. The NFL's initial partnership with CBS provided for all league games to be televised, with home games blacked out, away games shown in the team's viewing area, and the rest of the network's outlets showing a game most likely to appeal to local audiences. These arrangements accelerated the development of extensive followings for some teams; the Dallas Cowboys became America's team in the 1970s, drawing the largest television audiences of any football team. Organization of television on a national basis combined with the wide appeal of the NFL's basic product to nurture a growing audience interested in watching professional football rather than a particular team. As a result, the NFL has developed a much larger audience for its games than other sports, and the most lucrative television deals in professional sports, including contracts for broadcasts of games scheduled for nationwide television on Sunday and Monday evenings.

Baseball, by contrast, continues to appeal primarily to hometown fans during the regular season. "Baseball," in the view of Roone Arledge, who built ABC Sports, "is essentially a local sport, a home-town sport, which mitigates against national television."[15] About three times as many people watch telecasts of the home team as tune in national games.[16] Networks have continued to concentrate on postseason play, which attracts national audiences. And baseball teams, especially those in the largest markets, have been reluctant to have national telecasts preempt local broadcasts, and thus reduce their income from local television, which totaled more than $350 million in 1993.

The NBA has carved out a position somewhere between baseball and football. Network television has concentrated primarily on postseason play, which in the early 1990s added up to a lot of television, since the playoffs lasted more than a month and involved the eventual contenders for the championship in three preliminary rounds before the final seven-game series. Unlike the baseball leagues, the NBA worked diligently to market the league and its superstars; and the emergence of performers like Michael Jordan and Shaquille O'Neal, whose appeal transcended their teams, steadily increased the NBA's attraction to national audiences. But like baseball clubs, NBA teams have been reluctant to have national telecasts reduce lucrative local broadcasts; "teams," an owner emphasizes, "must preserve as much local rights as possible because there's a market for it."[17] Hockey owners also have been wary of forfeiting local television revenues, a view reinforced by the NHL's difficulties in developing national broadcasting markets in the United States. While other leagues were hitting the television jackpot in the 1980s, the NHL had to settle for modest contracts with cable networks until the mid-1990s.

Despite these national-local variations, all four sports have been significantly affected by the desire of national broadcasters to maximize the market for sports telecasts. National networks want leagues with teams in large metropolitan markets throughout the United States; and professional sports revenues from national television depend on audiences that sports telecasts can deliver to advertisers. Television reinforced the importance of market size for professional sports; more than ever, leagues needed to be represented in major media markets. Leagues are also more attractive to television networks when teams in the largest markets are successful, thus enhancing the prospective audience for postseason play.

Media market considerations played an important role in shaping the National Football League after the merger with the American Football League. Before the merger, the sixteen NFL teams played in metropolitan areas that were twice the size of the ten AFL markets; as a result, CBS's contract with the NFL provided more revenues per team than the AFL's deal with NBC. Fearful that unequal television revenues would condemn the AFL teams to second-class citizenship, some AFL owners rejected the initial merger plan, which maintained two leagues with their own network contracts and provided for inter-league play.[18] At their insistence, a single league was created that was divided into two conferences with equal television revenues for all; the switch of Baltimore, Cleveland, and Pittsburgh from the National to American put thirteen teams in each conference and reduced the disparity between CBS's markets and those served by NBC.

Television's need for nationwide markets has intensified pressures for expansion and relocating teams. Professional sports were narrowly defined geographically when television arrived on the scene in the 1950s; the westward and southward movement of population placed more and more of the national television audience outside areas served by the major leagues. Some observers see television as the prime factor in the spread of sports leagues; an examination of the sports business in the *Washington Post* in 1983 concluded that "television in the 1950s became the catalyst that forced the expansion of major sports into all regions of the land."[19] "Forced" is too strong a term; professional sports were pressed to expand by a variety of considerations in addition to television, including internal pressures from owners, fears of rival leagues, the attractions of the new markets of the west and south, and the political muscle of places that wanted big league teams. Still, television clearly was important. Roger G. Noll emphasizes the role of television in the reorientation of professional basketball through "relocations and expansions between the mid-1950s and the late 1960s," which placed "the NBA in all of the largest media centers, increasing the value of its product both at the gate and over the air."[20]

Television has had the most effect on the territorial reach of the NHL. Hockey's first expansion was heavily influenced by the lure of television money; before 1966, the NHL had teams in only four markets in the United States—Boston, Chicago, Detroit, and New York—large markets, to be sure, but limited in the kind of television audience they could deliver to national broadcasters and advertisers. The need to expand its television appeal in the United States led the league to bypass Vancouver and Quebec City in the initial expansion to twelve teams, since "the addition of the Canadian cities was not necessary to get an American TV contract."[21] In the 1990s, the NHL again sought to increase its attractions for national television in the United States by expanding into the Sunbelt; "if we ever want to get a bigger TV contract," explained an owner, "we have to get into more markets."[22] Four of the five teams added between 1991 and 1993 were in Florida and California. The NHL also encouraged movement of franchises from hockey's frozen heartland to metropolitan areas in the United States that would enhance what the league called its "geographic footprint" for television in the United States.[23]

Critics argue that television has had a bad influence on the location of professional sports teams. Donald A. Klatell and Norman Marcus see television as shifting franchises from places that valued their teams to locales that offered bigger television markets: "Teams and leagues have sprung up in cities chosen for their television potential, abandoning others after years of loyal fan support."[24] Rader contends that television dictated moves that made little sense demographically, indicating that "potential broadcast revenues rather than population concentrations often determined the location of major league baseball franchises"[25] Powers suggests that television led leagues into places that had no particular interest in a big-league franchise; leagues were "emboldened . . . to extend their empires, establishing franchises and building new stadiums in cities where no intrinsic demand for a major-league team had ever made itself known."[26] And Ira Horowitz regrets that "franchise location decisions are influenced by potential broadcast revenues, to the detriment of areas with a small broadcast audience."[27]

None of these criticisms is particularly persuasive, since leagues and broadcasters, by and large, have had similar market interests. Areas with large broadcast audiences have big populations, and were most attractive to sports leagues before the advent of television or radio. Sizable metropolitan areas like Los Angeles, San Francisco, Houston, Dallas, Miami, and Atlanta would have been prime candidates for major league teams even if broadcasting had not become a golden goose for sports. Small broadcast audiences, like modest populations, are a disadvantage in securing big league teams, although smaller metropolitan areas like Denver or Charlotte that can tap larger regional markets for ticket sales and broadcast audiences are proving increasingly attractive to sports leagues. Moreover, almost every franchise relocation or expansion has put major league teams in places that wanted big league sports sufficiently to provide new facilities at public expense; these were not teams being plunked, as Powers indicates, in places that exhibited no prior interest in a big league team.

As for relocation, few franchise moves have resulted primarily from a desire for television revenues. Perhaps the clearest case of a television-prompted move was the relocation of the Braves from Milwaukee to Atlanta, which tripled the team's television revenues. Atlanta offered the entire southeast as a television market, compared to Milwaukee, which was hemmed in by big league broadcasts in Chicago and Minneapolis; "we moved south in the first place because of TV," admits a Braves official, "we filled that gap in eight states which had been without a big league team."[28] Of course, the reach of Atlanta throughout the southeast would have been an attraction even if television had not been part of the picture, as would the fact that the Atlanta metropolitan area was growing almost four times faster than Milwaukee and its suburbs.[29] Pay television was a consideration in the move of the Dodgers to Los Angeles, where Walter O'Malley envisaged a bonanza that never materialized. Prospective television revenues also played a part in the decision to move the Raiders to Los Angeles, which offered greater market potential than Oakland in the event that NFL teams were able to secure unshared revenues from pay television; and the fading of this vision of vast local television riches was a factor in the Raiders' departure from Los Angeles in 1995.

Certainly television has had an enormous impact on the territorial framework of professional team sports; it has amplified the demand for franchises, increased pressures for relocating teams and expanding leagues, spurred the organization of new leagues, and reinforced the importance of market size and coverage. Television has also reduced the likelihood that more than one team in a sport will be located in a metropolitan area, since networks gain nothing in terms of national audience from having another NBA team in Chicago or a second hockey club in the Boston area. Still, to blame television for preferring large over small markets or more over less profitable places to play, or for exclusive territorial rights, is to ignore the shared interests of broadcasters and professional teams and leagues. The imperatives of large markets, national reach, and territorial exclusivity were not created by the broadcast partners of professional sports. Territorial rights that restrict access to markets already served by a team predate the electronic revolution in all four sports. Leagues that failed to pay attention to the massive shifts of population and the rise of major new metropolitan centers would have been faced with rival leagues as well as smaller checks from broadcasting networks.

Territorial Concerns

Changes in the television business have raised complicated territorial issues for professional sports. A team's territorial rights include exclusive control over broadcasts by other teams in the league within its area, with teams "exchanging broadcast rights so as to permit each club live broadcasts of its away games."[30] Local control over broadcasts can be superseded for games telecast under league contracts with national networks. As already noted, however, cable television networks did not fit neatly into this local-national division of territoriality; cable networks picked up local telecasts of games and distributed them to stations, including those within the territories of other teams in the league. Thus were born the superstations, beaming games into what had been exclusive markets of home teams.

Superstations challenged control of both local territories by teams and national broadcasts by leagues. Beaming telecasts into other major league baseball markets was denounced by Commissioner Peter Ueberroth as "a violation of another team's territory."[31] By jeopardizing teams' gate revenues and their local television audiences and revenues, superstations, warned Commissioner Bowie Kuhn, "could prompt franchise moves and otherwise destabilize an industry"[32] Superstation broadcasts also reduced the value of a sport to national television networks, since games on superstations competed with national games for viewers and saturated the market with games. Superstations rejected these arguments, contending that their broadcasts stimulated interest in baseball or basketball and the home team; "having the games on TV helps sell the product," insisted an official of the Chicago Tribune Company, owner of both WGN and the Cubs.[33] Klatell and Marcus in their 1988 study of television and sports conclude that the fears of the critics have little basis in reality: "Statistics show . . . that superstations have relatively little effect either on home team attendance or on the ratings of home stations."[34]

Convinced by neither the superstations' contentions nor data on attendance and audiences, professional sports have sought without much success to restrict superstations. Major league baseball sought and received assurances from Ted Turner when he bought the Atlanta Braves that he would "comply with the best interest of baseball in all matters including baseball's collective posting on cable television."[35] Turner, however, moved ahead with his plans to turn WTBS into a superstation with the Braves' games as a prime attraction. Internal efforts to limit superstations have been constrained by the considerable influence of cable television within professional sports. The two largest superstations—WTBS and WGN—are part of corporate empires that also own teams. WGN's owner, the Chicago Tribune Company, is the television partner of a number of baseball teams, as well as the Chicago Bulls. Teams such as the New York Mets and New York Yankees profit handsomely from their partnerships with superstations and regional sports cable networks. Other teams and owners have broadcasting interests or plans that temper their enthusiasm for restricting superstations. Efforts in Congress to curb superstations have been handicapped by these internal divisions and stymied by the political muscle of the cable industry.

Restrictions on cable broadcasts have also not fared well in the courts. An NBA plan to limit superstation broadcasts was challenged in federal court by the Chicago Bulls and WGN. A victory for the NBA would have opened the legal door to similar restrictions by other leagues to the detriment of superstations, teams whose games they broadcast, and cable stations whose audience ratings were bolstered by games on superstations. The judge, however, ruled that the NBA's proposal was "a significant restraint of trade" that did not "contribute to any legitimate objective . . . by increasing competition in the broadcast of NBA games or between NBA games and other forms of TV programming."[36] The ruling, which was upheld on appeal, was greeted by the victors as a "groundbreaking decision for superstations, fairness and freedom of choice for fans."[37]

New Connections

By the 1990s, professional teams and leagues were inextricably entwined with their broadcast partners. "If we had our druthers, we wouldn't want to be economically dependent on any one thing," Pete Rozelle confessed in 1987, "but as it stands 60 percent of our money comes from television."[38] Increased dependence has been accompanied by accelerating change in the connections between professional sports and broadcasting. The most lucrative partnerships of the 1990s, those between leagues and national networks, bore little resemblance to the relationships of a decade earlier. One new element was the cable networks, which had secured a piece of the national broadcasting action of each major league. Another change was the exit of CBS, a central player in network sports for more than three decades, from major league broadcasting. CBS dropped baseball after taking heavy losses on its billion-dollar contract in the early 1990s. In football, CBS was outbid by Fox Broadcasting for the flagship television properties of major league sports, the Super Bowl and the NFL's National Football Conference with its base in large metropolitan markets.

Traditional arrangements between broadcasting and professional sports are also in flux, as teams and leagues experiment with alternatives to selling broadcast rights to stations and networks that produce games, sell advertising, and deliver the finished product to audiences on free television. Driving these changes are rapid changes in communications technology, which multiply the number of outlets for sports broadcasts and offer more flexibility in how and to whom telecasts are transmitted. The appeal of these new technologies is enhanced by the desire of professional sports for more control over their product and more broadcasting revenue. These changes, like past developments in broadcasting, have important implications for the relationship between professional sports and the places where teams play.

One consequence is the repackaging of sports broadcasting to emphasize local and regional markets. Network television sought national markets for its sports broadcasts, even though strong markets for national coverage of regular season games have developed only for professional football. More revenues can be generated from local markets in baseball, basketball, and hockey; and new broadcasting arrangements promise teams increased income from local and regional telecasts. Cable television provides the means for extending local sports telecasts to larger regional markets, and the potential to raise local revenues significantly. Regional cable networks can be put together by teams rather than broadcasters, which provides a team with more control over its telecasts and greater revenue possibilities. Along with organizing cable networks, a growing number of teams are producing their own show. And a few teams like the Boston Celtics have moved even further by buying a local station.

For leagues, the parallel to producing games and acquiring stations is league operation of broadcast networks. League networks would organize local outlets, produce games, and sell advertising, and in the process regain control over the league's product. Leagues could broadcast games nationally as well as to local and regional markets. Networks controlled by leagues could operate over traditional television, cable, and pay-per-view. The pay-per-view possibilities are particularly attractive, since viewers would be able to buy telecasts of any team they wanted to watch regardless of where they happened to live. A Denver Bronco fan in Los Angeles, for example, could buy telecasts of individual Bronco games or all the team's games in a season package.

Baseball made the most dramatic move into the television business, the result of necessity when there were no takers among the major networks for a new contract after the expiration of CBS's disastrous venture in 1993. A new kind of partnership was created with ABC and NBC; unlike past arrangements with the networks, no money was guaranteed by the broadcasters and advertising would be sold by baseball rather than the networks. To increase the amount of commercial time to sell to national advertisers, baseball added another round of playoffs. During the regular season as many as fourteen games were televised at once so that local fans could watch the home team. Local telecasts were preempted by the national arrangement, which distressed teams in the largest markets, whose local broadcasts were worth less since fewer games were available; the New York Mets complained that the new deal took "money out of the pockets of individual clubs, most of them from large markets who televise heavily."[39]

More control for leagues and teams means trading the certainty of a contract for broadcast rights for the riskier business of assuming the costs of production and the necessity to sell advertising. Crippled by the 1994 strike that canceled postseason play and telecasts, baseball's venture with ABC and NBC dissolved the following year amidst disappointing revenues and disputes with the two networks. Risk sharing, however, is very attractive to broadcasters, especially after the losses experienced by networks in the glutted television sports market of the early 1990s. Networks are likely to bargain with leagues, and stations with teams, for revenue sharing as an alternative to higher rights fees. The NBA contract with NBC that went in effect in 1994 provided for a smaller increase than the league had sought in return for NBC sharing advertising revenue with the NBA in the fourth year of the contract.

For teams and leagues, pay-per-view rather than revenue sharing is the preferred approach of the future. Pay-per-view offers the most control over the product and the largest pots of gold at the end of the rainbow. As noted above, pay-per-view can be customized to the individual customer's preferences for what games are to be viewed; advertising on pay-per-view also can be tailored to the individual viewer or a particular class of viewers. Professional sports, at least in its video incarnation, will be free from the bounds of geography; home team allegiances as well as other preferences for particular teams can be exercised by anyone with the money to buy games on the tube.

6

Teams in Leagues

THE BUSINESS of professional team sports requires organization of teams into leagues. Leagues bring together a set of places that provide the primary market for the collective product; they provide the framework in which teams meet to produce games; they structure games into seasons, playoffs, and championships. Customers prefer organized games among teams competing for pennants, division titles, or a place in postseason play. As Commissioner Pete Rozelle constantly reminded NFL owners, "if you didn't belong to a league, and just had teams arranging scrimmages against one another, you couldn't expect many people to watch."[1]

The necessity for teams to be organized as leagues structures relations between professional sports and places. Leagues exercise controls over the location and relocation of teams, territorial rights, suitability of places for teams, the number of places that can have franchises, and who can own teams. They determine how revenues will be shared among members, negotiate national broadcasting arrangements, and bargain collectively with players. These league activities raise complicated issues of public policy, whose outcomes shape the way places connect with teams and leagues.

Structuring the Game

In performing their functions, leagues have developed a common organizational structure, composed of individual teams operating collectively under direction of a commissioner. Baseball has the most complicated arrangement, maintaining two separate leagues, each with its own president, umpires, and even playing rules in the case of the designated hitter. The bifurcated structure of baseball is important to places because relocation and expansion have been undertaken primarily by leagues rather than baseball as a whole. The result of these arrangements has been interleague competition for the most desirable new markets. In the initial relocations in the 1950s, the National League won the big prizes of Los Angeles and San Francisco, while the Americans wound up with Baltimore and Kansas City. Determined not to lose again, the American League jumped the gun in 1961, expanding a year ahead of the National League; and after both leagues added teams in 1969, the American League moved on its own to add expansion franchises in Seattle and Toronto.

Leagues are associations of teams rather than independent entities; they exist to promote the common interests of their member teams, which are separately owned and operated firms. League rules are determined by member teams, and are only effective as long as individual teams abide by them. Teams collectively make league decisions on relocation, expansion, revenue sharing, and network broadcasting contracts. Extraordinary majorities usually are required on important questions like moving or adding teams. These special voting requirements increase the power of individual owners or small groups of teams with common interests, such as large-market teams desirous of protecting their territories from competition and their revenues from sharing arrangements.

Team interests often conflict with the collective welfare of a league. Revenue sharing reduces income for some clubs in the interest of lessening economic differences among all teams in a league. Few teams can resist the attractions of unshared revenues from luxury boxes, better stadium and concessions deals, and broadcasting income outside league control, even though these revenues tend to increase disparities within a league. Conflict has been intensified by the rapidly increasing economic stakes of professional team sports. Newer owners who pay hefty prices for their teams and carry substantial debts are particularly interested in maximizing team revenues, which intensifies conflicts within leagues over revenue sharing, broadcasting deals, labor contracts, and expansion fees.

Differences among league members are amplified by the people who own major league franchises. Most are rich and powerful individuals who have been successful in other businesses and are used to having their way. Strong egos and personal animosities among owners exacerbate conflicts within leagues over relocation, expansion, and sharing revenues. Baseball owners, in the words of one, "never learned how" to be "both competitors and partners off the field."[2] Owners in the NFL have been more willing to subordinate individual for collective interests; they were the first to adopt an amateur playing draft, and developed the most extensive revenue-sharing arrangements in professional team sports. Still, sustaining collective concerns has been a constant struggle within the NFL. "We have a very fragile, delicate thing in this league," an owner emphasized in 1995, "that allows Green Bay to compete with the Giants, for Buffalo to compete with Chicago, for small cities to compete with the big ones."[3]

Leadership has been an important factor in the interplay of league and team interests. Formidable political and public relations skills enabled Pete Rozelle to expand league authority despite an increasingly diverse and contentious set of NFL owners. Another strong leader, David Stern, revitalized the NBA, turning a league plagued by drugs, weak franchises, and declining television appeal into a vibrant organization that pioneered the development of salary caps and league marketing, while expanding successfully and securing lucrative network television contracts. Under Stern, the NBA has emphasized league interests and league services to teams in marketing, promotions, and local broadcasting. National broadcasting revenues also have boosted the power of league officials. The dependence of NFL owners on the commissioner's ability to make good television deals greatly enhanced Rozelle's authority over all aspects of the game.

The dynamic relationship between teams and leagues affects connections between professional sports and places. Teams are located in a particular place, leagues are not. Leagues care about places, but their place interests are different from teams. League officials are concerned about a set of places; they worry about market coverage and being in major markets. Increasingly, the focus of leagues is national and international, while teams are preoccupied with their metropolitan and regional market. David Stern promotes the NBA as an entity rather than a set of teams—in Stern's words, as "a major business organization put together to produce a certain product."[4] Stern, reports Bill Saporito, "looks at his business as an entertainment—with a global brand" similar to "entertainment companies like Disney."[5] In Stern's approach, individual teams become units of the business like Disneyland or Disney World, and places where they play are the sites of particular business units in the same sense that Anaheim and Orlando are for the Disney empire. Of course, there are critical differences between the NBA and Disney; each of the NBA's twenty-nine teams is individually owned and operated, most play in public arenas, and the owners collectively hire and fire the league commissioner as well as pass judgment on league decisions affecting ownership of teams, relocation of franchises, expansion of leagues, suitability of arenas, national broadcasting deals, and sharing of revenues.

Competitive Leagues

Professional teams have a collective interest in producing games that involve enough uncertainty to sustain the interest of their customers. Competitive leagues are good business; close pennant races and more teams in contention for postseason play increase attendance and broadcast audiences. A league's ability to produce competitive games, teams, and seasons determines how many places will have successful teams at least some of the time. "It's important that the fan in the franchise city have a hope," emphasizes an official of a NFL team. "We have to have a system to hold the fans, to hold the ratings. Our product is close games. It has to be. We have to have an entertaining game for our fans and for television, or the money's not going to be there."[6]

A league's collective interest in competitiveness coexists uneasily with the desire of individual teams to be successful. Team success means doing better than other clubs by winning more games and championships. Winning teams attract more customers, command more local broadcast revenues, earn additional revenues from postseason play, and make more money for their owners. Both winning teams and competitive leagues are good for business, but teams that win most of the time reduce league competitiveness. This situation leads to arguments that teams have a rational interest in winning, but not so often as to dominate a league and undermine the viability of weaker teams. To maximize revenues, James Quirk and Mohamed El Hodiri suggest, "the owner will wish to field a team that is stronger than the league average, but not too strong, since revenues fall if the probability of winning is too high, reflecting the loss of public interest in contests that lack uncertainty of outcome."[7] Winning, however, can be a profitable business strategy even if a team dominates its league. Great teams and dynasties usually are good business for the triumphant team, if not the league. Henry G. Demmert finds that the "limit to how good a given team can become without adversely affecting its profitability by destroying the contest, or uncertainty aspect of the product . . . is beyond the range of observable data. Without exception, the popularly acknowledged 'super teams' appear to have had substantial economic success."[8]

For most teams, the incentives to win also are more powerful than the rewards of increased competitiveness. Although closely contested games, pennant races, and championships are collectively desirable, individual teams understandably are wary of the risks inherent in highly competitive enterprises. "The best of all possible worlds for a club may be to win the championship by the closest possible margin," notes Demmert; "however, in an uncertain world, the club faces obvious a priori risks of not winning in such a situation, and if there is a positive payoff to winning, such as playoff money, the maximization of expected profits will require winning by more than a close margin."[9] Noneconomic considerations reinforce the attractions of winning teams over competitive leagues. Most people who own teams are highly competitive; they are used to success, and success in professional sports is measured by won-lost records and championships rather than profits and losses. "Unlike most businesses," a baseball official points out, "the team which makes the most money is not highly regarded; the team that wins the World Series is."[10] Fans reinforce the drive for victory; fans care more about rooting for winners than whether the home team plays in a competitive league. And winning itself increases pressures to win again, heightening expectations of players for bigger contracts, of fans for another victorious season, and of owners for the thrill of another championship.

Among the four sports, the NFL has been most committed to increasing competitiveness. League control of television and sharing of most revenues were acceptable to NFL owners because these policies promised a more attractive product by increasing the ability of teams to compete regardless of market size. The NFL also uses scheduling to increase competitiveness, matching teams for games outside their division with opponents with similar records during the previous season. Most teams, however, cannot have winning records no matter how committed a league to competitiveness or how much tinkering is done with schedules and divisions. For every win there is a loss (except in football and hockey, where a few regular season games end in ties); and only one team can win the World Series, Super Bowl, Stanley Cup, or NBA championship. Leagues, however, can create more winners by increasing opportunities to participate in postseason play. Leagues can be subdivided into conferences and divisions whose winners make the playoffs, and "wild card" teams can be added to increase the number that advance to postseason play.

Critics insist that more playoff teams cheapen the regular season; Benjamin Rader argues that "the burgeoning number of playoff games sharply reduced the importance of regular season games" which become "more meaningless" as additional teams qualify for postseason play.[11] Purists also bemoan the possibility of teams with mediocre records winning championships. Additional playoff spots, however, sustain interest in more teams in more places; what might have been meaningless games by an also-ran team becomes a spirited battle for the last playoff spot in an NBA conference or an NFL wild card berth. And too few winners in a league certainly results in lots of "meaningless" games as the also-rans play out their schedule. Playoffs also are good business; postseason games draw larger crowds at higher prices, attract better media deals, and make substantial contributions to team revenues. NHL teams in 1988–1989 earned more than a third of their profits during playoffs; according to league figures, teams made $31.3 million for the regular season and another $17.5 million for the playoffs.[12]

Capable Owners

Every team in a league has a stake in the viability of the other members. Teams have a collective interest in the ability of each club to field a major league team, maintain a schedule, sustain a successful business, and carry its financial weight as a league member. Should a team fail or experience serious financial problems, the rest of the league typically has stepped in to insure continuity and maintain public confidence in the league. When the expansion Seattle Pilots collapsed after an unsuccessful first season, the franchise was taken over by the American League and then sold to Milwaukee interests who moved the team to Wisconsin. The NFL operated the Dallas Texans after its owners threw in the towel during the 1952 season, then arranged for its purchase at a bargain price and relocation to Baltimore. League funds had to be used to help the New

England Patriots meet its payroll in 1987, and the continuing financial problems of the debt-ridden franchise threatened to saddle the NFL with millions of dollars in obligations.

Leagues seek to protect their members' collective interests in having capable owners through a variety of procedures and policies. Ownership rules are set by members of the league; they make the rules, then apply or change them in deciding who can become a member of their club by buying a team, owning an expansion franchise, or joining a league in a merger. The power of leagues to determine who can own a team has been upheld in various courts. In 1974, a federal district court ruled that antitrust issues were not raised by the NBA's refusal to accept a group that wanted to buy a team; the judge concluded that "the plaintiffs wanted to join with those unwilling to accept them, ... the exclusion from membership in the league did not have an anti-competitive effect nor an effect on the public interest."[13] A federal judge also turned aside a challenge of the NFL's unwillingness to grant a franchise to the Mid-South Grizzlies of the World Football League.[14]

League members bring a mix of business, sporting, and personal concerns to the process of passing judgment on prospective new members. Prospective owners have to be acceptable to members of a league, with each league currently requiring approval by a three-fourths majority. New owners have to demonstrate their financial capability to acquire and operate a team and meet their league obligations. All leagues prohibit owners from having an interest in more than one team in the league. Common ownership of teams raises questions about the integrity of games, which is a critical part of what professional sports leagues are selling. Concern about integrity of their games also has led modern leagues to keep gambling interests from acquiring teams, in contrast with an earlier era when gamblers owned a number of baseball and football teams.

Single owners are favored over collective arrangements. Members of a league want to deal with an individual rather than a group of people; they want someone to be clearly in charge who has financial responsibility for the team. Until 1993, the NFL also prohibited corporations from owning teams on the grounds that "a corporation ... owning or controlling one of our football teams would make it impossible for us to control ownership in our League."[15] The prohibition was amended to permit ownership by privately held corporations after the ban on corporate ownership was challenged in federal court by a former owner of the New England Patriots, who contended that the league's policy lowered the selling price of the team by limiting the number of prospective purchasers.

Leagues vary in their concern about the connection between owners and the place where a team plays. Baseball has the strongest preference for local owners, seeing people with roots in the community as giving "a better promise of franchise stability."[16] Baseball has turned aside some prospective purchasers because they lived in the wrong place. A bid to purchase the White Sox in 1980 was opposed in part because Edward DeBartolo lived in Ohio; and inquiries by a possible buyer of the Kansas City Royals in 1990 were rebuffed because the individual was based in Arkansas. Baseball, of course, has accepted outsiders as owners. Sometimes there are no locals interested or able to purchase the home team. The New York Yankees, as Bowie Kuhn, a strong supporter of local ownership, indicates, "had been on the market for some time without local buyers coming forward when Cleveland's George Steinbrenner emerged."[17]

More troublesome than outside owners from elsewhere in the United States or Canada has been overseas ownership. Increasing flows of capital from abroad were bound to seek out investments in professional teams, following foreign buyers of domestic companies and real estate. The Seibu Saison Group, owner of the Inter-Continental Hotel chain, was interested in acquiring the Dallas Cowboys in 1989, but backed off because of the sensitivities involved in a Japanese firm purchasing America's team; "the Japanese," indicates a partner of the Cowboy's owner, "were very worried about a public backlash."[18] Although little notice was taken when Japanese investors became the principal owners of the NHL's Tampa Bay Lightning in 1991, the kind of public backlash that worried Seibu Saison erupted following a bid to keep the Mariners in Seattle by a local group headed by Minoru Arakawa, a Japanese citizen who ran Nintendo's operations in the United States. Some Americans were outraged by the prospect of Japanese ownership of a piece of the national pastime. Others noted that Arakawa would be the first owner of the Mariners who lived in Seattle. Baseball officials flailed about, initially indicating that sale of a team to a foreigner was not permitted, then retreating in the face of political pressures and negative publicity, and finally agreeing to let Arakawa and his partners buy the team after convincing themselves that "this venture is not going to be controlled outside North America."[19]

Another controversial policy has been the NFL's desire to prohibit owners from holding an interest in professional teams in other sports (see Table 6.1). Owning more than one team offers economies of scale, and when the teams are in the same place, there are opportunities for packaging season tickets, luxury seating, advertising, and promotions. Opponents of multiple ownership argue that owning professional teams in other leagues creates a conflict of interest, since leagues compete for customers and advertisers. Multiple ownership, like corporate ownership, is also seen as diluting the focus of owners who should have one game as their primary business. Within the NFL, owners with interests in other sports fought the league's dogged efforts to force them to sell their holdings. In the end, the league bowed to financial realities and gave up on cross-ownership, agreeing in 1994 to the acquisition of the Miami Dolphins by

Table 6.1   Owners of Multiple Major League Franchises in Same Market

Metropolitan Area	Owner(s)	Teams
Atlanta	Ted Turner	Atlanta Braves
		Atlanta Hawks
	Time Warner	Atlanta Braves
		Atlanta Hawks
Boston	Boston Garden Corporation	Boston Bruins
		Boston Celtics
Chicago	Jerry Reinsdorf and Eddie Einhorn	Chicago Bulls
		Chicago White Sox
Denver	Comsat Video Enterprises	Denver Rockets
		Colorado Avalanche
Detroit	Mike Ilitch	Detroit Tigers
		Detroit Red Wings
Los Angeles	Jack Kent Cooke	Los Angeles Kings
		Los Angeles Lakers
	Jerry Buss	Los Angeles Kings
		Los Angeles Lakers
	Disney	California Angels
		Mighty Ducks of Anaheim
Miami	Wayne Huizenga	Florida Marlins
		Florida Panthers
		Miami Dolphins
New York	Gulf & Western	New York Knicks
		New York Rangers
	Paramount Communications	New York Knicks
		New York Rangers
	ITT - Cable Vision Systems	New York Knicks
		New York Rangers
	Roy Boe	New York Islanders
		New York Nets
Philadelphia	Comcast Corporation	Philadelphia Flyers
		Philadelphia 76ers
Phoenix	Jerry Coangelo	Phoenix Suns
		Arizona Diamondbacks
		Phoenix Coyotes
San Francisco-Oakland	Charles Finley	Oakland Athletics
		Oakland Seals
Vancouver	Orca Bay Sports and Entertainment	Vancouver Canucks
		Vancouver Grizzlies
Washington	Abe Pollin	Washington Bullets
		Washington Capitals

Wayne Huizenga, who already owned major league baseball and hockey teams as well as a substantial interest in Joe Robbie Stadium, where the Dolphins played.

Most ownership limitations work against the interests of places in having teams. Restrictions reduce the pool of prospective owners of major league teams in a particular place. Cross-ownership bans limit opportunities for experienced sports operators in a metropolitan market to own teams. Ownership of more than one team in a city also reinforces place connections, since an owner is less likely to leave if one of a set of clubs is faltering. To be sure, multiple ownership has potential drawbacks as well as benefits for places: an owner with two or three teams is likely to have more leverage than a single owner in negotiations over stadiums, tax breaks, and other subsidies, and financial difficulties or death could pose the threat of a place losing more than one team.

Territorial Rights

Teams in a league have substantial shared interests in the location of franchises. As a result, league control of franchise locations has been a cardinal feature of professional team sports from the start. The National League limited franchises to cities with populations of 75,000, with each team granted exclusive territorial rights in its market area. The National League and American Association agreed in 1883 to preserve exclusive territories for teams in each league. Contemporary territorial rights generally include the city where a team plays and the surrounding area within fifty or seventy-five miles of the team's home turf. Each NFL team has "the exclusive right within its home territory to exhibit professional football games played by teams of the League," with two teams in the same territory, as in the New York area, having equal rights.[20] Territorial rights include broadcasts within a team's area, except for games covered by league contracts with national networks.

Territorial exclusivity enables teams to avoid competition for local fans, viewers, media, and broadcasting and advertising dollars. Exclusive territories focus fan loyalty and support for the home team. With the departure of the Dallas Texans of the American Football League to Kansas City, the owners the Dallas Cowboys "not only were . . . free of the financial competition of the Texans, but they were free of all the minor irritations of being one of two teams in the same town. They no longer had to worry about constant comparisons with the Texans, challenges from the underdogs who had little to lose, competition for newspaper coverage, and all the other bothersome aspects of a cross-town rivalry."[21] On the other side of the coin was the attitude of the Los Angeles Rams toward the move of the Raiders into their market; "they didn't want us here," a Raider official indicated, "they don't want the competition."[22]

Territorial controls are the basic instruments by which teams and leagues regulate their relations with places. Exclusive franchises are based on the notion that places belong to a league and its teams; territories are staked out and controlled by private league rules. Territorial controls are vigorously defended as indispensable to professional team sports; baseball commissioner Ford Frick told Congress in 1957 that territorial restrictions were one of the "keystones of organized baseball."[23] Without these protections, professional sports are seen as facing economic ruin and places could lose their teams; if teams could "shift around at will . . . several teams might move to a city that could support only one, and each would suffer financial hardship; possibly all would be driven out of business."[24]

Territorial restrictions insure that all but a few teams enjoy local monopolies protected by their league. Only 21 of 115 major league franchises in 1996 shared their local market with another team in the same sport. The ten instances in which more than one franchise in a league operates in the same territory are the five largest metropolitan areas: New York has two teams in three sports and three hockey clubs, Los Angeles has two in three sports, San Francisco-Oakland has two each in baseball and football, Chicago has a pair of baseball teams, and Washington-Baltimore has two football franchises. Three of these shared markets are the result of league mergers: consolidating the American and National Leagues in 1903 produced five multi-team cities, of which only Chicago remains; the merger of the AFL with the NFL and the NBA's absorption of the American Basketball Association resulted in two football and basketball teams operating in New York. Four shared markets are products of expansion: a second baseball team was placed in Los Angeles when the American League was enlarged in 1961, and in New York when the Nationals expanded the following year; the NHL expanded to Long Island in the New York area and Anaheim in the Los Angeles metropolis. Four multi-team markets resulted from relocation, with the NHL moving a team to the New Jersey portion of the New York area, the Clippers shifting to Los Angeles from San Diego, the Raiders moving back to Oakland from Los Angeles, and the transfer of the Cleveland franchise in the NFL to Baltimore.

In most of these instances, new teams were required to compensate existing franchises for the loss of exclusive territorial rights. In the football merger, AFL teams paid $18 million to indemnify the Giants and 49ers for agreeing to share their territories with the Jets and Raiders. The NBA's settlement with the ABA required the Nets to pay $4 million to the Knicks for rights to play in the New York metropolitan region, and another $4 million to move from Long Island to New Jersey. In the NHL, the expansion Islanders paid $4 million to the New York Rangers in 1972. Relocation of the Colorado Rockies to New Jersey in 1982 impinged on territorial rights of the Rangers, Islanders, and Philadelphia Flyers, who shared $12.5 million in indemnification fees. In 1993, half of the NHL's $50 million admission fee for the Mighty Ducks of Anaheim went to the Los Angeles Kings as compensation for sharing their

Figure 6.1   Baseball Attendance in the Bay Area: 1958–1995

territory with the expansion team. The Kings termed Disney's involvement "unbelievable for hockey," emphasizing that "anything that's good for hockey is good for the Kings."[25] And $25 million made it even better.

Owners clearly prefer local monopolies; and sports officials and sympathetic analysts underscore the perils of teams sharing a market. Baseball in the San Francisco-Oakland area has attracted the most attention. Bowie Kuhn writes that "attendance figures were emphatically telling us that the Bay Area could not support two clubs."[26] Jesse W. Markham and Paul V. Teplitz emphasized in 1981 that "the San Francisco Giants and the Oakland Athletics have shared the Bay Area market, with unfortunate results for both teams."[27] Attendance figures for the first dozen years after the arrival of the Athletics from Kansas City in 1968 support these conclusions; as shown in Figure 6.1, the Giants and A's were clearly splitting the market during this period to the detriment of both teams. In the late 1980s, however, an improved team in San Francisco began drawing in the same range as before the A's arrived, while the Athletics, under new ownership that skillfully rebuilt and promoted the team, outdrew the Giants. By 1990, attendance for both teams was pushing the five million mark, and less was heard about the Bay Area being too small to support two teams, even though attendance for both teams fell in the wake of the 1994 strike.

Territorial rights have been relatively static during the rapid expansion of metropolitan areas and urban regions. Fifty or seventy-five miles, which once extended the control of most teams well beyond the urbanized portion of their home territory, now encompass a diminishing portion of the far-flung regions that supply teams with customers and viewers. The move of the Braves to Milwaukee, for example, cut into the fan base of the Chicago teams, located only ninety miles from Milwaukee. Metropolitan growth and overlapping markets have linked the fortunes of Baltimore and Washington in a number of sports. The cities are only forty-five miles apart, and the two metropolitan areas have merged into a belt of continuous urban development. Relocation of the St. Louis Browns to Baltimore in 1954 was one of the factors undermining the Washington franchises that left for Minneapolis in 1961 and Dallas-Fort Worth in 1972. Washington's subsequent efforts to get back into baseball have been hindered by the Orioles' desire to preserve their monopoly in the area. And Baltimore's search for a replacement for the Colts was not welcomed by the Washington Redskins, who preferred to be the only NFL franchise in what is now the nation's fourth largest metropolitan complex.

Territorial rights have the most substantial impact on the location of professional teams in large metropolitan areas; with or without exclusive territories, smaller areas can sustain only one team in a sport. But territorial rights mean fewer teams than could be supported in markets like New York, Los Angeles, Chicago, San Francisco-Oakland, and Washington-Baltimore. "The largest cities," Roger G. Noll argues, "have too few teams."[28] In ruling against the NFL's territorial controls in 1984, a federal court agreed, concluding that "Los Angeles is a market large enough for the successful operation of two teams."[29] For Noll, "the exclusive territorial rights of big-city teams act as an important restriction to competition that benefits teams at the expense of sports fans and players."[30] Chicago, which supports two major league baseball teams, presumably would be attractive to potential team owners if other leagues permitted additional franchises in the third largest area in the United States and Canada. In the case of the Washington-Baltimore complex, prospective owners have been eager to invest in another baseball and football team, but were passed over when baseball and football expanded in the 1990s.

Markham and Teplitz disagree with Noll, arguing that economic realities rather than franchise controls limit the number of multi-team cities in baseball: "The historical record of two-team cities such as Boston, Philadelphia, St. Louis, and San Francisco-Oakland would suggest that economic considerations, rather than league rules, have been the main deterrent to multiteam cities."[31] The recent historical record in large metropolitan areas, however, does not support the conclusion that multi-team markets are economically unfeasible in baseball. Two teams thrived in the Bay Area after 1985, and in Los Angeles, as shown in Figure 6.2, arrival of the expansion Angels had little

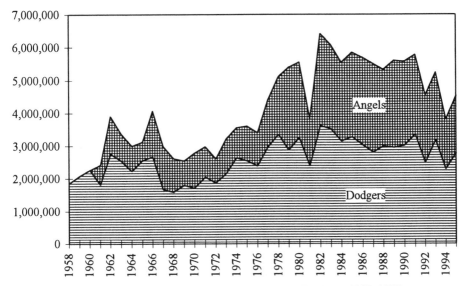

Figure 6.2   Baseball Attendance in the Los Angeles Area: 1958–1995

impact on the Dodgers, who maintained their customer base as the Angels eventually established a solid market in the eastern portion of the vast Los Angeles basin.

Because territorial exclusivity primarily protects franchises in the largest markets from competition, these rights reinforce the advantages of teams in the major urban centers. Limiting the number of teams in large metropolitan areas exacerbates market differences by forcing most owners to operate in smaller areas with less revenue potential. League controls also severely constrain the ability of small-market teams to move to larger markets that could sustain another franchise or support a more successful team. Noll points out that "during most of the 1980s the New York Knicks were weak or mediocre"; without league restrictions on movement, ""a strong but poorly drawing team in Miami or Minneapolis might go head to head against the Knicks in New York."[32] The other side of this coin, of course, is that more places have teams because the number of franchises in the largest metropolitan areas is limited by leagues.

Territorial restrictions also reduce competition among teams to be in a particular place, thus increasing the leverage of teams on places. Most places have to deal with a single team in each sport. In the absence of competition from other teams for stadiums and arenas, holders of exclusive franchises are able to drive harder bargains with public agencies for leases, tax concessions, and other subsidies. Franchise controls, however, do not guarantee that a team will be able to capitalize on its market monopoly. In New York, as indicated in Figure 6.3, departure of the Dodgers and Giants had no appreciable effect on

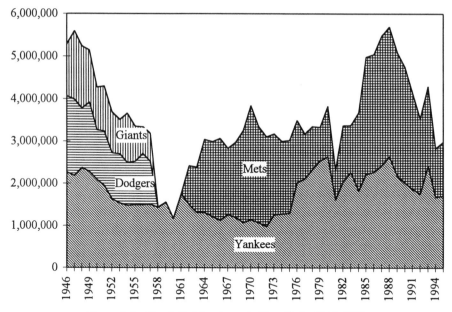

Figure 6.3   Baseball Attendance in New York: 1946–1995

the Yankees' attendance, although the Yankees were the only team in the huge New York market. Many National League fans who had supported the Dodgers and Giants had little interest in the Yankees, but they returned to the fold when the Mets arrived in 1962. Subsequent variations in attendance for the two teams have resulted primarily from team performance rather than competition for the same set of customers.

Leagues and the Law

As illustrated by territorial rights, restricting business competition is a primary objective of the collective activities of professional sports leagues. The four leagues are monopolies; they are the only sellers of major league baseball, basketball, football, and hockey. Leagues operate as cartels in their relations with places where teams play; they restrict entry into their business through territorial rights and control over the number and location of franchises. Leagues also function as a cartel in selling national broadcasting rights, with a single seller peddling rights to national networks. And professional sports leagues have sought with considerable success to maintain a monopsony, a one-buyer market, with respect to labor.

Since 1890, restrictive practices of professional sports leagues in the United States have been clouded by the provisions of the Sherman Antitrust Act. Baseball, however, did not curb its labor, territorial, and franchise policies in the wake of the Sherman Act; instead monopolistic control was extended by the triumph of the National League over rival leagues in the 1890s and the merger that brought the American League into the fold in 1903. Baseball was eventually challenged under the Sherman Act, over a dispute growing out of the deal that ended the upstart Federal League in 1915. Owners of the Baltimore entry in the Federal League claimed that major league baseball did not honor a promise to permit them to buy the St. Louis Cardinals; and sued under the provision of the Sherman Act, which prohibits conspiracies to restrict trade in interstate commerce. The aggrieved Baltimore group won in federal district court, but was turned back by the U.S. Supreme Court, which ruled in 1922 that "exhibitions of baseball . . . are purely state affairs" rather than interstate commerce, and thus outside the reach of the Sherman Act.[33]

Baseball has retained its antitrust exemption despite the growth of broadcasting and other interstate aspects of the sports business. The Supreme Court acknowledged in 1953 that baseball was a business engaged in interstate commerce, but declined to set aside the exemption because baseball had operated for thirty years on the basis of the previous ruling.[34] In 1972, the Court reiterated that baseball's treatment under the antitrust laws was an anomaly, but concluded that remedies would have to come from Congress.[35] Immunity from antitrust laws, however, was not extended to other professional sports. Baseball decisions, the Supreme Court decided in 1957, applied only to baseball, even though professional football was a similar enterprise.[36] Subsequent federal court rulings placed professional hockey and basketball under the antitrust laws.[37] These decisions produced a bizarre legal situation in which four essentially similar businesses are not subject to the same legal constraints. As a result, baseball has more freedom of action on place issues, while the practices of the other leagues are more vulnerable to antitrust challenges.

League broadcasting policies raised new antitrust issues that grew in importance as television changed the nature of watching and financing professional sports. Worries about the consequences of unrestricted broadcasting led professional sports to ration broadcasts, black out home games, restrict telecasts of outside games into a team's home market, and deal collectively as leagues with national broadcasters. In 1952, the U.S. Department of Justice challenged league blackouts of telecasts within a seventy-five mile radius of a home game as an unlawful restraint of trade. In court, the NFL insisted that unfettered telecasts would undermine live attendance, persuading a federal district court that "reasonable protection of home game attendance is essential to the very existence of the individual clubs, without which there can be no League and no professional football as we know it today."[38] A decade later, the Justice Department contested the NFL's first national television contract with CBS, arguing that a single league package for televising games violated the Sherman Act. This time the NFL lost, as the court ruled that the national contract was an undue restraint on trade because the arrangement eliminated competition among teams to sell television rights.[39] The NFL, eager to protect its promising national television gold mine and supported by the other leagues, decided to try an end run around the courts in Congress.

Leagues and Congress

Before the leagues came to Washington in 1961 to seek relief from the adverse television decision, Congress had never enacted legislation dealing directly with professional team sports. Congress took its first serious look at professional sports only in 1951, when the Judiciary Committee in the House of Representatives examined baseball's legal status following introduction of bills providing professional sports with a blanket exemption from antitrust laws. After extensive hearings, the committee proposed no legislation and Congress took no action on the exemption bills. After the Supreme Court declined to extend baseball's exemption to football in 1957, the NFL lobbied Congress for an extension of antitrust immunity to all professional sports. This effort led to new legislative proposals and another round of hearings by the House Judiciary Committee, which this time endorsed legislation, recommending an antitrust exemption for league activities to equalize competition, protect the integrity of sports contests, and operate in specific locations.[40] The latter provision would have placed league control over territorial rights, franchise location, and expansion beyond the reach of the antitrust laws. Legislation embodying these provisions, however, was never enacted.

Professional sports put its first points on the board in Congress with enactment of the Sports Broadcasting Act of 1961, which circumvented the federal courts by permitting professional leagues to sell national television rights and share revenues among teams without violating the antitrust laws.[41] Congress accepted the NFL's argument that failure to authorize collective television contracts would "seriously impede the league's effort to maintain a balanced league."[42] The Senate report on the legislation concluded that pooled television revenues were necessary to "assure the weaker clubs of the league continuing television income and television coverage on the basis of substantial equality with the stronger clubs."[43] Five years later, Congress again came to the aid of professional sports, this time exempting the merger of the NFL and AFL from antitrust challenges.

Approval of these antitrust exemptions reflected the substantial political influence of team owners, leagues, and their corporate allies. Most teams are owned by rich individuals or big corporations; individual owners often have other substantial business interests. Many have political connections, which they nurture with hefty campaign contributions and other goodies. Ownership changes have added the political clout of broadcasters and brewers to the influence of sports interests. Owners have bolstered their influence in Washington by hiring league commissioners, lawyers, and others with political connections and skills. Similar links cross the Canadian border, where professional sports are "closely tied to Canada's corporate elite and its structural alliances with American capital."[44] Sports also have special benefits to offer political supporters: tickets to games, seats in the owner's luxury box with other important people, access for politicians to locker rooms to share the victors' limelight, and even teams for the constituencies of members of Congress who provide exceptional services. In the case of the football merger bill, strong support came from two powerful Louisiana Democrats, and their backing was instrumental in securing an NFL expansion franchise for New Orleans the following year.

Congressional consideration of sports issues has been influenced by the lack of organized consumer interests. Fans, as indicated above, have not been effectively represented, despite the existence of organizations that aspire to be the voice of the fans. As a result, contests over broadcasting, mergers, and antitrust exemptions have largely been fought by teams, leagues, players, broadcasters, and government agencies. Claims by teams and leagues to represent fans rarely are countered by congressional testimony or lobbying by consumer organizations; and professional sports clearly benefit politically from cloaking themselves in the mantle of the devotion of millions of Americans to this or that game.

Constituency interests have also been weakly articulated in Congress on sports issues. On matters such as broadcasting and mergers, owners have been the most vocal constituents, and members of Congress often have considered the interests of their home team and their constituents to be the same. An exception are pressures on local representatives and senators to do something about loss of a team or to help secure an expansion franchise. But these pressures typically cancel each other out in Congress. In the zero-sum games of relocation and expansion, one place's victory is bound to be another's loss, so outraged members of Congress from Ohio were offset by a delighted Maryland delegation in the wake of the Browns' move from Cleveland to Baltimore.

Constituency concerns have had the most influence on the issue of the availability of telecasts, the only area of sports policy in which Congress has enacted legislation opposed by leagues. Dissatisfaction with television blackouts of home games mounted as the NFL's popularity grew, generating increased pressures on Congress for limitations on blackouts, especially on sold-out home games. An additional factor was the unhappiness of many members of Congress unable to watch the home games of the Washington Redskins on local television. Brushing aside league objections, Congress passed legislation in 1973 that prohibited blackouts when games were sold out seventy-two hours before kickoff; and the bill was enthusiastically signed by President Richard Nixon, an avid follower of the Redskins on television.[45] The law expired in two years; but fear of facing even more restrictions persuaded the NFL to maintain the seventy-two hour policy voluntarily. Returning to the old blackout policy would also have been bad for business, since televising more NFL games to hometown fans increased ratings and the value of the league's television contracts.

Continuing concern in Congress over the future of free sports television looms over plans of teams and leagues to extract more revenues from cable television and pay-per-view. Responding to constituents unhappy about the prospects of paying for what they were watching without charge, members of Congress have introduced bills and threatened legislation to keep sporting events on free television. When the Philadelphia 76ers went to cable, Representative Peter Kostmayer, whose suburban district reached north from Philadelphia, introduced the Fairness to Fans Act of 1991, which would have lifted professional sports' antitrust exemptions if games were shifted from free to pay television. "The average fan," argued Kostmayer, "is losing his ability to follow the hometown team on television."[46]

In pressuring teams and leagues on blackouts, pay television, and team location, Congress can always brandish its antitrust weapon, as in the Kostmayer bill, telling leagues to do this or not do that or risk loss of antitrust exemptions. Dissatisfaction with franchise moves or league actions on relocation and expansion prompt periodic antitrust threats from senators and representatives from affected states and districts. Congressional threats, along with legislative proposals and hearings, attract publicity and demonstrate that members of Congress share their constituent's outrage at Cleveland's losing the Browns or St. Petersburg's failure to secure the Giants. But threats are very difficult to turn into legislation likely to be supported by a majority of both houses, and thus usually lack credibility with teams and leagues.

Private Government

Professional sports have successfully fought to maintain private control through private teams operating collectively as private leagues. Like teams, leagues are private rather than public entities; they conduct their business behind closed doors, determine their rules privately, apply the rules as they wish, and change them as needed. The leagues' self-regulation is particularly important for places; leagues exercise substantial power over relocation, total authority over expansion, and considerable freedom of action in contests with rival leagues; they set and apply standards for markets, arenas and stadiums, acceptability of owners, and transfer of franchises.

Government intervention more often than not has enhanced the private powers of leagues. The exemption from the antitrust laws in the Sports Broadcasting Act of 1961 empowered leagues in two critical areas, national broadcasting contracts and revenue sharing. With respect to revenue sharing, the law established no public standards or regulations, permitting leagues to determine whether to share revenues, what revenues to share, and how to allocate revenues among teams. Since enactment of the 1961 legislation, leagues have resisted efforts by Congress to substitute public rules for private determinations about sharing revenues. In considering a basketball merger bill in 1971, Congress added a provision that required home teams to share at least 30 percent of gate receipts with visiting clubs.[47] Both the NBA and the ABA opposed this provision, which helped doom the merger legislation. Nor did baseball welcome the proposed Major League Baseball Equity Act of 1991, introduced by two members of Congress from Washington worried about the fate of the Mariners in Seattle's small market, which would have required teams to share half of their local television revenues.[48]

The position of teams and their leagues was pungently expressed by the president of the ABA during consideration of the basketball merger legislation: "owners argue . . . that the decision whether to share gate receipts is a business determination within their province and of no public interest whatsoever."[49] For most of what professional sports leagues do, little has changed since John W. Stayton described major league baseball in 1910 as having created an entity to "govern and control itself by its own decrees, and enforcing them without the aid of the law, and answerable to no power outside its own."[50]

7

Big League Cities

M AJOR LEAGUE teams are very attractive to places. Having a team is widely seen as the mark of being a big league city, losing one is perceived as a serious blow to a place's status. The symbolic importance of major league teams to places, along with the strong emotional attachments between teams and home town fans, makes professional sports a special kind of business everywhere in the United States and Canada. Teams attract far more attention in the local press than do other businesses; they carry the local banner to stadiums, arenas, television screens, and sports pages across the continent. "A National Football League franchise," Oakland argued in seeking to persuade a federal court to nullify the Raiders' move to Los Angeles, "is an enterprise with unique economic, civic, cultural, recreational, and psychological effects . . . unparalleled by other business activities."[1]

The distinctive nature of professional sports is critical to understanding the success of teams and leagues in getting much of what they want from the places where they play. Major league teams command more public attention and resources than other businesses that threaten to leave town or that places are trying to attract. To keep or entice a team, and thus to remain in the major leagues or secure recognition as a big league metropolis, cities and other places have been willing, often eager, to commit growing amounts of public funds to stadiums, arenas, and other subsidies to existing or prospective home teams.

Major league teams have become a critical talisman of the status of cities and metropolitan areas because of the popularity and visibility of professional sports. Art museums, symphony orchestras, theaters, and zoos are all marks of major cities, as are libraries and universities, leading law firms and banks, and great commercial and industrial corporations, but big league teams are seen by many as more easily and widely recognized symbols of a place's importance. "How can I bring people to Pittsburgh to work for Westinghouse," asks a business executive, "if I can't tell them we have a major league community?"[2] After his city was anointed by the NFL, Mayor Ed Austin of Jacksonville proclaimed "we are now a big-league city."[3] States as well as cities fret about big league labels; "Wisconsin," argued Governor Tommy G. Thompson in unveiling plans for a new ballpark for the Milwaukee Brewers, "can't afford to lose its major league status."[4] Not having major league teams marks a place as minor league. A booster of seeking big league sports for Raleigh speaks of the need for "a unified effort if Raleigh is to move out of the minor leagues."[5]

A major league team means being listed with other big league places in standings, scores, and other daily items on sports pages and news shows. Media coverage of professional sports publicizes cities, metropolitan areas, states, and provinces that have major league teams. Televised games display a place's skyline, amenities, and climate for regional and national audiences. "Tonight, on every single television and radio station in the USA, Seattle will be mentioned because of the Mariners' game," a baseball owner told a reporter, "and tomorrow night and the next night and on and on. You'd pay millions in public-relations fees for that."[6] Sports teams, moreover, usually generate good news and favorable publicity; as Robert Lipsyte notes, teams plug troubled cities into "the good news network. . . . We're O.K., say the sports pages."[7]

Being in the big leagues also offers cities opportunities to host special events—the Super Bowl, World Series, other championships, and all-star games—which publicize a place and showcase its attractions. For Houston, baseball's 1986 All-Star game made "people think of Houston as a place to visit" by showing "that things are going on all the time and that exciting things are happening."[8] Tampa leaders saw the 1984 Super Bowl "as the biggest thing that has ever happened to us," offering an unparalleled opportunity to boost economic development and tourism in the area.[9] The 1988 Super Bowl provided San Diego with exposure that a hyperbolic businessman found "hard to imagine" and "almost beyond comprehension."[10] Major league facilities are also essential for cities that seek to host the Olympic Games. New stadiums for their baseball teams were the centerpieces of the successful quests of Montreal and Atlanta for the games in 1976 and 1996. And the promise of the prestige and economic benefits of the Olympics was critical to winning political backing for the stadium projects in both cities. In New York, Mayor Rudolph Giuliani has dangled the potential riches of the 2008 Olympics in seeking support for investing $1.5 billion in new parks for the Mets and Yankees.

Using sports to get into the big leagues is particularly important to smaller cities and newer metropolitan areas. Baseball's first professional team was organized by boosters who sought to attract attention to Cincinnati. To be one among the ten places with big league baseball teams differentiated Cincinnati from cities that were not represented in the National or American League. Indianapolis invested $77 million in the Hoosier Dome because "it puts us on the map to be in the National Football League."[11] For the leader of Yes for Nashville, which spearheaded the successful campaign for a new stadium, luring an NFL franchise was "a way for us to get noticed as something other than a small town with good country music."[12] Because of these considerations, and because small markets are inherently less attractive to team owners, smaller places generally are willing to do more than larger areas to secure a place in the big leagues; they are more likely to build arenas and stadiums in an effort to lure a team and offer generous subsidies to attract or retain a major league franchise.

Big league teams also offer a means of reshaping the image of a city or suburb or metropolitan area. Houston's Astrodome, the self-proclaimed "eighth wonder of the world," helped recast the city's image from sleepy bayou town to space-age Sunbelt dynamo. Leaders in Indianapolis saw the Colts as a means of changing outside perceptions and enhancing Indiana's attractions to growth industries: "We're pretty much a smokestack state. We need to do something to project a major league image so we can attract new industries. Otherwise, we may be left at the post."[13] Irwindale, a working-class Latino suburb known mostly for its dusty gravel pits, gambled $10 million on an aborted bid for the Los Angeles Raiders, which promised to change its image from "the armpit of the San Gabriel Valley" to the "crown jewel."[14]

Prestige is enhanced by having teams in more than one league; "having a professional sports team puts you on the map," notes an executive of the Orlando Magic, "having two teams puts you on a bigger map."[15] And a full set of four provides membership in the elite of big league places. Some sports, however, are more valuable than others to status-seeking places. Basketball and hockey teams remain lesser prizes than baseball or football franchises. Explaining why the city was less responsive to the demands of its basketball than baseball team, an Atlanta official emphasized that the "economic impact . . . and the prestige factor . . . are just not as great" with the Hawks.[16]

Along with prestige and publicity come risks for big league places. Cities can be tagged as losers as well as winners, and attract as much publicity for futility as for success. Cleveland's image as a failed city was reinforced by a long string of losing seasons by the Indians, who played in a dingy stadium tabbed the "mistake by the lake." Even the local media took to calling Atlanta "Loserville, U.S.A." during the years when the Braves, Falcons, and Hawks were going nowhere.[17] Television also is a mixed blessing, despite efforts of local boosters to accentuate the positive for national audiences. No amount of public relations blather can disguise the fact that the weather in Buffalo is far from balmy during the football season, as viewers across the land watch games played in blizzards and Arctic cold. Television can project images of urban disorder as well as economic vitality, as did the 1989 Super Bowl in riot-torn Miami, reinforcing the city's reputation as a violent and dangerous place rather than reflecting, as the mayor and other leaders had hoped, "the changed reality and the changed image of Miami."[18]

The biggest risk of being in the big leagues is losing a major league team; not only do places lose whatever status came with the team, but take the chance of being "ridiculed and pitied as cuckolds."[19] Losing the Oilers, the only big league team in a relatively small Canadian metropolitan area, whose owner was threatening to move in the early 1990s, meant "Edmonton will suffer from an economic and status point of view."[20] A more graphic expression of the same concerns was expressed by a Minneapolis business leader some years ago: "If the Vikings and Twins left . . . we'd be well on our way to becoming a frozen Omaha."[21] Peter Richmond characterizes the loss of the Colts to Indianapolis as representing "Baltimore's worst fear about itself: It was a second-rate town again."[22]

Economic Benefits of Professional Sports

Promoters of professional sports incessantly trumpet the economic benefits that come to places that have major league teams. Sports teams, along with arenas and stadiums, are substantial enterprises with sizable payrolls. Games attract people to the place where the home team plays, generating customers for all kinds of businesses. Construction of arenas and stadiums creates jobs, and can spark development of city or suburban areas. Most generally, professional teams are seen as stimulating economic activity by increasing the attractiveness of a place for commerce and industry. All this from a nonpolluting business that also offers a variety of intangible benefits to a place and its people.

Economic rewards for places from professional sports are both direct and indirect. Direct economic benefits include rent on an arena or stadium, income from suites and other preferred seating, parking fees, concessions sales, jobs with teams, local purchases by teams, and tax revenues. Indirect benefits, which typically account for a substantially larger share of the overall economic benefits, encompass general economic activity such as spending on food, lodgings, and transport.

Estimates of economic impact vary considerably among places and sports. A 1983 study for the Montreal Expos indicated that the team accounted for $100 million in direct and indirect economic activity.[23] About the same time, the chamber of commerce in Denver underwrote a study that concluded that major league baseball would contribute $75 million to the local economy. In Milwaukee, a 1987 study for the Brewers calculated that the team generated $212 million, including $153 million in sales, $47 million in wages, and $12 million in taxes. Philadelphia's four major league teams in 1988 were estimated to produce $343 million in direct and indirect benefits for the city and $576 million for the metropolitan area as a whole.[24] Topping these numbers was a study which indicated that St. Petersburg's domed stadium would contribute $750 million annually to the local economy.[25]

Additional benefits from the World Series, Super Bowl, and other special sporting events have been estimated for a number of local economies. Expectations that out-of-towners would contribute $5 million for each home game led the head of the Atlanta Convention and Visitors Bureau to herald the 1991 World Series as "economically . . . a home run for Atlanta."[26] Benefits from the 1987 World Series have been calculated at $93 million for Minneapolis and $105 million for St. Louis.[27] With fans spending almost four times as much as the average visitor to Los Angeles, the city's convention bureau put the Super Bowl in a class by itself, emphasizing that "there is not a single convention or event that comes into Los Angeles that compares to the Super Bowl."[28] Estimates of the local economic bonanza from recent Super Bowls range from $119 million for the 1992 game in Minneapolis to $226 million for 1986 in New Orleans.

Costs typically receive far less attention than benefits in studies of the economic impact of professional sports. As Arthur T. Johnson notes, the "assumption of economic benefit appears to be blind to auxiliary costs which diminish or eliminate positive economic impacts."[29] Costs include public operating expenses for arenas and stadiums, amortization of stadium debt, and subsidies for stadiums and teams. The public also bears the cost of police protection, traffic control, and roads for arenas and stadiums. Other costs involve taxes foregone on sports facilities and revenue lost from tax exemptions granted to professional teams.

Treatment of benefits as well as costs is questionable in most studies of the local economic impact of professional teams. The "fundamental issue," write Robert A. Baade and Richard F. Dye, "is the extent to which the stadium causes a net increase in area activity rather than a mere reallocation or redistribution of the same level of activity."[30] Most money spent on professional sports would be spent on some other form of entertainment or leisure activity if there was no team in town; only expenditures by visiting teams and out-of-town customers constitute a net addition to the local economy. Different assumptions about these additions to the local economy produce wide variations in estimations of economic benefits; in Seattle, the chamber of commerce concluded that the Mariners added between $75 million and $100 million to the economy in 1984, but a report prepared for the city council argued that only $22 million was "new money."[31] Critics also question the value of the jobs created by professional teams. Aside from construction jobs and a relatively small number of executive and administrative posts in team and stadium front offices, most employment generated by professional sports is in low-wage seasonal service jobs.

Benefits to particular places depend on where money generated by professional sports is spent. With the spread of metropolitan areas, the locality that invests in professional sports does not reap all the economic benefits that accrue to an area. Benefits are particularly difficult for suburbs to capture because suburban jurisdictions tend to encompass relatively small portions of a metropolitan area. A study of the suburbs that host the Dallas Cowboys and Texas

Rangers concluded that "the economic benefits of professional sports have spilled over the boundaries of Arlington and Irving and are affecting the economies of many different cities in the region."[32]

Under the best of circumstances, determining benefits, particularly indirect benefits, of a complex economic activity in a large city or metropolitan area is a difficult assignment. Studies rest heavily on assumptions with lots of guesstimates; further muddying the waters is the fact that most of the guesstimates are made by or for interested parties. Studies typically are undertaken for governments that want to attract or retain a team, business interests that want to build a stadium or arena, or teams that want more public subsidies. Such studies almost always are highly favorable to what the sponsors seek; "it's all to sell the local community on making an expenditure," admits an activist in the effort to bring major league baseball to South Florida.[33]

Studies of the economic impact of professional sports rarely indicate that the principal beneficiaries will be teams and their wealthy owners. Public investments in arenas and stadiums, along with sweetheart leases and other subsidies, reduce the operating costs of teams, thus increasing their profitability. New facilities usually result in larger crowds and more concession sales, which bolster team revenues. Attractive stadiums and higher revenues increase the market value of teams. Construction of Camden Yards by Maryland produced enormous benefits for the Baltimore Orioles, as attendance and revenues soared at the beautiful ballpark; and the riches that flowed from the new stadium were a principal factor in the sale of the Orioles in 1993 for a record $178 million, none of which was shared with the people of Maryland who built Camden Yards.

Risks also receive little attention in studies that emphasize the economic benefits of professional sports—risks that are borne largely by the public. The biggest risk for a place is to build a stadium or arena and wind up with no team because the home team relocates, or because efforts to lure a team or land an expansion franchise fail. Risks exist for places even when teams are safely in the fold, since new demands from teams can increase costs through renegotiated leases, other subsidies, or public construction of new arenas or stadiums. Labor disputes are another risk for places; in recent years, strikes and lockouts have shortened seasons, with resulting losses of rent and concessions income to governments that provide arenas and stadiums, as well as fewer of whatever other economic benefits are generated by the home team.

Economic Development and Professional Sports

Along with the specific economic benefits generated by teams, professional sports are vigorously promoted as a means of stimulating economic development. Places with professional teams are widely viewed as more attractive business locations than places that are not in the big leagues. The Cowboys make Dallas "a more exciting and attractive city" for business; "a corporation seeking to locate a plant or home office in the Southwest could be influenced in favor of Dallas because a nationally-known professional football team is located there."[34] A business booster of major league baseball in the Miami area was confident that "a big-league team" would "bring big-league companies."[35] Baseball also promised to bolster tourism, Florida's biggest industry, during the slack summer months. In ardently supporting Denver's successful quest for a major league baseball team, Mayor Federico Pena insisted that "you have to have all the major sports teams in your city . . . if you're going to compete in the global marketplace."[36]

Whether the presence of major league teams affects locational decisions of major businesses is difficult to determine. Many factors influence the location of firms—markets, labor force, transportation facilities, schools and other public services, tax rates, climate, and personal preferences of top executives. At the margin, a major league team may be a factor in deciding whether to locate in Charlotte, which has teams in the NBA and NFL, over Memphis, which has no representation in the big leagues, but there is little evidence that the presence of professional sports is a determining factor in such decisions. Unraveling cause and effect in the case of most places that secure teams is further complicated, as T. Keating Holland notes, because "new teams and boom times usually arrive hand in hand, so it's a chicken-or-egg question."[37]

Development goals for specific parts of a city or metropolitan area may be tied to professional sports facilities. Arenas and stadiums are seen as magnets that will bring business and tourists into a particular area, revitalizing decaying neighborhoods, enhancing the appeal of downtown to investors, or fostering economic development in suburbs. Traditionally, ballparks were located on the urban periphery where land was relatively cheap, but using sports to bolster downtown development has brought stadiums into the heart of many cities. Downtown stadiums, promoters hope, will attract people to the central business district in the evening and on weekends, in the process bolstering tourism, restaurants, and hotels. Minneapolis officials saw the Metrodome largely in terms of its contribution to the vitality of the central business district; "a lot of people are afraid to go downtown," emphasized the president of the city council, "if they come to watch the Twins and the Vikings they will be more apt to visit again."[38] Suburbs also have sought stadiums to prime the development pump, as well as put a particular community on the map. Arlington and Irving built stadiums for the Rangers and Cowboys "in hopes of gaining prestige, revenue, and entertainment for local residents, much of the same way they sought to attract industry and businesses to improve their community's tax base and quality of life."[39]

The impact of professional sports facilities on particular sections of a city or metropolitan area, like the more general effect of teams on economic development, are not easily disentangled from other factors that affect local economies and land-use patterns. Arenas and stadiums have had a positive effect on adjacent development in some places. Busch Stadium was a central element of an ambitious plan to renew downtown St. Louis; as John F. Rooney Jr. notes: "Ramshackle tenements and marginal business establishments have been replaced by the stadium, parking structures, stores, and restaurants. The success of the Gateway Arch and Spanish Pavilion have also been influenced by the stadium location, not to mention the impact of three million fans who look to the downtown area each year."[40] In New Orleans, the Superdome sparked nearby hotel, retail, and office development, and development of three stadiums and an arena in downtown Atlanta contributed to the expansion of the central business district.

In most of these places, however, stadiums have been part of larger development efforts that presumably would have proceeded even if sports facilities had not been developed. In Baltimore, Camden Yards has been icing on the cake for a city which had been successfully rebuilding its center around the waterfront for more than a decade before the new ballpark was located within walking distance of the aquarium, restaurants, shops, and hotels that flank the harbor. Busch Stadium, as Steven A. Riess indicates, was "just one part of the city's major effort at rejuvenating the downtown, best symbolized by the Gateway Arch, built in 1965 before the stadium was completed."[41] New Jersey's development scheme for the Hackensack Meadowlands was well underway when plans were modified to include Giants Stadium and other sports facilities; as a result, the sports complex has increased the attractions of the area for investors rather than determining its fate. "There would have been development . . . without the stadium," acknowledges an official, but emphasizes that "it would have more difficult to attract blue-chip corporations to the area had it not already been pre-sold . . . by the sports complex."[42]

In many places, sports facilities have done little for the surrounding economy. Expectations that Houston's Astrodome would "become a center for public entertainment and an attraction for conventions and other businesses . . . were overly optimistic."[43] Rich Stadium, built by Erie County for the Buffalo Bills, has had little impact on development in suburban Orchard Park. Even downtown stadiums, typically built as part of larger redevelopment plans involving additional public and private investment, do not guarantee success. In Minneapolis, where "optimistic stadium promoters forecast an economic boom for the area surrounding the dome, the stadium has failed to generate any sizable development."[44] And in Indianapolis, often pointed to as an example of downtown rebirth spurred by sports development, a 1994 study concluded that "Indianapolis's sports strategy" produced "no significant or substantial shifts in economic development."[45]

Economically, the bottom line for major league teams and their arenas and stadiums is that at best they make modest contributions to the economies of cities and metropolitan areas. Almost always, the purported benefits in terms of jobs, tax revenues, and general economic development are overstated, and the costs understated. And with rapidly rising price tags for sports projects, particularly those located in central business districts, economic benefits have become even harder to realize. Selling these increasingly expensive sports palaces to those who will pay for them, however, leads advocates to ever more grandiose claims of economic riches and revitalized cities.

Social Benefits

Major league teams are an important addition to an area's entertainment, recreational, and leisure activities. Bringing major league baseball to Denver, argues a city official, "was about fun, about quality of life, building a community that had a lot of diversity, a lot of activities."[46] Substantial numbers of people enjoy professional sports, and that enjoyment is enhanced when there is a home team to support. But residents of a city or metropolitan area are interested in a very wide range of leisure and recreational activities, from archery to zoos. And facilities for users of these activities usually make far more modest claims on the public treasury than major league sports.

Major league teams also foster civic pride and communal identity; the "home" in home team is an important part of the collective experience of urban dwellers. "The Buffalo Bills," emphasizes a local politician, "are the very soul and fiber of this community."[47] Sports provides one of the rare opportunities for people to emphasize their communal ties. "We have to have things that create a sense of community," argues Baltimore's Mayor Kurt Schmoke, who sees sports "as the glue . . . to help hold the community together."[48] Reflecting on 1948, when his Indians swept to the American League pennant, Bill Veeck writes of "that feeling of reflected glory in a successful baseball team. Cleveland is winning the pennant, the eyes of the whole country are upon Cleveland, upon us, upon me and you."[49] And when the Mets won their improbable championship in 1969, "it seemed as if the ball club had actually pounded a few more beats into New York's sick old heart. Anyway, that's what the press told us. We're gonna be all right. If the Mets can do it, so can New York. We're number one."[50]

This shared interest in the home team bridges other divisions in society. "Sport is one of the few things in life that transcends all strata of the community," contends a city official in St. Petersburg in explaining his city's dogged efforts to secure a major league baseball team; "it is one of the few things left in society that ties us together, regardless of race, economic standing or gender."[51] Oakland's representative in Congress saw the city's "professional sports franchises . . . as a unifying factor between labor and management and between poor and rich."[52] The mayor of San Francisco told a congressional committee that a Super Bowl victory parade attracted a million people who "represented every age group, every racial background, every economic and social value on earth."[53]

Bringing ethnically and racially diverse populations together to support and celebrate the home team can mitigate social conflict. "Hostile groups," Allen Guttmann writes, are brought "together in the community of fandom. Cities wracked by racial tensions can find moments of release in the joys of sports championship."[54] Benjamin Rader thinks the "outbursts of civic pride" that accompanied the successful pennant drives of the Cardinals in 1967 and the Tigers in 1968 may be why St. Louis and Detroit "escaped massive racial riots" during a period when violent upheavals scarred many American cities.[55] A study of the Dallas Cowboys sees the presence of blacks as capable and respected team members "whose ability commanded the respect of all fans, white and black" as having "undoubtedly helped shake the more fundamental psychological blocks on which segregation was built" in Dallas.[56]

Not all the social implications of professional sports are positive, however, nor are the benefits as unalloyed as some enthusiasts claim. Community pride and solidarity usually are discussed in terms of bringing people together behind a winning team. But some places will have losing teams; for every World Series or Super Bowl winner, there are last-place finishers and habitually weak teams. Occasionally, a city will rally around a losing team, usually in the midst of a horrendous losing streak, but most mediocre teams are communal embarrassments rather than community assets. Places also can lose teams, a more serious blow to community pride than a losing team, often leading to divisive finger-pointing in an effort to find someone to blame. Even when teams stay, communal solidarity is frayed by recurrent threats to move by footloose owners and by bitter conflicts over new sports facilities.

Triumphs by the home team can trigger destructive riots as well as joyous celebrations.[57] In Detroit, celebrations turned nasty following championship seasons for the Tigers and Pistons. Three women were raped and a man killed in 1984; six years later eight died, including four children, three of them by a car driven on the sidewalk into a celebrating crowd. Three consecutive NBA championships for the Chicago Bulls resulted in three nights of violence; over a thousand people were arrested in 1992 in riots that injured more than 100 police officers and caused an estimated $10 million in property damage. Most of the riotous celebrants in Chicago and Detroit were inner-city blacks, but race was not a factor when hundreds of young men rampaged through downtown Montreal following the Canadiens' capture of the Stanley Cup in 1993, injuring scores of people and destroying or stealing $10 million worth of property. Whatever the reasons for these violent episodes, riots are the antithesis of bringing a community together, particularly when there is a substantial racial component.

More generally, the integrative role of professional sports is questionable; happy images of everyone coming together behind the home team gloss over the role of socio-economic factors in separating sports fans along class, income, ethnic, and racial lines. Variations in ticket prices combined with differences in income to keep the classes apart in the early decades of baseball.

Today, luxury boxes and other premium seating arrangements physically divide the well-off from ordinary fans, and rising ticket prices prevent lower-income groups from attending most major league games. Arenas and stadiums have been battlegrounds as well as meeting places for whites and blacks. Professional sports shunned African Americans, both as players and spectators, until well into the twentieth century. "Shibe Park was a typical place of prejudice," notes Bruce Kuklick, "blacks were not fans of the A's or Phillies, and the franchises did not attract blacks to the ball park."[58] With the breaching of baseball's color line in 1947, blacks came to see Jackie Robinson, and often were greeted with hostility from whites at Ebbets Field and other ballparks; as one Dodger fan recalls, "when the blacks started coming to the game, a lot of whites stopped coming."[59]

Race continues to have a pervasive divisive impact on professional sports, affecting issues from differences in salaries for black and white athletes of comparable ability to the reluctance of some white fans to support heavily black teams. Pittsburgh's unwillingness to embrace excellent Pirate clubs in the early 1970s was widely attributed to the team's large number of black and Latino players. Whether games are played mostly by blacks, in the case of pro basketball, or whites, as in the NHL, the crowds everywhere are largely white, even though the cities in which most major league teams play are increasingly populated by blacks and other minorities. In Atlanta, which counts substantial numbers of well-off residents among the blacks who constitute 60 percent of the city's population, African Americans bought only 4 percent of the tickets to Braves' games in 1991; through marketing directed at blacks, the Braves doubled the proportion of black ticket buyers in 1992.[60] Some teams have reacted to racial change in their immediate environs by moving closer to their white customer base rather than by marketing their product more effectively to blacks. And teams that have stayed in black areas, like the Blackhawks, Bulls, and White Sox in Chicago, have designed their facilities so that white fans will not have to venture into black neighborhoods.

Political Attractions

Professional sports are politically attractive; big league sports are popular, and politicians like to be associated with popular activities. Politicians support professional sports regardless of their personal feelings about this or that game, seeking to benefit from the civic pride generated by the home team. Particularly attractive to politicians is association with winners, which is why they turn up in locker room celebrations and greet the champions at city hall after the victory parade. Mayor John Lindsay's participation in the wild locker room scenes that punctuated the New York Mets' unlikely march to baseball's world championship in 1969 was widely credited with providing a critical boost to his uphill reelection campaign that November.

Politicians also want their city or state or province to be in the big leagues. At the turn of the century, city officials joined with civic and business boosters in seeking teams as baseball leagues expanded, contracted, and merged. Today, mayors and governors typically are the chief boosters for their city or state, as are their counterparts in Canada, usually leading the charge in the competition for expansion teams, in efforts to lure or retain a team, and in campaigns to build the arenas and stadiums expected of big league places.

Everywhere, the political appeal of sports is reinforced by influential constituencies that support big league teams and facilities. Business provided backing for the first professional sports teams, and local business elites continue to be a primary source of support. Connections between business leaders and city hall typically are close when a place's status, competitive position, economic health, and downtown vitality are at issue, which usually means that local political and business elites have shared interests in teams, stadiums, and arenas. Alliances of political and business leaders have dominated the politics of development in most American and Canadian cities; the overriding concerns of these alliances have been to enhance their city's competitiveness and focus resources in downtown areas, priorities that have both increased the importance of professional sports and concentrated sports facilities in center city. Local newspapers and television stations, critical constituencies for politicians, usually strongly support professional sports. Like a city's business and political leaders, the press wants to be in the big time; and newspapers almost always are enthusiastic boosters of the economic growth and downtown development promised by sports facilities.

Professional sports have offered attractive rewards to politicians from baseball's earliest days. Complimentary passes for White Stockings' games in 1880 "included all of the city's aldermen as well as the city clerk, the commissioner of public works, the chief of police, and Carter Harrison, Chicago's mayor."[61] Teams had jobs for the politically connected as ticket sellers, ushers, vendors, guards, and grounds keepers. Land for ballparks, building and maintenance contracts, and transit connections offered politicians opportunities for payoffs and profitable deals. For their part, teams welcomed beneficial political links; in most industrial cities, machine politics was the only political game in town, offering protection and favorable treatment. The resources that politicians controlled became increasingly important as city governments expanded, providing additional public services and facilities, and regulating more private activities through building, fire, safety, and health codes. Friendly city governments could provide police protection at the ballpark, sympathetic inspections of often unsafe facilities, and help with building arenas and ballparks.

In the early days of professional sports, politicians often cemented these relationships through owning all or part of a team, thus securing more control over the distribution of rewards. Steven Riess has detailed the pervasive involvement of Tammany Hall in the ownership of baseball teams in New York from Boss Tweed's control of the New York Mutuals, a charter team in both the National Association and the National League, until well into the twentieth century.[62] In Cincinnati during the early years of the twentieth century, the Reds were controlled by the local Republican machine. Alliances between machine politicians and gamblers provided another political linkage to professional sports. One of the leaders of the Tammany-backed syndicate that obtained the New York franchise in the American League in 1903 was Frank Farrell, a big-time gambler. Among the early owners of NFL franchises were Tim Mara, a bookmaker with Tammany connections, and Art Rooney, a gambler active in Pittsburgh politics.

As the twentieth century unfolded, political machines faded and urban politicians sought new allies, especially among powerful local business interests. In a number of places, acquisition of teams by such interests—the Chicago Tribune Company in Chicago, Anheuser-Busch in St. Louis, Ted Turner and his Atlanta-based broadcasting empire, Wayne Huizenga in south Florida, and the Walt Disney Company in Anaheim—has increased the responsiveness of mayors and other local political leaders to professional sports. And regardless of their local economic clout, team owners can usually command political attention because they decide what places will be in the big leagues.

The attraction of politicians to professional sports has grown with expanding governmental involvement in stadium building and associated activities. Concomitantly, the political opportunities offered by publicly financed sports facilities have spurred politicians to favor bigger roles for government in seeking and sustaining home teams. Leading the quest for a professional sports team is very hard to resist; officials, as Arthur T. Johnson points out, "welcome the rare issue that promises community consensus and will allow them to demonstrate leadership. If the issue also permits them to manipulate political symbols and promotes economic development, it will be even more attractive. The pursuit of a sports franchise is just such a policy for cities without one."[63] Bringing a big league team to town is almost always enthusiastically endorsed by business leaders, local media, and sports fans; opponents, at least in the early stages, are likely to be few in number and unorganized. The political calculus of relocation is similar; more vocal interests will support than oppose efforts to keep a team from moving.

Stadium building also is very attractive politically, particularly if tied to development goals such as downtown renewal favored by influential business interests. Arenas and stadiums generate a variety of opportunities for political and economic gain. The construction industry strongly supports large public works, and backs its interests with substantial political contributions, as do the building trades unions. Development and operation of public stadiums involves myriad opportunities for patronage and other benefits, from free tickets for local officials to multi-million dollar bond issues and construction contracts to politically favored firms. Arenas and stadiums, moreover, are tangible accomplishments; in rebuilding downtowns, Bernard J. Frieden and Lynne B. Sagalyn note, "mayors wanted projects with broad popular appeal, places that the voting public would visit. Festivals, fairs, and celebrations were right for this purpose, and big league sports were even better."[64]

Securing these benefits, however, can involve substantial political costs and risks. Sports issues usually become controversial when discussion moves from general goals to specifics involving substantial sums of public funds and the impact on areas where arenas or stadiums are located. The result is likely to be disagreement over whether sports facilities and subsidies are desirable or necessary, over who should bear the costs of new facilities, and over the pluses and minuses of particular sites. Teams inevitably become dissatisfied with their arrangements, seeking more concessions and better facilities, which will increase the cost to taxpayers of staying in the major leagues. The triumph of securing a big league team, as Johnson notes, can become "one of many potentially harmful issues over which" city officials "have little control. The team owner is no longer bearing idealized gifts to the city but has been reduced to one of many interests scrambling for scarce public monies."[65]

Looming over the process is the possibility of failure—that a place will not land a footloose or expansion team, or that the home team will depart, or that a promised stadium or arena will not get built, or that a facility will be constructed without a team to play in it or help pay for it. For elected officials, the biggest perceived risk is being blamed for losing a home team, regardless of whether there was anything that could have been done to keep the team in town. This wariness is based more on possibilities than actual experiences, since loss of a team has rarely been an election issue, and does not seem to have been a significant factor in the defeat of any incumbent who "lost" a team. Politicians, however, seek to minimize risk; thus, the prudent response to a threatened departure is to make a strong effort to do whatever can be done to keep a team, or to appear to be doing all that is possible or even more, as in the case of Governor James R. Thompson of Illinois who promised that "I'll bleed and die before I let the Sox leave Chicago."[66]

Emphasizing the Positive

Political leaders usually conclude that the benefits of professional sports outweigh the costs. Regardless of the doubts expressed by almost every impartial study, public officials behave as if economic benefits were substantial and economic stakes were vital. Positive studies are emphasized, usually by stressing the most optimistic projection of benefits that will get a headline or sound bite, while negative studies and critical evaluations are ignored. The result is a political litany of expressions of unshakable faith in the economic benefits of professional sports. "One World Series in Los Angeles," promised Mayor Norris Poulson who made the deals that brought the Dodgers west, "and every cent that Los Angeles has invested in this project will be repaid many times over. Progress must not be stopped in Los Angeles."[67] Mayor Federico Pena, explaining why he energetically campaigned for a new baseball stadium in Denver, insisted that "it's a pure business deal. That's the only way I can do it. If I didn't think it was a moneymaker for the city, I would question using public dollars."[68]

Politicians also give substantial weight to intangible benefits in weighing the pros and cons of sports issues. Professional sport is not an enterprise that places or public officials, any more than fans or journalists, or owners and players for that matter, approach as purely economic endeavors. New York City's top economic development official, who was orchestrating efforts to build new stadiums for the Mets and Yankees in the mid-1990s, termed his mission "more than economic, . . . it's psycho-economic."[69] New Orleans' Mayor Moon Landrieu called the "Superdome . . . an exercise of optimism. A statement of faith. It is the very building of it that is important, not how much it is used or its economics."[70]

Baade and Dye, whose work is highly critical of the proclaimed economic benefits of professional sports, concede "the possibility of 'intangibles' or external benefits from 'civic pride' or psychological identification with big-time sports," but they "prefer to leave intangibles as a residual explanation after direct or indirect economic activities have been explored."[71] This residual, however, is a primary factor in understanding the politics of professional sports. Intangible benefits are centrally important because prestige, communal identification, community pride, and emotional attachments matter when places wrestle with sports issues. And the value of intangible benefits to so many of the most interested participants reinforces the attractions for public officials of luring and keeping teams, building and improving stadiums, and remaining competitive in the turbulent world of big league sports.

8

Competing for Teams

D EMAND by places for big league teams exceeds the number of major league franchises. Urban growth and regional change continue to bolster the ranks of places that want to play in the big leagues, while cities that secure a team typically seek franchises in other sports. Underlying the mismatch between supply and demand for teams is control of franchises by sports leagues. Control over supply and location of franchises is the basis for most of the benefits that professional sports extract from places where they play. And insuring that some sizable metropolitan areas do not have teams makes threats to relocate credible.

The result of this mismatch is pervasive competition for the limited number of big league teams. Places seeking teams compete with other places, both for existing teams and for new ones when leagues expand or merge; places with teams have to compete to retain them. Competition bids up subsidies for playing facilities and other inducements, steadily increasing the public cost of major league sports. Construction of new stadiums and arenas and a lengthening list of lucrative incentives intensifies competition, while creating pervasive uncertainty for places with teams.

Competition for teams skews the relationship between places and professional sports heavily in favor of teams and leagues. A city official in Florida underscores the weakness of the competitors: "It's a game of leverage and those that are competing on the outside have none, except to offer their wares in the most attractive way."[1] Norris Poulson, mayor of Los Angeles when Walter O'Malley moved the Dodgers west, emphasized that "since O'Malley needed us much less than we needed him, he obviously held the trump cards."[2] Teams and leagues have become increasingly adept at using their leverage to extract concessions. O'Malley was a pioneer in exploiting the inherent advantage of teams over places; Los Angeles "officials promised O'Malley the moon," Poulson notes, "and Walter asked for more."[3] By the 1980s, owners were routinely playing communities off against one another in the quest for better deals. Al Davis moved the Raiders south after Los Angeles topped

Oakland's offer, then encouraged a bidding war for the Raiders among Los Angeles and competing cities, and finally returned to the Bay Area in 1995, when Oakland put together a winning package.

Competitive Environment

Competition for major league teams is part of the larger contest among places for economic development. States and most localities are involved in an unremitting quest to attract and retain business, bolster the local economy, and enhance the tax base. Cities and suburbs compete with localities across the United States, as well as among themselves within metropolitan areas; states battle other states, usually in alliance with localities within the state. Canadian cities, metropolitan areas, and provinces similarly compete with each other and places in the United States. Businesses, for their part, seek to extract concessions from existing locations with threats to move and by fostering competitions among places for new facilities. Underlining this competition is the fundamental reality of immobile places and footloose businesses; in the case of professional sports, cities cannot move while teams can.

In competing for teams, places employ the same inducements they use to woo and keep businesses in general, including free or subsidized land, publicly constructed buildings, favorable leases, tax breaks, improved roads, and other public facilities. Political and economic heavyweights—including governors, members of Congress, mayors, bankers, corporate executives, and publishers—are mustered to sell a place to coveted businesses or sports teams. Consultants sell their expertise and connections to competing places, and interested parties gather to ponder the tactics and strategy of securing major league franchises, such as a four-day conference in 1996 on the theme of "If You Build It, Will They Come" organized by the National Council for Urban Economic Development. Public funds provide the principal resource in the competition for teams as for business more generally; thus, competition escalates the public stake in professional sports. And the more places that offer similar inducements, the less advantage a particular locale gets from its package of goodies, and the higher the expectations and demands of teams and leagues.

As with other businesses, competition constrains places in dealing with professional sports. Cities and states have to remain competitive with rival places, most obviously in deals for arenas and stadiums but also with respect to other matters. Teams, like other enterprises, want a favorable tax climate, which usually means as few taxes as possible. Local regulations that impinge on more general league policies or preferences, such as requirements that games be broadcast on free television or proposals mandating alcohol-free sections in stadiums and arenas, can be liabilities for places. Professional sports have been particularly sensitive about legalized gambling on major league contests, fearful of a recurrence of scandals that have periodically tarnished their games.

Leagues have strenuously opposed sports lotteries, warning that places with sports gambling would be at a serious disadvantage in securing and keeping major league teams. Threats by the NBA to move the Portland Trailblazers persuaded Oregon to drop basketball from its sports lottery. In 1993, the NBA forced two Canadian provinces to choose between sports lotteries or NBA teams in their largest cities. After a lot of grumbling about having public policy dictated by a sports league, and an American one at that, Ontario and British Columbia eliminated basketball from their lotteries, paving the way for approval of expansion franchises in Toronto and Vancouver.

Competition for professional sports franchises frequently raises questions of parity when two or more teams play in a place; as with business in general, a good deal for one team prompts demands from the others. Municipal construction of a stadium to bring the National League back to New York opened the door for the Yankees to lever substantial concessions from the city government. In Baltimore during the 1970s, city officials were caught in what Charles C. Euchner calls "a protracted game of 'me-tooism' by the Colts and Orioles"; after the Orioles badgered the city into a better deal for Memorial Stadium, the "Colts responded by demanding a new lease based on dollar parity with the Orioles."[4] The same game began in Minneapolis after $80 million in public funds kept the Timberwolves in town: the Vikings pressed for a better lease at the Metrodome and the Twins campaigned for a new ballpark.

Competition for big league teams attracts a steadily enlarging number of participants. Rapid urban growth in the Sunbelt has swelled the ranks of metropolitan areas with big league ambitions. Suburbanization has multiplied the number of competing places, particularly in the largest metropolitan areas. City governments have been the primary competitors, but other local governments have gotten into the act, reflecting the complex sharing of responsibilities and financial resources in most metropolitan areas. County governments were key players in moving the peripatetic Braves from Boston to Milwaukee's County Stadium and then on to Atlanta-Fulton County Stadium. State and provincial governments have become increasingly important participants in the competition for teams, in some cases as partners with localities, in others as the principal agent seeking to lure or keep a team. Stadium agencies add another element to the cast of competitors, one with an intense interest in securing major league tenants for public arenas and stadiums.

Government officials are typically allied with local business interests in the quest for major league teams, as they are in the competition for economic development more generally. The relative roles of public and private parties vary from place to place. In Los Angeles, the key parts in the successful campaign for the Dodgers were played by elected officials. The Denver Baseball Commission, created by Mayor Federico Pena, was composed largely of business leaders and was financed by major corporations. Business interests took the lead in organizing the Phoenix Sports Alliance to direct the metropolitan area's efforts to increase its representation in the big leagues, and businesses were the driving force behind the aggressive efforts of Touchdown Jacksonville! to bring the NFL to northern Florida. Milwaukee's successful bid to get back in the major leagues was spearheaded by a group of local businessmen who were interested in owning a baseball team in their hometown. The Committee to Relocate the Rams to Anaheim brought together a broad spectrum of business interests and political figures in Orange County. And the successful effort to move the Rams from Anaheim to St. Louis was managed by FANS (Football At the New Stadium), an organization created by city, county, and state political leaders, directed by a former United States senator, and backed by the area's major businesses.

All of these competitive efforts are shaped by the nature of the prize. The visibility, emotional links with fans, and value as communal status symbols of major league teams heightens competitive stakes. Places typically offer far more to secure or retain teams than they would for a comparably sized business. And because places are so determined to win these high-stakes competitions, their bargaining position with teams and leagues is further weakened, especially in the case of older cities that have lost so many other businesses to suburbs and newer urban areas in the south and west.

Competing Places and Cohesive Leagues

Competitions for major league franchises are zero-sum games in which one place's gain is another's loss. When a team relocates—or is persuaded to stay—one place gets a team at the expense of another. Expansion involves winners and losers whenever more places seek expansion franchises than a league makes available. Merging leagues usually involves winning and losing places, since the full set of franchises in the weaker league rarely survives.

Because one's gain is another's loss, places have few common interests in the competition for major league franchises. The result is cutthroat competition. Places that want teams are constantly on the lookout for opportunities provided by souring relationships between clubs and their current locale. When negotiations over a new arena between the Seattle SuperSonics and city officials bogged down in 1990, suitor cities quickly appeared to woo the Sonics. Memphis offered a rent-free lease on its new arena, guaranteed 10,000 season tickets and $3 million for radio and television rights, and proposed a sweetheart deal on luxury boxes. Another bidder was San Jose, eager to find a major league tenant for a downtown arena that was under construction.

So many places have tried to steal teams that very few competitors have clean hands, or evoke much sympathy when faced with threats to teams that were lured from somewhere else. Those who criticized Indianapolis for purloining the Colts were reminded by Mayor William Hudnut that Baltimore had played the same game in the past: "Where did the Colts come from? Texas.

Where did the Orioles come from? St. Louis. Franchises move around. It's just as moral now as it was then."[5] And Baltimore displayed few moral qualms about replacing the Colts with another city's team. A state legislator from Los Angeles complained in 1987 about "our own Los Angeles Raiders being lured away from the Coliseum by an unbelievable favorable financial proposal by the City of Irwindale."[6] Of course, Los Angeles' "own" Raiders were once Oakland's "own" Raiders before being lured south to the Coliseum; Los Angeles also used public money to pilfer the Dodgers from Brooklyn, and took the Rams from Cleveland and the Lakers from Minneapolis.

Leagues are more cohesive than places; whereas places compete for teams, league members generally cooperate. They have common interests in regulating the supply and location of teams. Competition among places increases financial benefits and locational options for teams, as well as enhancing the value of existing franchises and raising expansion fees, which are shared by all members of a league. Control over the number and location of franchises enables leagues to determine the terms of competition among places, and thus further advance the mutual interests of teams.

Within this framework, teams have strong incentives to play places off against one another, while places lack attractive alternatives to bidding against other contestants. The quest for a replacement franchise for the Rams by Los Angeles "led to a series of quasi-blackmail capers by several owners" who "used the threat of relocation as a club to win valuable concessions from their respective home cities."[7] Robert Irsay dangled the Colts in front of Indianapolis, Jacksonville, Memphis, and Phoenix, each of which responded with an attractive bundle of goodies, as did Baltimore in a futile effort to keep the team. In these bidding wars, teams are in the driver's seat; they decide which offers to entertain and whether to proceed with this or that ardent suitor, and they largely determine the outcome of the competition. Memphis offered Irsay $65.5 million in inducements to move the Colts, but as a participant in the negotiations tells the story, "Irsay just excused himself to go the bathroom, and he never came back again."[8] The Nordiques left Quebec after the team's owners unilaterally concluded that "the offer of aid we received from the government was not in line with what it takes to keep a professional NHL club in Quebec City."[9]

Professional sports make no apologies for taking advantage of the benefits that result from competition among places; instead teams and leagues have welcomed the opportunity to join the rest of the business world on the gravy train. "Cities spend fortunes to bring in industries," points out an owner, "why should the baseball industry be looked upon as different?"[10] Places have to be competitive or face the consequences: "You can't be lagging behind other cities," warned the owner of the Browns long before he left Cleveland, "if we don't have a new facility, it will be a major problem for city fathers because of mobility of franchises and because of cities trying to lure franchises."[11] Teams also argue that they need bidding among places in order to remain competitive within their leagues. For Harold Katz, who encouraged offers from New Jersey to move his Philadelphia 76ers across the Delaware River, a bigger arena meant the 76ers would "be able to generate the money that's needed to compete against other cities."[12] Threats to move, owners insist, are necessary to secure adequate support: "We had to make threats to get the new deal," explains White Sox owner Jerry Reinsdorf, "if we didn't have the threat of moving, we wouldn't have gotten the deal."[13]

Leagues foster competition at every turn. Teams usually have free rein from their leagues to use relocation as a means of levering better deals. League officials can be counted on to help teams extract as many benefits as possible, usually with dire predictions about the consequences of failing to meet team demands. In addition, as Euchner notes, "league officials do their best to make sure that the more favorable lease terms serve as the minimum standard for future negotiations of other teams."[14] As a result, minimum league "standards" keep rising, forcing places to offer more favorable terms, more luxury boxes, larger arenas, bigger football stadiums, and new ballparks for the exclusive use of baseball teams. Professional sports have also expanded the scope of competition among places to all-star contests and the Super Bowl. Bids for the 1992 Super Bowl from four cities ranged from $9 million to $10.8 million, and contestants mustered mayors, governors, senators, and business leaders to boost their prospects.

Pervasive Uncertainty

Places compete for professional sports teams in a highly uncertain environment. Places become more or less attractive to teams and leagues as a result of changes in local populations, economies, and social conditions. Stadiums and arenas age and become obsolete in terms of capacity, amenities, location, parking, sharing with other users, and revenue generation. Relations with fans, community, press, and politicians also change, as do broadcast markets and revenues. Leases, subsidies, taxes, and other local arrangements typically become less attractive to franchises over time, particularly as other teams get new facilities and better deals. These dissatisfactions fuel demands for new arenas and stadiums, lower rent, luxury seating, additional revenues from concessions, more favorable tax treatment, and other inducements.

Intensifying uncertainty is the persistent and credible threat of relocation. Efforts to secure major league baseball for St. Petersburg and Tampa involved almost enough teams to form a separate league—the Chicago White Sox, Minnesota Twins, Oakland Athletics, San Francisco Giants, Seattle Mariners, and Texas Rangers—with most using the possibility of a move to demand new facilities, better leases, or other concessions from their hometowns. Competition heightens instability, since more places chasing a fixed number of teams increases the likelihood of attractive offers, serious threats to move, and actual relocation. So does absence of any rules for the competitive game other than those adopted and applied by sports leagues, rules designed to enhance the bargaining power of teams and leagues rather than protect the interests of places. "If anyone can go out and bid for a team and there are no bylaws owners must comply with," an official in Oakland argues, "every city . . . is threatened."[15]

For teams, past support in a place is less important than future prospects. Although the Rams did well in Los Angeles, the team moved to a newer stadium in Anaheim with luxury boxes and the opportunity to develop ninety-five acres of prime commercial land adjacent to the stadium. Winning the competition for a franchise, moreover, is not the end of the game—only the beginning of a new one to hold a team. In seeking a new stadium, the Twins' owner reminded Minneapolis that "I was wined and dined when they succeeded in getting me to move. . . . I'd like to be convinced the business leaders in this area are as interested in keeping us here as they were in getting us to move here."[16] Only a few weeks after finally getting a major league baseball team, St. Petersburg was reminded that staying in the big leagues can be as stressful as getting there; "I've already been contacted by other parties from outside Pinellas County," the owner of the Devil Rays announced in demanding $48 million in additional public funds for the Thunderdome; "as long as other people fulfill their obligations, I'll be here."[17] And if not . . .

Smaller cities and metropolitan areas face the most uncertainty. Whereas leagues want to be in the largest metropolitan areas, they do not need particular small urban areas. As a result, lesser places face more intense pressures than larger ones in the competition for teams; they have the most difficulty attracting teams and retaining them, and often are asked to compensate teams for the inherent disadvantages of small-market locations. Uncertainty is further increased for smaller places because weak teams tend to make the most insistent demands for help, and such teams are more likely to be located in lesser markets.

Rising Stakes

Increasing competition for major league teams has rapidly escalated the stakes for places. The targets during the initial round of baseball relocations were weak teams in shared markets that demanded little and moved in response to modest offers involving modern facilities, conventional leases, and little else. Four decades later, places were offering a cornucopia of inducements to major league teams. Stadiums and arenas are proffered at low rent or no rent, with lenient leases and lucrative shares of concessions and parking fees. Phoenix lured the Cardinals with a package that gave the team 90 percent of regular ticket revenues, half the take on parking and concessions, all the income from sixty luxury boxes, and a lease that provided considerable freedom of action if the team decided to move elsewhere. Offers increasingly include revenue guarantees for ticket sales, luxury seating, and broadcasting. Indianapolis assured the Colts $47 million in ticket sales and preseason radio and TV revenues. Jacksonville pledged ten years of sellouts at the 80,000-seat Gator Bowl in an unsuccessful bid for the Cardinals. Competing for an expansion baseball franchise, New Jersey guaranteed two million paid admissions; as Commissioner Peter Ueberroth noted, "guaranteeing substantial revenue . . . gets people to sit up and pay attention."[18]

Additional inducements run the gamut from training facilities to land to loans to cash on the barrel head. Among the goodies the Cardinals collected in Phoenix was a $5.5 million practice facility. An option to buy $33 million of developable land for $7.6 million enhanced Anaheim's appeal to the Rams, leading an official of the jilted Los Angeles Coliseum to grouse that the Rams' owner "didn't move a football franchise, he made a real estate deal."[19] Pittsburgh's Urban Redevelopment Authority lent the Pirates $20 million in 1985 as part of a package to keep major league baseball in Three Rivers Stadium; and Montreal advanced $28 million at 2 percent interest to insure that the Expos were sold to a buyer who would not move the team. Sacramento was willing to pay the Los Angeles Raiders $50 million to relocate, a bid that upped the cash that other places promised Al Davis in return for a place in the NFL.

Each new sweetheart deal raises the stakes the next time around. "Competitive bidding by cities," James Quirk and Rodney D. Fort emphasize, "produces pressures to reduce rental rates in all cities to the lowest rates being offered by any city."[20] Denver enhanced its successful bid for an expansion baseball franchise for 1993 with a stadium deal that offered a public stadium for private use at almost no cost. The new team would pay no rent for five years and very little thereafter, as well as receive all the income from concessions, parking, luxury boxes, and advertising; the team would also keep all income from nonbaseball uses in return for operating and maintaining the stadium. Understandably impressed, baseball officials saw Denver's lease as "the prototype of what we ask our teams to look at . . . in negotiating" in the future.[21] Who has the best deal, notes a stadium official, "depends on who has the last deal."[22]

Counter offers from places with teams jack up bidding for particular franchises, while raising stakes more generally. Places bid to retain their teams because they do not want to lose major league sports, and because keeping a team is easier than getting a replacement. State and city officials kept the White Sox in Chicago with a new stadium deal that included no rent for the first 1.2 million admissions and a promise to buy up to 300,000 tickets if attendance fell below 1.5 million during the second half of a twenty-year lease. Losing a franchise further ups the ante, typically leading to relentless efforts to get a replacement team. Following the departure of the Rams to Anaheim, Los Angeles snared the Raiders with the lure of $25 million in luxury boxes and other improvements to the Coliseum. After the loss of their NFL teams, Baltimore and St. Louis bid for expansion franchises and wooed exiting teams with state-of-the-art stadiums, extensive revenues, and other goodies that set new highs in the ever-escalating bidding for big league sports.

Stadiums and arenas drive the rising stakes in the competition for teams. Teams and leagues demand, and places provide, new facilities with luxury boxes and other premium seating; baseball and football increasingly seek exclusive stadiums rather than the shared facilities that were the norm from 1950 into the 1980s. New baseball parks in Baltimore and Cleveland, and a football dome in St. Louis, have replaced dual-purpose stadiums, and Atlanta built new facilities for the Falcons and the Braves, who had been sharing Atlanta-Fulton County Stadium. Denver's successful bid for an expansion baseball team was premised on the need to be competitive with places offering new stadiums; David Whitford writes that "it was plain to everyone that until Denver built a stadium, it had a problem in baseball's eyes, especially in view of what other cities were apparently willing to do."[23] So Denver promised to build a baseball park, even though Mile High Stadium, originally built for baseball and expanded substantially for football, could be easily upgraded to major league standards.

If jazzy new buildings are more competitive than existing facilities, then actual stadiums or arenas offer a better chance of attracting major league teams than promises to build—or so more and more places have concluded. As a result, stadiums and arenas are increasingly being constructed with no commitment from a team or league, in the process dramatically raising the stakes and risks for competitors for major league teams. Professional sports have insisted that places secure no competitive advantage from speculative stadium development. "You would be foolish to build a stadium before you have a team," was Commissioner Peter Ueberroth's advice to Mayor Pena of Denver, as contestants lined up for the race for a baseball expansion franchise for 1993.[24] Perhaps, but the list of the foolish keeps growing, as do the number of places that find teams to put in their new stadiums and arenas. Speculative stadium development in Milwaukee, Baltimore, and the Twin Cities in the 1950s was a critical factor in bringing major league sports to these metropolitan areas. Indianapolis built the Hoosier Dome and then sought a team; as Thomas W. Moses, a business leader explained: "we are taking a chance. Let's cross our fingers and hope we get a franchise. At least the dome is not a dream anymore. They can come to town and see it."[25] And the Colts came, which would not have happened without the Hoosier Dome. St. Petersburg believed that its only chance for a major league baseball team was to "offer a truly competitive alternative by investing $110 million in the Suncoast Dome."[26] Despite unsuccessful courtships of a number of teams, as well as a failed bid for a 1993 expansion franchise, the gamble eventually paid off when baseball next expanded.

Other places have taken the risk and come up empty. Memphis built the Great American Pyramid, a 20,000-seat arena, in the hope that "if you build it they will come and play," but the $85 million building attracted neither the NBA nor NHL. San Antonio's $160 million Alamodome has failed to lure an NFL team. And Sacramento has only a hole in the ground to show for a stadium project designed to snare the Raiders. Nonetheless, the lesson that emerges from the experience of both winners and losers among places that have built speculative facilities is less the riskiness of these ventures than the competitive advantage that they can offer, particularly to places that are marginal prospects for the big leagues.

Competition within Metropolitan Areas

Intercity competition for major league teams attracts more attention than competition within metropolitan areas, but intrametropolitan competition increasingly influences where teams play, particularly in the largest urban areas. Competition within metropolitan areas involves contests between central cities and suburbs, among suburbs, and between cities in areas with two or more major urban centers. Intrametropolitan competition poses issues different from those of intercity competition. Teams that shift locales within a metropolitan area remain in the same market; they retain their general fan base and broadcasting audience. For some customers, the new location will be more accessible, for others less so; but the team will still be the Miami Dolphins or Detroit Pistons, wearing the same uniforms, covered by metropolitan newspapers, and broadcast on local stations. Because no significant changes in market or broadcast revenues are involved in moves within metropolitan areas, competition among places focuses almost exclusively on facilities—design, size, location, amenities, accessibility, revenue potential, and the attractiveness of the deal in a particular place. Intrametropolitan shifts are also treated differently by leagues, with teams generally free to determine their specific location within the area encompassed by their territorial rights. Teams understandably downplay the significance of intrametropolitan shifts; "New York is not losing a team," insisted the owner of the Giants when criticized for moving to New Jersey, "but gaining a sports complex."[27]

More places in metropolitan areas are able to compete for teams because of the growing attraction of suburban locations for professional sports. For major league teams, like other businesses, suburbia offers an escape from cities and their problems. "We want a place where you feel 100 percent safe to let your kid go to," emphasized the owner of the Mavericks in exploring suburban alternatives to Reunion Arena in downtown Dallas.[28] A suburban location was a means for the Florida Marlins to minimize the negatives of Miami: "No longer were we just Miami and the vision of *Miami Vice* and Cuban refugees and riots. We were in fact South Florida, a blended community of almost four and a half million people."[29] In Miami as elsewhere, suburbia is where an increasing portion of the customers of professional sports lives and works, and sites for stadiums and their parking lots and highway connections are more plentiful in suburbs than in cities.

Complementing the attractions of suburbs for professional sports are the desires of many suburbs and lesser cities to get into the big leagues. In suburbia, major league teams offer status to places whose names are little known, despite growing populations and substantial concentrations of economic activity. Suburban Irving jumped at the opportunity to build a new stadium for the Cowboys after Dallas balked at replacing the Cotton Bowl. Having the Cowboys meant exposure on national television, thousands of customers for local businesses, and hopes that "the Cowboys will mean as much to Irving . . . as Disneyland does to Anaheim."[30] Local interests fought to keep professional sports in suburban Metropolitan Stadium because "the Vikings and the Twins were literally Bloomington's lease on national fame and glamour."[31]

Cities, on the other hand, strongly resist the movement of professional sports franchises to the suburbs. City interests insist that cities are the appropriate place in the metropolis for major league teams, and that cities whose names are borne by teams have a right to host the home team. Exclusive claims to major league sports are part of the broader effort by cities to hold on to activities that once defined a city and underscored its importance. In the view of the federal government's top urban official, losing a team to the suburbs "is a major blow to the heart of the city."[32] Sports teams are particularly important because of their visibility and symbolic roles; teams leaving cities for the suburbs dramatically underscore the outward flow of people, jobs, and activities. "Each team that leaves for a larger stadium," wrote a New York judge in a case arising from the Jets' desire to move to New Jersey, "is another drop of the City's life's blood."[33]

Criticism of suburban sports development echoes general concerns about suburbia and its impact on cities. John Bale argues that "suburban stadium development has encouraged sprawl and polynucleation and requires massive car parking facilities in order to operate efficiently in a car-oriented society."[34] Auto-friendly suburban locations also tend to be less accessible to diverse urban populations than city stadiums and arenas; a business leader in Minneapolis emphasized that "putting the stadium downtown provides much greater opportunities for poor and old people, for blacks, for people without cars."[35] Stadiums for suburbanites are attacked for separating sports from the community; "baseball parks once linked the team and community, but suburbanization and the automobile have given rise to stadiums with no connection to residential areas," writes Euchner, who concludes that "the result has been a disaster for both the game and the neighborhoods."[36]

Table 8.1   What's in a Name? 1996

Type (number of teams)	Team
City teams with state or regional names (14)	Arizona Diamondbacks
	Carolina Panthers
	Colorado Rockies
	Colorado Avalanche
	Florida Panthers
	Golden State Warriors
	Indiana Pacers
	Minnesota Timberwolves
	Minnesota Twins
	Minnesota Vikings
	Tampa Bay Buccaneers
	Tampa Bay Devil Rays
	Tampa Bay Lightning
	Utah Jazz
Suburban teams with state or regional names (7)	Arizona Cardinals
	California Angels
	Florida Marlins
	New England Patriots
	New Jersey Devils
	New Jersey Nets
	Texas Rangers
Suburban teams with city names (12)	Buffalo Bills
	Dallas Cowboys
	Detroit Lions
	Detroit Pistons
	Los Angeles Kings
	Los Angeles Lakers
	Miami Dolphins
	New York Giants
	New York Islanders
	New York Jets
	Washington Bullets
	Washington Capitals

NOTE: Table includes 1998 MLB expansion teams.

Because professional teams have so much symbolic importance, team names have been an especially sensitive issue. Cities understandably seek the identification that comes with having their name on a team's jerseys, and in the boxscores and standings. As a result, cities have been unhappy over the loss of big-league identity that comes with regional and state names (see Table 8.1). After years of trying to get a major league baseball team to boost Denver, the city wound up with the Colorado Rockies rather than the Denver whatevers. City interests in Miami wanted their team to be the Miami Marlins, and pressed their case with a poll in the *Miami Herald* in which almost 82 percent of 3,482 respondents favored Miami over Florida or South Florida, none of which had any influence on Marlin owner Wayne Huizenga, who preferred to have his suburban-based Florida Marlins stake a claim to the entire state.[37]

Cities have been particularly incensed by the use of their name by teams that have moved beyond the city limits. "Chicago is Chicago," insisted Mayor Harold Washington in arguing that the White Sox would need a new name if they moved to suburban Addison; "if you go beyond the border, you can't take nothing with you."[38] Mayor John Lindsay threatened to sue if the New York Giants did not change their name, and the New York legislature considered a proposal that would have forced the Giants and Jets to drop New York from their name. After the Giants won the Super Bowl, New York City refused to honor the team with a traditional ticker tape parade for its champions because the Giants played in New Jersey; "we cannot spend $500,000 on a foreign team," explained Mayor Edward Koch.[39]

Aside from its political appeal to municipal chauvinists, fretting over city names for teams that play in the suburbs is not very rational. Given the symbolic importance of team names, cities should be grateful rather than spiteful over the retention of their name by teams that relocate to the suburbs. For most fans, television commentators, and sportswriters, the Giants and Jets are from New York rather than East Rutherford, New Jersey, and the Pistons and Lions represent Detroit rather than Auburn Hills and Pontiac. Despite the New York legislature's unhappiness with the Giants and Jets, the state's Department of Motor Vehicles considers the teams part of New York's sports family, offering vanity license plates for the Giants and Jets along with the teams actually located in the state.[40] Moreover, considering the costs involved in subsidizing teams, cities may well be getting a bargain by having their names on teams that other places underwrite. The communities that have the most complaint are those that bear the burden of supporting a team without the glory of having their name on the team banners. Anaheim, for example, wound up with baseball and football teams that had emigrated from Los Angeles, one calling itself the California Angels and the other remaining the Los Angeles Rams during its sojourn in Anaheim. Not until the Anaheim-based Walt Disney Company acquired an NHL franchise did the suburban center have a team to call its own, the Mighty Ducks of Anaheim.

Competition for teams within metropolitan areas involves benefits as well as symbols, but here too metropolitan interdependence muddies the waters for particular places. Spectators, viewers, and advertisers are drawn from a metropolitan market and beyond; none are bound by the political lines that separate cities and suburbs. Economic benefits typically are generated beyond the boundaries of the place where the team plays its games, particularly if that place is relatively small, as are most suburbs. As a result, net benefits for metropolitan areas are not changed much by the movement of teams from city to suburbs. To be sure, benefits and costs are redistributed, with places that capture teams reaping more benefits than most other jurisdictions in a metropolitan area, but such places typically bear heavier costs in terms of taxes, traffic, and tranquillity.

The most intense and focused battles over professional sports within metropolitan areas involve competition between large cities that share an urban region. Major league teams become another prize to be contested by traditional rivals like San Francisco and Oakland or Minneapolis and St. Paul. In the Bay Area, San Francisco got the first team in each sport, but none was seen by Oakland as its home team. Instead, Oakland scurried to get its own place in the sun, landing the AFL's Raiders, the Athletics from Kansas City, and the Warriors from San Francisco. Baseball's efforts in the 1970s to relocate one of the teams and have the other play in both places foundered on the bitter rivalry between the two cities. "San Francisco never gives us anything but problems," insisted an Oakland businessman who chaired the city's stadium commission, "why should we give up half our games?"[41] By the 1980s, a third city had entered the competition, as San Jose in the booming Silicon Valley flexed its muscles, seeking to lure the Giants forty-five miles south with the promise of a new stadium and bringing hockey back to the Bay Area in a spanking new arena. In the Twin Cities, Metropolitan Stadium was built in suburban Bloomington because of St. Paul's opposition to locating the project in Minneapolis. When pressures grew for a new stadium, Minneapolis and St. Paul were again rivals, each promoting local sites as well as competing with Bloomington, which wanted to keep the Twins and Vikings in the suburbs.

Another pair of cities unhappily sharing the same metropolitan area, Tampa and St. Petersburg, engaged in a bitter battle for major league baseball in the 1980s. St. Petersburg regarded the competition with Tampa for a baseball team as "an issue of pride in our county and city."[42] The competition was the starkest kind of zero-sum game, since the area was too small to support two teams; baseball warned both sides that "there's no possibility in the foreseeable future . . . that we'll consider two franchises in that area."[43] After a protracted conflict, St. Petersburg emerged the victor in the competition, building its speculative dome and eventually bringing major league baseball to the area. But the victory was partial at best, since the expansion team would carry the banner of Tampa Bay rather than St. Petersburg in order to increase the team's appeal to fans and businesses throughout the bifurcated metropolitan area.

States in the Game

Twice as many states and provinces had major league teams in 1996 than in 1950.[44] More players, along with rising stakes, intermetropolitan conflict, and regionalization of professional sports have brought states and provinces into the competition for major league teams. Three decades ago, no state or provincial government was a significant player in the quest for big league sports. Today, states and provinces finance and build and operate stadiums, provide tax and other subsidies to teams, mediate competition for teams by localities, and compete with other jurisdictions for franchises. States vie with neighboring jurisdictions, most notably in the case of New Jersey's efforts to lure teams from New York City and Philadelphia; they also compete with other states and their localities, as in the case of Illinois joining forces with Chicago to outbid St. Petersburg and Florida for the White Sox.

Legal, financial, and political considerations draw states into the competition for major league teams. State approval is usually required for localities to undertake big league sports projects; stadium agencies typically have to be empowered by the state government, and bond issues and taxes for stadiums normally require state authorization. As costs have risen, hard-pressed local governments have turned to states for help in financing new stadiums and arenas, and states in turn often have taken direct control, building and operating stadiums through agencies like the Maryland Stadium Authority and the Illinois Sports Facilities Authority. Territorial scope also draws states into the competition for major league teams. States encompass far more of the metropolitan and regional markets of professional sports franchises than cities and other local governments. As a result, states increasingly are the target of those who want government action to keep or secure teams. Politics also plays its part; governors and legislators no less than mayors and city councils want credit for keeping or luring a team, and seek to avoid blame for losing one. Governor Lowell Weicker invested $25.5 million in state funds to keep the Whalers, Connecticut's only major league team, then supported spending $252 million in an unsuccessful effort to bring the New England Patriots to Hartford. Florida's legislators, eager to help snare expansion franchises and teams on the move, provided $60 million in sales tax rebates for any team locating in the state.

Superior resources and territorial scope permit states to compete more effectively than local governments, especially for sports development in the suburbs. Four of the New York metropolitan area's nine teams play in East Rutherford, New Jersey, because the state created the New Jersey Sports and Exposition Authority, built a stadium and arena, lured the Giants and Jets from New York City, and provided the Nets and Devils with a place to play. Capitalizing on its statewide scope, the New Jersey sports authority also bid for Philadelphia's Flyers and 76ers, offering to build a modern arena in Camden. These efforts spurred vigorous responses from New York and Pennsylvania. Officials in New York attempted to stop the New Jersey sports complex by passing the word that financial institutions that bought the authority's bonds would be cut off from state and city business, a tactic that almost killed the project. Pennsylvania joined Philadelphia in putting together a deal for a new arena that kept the Flyers and 76ers on the west bank of the Delaware River.

State involvement in professional sports is complicated by intrastate competition for teams. Backing one contender over another can be politically risky, particularly if spurned competitors have clout in state politics. Florida's eagerness to attract teams produced subsidies for new franchises, but not a willingness on the part of state officials to choose among Miami, Orlando, and St. Petersburg in baseball's 1993 expansion derby. Similarly, California largely stood on the sidelines as Los Angeles, Anaheim, Oakland, Sacramento, and a bevy of suburbs fought a series of battles over the Rams and Raiders, although individual state legislators maneuvered to advance and defend the interests of their constituencies. Keeping the White Sox required Illinois to find a path of least resistance among city and suburban interests. Initially, Governor James R. Thompson backed the team's plan to relocate in suburban Addison, where the White Sox had acquired land, and promised roads and other infrastructure to support a new stadium. But state help for a move to the suburbs was opposed by legislators from Chicago, and then killed when suburban support eroded in the wake of environmental problems with the site and rejection of the plan by voters in Addison.[45] With the suburbs neutralized, Thompson joined forces with Mayor Harold Washington to provide the resources for the stadium deal that keep the Sox in Chicago.

Winners in the Big Metro Game

Competition within metropolitan areas and between adjacent states occurs largely in major urban areas; and almost all teams located outside central cities are in the largest areas, as indicated in Table 8.2. Big metropolitan areas have more suburbs and more local governments interested in playing in the major leagues; these areas are also more likely to spread across state boundaries. Major urban regions typically are multi-centered, with concentrations in secondary cities and new suburban "edge cities," thus multiplying potentially attractive locations for big league sports facilities. The size and complexity of the largest metropolitan areas also lessen ties to the traditional center; increasingly vast urban realms like the New Jersey and Long Island portions of the New York area, and Orange County in the Los Angeles megalopolis, seek their own identity and recognition and place in the big leagues.

Internal competition in the largest metropolitan areas permits teams and leagues to reap the benefits of competition in markets where teams are least likely to leave. Sports leagues want to be in the biggest markets; a major league is expected to be in New York, Los Angeles, Chicago, and other large metropolitan areas; and broadcasters need leagues to have strong bases of support in the largest markets. Threats to leave major metropolitan areas are less persuasive than talk of abandoning Minneapolis or Seattle, and are likely to be actively opposed by a league. But teams do not have to threaten to leave the best markets in order to reap the benefits of competition; all they need is to be wooed by other jurisdictions in the same metropolis. The Redskins played the District of Columbia off against suburbs and the states of Maryland and Vir-

Table 8.2   Metropolitan Areas with Major League Teams in Suburbs: 1996
(Ranked by 1990–1991 Population)

Rank	Metropolitan Area	Population	Total Teams	City	Suburb
1	New York	19,342,013	9	4	5
2	Los Angeles	14,531,529	6	2	4
4	Washington-Baltimore	6,727,050	4	2	2
7	Boston	5,455,000	4	3	1
8	Detroit	4,266,054	4	2	2
9	Dallas	4,037,282	4	2	2
12	Miami	3,192,582	4	2	2
19	Phoenix	2,238,000	3	2	1
36	Buffalo	1,189,288	2	1	1

NOTE: Table includes 1998 MLB expansion team in Phoenix. U.S. populations are for 1990; Canadian for 1991.

ginia in an effort to get the best deal in a lucrative market the team has no desire to leave. In Atlanta, the Braves successfully played the suburban card in securing almost total control over the city's new Olympic Stadium, and the Hawks explored arena sites in suburban Gwinnett, DeKalb, and Cobb counties in pressuring city officials to replace the aging Omni. Intrametropolitan competition means that any place with a team, regardless of market size, is vulnerable to competition from other places; and all teams are in position to benefit from the competition for teams, whether they play in small or large markets, and irrespective of whether they are prepared to move across the continent or just across a local or state boundary.

9

Changing Places

RELOCATION is the most painful aspect of the relationship between places and professional sports, and threats by teams to move are the most potent weapon employed to extract public concessions. Movement of teams to bigger markets was a critical element in the transformation of the Western League into the American League at the turn of the century; similarly, shifting of franchises to large cities was central to the emergence of the NFL, NHL, and NBA as viable major leagues. Today, relocation is how almost all places lose teams.

In the past, places frequently fell out of the big leagues as a result of the financial collapse of local teams or their merger with other franchises. Buffalo, Kansas City, Indianapolis, and Minneapolis muffed their shot at the big time with the new American League when their teams bellied up after the league's first season in 1900. A number of cities lost professional basketball franchises in the shakeout following the merger that created the National Basketball Association in 1949; and the original Baltimore Colts, one of the three teams absorbed into the NFL from the All-American Football Conference in 1950, lasted only one season. No major league team, however, has gone out of business since the NBA's Baltimore entry folded in 1954, although the bankrupt Seattle Pilots had to be relocated to Milwaukee in 1970. Mergers of teams are also rare in recent years, the last being absorption of the NHL's Cleveland Barons by the Minnesota North Stars in 1978.

Of the 113 major league teams playing in 1996, 25 have moved to their current home since 1950, and one other franchise was planning to move by 1998.[1] By contrast, 46 teams were expansion franchises playing in their original locations. Of the remaining teams, 13 came from merged leagues, and 28 were in the same place in 1950 (see Figure 9.1). Relocation, expansion, and merger are interconnected processes. Franchise moves preempt locations for expansion, whereas adding teams to a league reduces opportunities for relocation. Availability of expansion franchises affects efforts to lure existing teams, with expansion losers often turning to existing teams in an effort to get into the big leagues. Franchise shifts generate pressures for expansion, both to

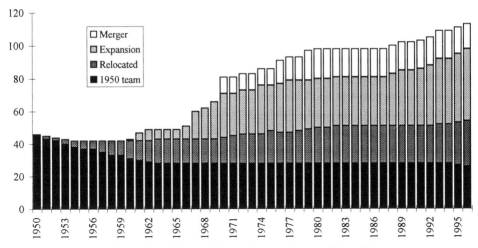

Figure 9.1   Origins of Major League Teams: 1950–1996

provide teams for other places that want to be in the major leagues and to supply teams for the jilted places. Rival leagues can spur existing leagues to expand; new leagues also offer an alternative route to the big time, which may affect the appeal of relocation or expansion to places and prospective team owners.

Although expansion has more effect on which places have teams, relocation is the most dramatic and controversial route to the big league. Relocation involves the most intense competition among places, results in the bitterest conflicts, and has stimulated most of the concern about changing the rules of the game for locating franchises. Observers of the sporting scene rarely welcome relocation. At best, moving teams is considered to be a necessary evil in a world governed by profit; at worst, shifting franchises is seen as the result of greedy manipulations by money-grubbers like Walter O'Malley who moved the beloved Dodgers to Los Angeles. Arthur Daley wrote in 1971 that "the quick-buck men have taken over to a sickening degree and they cynically play a game of musical chairs, pouncing on whatever perch is attractively plastered with dollar bills."[2] David A. Karp and William C. Yoels believe that franchise shifts attenuate ties between teams and places, making it "increasingly difficult for sport to serve the cultural function of creating community integration in as powerful a way as it did during the formative years of city and sports building in America."[3] Critics argue that relocation reduces external and internal cohesion; "the incessant franchise shuffling of the past few years," Lance Davis concluded in 1974, "has reduced fan interest, almost split the cartel apart, and produced an immeasurable amount of political ill will on Capital Hill."[4]

Franchise shifts have been particularly painful in baseball, reflecting both the game's reverence for tradition and its extraordinary franchise stability during the first half of the twentieth century. David Q. Voigt calls the initial relocation in 1953 a "tradition-shattering move"—abandoning "an established franchise to move to a more lucrative site, thus destroying the myth which held that baseball's success depended on maintaining permanently stable franchises in old, established communities."[5] Like others who rue the changes that began with the Braves' move to Milwaukee, Voigt overstates the viability of baseball's traditional arrangements; the Browns were a pathetically weak club on the field and box office for a quarter century before they moved, as were the Braves and both Philadelphia teams for most of the 1930s and 1940s. Although Voigt recognizes franchise moves as inevitable responses to changing population and settlement patterns, many critics are oblivious to the need for professional sports to adapt to demographic and urban change. For them, real baseball was sixteen teams frozen in ten eastern and midwestern cities. Anything else is not the real thing: Dodger fans in Los Angeles were counterfeits, less loyal and knowledgeable than the faithful in Brooklyn; San Francisco was unworthy of the proud tradition of the New York Giants and their seventeen pennants and five World Series victories. Real rivalries were the traditional ones; "the movement of the Giants and Dodgers to California," contends Ralph Andreano, "has done damage to the natural rivalries that had been built up over several generations."[6]

Much of this criticism is overwrought, revealing more about the anguish of losing major league teams than the reality of franchise shifts. The rivalry between the Dodgers and Giants did not end when the teams moved west, but was refueled by the fierce competition between Los Angeles and San Francisco. Franchise shifts have not undermined fan support; relocated teams typically have drawn more rather than fewer customers; and there is no evidence that aggregate attendance has been adversely affected by team moves. Nor is the argument concerning political costs very persuasive; relocation has generated a great deal of political talk but little action outside of the courts, where rulings have limited the powers of both leagues and places to restrict franchise movements. By and large, relocation has produced a draw, with places gaining teams neutralizing those that lose franchises.

Despite conflict, relocation remains alive and well because team movement appeals to many participants in the major league franchise game. Relocation is a highly attractive option for places seeking a big league team. Most aspiring places want to be in the real big leagues, not in the second-rate version offered by rival leagues. Relocation gives places an established team that almost always performs better than an expansion outfit. Relocation also offers places more control. Luring an established team does not depend on league timetables and procedures, as in expansion; timing and process are determined by the particular team, owners, and places involved. Efforts to lure an existing team, moreover, have a single target; they are focused on one team rather than an entire league and its team owners; and usually succeed if the target team's owner agrees to move.

What appeals to places also leads prospective owners to favor relocation over new leagues and expansion. Rival leagues are easy to get into, but do not guarantee membership in the exclusive club of big league owners, and expansion is a complicated crap shoot controlled by leagues. Buying an established team only requires finding an owner willing to sell and meeting his price; "you find the team," oil billionaire Marvin Davis told the people involved in trying to bring major league baseball to Denver, "I'll write the check."[7] Neither finding a team nor meeting the owner's price is easy, as indicated by Davis' unsuccessful efforts to buy the Athletics, Orioles, and White Sox; still, established teams offer entrepreneurs as well as places the surest bet at getting into the big leagues.

Last but hardly least, franchise mobility is highly desirable for teams and leagues. The ability to move, and thus to threaten relocation, critically enhances the bargaining power of teams and leagues with places, thereby increasing benefits, revenues, and franchise values for both the particular team and the rest of the league. Al Davis told fellow NFL owners that his disputed move to Los Angeles "won for all of them" because "franchises now had more leverage than ever."[8] Mobility also increases the value of teams by enlarging the pool of potential buyers to include prospective owners who would move the franchise. And, of course, freedom of movement permits owners to relocate when they find what promises to be a greener pasture.

Why Teams Move

Teams move primarily to improve the bottom line; they seek more customers, higher revenues, lower costs, and better deals in new locations. "The typical franchise move," concludes James Quirk in an analysis of relocation, "has been one in which the franchise owner sees higher profit potential in some other location."[9] An official of the Edmonton Oilers, discussing the team's threat to leave town, wondered why relocation "always comes as a great shock to people. . . . You either make it in business or you move."[10] Each of the first three baseball teams to relocate was the weaker franchise in a two-team city. The Boston Braves and St. Louis Browns had the worst cumulative records in the major leagues during the twentieth century.[11] Despite the baseball boom following World War II, the Browns struggled to draw 250,000 fans a year, less than some minor league teams. In Philadelphia, the once proud Athletics languished in or near the cellar following their last pennant in 1931, and their troubles worsened as the Phillies built a strong team that won a flag in 1950. None of these teams was able to attract sufficient fans or capital to survive economically where they were located.

Neil J. Sullivan questions whether relocation enhances the bottom line, contending that "moving a franchise to improve its earnings has almost always been a mistake born of the false conclusion that the abandoned community will no longer support baseball."[12] The trouble with this argument is that there is no way of knowing what difference a winning team, better owners, or more effective management would have had in Boston, Philadelphia, or St. Louis. What is clear is that these teams found a better place to do business, most strikingly in the case of the Braves, where a deficit-ridden operation became profitable as attendance soared in Milwaukee. The Braves' success increased the business appeal of relocation, attracting the attention of owners whose teams were doing well economically but might do better by moving to more fertile ground. Particularly impressed was Walter O'Malley, owner of one of the most successful and prosperous teams in baseball; O'Malley would move the Dodgers not to escape financial distress but to reap even larger economic rewards. As O'Malley put it, "if I'm going to [be called] a carpetbagger, I might just as well carry the satchel."[13]

An essential part of the business motivation of relocation is the quest for more attractive markets. Teams generally have moved in the direction of people and jobs, westward and southward and outward toward the suburbs. The Rams, Dodgers, and Lakers were drawn to southern California by the prospects of a huge market in a rapidly growing area. For some teams, relocation offered an escape from a shared market. Baseball's Giants wanted to move out of New York, where they competed unsuccessfully with the Dodgers and Yankees after World War II. Playing second fiddle eventually pushed the Chicago Cardinals—who drew fewer fans, attracted less attention, won fewer games, and were a less successful business than the Bears—to St. Louis. Relocation also is a way out of small markets with their inherent limitations. Getting out of a small market, however, usually means moving to another marginal market, as long as leagues control relocation and teams exercise territorial rights to exclude competitors from larger markets. The result is considerable franchise instability in smaller metropolitan areas; baseball teams have come and gone in Kansas City, Milwaukee, and Seattle, to be replaced with teams that also have struggled to survive in these limited markets.

Unattractive local settings as well as more general market considerations have influenced decisions to relocate. Both the Dodgers and Giants were playing in obsolete ballparks located in decaying inner city neighborhoods; Ebbets Field had fewer than 32,000 seats, parking for no more than 700 cars, and poor connections to major highways; the aging relic of the Polo Grounds lacked parking and shared Coogans Bluff with a housing project. Both incarnations of the Washington Senators were eager to get out of the nation's capital and its growing black population; the original team was moved to Minneapolis by an owner who worried that "the trend in Washington is getting to be all colored," and the replacement Senators were moved to Texas by an owner who complained that whites would not come to the ballpark because "no place in Washington is safe at night."[14]

New arenas and stadiums have become an increasingly important element in the relocation equation. Moving to Milwaukee put the Braves in a modern public stadium, as did the relocation of the Browns to Baltimore. Los Angeles provided a 300-acre site for the Dodgers to build a new stadium, and invested $5 million in access roads and other public works; San Francisco constructed a stadium for the Giants. In none of these cases were stadiums the primary factor; but new ballparks enhanced the economic and market attractions of relocation, as well as establishing expectations that a relocating team would be handsomely housed and treated, expectations that would constantly rise as competition for teams intensified. And in the process, new playing facilities and associated benefits would become increasingly important considerations in relocation decisions.

Along with new arenas and stadiums have come better television and radio deals, especially in the untapped media markets of the west and south. David A. Klatell and Norman Marcus see television money as the principal factor in the initial baseball relocations, concluding that "the growing competition among franchises for broadcast revenues spurred the first wave of migrations to new markets."[15] Certainly radio and television was a factor in these moves. In Los Angeles, the Dodgers commanded broadcasting revenues second only to the Yankees, even though O'Malley blacked out home games. Television also exacerbated the problems of weaker teams in cities with two baseball franchises; Lou Perini, who moved the Braves to Milwaukee, felt "that since the advent of television Boston has become a one-team city."[16] But none of these shifts was primarily driven by the promise of broadcasting riches; the Braves, Browns, and Athletics would have moved to more promising markets with or without better television deals. The Browns, in fact, were prepared to move to Los Angeles in 1941 when broadcast revenues were a relatively unimportant consideration. The fundamental attraction of Los Angeles to O'Malley was the size and potential of the market, both to fill his new stadium and generate broadcasting revenues.

Owners, of course, move teams, and it is they who determine what weight is given to economics, markets, stadiums, and television deals. In some cases, teams are acquired so they can be moved; the Browns were sold to a group in Baltimore with relocation as part of the deal; similarly, the Athletics were bought by a Kansas City sports entrepreneur with the understanding that the team would be moved; and the bankrupt Seattle Pilots were sold to a group that had been trying to bring major league baseball back to Milwaukee ever since the Braves left. Other owners want to be somewhere else; Robert Irsay had no roots in Baltimore and little interest in keeping the Colts in town regardless of what the city offered. In the end, owners can leave for whatever reasons they choose, providing their fellow owners approve the move or are forced by the courts to acquiesce.

Patterns of Franchise Relocation

Since 1950, major league teams have moved forty-three times between metropolitan areas, with thirty teams involved in these relocations (see Table 9.1). When comparing major leagues over any period, the problem arises that different sports are in different stages of development at any given time. When 1950 is used as a base, the period includes the NBA's formative years, a time typically marked by franchise instability; as a result these data inflate the frequency of franchise movement in the NBA compared with other leagues. For baseball, football, and hockey, 1950 provides a convenient watershed. Baseball was ending an era of remarkable franchise stability in 1950, with no moves since 1902. The NFL had merged with the rival All-American Conference in 1949. And the NHL, by 1950, had begun a long period of franchise stability in which teams neither moved, dropped out, nor were added to the league.

Basketball, as expected, has had the most intermetropolitan shifts since 1950; the sixteen NBA moves account for 37 percent of all moves. Ten teams have moved, with the Hawks and Kings relocating three times and the Bullets and Clippers twice. Half the NBA shifts occurred between 1950 and 1963, a period when the new league was replacing small cities with larger markets. The NBA continued to be less stable than the other leagues for the next two decades, accounting for 44 percent of all franchise moves from 1964 to 1985. No NBA teams, however, have moved since 1985. Baseball accounts for ten of the intermetropolitan franchise shifts since 1950, with six teams moving once, and two—the Athletics and Braves—relocating twice. Half of these moves were in the 1950s, and no team has relocated since the Washington Senators went to Texas in 1972. Seven relocations have involved NHL teams, with five teams moving once and the team that is now the New Jersey Devils shifting locations twice; in addition, one relocating team disappeared as the Cleveland franchise was merged with Minnesota after moving from Oakland. Six NFL teams moved across metropolitan boundaries between 1950 and 1995, accounting for ten moves, with the Colts moving three times and the Cardinals and Raiders twice. Two of the moves were in the early 1950s, and were the culmination of a series of shifts that had moved a franchise from Boston to New York to Dallas before the team settled in Baltimore in 1952. No NFL team then moved for three decades until the Raiders relocated to Los Angeles in defiance of the NFL, a move that opened the door for the shifts of the Colts to Indianapolis, the Cardinals to Phoenix, the Rams to St. Louis, the Raiders back to Oakland, the Browns to Baltimore, and the Oilers to Nashville.

Franchises moved most often in the 1950s, and eleven of the forty-two relocations occurred between 1950 and 1959. Fewer teams have moved in succeeding decades; and the percentage of teams moving has dropped since all of the leagues expanded substantially after 1960. The pace of relocation quick-

Table 9.1   *Intermetropolitan Franchise Relocations by League: 1950–1996*

	Number of Relocations	Percent of All Relocations	Number of Relocated Teams	Percent of All Teams
MLB	10	23.3	8	26.7
NBA	16	37.2	10	33.3
NFL	10	23.3	6	20.0
NHL	7	16.3	6	20.0
Total	**43**	**100.0**	**29**	**100.0**

ened in the 1990s; seven of the hundred and two teams that were in business at the beginning of the decade had relocated or were about to move by the end of 1996, three in the NHL and four in the NFL Still, the relocation rate for the 1990s is less half the rate in the 1950s, when nine of the forty-four teams that began the decade moved, including five of the sixteen baseball franchises.[17]

Thirty-five metropolitan areas have gained or lost teams through franchises shifts since 1950. Ten of these areas added more than one team, and eleven lost two or more franchises. Eight metropolitan areas were involved in almost half of these moves: Baltimore, Los Angeles, San Francisco, and St. Louis had six each; Kansas City and Milwaukee had five; and Dallas and New York four. Among metropolitan areas obtaining more than one team through relocation, only Baltimore, Dallas, Los Angeles, Phoenix, and San Francisco had net gains of more than one franchise; Phoenix snared two with no losses, Dallas gained three teams and lost one, and Baltimore, Los Angeles, and San Francisco had four wins and two losses. Eight other metropolitan areas had a net gain of one team, five of them without any losses.

New York, Kansas City, and St. Louis were the biggest losers through franchise shifts, each having three teams move away. In the case of both Kansas City and St. Louis, two of three teams that left town had earlier relocated from elsewhere—the Athletics and Kings in Kansas City and the football Cardinals and Hawks in St. Louis. New York and Chicago were the only net losers of more than one franchise. New York's three losses (the Dodgers and Giants and the NFL entry that moved to Dallas in 1952) were offset by one team moving into the area, the NHL's New Jersey Devils. Chicago lost the football Cardinals and its original NBA franchise, and no teams moved to Chicago. Thirteen losses offset gains, as teams secured through relocation later moved; these pass-throughs account for 30 percent of all franchise moves (see Figure 9.2).

Market size is a factor in relocation, with teams generally seeking to exchange smaller for larger markets. More often than not, however, relocating franchises go from larger to smaller metropolitan areas. All of the initial baseball moves were to smaller markets, although some of these were large metropolitan areas, particularly Los Angeles and San Francisco, and each provided an exclusive market for a team that was previously sharing a metropolitan area with one or more teams. NFL moves since 1950 have been to smaller areas,

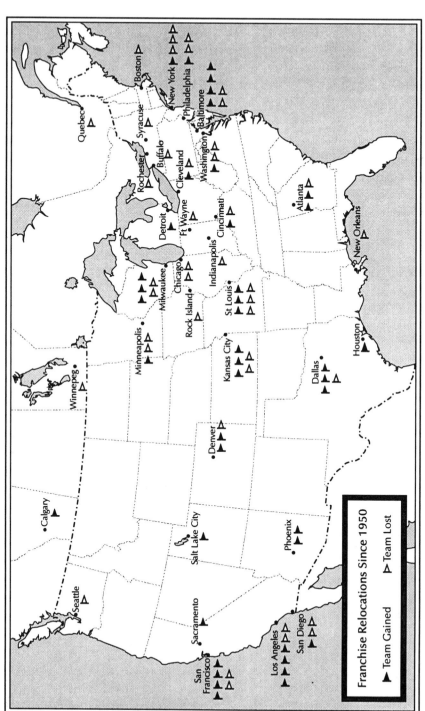

Figure 9.2 Franchise Relocations since 1950

Table 9.2   Total Franchise Relocations by League: 1950–1996

	Intermetropolitan Relocations	Intrametropolitan Relocations	All Relocations	League Percent of All Relocations
MLB	10	2	12	20.3
NBA	16	5	21	35.6
NFL	10	9	19	32.2
NHL	7	0	7	11.9
Total	**43**	**16**	**59**	**100.0**

with the exception of the Raiders' shift to Los Angeles in 1982. NBA teams have moved more often to larger than smaller markets, but four of the NBA moves to larger metropolitan areas were part of the league's shakeout of small cities; since 1963, NBA shifts have been split between moves to smaller and larger areas.

Underlying these patterns is the lack of big metropolitan areas for teams to move to; most large areas have teams and league rules protect existing teams from competing franchises. Two of the most recent moves from smaller to larger markets, the relocations of the Raiders and Clippers to Los Angeles, were made in defiance of league rules concerning relocation and territorial rights. Baseball has teams in the twenty largest metropolitan areas in the United States and Canada; and the NFL is represented in twenty-one of the twenty-two largest areas in the United States. The NBA has teams in all but four U.S. metropolitan areas with populations over two million, and two of these unrepresented areas, San Diego and St. Louis, have had teams and lost them. Opportunities for relocation to larger markets have been most numerous in the NHL, reflecting its tardiness in moving to the Sunbelt. All of the NHL shifts in the 1990s involved a move to a larger metropolitan area: to Dallas from Minneapolis-St. Paul, Denver from Quebec, and Phoenix from Winnipeg.

Most of the anger of jilted fans, distressed politicians, and critical commentators has focused on intermetropolitan franchise shifts. Moves within metropolitan areas have aroused less interest and passion because they are different; they involve no significant change in a team's market or broadcasting arrangements, or even in most cases a change in the team's name; fans are not abandoned, only convenienced or inconvenienced depending on where they live. Nonetheless, moves within metropolitan areas are relocations, typically motivated by considerations similar to those involved in other franchise shifts. New locations in the same market promise more profits, better facilities, and higher subsidies; such locations also typically offer greater accessibility for customers than older arenas and stadiums. Between 1950 and 1996, sixteen teams relocated across local political jurisdictions within metropolitan areas. Moves from cities to suburban areas accounted for thirteen of these shifts. Football teams have moved most often within metropolitan areas, with nine of the sixteen moves, all but one from city to suburb. Including franchise moves within metropolitan areas alters the overall picture of locational stability. This is particularly the case with the NFL, in which moves within metropolitan areas have been almost as numerous as intercity shifts; the league accounted for only 23.3 percent of intermetropolitan relocations, but its share of all franchise moves between 1950 and 1996 was 32.2 percent (see Table 9.2).

Performance of Relocated Franchises

Places that land franchises relocated across metropolitan boundaries often receive damaged goods, teams that were doing well neither on the field nor at the gate. In baseball, every American League club with a cumulative losing record between 1903 and 1970 shifted locations.[18] When the Dallas Texans arrived in Baltimore for the 1953 NFL season, the team was making its second move in two seasons; as the New York Yankees the club had posted a 1–9–2 record in 1951 before being relocated to Dallas and losing eleven of twelve games. Exceptions exist, most notably in the case of the Brooklyn Dodgers, who copped six National League pennants in their last dozen years in Brooklyn, and lost three other flags on the last day of the season. And the Raiders, one of strongest teams in the NFL, won the Super Bowl two years before leaving Oakland and again in their second season in Los Angeles.

Relocated teams generally play about the same before and after a move; changes in scenery, including a new place to play and different fans and press, do not significantly improve performance. In a few cases, teams have played much better after moving. The Braves won an average of fourteen more games in their first three seasons in Milwaukee than in their last three in Boston. Minnesota and Oakland did even better, with the Twins winning an average of fifteen more games during the initial three seasons after moving, while the A's averaged twenty-one more victories for the same period. The Dodgers, on the other hand, plunged from second to seventh place in their first year in Los Angeles, and averaged twelve more losses in their first three seasons in the west compared with their last three in Brooklyn, despite winning a pennant their second year in Los Angeles.

Moving to a new market is expected to draw more fans and thus increase revenues and profits but, gauging the relationship between relocation and attendance is difficult. A host of factors affect attendance, including team performance, stadium or arena size, and changes in the length of seasons; in addition, attendance data are spotty, with insufficient information to include the NHL or early moves in the NBA in a general comparison. Relocation appears to have had the most effect on baseball attendance, as shown in Figure 9.3. On average, baseball teams have drawn 66 percent more customers in the three years following a move than in the same period before relocation, compared to 26 percent for NFL clubs and only 4 percent for relocated NBA franchises for

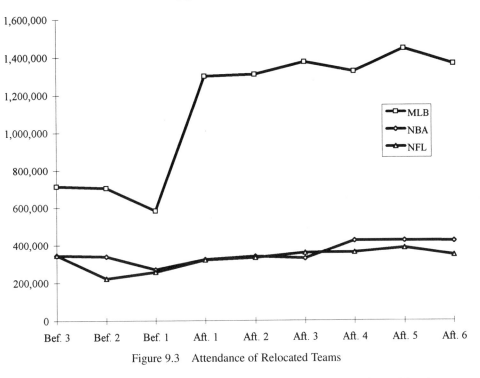

Figure 9.3   Attendance of Relocated Teams

which data are available. The most striking increases were registered by the Braves, who drew over 1.8 million in their first year in Milwaukee, 100,000 more than the combined total for the last three seasons in Boston. Some observers have suggested that relocation only provides a temporary boost in attendance. Voigt argues that the Baltimore Orioles and Kansas City A's "enjoyed a short honeymoon, followed by years of disappointing attendance."[19] Lee Lowenfish emphasizes that both these teams "suffered drops of over 20 percent in their second years after the novelty of the new team wore off."[20] The Orioles and Athletics, however, were drawing around twice as many fans five or six years after relocation than in the years immediately preceding their moves. Overall, relocated baseball teams drew slightly larger crowds on average in their sixth year than in the first or second seasons in their new home town.

Teams that move tend to be less stable in their new locations than franchises in general. Relocated teams have moved at about twice the rate of all teams. Eleven of the twenty-seven franchises that moved across metropolitan boundaries subsequently relocated, for a relocation rate of 41 percent compared with 24 percent for all teams. Repeat moves underscore the fact that teams that leave tend to be marginal franchises in smaller markets, and that these teams often relocate to other marginal locations.

Teams, Leagues, and Relocation

Decisions about moving rest primarily with team owners. Leagues generally react to team initiatives, informally as an owner sounds out relocation possibilities and reviews the bidding, and formally when approval is sought under league rules. Should a league desire to move a team, it has to have an owner agreeable to moving; in the rare instances in which a league has acquired a team it wanted to move, as with the Dallas Texans and Seattle Pilots, the league needs a buyer interested in doing business in a new location. Places seeking an existing team have to find an owner who desires to be in that location, or is ready to sell to someone willing to move to the place. Similarly, local interests that want to foreclose a move have to convince an owner to remain or sell the team to buyers who will keep the franchise in town.

All franchise shifts to a new territory prior to 1982 were undertaken with league approval. Leagues generally have required that relocation be approved by extraordinary majorities or unanimous votes of member teams, usually with more stringent provisions applying to moves that encroach on another franchise's territorial rights. Before 1952, baseball required a unanimous vote of the league in which the move was proposed and a majority vote in the other league; these provisions helped freeze baseball's map for half a century. Changes adopted in 1952, providing for a three-fourths majority in the affected league and no role for the other league except when its territorial rights were involved, paved the way for the franchise moves that began with the Braves in 1953.

Moves within metropolitan areas have not been subject to these league controls. Exclusive rights to a territory, in effect, provide teams with freedom of movement within their market. Commissioner Pete Rozelle kept the NFL out of the Rams' move to Anaheim because the relocation was a "stadium shift" within a market rather than a departure from a metropolitan area.[21] Leagues also have accommodated intrametropolitan moves by extending territorial rights, as baseball did in 1990 by expanding the San Francisco Giants' exclusive territory to include Santa Clara County, where the team planned to move if a proposed stadium had been approved.

Leagues have exercised their controls over franchise movement in the absence of either criteria for relocation or analyses of the implications of moving franchises. Relocation rarely has been guided by comprehensive market strategies; little systematic attention has been paid to broader issues of regional growth, market size, and intercity rivalries. Nor has much effort been made to link relocation to expansion except after the fact, in order to fend off political retribution and potentially damaging lawsuits. In ruling against the NFL's effort to prevent the Raiders from moving to Los Angeles, a federal appeals court criticized the league's lack of specific criteria for evaluating franchise moves: "No standards or durational limits are incorporated into the voting requirement" concerning the protection of "an owner's investment in a football franchise. . . . Nor are factors such as fan loyalty and team rivalries necessarily considered."[22]

Baseball's approach has been particularly chaotic, as teams have moved from large to small markets, expansion franchises have been promised to replace teams that moved elsewhere, and some markets have been crowded while others were ignored. One of the most damning critiques of baseball's haphazard approach to franchise movement came from Commissioner Fay Vincent: "We moved from Kansas City to Oakland and replaced it with a team in Kansas City. What was the point of that? We moved from Washington twice and now Washington makes an effort to get a team. We moved from Milwaukee, we moved from Seattle and in each case the teams were replaced."[23] Underlying this haphazard approach in baseball as in the other sports has been the desire of individual teams to move in search of bigger bucks. Baseball's two decades of musical chairs were an unplanned series of moves set in motion by individual owners; as baseball's commissioner on the eve of the first franchise shifts later characterized the process, "a fellow said, 'I'm going here,' another said, 'I'm going there,' and the gold rush was on."[24]

The usual response to a proposed shift is favorable from owners who expect to be similarly treated should they wish to move or make a credible threat to relocate. Owners, moreover, are members of a club, with collective interests and personal connections that usually produce supportive responses to matters that are important to a fellow owner. Support for relocation is reinforced when a move serves the interests of other teams, particularly those in the same market. Strong backing for moving the Cardinals out of Chicago came from George Halas, owner of the Bears and one of the powers of the NFL. The owner of the Philadelphia Phillies, Robert Carpenter, played a key role in the transfer of the Athletics to Kansas City, with Carpenter buying a ballpark he did not want to help get the rival Athletics out of town. Leagues also usually accommodate owners who wish to move because blocking relocation can be costly for all league members once word of a proposed move leaks. Attendance for lame-duck teams often falls sharply; and the longer the period between public knowledge of the intention to move and actual relocation, the more substantial the financial bleeding.

Owners who want to move are least likely to be accommodated when a relocation adversely affects an existing franchise. During the 1930s, the St. Louis Cardinals explored moving to Detroit, shifting from an overcrowded market to a larger area with only one team, but the Tigers' owner was unwilling to share his territory. One factor leading the National League to reject the sale of the San Francisco Giants to buyers from St. Petersburg was objection from Wayne Huizenga, who did not want his expansion Marlins to face competition in Florida from an established team. League interests in controlling a major market came into play when the NHL blocked relocation of the Seals from the Bay Area to Vancouver, with the Seals claiming in court that the league acted to maintain a team "in San Francisco, thus discouraging the formation and growth of teams from rival leagues in that location."[25]

Financial stakes have become increasingly important in relocation as the prices for expansion franchises have escalated. For NFL owners, as Pete Rozelle explained in discussing the league's opposition to moving the Raiders, "an expansion franchise in Los Angeles would be worth more to the other cities in the league" and "that money should be shared by the twenty-eight partners and they felt that they would be excluded if Oakland took it."[26] By the 1990s, leagues were seeking to extract compensation from teams that moved into prime expansion markets; the Rams agreed to forfeit some future expansion fees as part of the agreement in which the NFL reluctantly permitted the team to relocate to St. Louis.

Leagues are most likely to reject relocations when members do not care about accommodating the owner who seeks to move. Mavericks like Bill Veeck, Charles O. Finley, and Al Davis encountered more difficulty in moving teams than members in good standing in the owners' club. Veeck was blocked from moving the Browns, not out of concern for St. Louis or the team's fans but because the owners wanted to get rid of Veeck and his unconventional approach to the national pastime. The obstreperous Finley was the only baseball owner between 1950 and 1990 to have a proposed move formally rejected; he failed to win a single vote for shifting the Athletics to Louisville in 1964. The sole franchise shift formally defeated in the NFL was the Raiders' fateful move to Los Angeles, an outcome heavily influenced by the dislike of Davis by most NFL owners.

Rising financial stakes have made owners more likely to challenge or bypass league controls. After Finley's move to Louisville was rejected, the A's owner blustered and threatened to sue the American League, which then grudgingly approved relocation to Oakland. When the National Hockey League refused to permit the Seals to move in 1968, the team sued the league in federal court, contending that the action violated the Sherman Act. The Seals lost when the judge ruled that the NHL's control over franchise locations "imposes no restraint upon trade or commerce."[27] Six years after the Seals were checked in federal court, Al Davis, knowing that his fellow owners were unlikely to let him move to Los Angeles, decided to bypass the NFL's relocation procedure. In directly challenging league control, Davis was risking his franchise; at one point the NFL went to court in an effort to take over the team. For the NFL, the struggle with Davis put league control over team movement on the line, as well as endangering territorial rights since the Raiders were moving to Los Angeles without the permission of the Rams. And beyond the questions of league authority over franchise shifts and territorial rights was what Rozelle called "the greater issue of anarchy," the ability of a league to function collectively.[28]

The main battle was fought in federal court, where Davis joined forces with the Los Angeles Memorial Coliseum Commission in challenging the NFL for restraint of trade in violation of the Sherman Act. Both the district court and an appeals panel disagreed with the ruling in the Seals case, holding that territorial rights impeded competition and that the requirement that three-fourths of the NFL's members approve relocation violated antitrust laws. "Exclusive territories," concluded the appeals court, "insulate each team from competition within the NFL market" and "effectively foreclosed free competition among stadia such as the Los Angeles Coliseum that wish to secure NFL tenants."[29] The decision freed the Raiders to move to the Coliseum, and wound up costing the NFL $18 million in damages, as well as $10 million for plaintiffs' legal fees.[30]

Dire predictions followed the ruling in the Raiders case, ranging from those who saw franchises moving at will to an NFL lawyer who predicted the "unraveling of sports leagues."[31] Certainly, the Raider decision substantially strengthened the hand of teams in relocation controversies with the three leagues that do not share baseball's general antitrust exemption. In the case of the NFL, teams have been much more likely to move since the league's loss in federal court. No team had moved out of a metropolitan area in more than two decades when the Raiders decamped for Los Angeles in 1982; six teams relocated in the dozen years following the court ruling in 1984. The first to go was the Colts; Robert Irsay moved the team to Indianapolis in 1984 without league permission; "we just weren't in a position to stop him," Rozelle claimed, because "our rules on franchise moves have been suspended because of the Oakland situation."[32] After the Colts' move, the NFL sought to monitor relocation informally; teams considering a move were asked to inform other league members of their plans, with the league providing official blessings once a decision had been made. This procedure was followed when the Cardinals moved to Phoenix in 1988; "Bill Bidwell," reported one executive before the vote, "has done a real good job keeping the membership apprised of his problems from a stadium standpoint. I imagine he'll get an attentive audience."[33] What would have happened had Bidwell gotten a less attentive audience was not clear, since the Cardinals' owner had indicated his intention to move regardless of the league's action. Another round of moves began in 1995, when the Rams went to St. Louis, followed by the return of the Raiders to Oakland and the shifts of the Browns to Baltimore and the Oilers to Nashville. None of these moves was welcomed by the NFL, all were accompanied by threats of lawsuits, and in each instance the league acquiesced despite substantial internal misgivings.

The Raider decision has had less impact on league control of relocation by the NHL and NBA. All of the recent hockey franchise moves have been acceptable to the NHL, if not encouraged as part of the league's effort to expand its presence in the growing markets of the Sunbelt. The NBA faced an immediate challenge following the Raiders ruling, as the Clippers moved from San Diego into the Lakers' territory in Los Angeles without league approval. The NBA promptly sued in federal court, seeking to rescind the Clippers franchise and $25 million in damages. "They can't win," was the confident prediction of the Clippers' owner based on the outcome of the Raiders case.[34] The Clippers took the first round when a federal district court dismissed the NBA's suit on the grounds that a favorable verdict was precluded by the Raider ruling, but an appeals court sent the case back for trial, ruling that league control over franchise shifts was not automatically invalidated by the Raider ruling, and that the antitrust implications of league rules had to be evaluated on a case-by-case basis.[35] At this point, the Clippers decided to settle out of court; the team forfeited its $3 million share of the entry fees when the NBA next expanded in return for league permission to stay in Los Angeles. Since the Clippers episode, only one NBA team has sought to relocate, and the move of the Minnesota Timberwolves to New Orleans was successfully blocked by the league despite threatened legal action.

In this murky legal situation, lawsuits are more useful to teams and leagues as bargaining chips than as battlefields, given the costs, delays, and uncertainties involved. The Rams, for example, combined the threat of litigation with financial concessions to persuade the NFL to reverse a preliminary vote against the team's shift to St. Louis. In the move of the Browns from Cleveland, the NFL avoided legal action by negotiating the compromise that shifted the franchise to Baltimore, and promised Cleveland a replacement team. Also unclear is the role of league relocation criteria in future legal battles. In the Raiders' case, the appeals court indicated that league controls over relocation might pass judicial muster if standards for franchise moves were specified; suggesting "an express recognition and consideration of those objective factors espoused by the NFL as important, such as population, economic projections, facilities, regional balance, etc. would be well advised."[36] The NFL then developed a set of standards dealing with a franchise's financial condition, stadium suitability, and fan support, but these rules had little impact on subsequent moves, in part because of the league's unwillingness to risk another expensive defeat in court.

Baseball has also been leery of lawsuits challenging its control over relocation, fearing that its general antitrust exemption could be lost if franchise controls failed to pass muster in federal court. The major leagues established what Commissioner Fay Vincent called four "hard and tough criteria" to judge franchise relocations: teams could move only if the franchise had "a long history of substantial operating losses," played in a stadium "substantially below standard, with no immediate solution in sight," was located in a city that made "some overt act evidencing no continuing interest in baseball, like voting down funding for a new stadium," and when there was "no immediate prospect for reviving baseball or the franchise in that community."[37] Vincent's "hard and tough criteria," however, provided no specific standards, relying instead on judgments about the adequacy of stadiums, fan support, and local interest. And these judgments, in baseball as in the other sports, would continue to be made by league members, based on what was best for a league and its teams, with places having neither formal roles nor legitimized interests in the process—realities that are examined in the next chapter.

10

Playing for Keeps

Owners determine which teams can and cannot move; and they make these decisions primarily to advance their individual and collective interests. Places, fans, community identification, and public investments in arenas and stadiums are not usually central considerations in a relocation process that has determined the location of more than a score of big league teams, as well as sweetened arrangements for many other teams that threatened to move.

Professional sports talk a better game about loyalty to places than teams and leagues play. "The Senators will never move in my lifetime," promised Calvin Griffith, who was alive and well when he moved the team to Minneapolis a couple of years later.[1] "We'll always remain the New York Yankees," gushed George Steinbrenner after his syndicate acquired baseball's most illustrious franchise, but Steinbrenner soon was flirting with New Orleans and entertaining proposals from ardent suitors across the Hudson in New Jersey.[2] "This is the hockey heartland of the United States," proclaimed the new owner of the North Stars in 1990, who promised that "down the road" Minnesota would have a Stanley Cup; but the road led the team to Dallas in 1993 rather than to a championship for hockey's heartland.[3] Owners alone determine the nature of their obligations to places where they play; and these bonds normally take a back seat to business calculations and personal desires.

Leagues, Relocation, and Places

During the 1950s and 1960s league officials largely ignored places that were left behind as baseball teams came and went. The president of the National League told a congressional committee on the eve of the departure of the Dodgers and Giants that he was "not interested" in the matter.[4] For Commissioner Ford Frick, teams were not responsible to places where they played; "an owner has a responsibility to his partners and stockholders, . . . he has no responsibility to lose money or to stay where he can't get by or where it appears the city is not going to support big league baseball."[5] Frick's successor made no effort to keep the Braves in Milwaukee because of his conviction that "in this great democracy we live in, if a man wants to take his property somewhere else and can do it legally, then I could not stop him."[6]

More recently, leagues have professed greater concern for places with teams and their fans, as well as the need for franchise stability. "We owe the fans considerable obligations," Commissioner Fay Vincent emphasized in explaining his general opposition to relocation.[7] The NBA also stresses franchise stability and place loyalty; "our first choice is for teams to stay where they are," emphasized Commissioner David Stern in 1994, "we're not putting teams up for the highest bidder."[8] During the Raiders case, the NFL argued that it had "an interest in preventing transfers from areas before local governments, which have made a substantial investment in stadia and other facilities, can recover their expenditures."[9] Soon after the Raiders ruling, the NFL condemned a proposed relocation of the Philadelphia Eagles, emphasizing that "such a move would abandon a community that has supported its team superbly for more than half a century."[10] When the flight of the Raiders and Rams from Los Angeles triggered another round of moves and threatened franchise shifts, Commissioner Paul Tagliabue warned NFL owners in 1996 that "franchise free agency angers the public" and spoke of the league's "need to put ourselves in the fans' shoes."[11] But owners are more comfortable in owners' shoes; the same meeting that aired the concerns over franchise free agency approved the deal that permitted Arthur Modell to move from Cleveland to Baltimore, and two months later the league blessed the relocation of the Houston franchise to Nashville.

League officials have occasionally intervened to prevent teams from moving. Vincent's efforts were instrumental in keeping the Mariners in Seattle and Giants in San Francisco; Commissioner Peter Ueberroth successfully opposed moving the Twins to Tampa. Opposition within the NFL to the Raiders' move was motivated in part by concern for Oakland and Raiders fans who had loyally supported the team for years. Aggressive intervention by the NFL in cooperation with city officials kept the Eagles from relocating to Phoenix in 1985, and league opposition helped block a move by the Seattle Seahawks to Los Angeles. The NBA turned down the proposed sale of the Minnesota Timberwolves to a New Orleans syndicate that planned to move the team south, citing solid local support of the team.

Protecting places and fans with teams, however, is neither the only nor most important reason why leagues may oppose relocation. In contesting the Raiders' move to Los Angeles, the NFL's primary concern was retaining league control over relocation, not Oakland's loss of its team or public investment in stadiums. Commissioner Bowie Kuhn, who grew up in the nation's capital rooting for the Senators, cared about Washington losing its team, but his opposition to moving the franchise also reflected his concerns about political and public relations damage to baseball; as he later wrote, "if baseball was going to repair its wounded image, the time had come to stop moving franchises. . . . If the fans were to start believing in us again, they had to be convinced we were intent upon franchise stability."[12] Leagues are also not eager to be seen as at the mercy of footloose owners; "our league has built its success on continuity and stability," claimed one in opposing the Raiders' invasion of Los Angeles, while another insisted that "we're not like other sports leagues that are constantly moving."[13] But soon the NFL was under siege as owners scrambled for new places to play, including the Browns' Arthur Modell, who had preached continuity and stability when someone else had taken the money and ran. "The whole thing has turned into a broad comedy," lamented the owner of the Buffalo Bills in 1996, "each day I wake up waiting to see who is going to throw the next pie."[14]

Leagues, as has been indicated, also have distinctive place interests; these result in a different perspective on relocation from that of individual teams, particularly those seeking to move. League officials are more concerned than individual owners with the network of places in which a league plays, particularly with being represented in major markets. When the proposal to move the White Sox to Seattle was considered, the president of the American League asked Kuhn: "Commissioner, do you really want to see the American League abandon Chicago, one of the finest baseball cities on the continent?"[15] And Kuhn's answer was no. Consideration of a move to Phoenix by the financially strapped owner of the Philadelphia Eagles produced a threat from the NFL of legal action to keep the team in the fourth largest metropolitan area. "If you put the Eagles in the Phoenix market," an NFL attorney explained, "from a television standpoint that is a significantly less attractive market to sell the national package than having them in Philadelphia."[16] Leagues also worry more than individual owners about the political and legal repercussions of franchise moves, and the broader implications of relocation for treatment of leagues under antitrust and broadcasting laws.

These distinctive league concerns help some places with teams and hurt others. The NFL's desire to reestablish a presence in Los Angeles after the departure of the Raiders and Rams in 1995 put a number of lesser places on the endangered team list, as owners in Cincinnati, Minneapolis, Phoenix, Seattle, and Tampa Bay cast envious eyes on the huge Los Angeles market. The NHL's drive for more franchises in larger metropolitan areas greased the skids for shifting the Minnesota North Stars to Dallas, the Quebec Nordiques to Denver, and the Winnipeg Jets to Phoenix, as well as clouding the future of major league hockey in Calgary, Edmonton, Hartford, and Ottawa. Kuhn's persistent effort to placate Congress by restoring major league baseball to Washington threatened places whose teams were targeted for relocation to the nation's capital. And what the National League heralded as the "public service" of putting "a team in the great Southeast" meant moving one out of Milwaukee.[17]

On relocation as on other issues, league officials normally promote the interests of their bosses, the team owners. Proposed moves typically are facilitated rather than obstructed by commissioners, as are threats to move. League officials can be counted on to enhance the leverage that franchise relocation provides teams in their dealings with places. "The league will allow teams the threat to move to get the concessions," admits a Raiders' official, "that's the unwritten rule for most of the brethren."[18] Commissioner Ueberroth bolstered the White Sox in their bargaining with Chicago by indicating he would not block a move if Chicago failed to provide a new stadium. Pete Rozelle jumped into the battle over a new stadium in Minneapolis, underscoring the readiness of the NFL to let the Vikings move if a new stadium was not approved; Rozelle listed all the places that wanted to get into league, while emphasizing that "it is untrue that teams never get permission to move."[19] And, in the end, leagues emphasize the positive; despite widespread unhappiness within the NFL over restless owners, as well as concern over the Oilers leaving Houston, the eleventh-ranked television market, for Nashville, the thirty-third largest, Commissioner Tagliabue heralded the league's approval of the move as a "historic" breakthrough with "the first major sports franchise in Tennessee."[20]

Leagues typically agree with owners who justify relocation on the basis of inadequate local support. Places are faulted despite losing records, poor management, lousy public and community relations, and threats to move that alienate local customers. In St. Louis, owner Bill Bidwell demanded a bigger stadium despite his inability to field a team that could fill one of the NFL's smallest facilities; and when St. Louis failed to satisfy Bidwell, his fellow owners concluded that the problem was the city rather than Bidwell's losing team and inept management: "Obviously, he got to a point where he couldn't stay in St. Louis."[21] Discussing the move of the Senators to Texas, Bowie Kuhn concedes that "the area had not failed; management had failed to provide attractive baseball."[22] Nonetheless, the American League accepted owner Robert Short's claim that Washington could not support his team.

Declining attendance, regardless of the reason, is likely to hasten departure of teams. As a result, fans who express their displeasure with a losing team or bad management by not buying tickets may well wind up with no team at all. Attendance plummeted in Oakland after Charles O. Finley dismantled the powerful team that dominated the American League in the early 1970s, leading Finley to argue that Oakland could not support major league baseball. As the Baltimore Colts settled into mediocrity under the erratic ownership of Robert Irsay, attendance dropped sharply, prompting Pete Rozelle to indicate that Irsay now had "a stronger case for moving than he would have had in the past."[23] And fans that stay away after teams threaten to move usually increase the prospect that a franchise will relocate. In St. Louis, strong indications that the football Cardinals were going to fly the coop led to an informal fan boycott that reinforced the team's argument that local support was inadequate.

Consideration of local backing also underscores the lack of systematic standards for relocation. Local support tends to be a factor only when a team claims that backing is inadequate; places generally get little credit for strongly supporting a team that wants to move. When leagues make positive judgments about local support, as in the case of the Timberwolves, the criteria tend to be ad hoc and post facto, providing little guidance about what standards might be applied in future cases. And the local support that increasingly matters to leagues is willingness to commit public millions to new stadiums and arenas. "We recognize tradition and loyalty," insisted the NFL in 1996, "but we also have to enable our teams to go forward in facilities to keep our traditions going in the right way."[24]

Politicizing Franchise Relocation

Before the Dodgers and Giants left New York in 1957, franchise moves caused little stir in places that lost their team. Franchises came and went during the early years of all leagues with little public outcry. Boston shed few tears when the Redskins departed for Washington after the team's prowess on the field in 1936 was not matched by success at the gate. None of the NFL moves in the years immediately after World War II provoked much response, either because the team was a civic embarrassment, as in the case of the Dallas Texans, or because another team was playing in town—the established Giants in New York when the Yankees left, and the triumphant Browns of the upstart All-American Football Conference, who quickly replaced the departed Rams in the affection of Cleveland football fans.

Professional basketball's franchise moves during the NBA's early years were rarely controversial. Officials and fans in Fort Wayne, Rochester, and Syracuse recognized that the cards were stacked against smaller cities as the league stabilized its operations in big league metropolitan centers. When the Syracuse Nationals moved to Philadelphia in 1963, locals were saddened but grateful to the team's owner for keeping Syracuse in the big leagues as long as he did; as one emphasized, "that the Nats have continued to represent Syracuse these latter years is due largely to the loyalty of Danny Biasone to his community."[25] In Minneapolis, where the Lakers had dominated professional basketball in the early postwar years, the team had fallen on hard times before leaving quietly for Los Angeles in 1960, "a troubled, disorganized and impoverished club" whose "departure from Minnesota was mourned by only a few diehards."[26]

Negative responses to baseball's initial moves out of Boston, Philadelphia, and St. Louis also were muted. Each city retained a team, and thus a place in the big leagues. Moreover, the departing team was the weaker of the two, so the Braves, Athletics, and Browns were bid good-bye with heavy hearts by loyal fans but little civic response. In Boston, the mayor, governor, and chamber of commerce all responded to the Braves' sudden move with fighting words, but nothing came of these predictable responses. Bad teams were hard to rally around; as a Philadelphia sportswriter emphasized as the Athletics left, "no city, no matter how large and charitable, can be whipped or cajoled into supporting a team that has finished in the cellar eight times in the last thirteen years."[27] And the lack of opposition to baseball's initial franchise shifts encouraged other teams to consider relocation; "the ease with which all moves were accomplished and the resulting profits," notes David Q. Voigt, " convinced owners that the time was ripe for a more dramatic break with the past."[28]

That more dramatic break with the past came in 1957 with the Dodgers' move to Los Angeles in tandem with the Giants' departure for San Francisco, and with these franchise shifts came public outrage, journalistic fulminations, and cries for political action. New York was the nation's largest city and media capital; the Dodgers were profitable winners, while the Giants had won two of the four pennants the Dodgers had failed to capture between 1947 and 1956. Dodger fans, in keeping with the team's raucous tradition, were the more vocal; they circulated petitions, rallied at Brooklyn's Borough Hall, and picketed Ebbets Field and the team's offices. Politicians responded to the outcry with speeches, investigations, threats, and legislative proposals. And relocation would never be the same. Now franchise shifts would be countered with injunctions and lawsuits, attempts to acquire teams through condemnation, demands that leagues block moves, threats of antitrust action, and legislation designed to protect communities with teams.

Public and political concerns over franchise relocation have been intensified as more and more teams play in government-built facilities and receive other subsidies. Increasingly, moving a franchise has meant abandoning not only a city and its fans but a public stadium or arena, usually built for the team that now wants to leave. As result, places battle to keep their teams for tangible as well as intangible reasons, with millions of dollars of public investments and revenues at stake; and the affected parties include taxpayers, politicians, and stadium agencies as well as fans who face loss of their team.

Politicization has underscored the power of teams and their leagues over franchise location, and the lack of legitimate roles in the process for places and fans. Places have responded to their unequal bargaining power primarily by seeking to change the rules of the game through the courts and the political process. Relocation, critics contend, should not be an unilateral process that ignores public investments in arenas and stadiums, economic benefits generated by teams, civic stakes in being in the big leagues, and emotional ties to the home team. "Professional sports franchises should not be able to pull up stakes and abandon communities with no questions asked," argued Senator John C. Danforth of Missouri, who saw teams and their leagues as "unique enterprises" because "they often operate in facilities built at public expense, and they capitalize in a singular way on identification with localities."[29]

Turning these general concerns into specific measures that would protect place interests in relocation has proved extremely difficult. Aggrieved localities faced with losing their team have limited ability to control the activities of sports leagues. Governments have jumped into the fray to try to save the home team, but have lacked effective means of blocking what are usually interstate moves by members of national or international leagues. Once the various financial, land, and infrastructure incentives that places use to lure and retain industries are exhausted, state and local governments do not have a ready arsenal of weapons that can prevent businesses from moving. Moreover, using the limited means available runs the risk of reprisals from professional sports leagues, including the possibility that a place that fights relocation will scare off other teams or be blacklisted by major league sports.

Among the limited means available to keep teams from moving, neither state antitrust restrictions nor laws authorizing public acquisition of private property have passed muster with the courts. Wisconsin sued the Braves and the National League to keep the Braves in Milwaukee, charging that the decision to move the franchise constituted an illegal monopoly under state law and that the league's refusal to replace the Braves was an illegal boycott. A local judge agreed, ordering the Braves to play their home games in Milwaukee unless the league granted a replacement franchise for the 1967 season.[30] Baseball appealed to the Wisconsin Supreme Court, which overturned the lower court, ruling that state antitrust laws did not apply because major league baseball was interstate commerce subject to federal rather than state regulation.[31]

The Wisconsin ruling, which the U.S. Supreme Court declined to review, effectively exempted baseball's franchise controls from regulation by any level of government. State regulation was precluded because professional sports were interstate commerce; but baseball was exempt from federal antitrust controls under the 1922 ruling of the U.S. Supreme Court that baseball was not an interstate business. Other sports did not enjoy baseball's exemptions, but were engaged in the same kind of interstate activities that convinced the Wisconsin court that state antitrust restrictions could not be applied. A Louisiana appeals court rejected a claim that relocation of the New Orleans Jazz to Salt Lake City violated the state's antitrust law on the grounds that federal law preempted the state's statute, because the NBA was engaged in interstate commerce.[32]

Eminent domain has proved equally fruitless as a means of retaining professional sports franchises. Governments generally are authorized to acquire private property for public purposes; the basic question raised by the use of eminent domain to condemn a sports team is whether such an acquisition serves a valid public purpose. Oakland justified condemnation to keep the Raiders on the grounds that a public stadium had been built for the team and that the Raiders were "important to the social, economic, sociological and psychological life of the city."[33] The city, however, failed to convince the state courts that seizing the Raiders was essential to the city's welfare or that acquisition of the team was a public use under the provisions of California law.[34] An attempt by Baltimore to acquire the Colts through condemnation also failed. Unlike the general California law under which Oakland sought to take the Raiders, Maryland acted under an eminent domain statute that specifically authorized condemnation of sports franchises for resale to owners who promised not to relocate. Developed as a counterweight to the Colts' threats to leave, the law was enacted the day after the Colts fled to Indianapolis. But the timing of the law led a federal court to rule that Baltimore had no jurisdiction over the team at the time the condemnation action was filed.[35]

Condemnation continues to attract periodic attention from jilted and threatened places and their champions. Some lawyers see the possibility of more successful outcomes by avoiding the pitfalls that brought down Oakland and Baltimore. Perhaps—but the obstacles to successful condemnation of a professional sports team are likely to dissuade all but officials determined to demonstrate that they have gone the last futile mile to keep a team in town. The Baltimore case indicates that teams that move across state lines are almost certainly gone for good unless a place acts before a team departs. Preparing in advance to condemn a team, however, seems certain to poison negotiations and hasten departure of a franchise; in Baltimore, as Charles C. Euchner notes, the city's decision to seek special legislation gave "the Colts notice of impending legal war. The legislative process gave Irsay enough time to arrange the team transfer. Irsay later said that he moved the club as a direct result of the legislation."[36] Condemnation also involves substantial financial risks to places for little likely gain; Oakland wound up paying the Raiders $3.2 million for legal fees and another $4 million in damages.

Leases on public arenas and stadiums have been more useful weapons than condemnation or state antitrust laws. Legal action or threats of lawsuits over lease provisions has helped deflect some moves, and bought time for places in other proposed relocations. After the Padres were sold in 1973 to buyers who planned to move the team, San Diego went to court to enforce a lease that ran until 1988, a move that helped block the sale and keep the team in San Diego. In 1976, San Francisco secured a preliminary injunction that prevented the Giants from moving to Toronto in violation of their lease after the team had been sold to Labatts Brewing Company. A year later, the Oakland-Alameda County Coliseum Commission secured a temporary restraining order to prevent the sale of the Athletics to a buyer who planned to move the team to Denver. Philadelphia's threat of court action to force the Eagles to honor the team's lease at Veterans Stadium was a factor in deflecting a move to Phoenix. Leases also provide a legal weapon to brandish against places seeking a team; Pittsburgh went to federal court to block efforts by New Orleans to lure the

Pirates south, and warned "any other city that attempts to breach our contractual rights with the Pirates . . . will be buying a lawsuit and should be prepared to go to court."[37]

Enforcing leases, however, has to be coupled with other actions to keep a team in town. The Eagles, for example, were also pressed by the NFL, which filed suit to prevent the team from moving; and the city made substantial concessions, including luxury boxes, a new practice field, and deferring the Eagles' $800,000 annual stadium rent for ten years. San Diego needed a buyer willing to stay put, or the team would have left, since the existing ownership was on the ropes financially; similarly, new owners were required to insure that the Giants and Athletics would remain in the Bay Area. Without buyers or substantial concessions, leases provide places with reprieves rather than solutions. New York City sued in 1977 to prevent the Jets from violating the team's lease on Shea Stadium; after the city won the first round in court, a settlement was reached that kept the Jets in New York for the lease's duration, but the team moved to New Jersey once the lease expired.[38]

Leases, of course, offer no protection for places when teams move after expiration, or if the agreement contains buyout provisions, or permits a team to leave if attendance or revenue fall below specified levels. As the price places are willing to pay for big league sports has escalated, leases have become more and more favorable to teams, offering reduced opportunities for using leases to buy time or increase leverage on teams. Moreover, as the rewards offered by places seeking teams increase and the prices buyers are willing to pay for teams continue to rise, buyout requirements become less significant barriers to moving teams. And staying in the big leagues only for the duration of a team's lease—as Houston did following the NFL's approval of the shift of the Oilers to Nashville after the expiration of the team's lease on the Astrodome at the end of the 1997 season—serves only to rub salt in everyone's wounds.

Relocation and the Sherman Act

Limited local and state means of preventing teams from moving have meant that places and their champions in the United States have turned to Washington for help in keeping major league franchises. Much of this effort has focused on federal antitrust laws, as places have argued that league controls over location of teams constitute an unlawful restraint of interstate commerce under the Sherman Act. Almost every modern franchise move has resulted in some kind of threat to baseball's antitrust exemption. Brooklyn's most influential member of Congress, Emanuel Celler, chairman of the House Judiciary Committee, responded to indications that the Dodgers would be moving with a bill that put all professional team sports under the antitrust laws. Charles O. Finley's wanderlust prompted threats by Senator Stuart Symington of Missouri to strip baseball of its antitrust immunity if Kansas City were abandoned; and the decision to move the Seattle Pilots to Milwaukee was clouded by promises of reprisals by the state's powerful senators, Warren Magnuson and Henry Jackson. Baseball's antitrust vulnerability was increased by congressional unhappiness over franchise shifts that left Washington without a place in the big leagues in 1971. On the day that the American League approved the move to Texas, legislation was introduced to end baseball's antitrust immunity. "Running through" these moves, reported an owner following a meeting with members of Congress, "was a threat. They made known their political clout."[39]

Congressional threats did not get Washington a team, but antitrust fears led baseball to promise to replace relocated teams with expansion franchises for Kansas City and Seattle. Senator Symington's warning of congressional action, combined with the city's threat of court action, persuaded the American League to package approval of the Athletics' move with an expansion team for Kansas City. Seattle, King County, and the state of Washington sued the American League under the Sherman Act for moving the Pilots to Milwaukee, which added to the pressures generated by Senators Magnuson and Jackson. Fearful of jeopardizing its antitrust immunity, baseball settled out of court with a promise to put another expansion team in Seattle.

Despite the leverage provided Kansas City and Seattle, federal antitrust law has not been a very useful weapon to most places that have lost teams. No city has ever retained a team because of a court ruling under the Sherman Act. Places losing teams also are not the only parties in the relocation game that can use antitrust to advance their interests. Teams that want to relocate can sue leagues that seek to prevent them from moving. Places that want teams can challenge league actions under the Sherman Act, as the Los Angeles Memorial Coliseum Commission did in a series of court actions that resulted in the most successful antitrust litigation affecting the location of professional sports teams.

In the wake of the Raiders ruling, the NFL argued that antitrust protections for league controls were essential to safeguard places against unilateral moves by teams, proposing the Professional Sports Community Protection Act of 1982. Leagues, insisted the NFL and its supporters in Congress, offered the only viable protection for communities with professional teams. Under the proposed antitrust exemption, leagues would decide whether teams could move, and leagues would determine what criteria to use since the legislation did not contain any public standards to guide league action in dealing with locational issues. Places with teams would have to rely on what a Senate sponsor of the bill termed "the collective wisdom of team owners who have experience and expertise."[40] The bill also protected leagues from communities, by shielding league actions from lawsuits by cities that lost their team or did not obtain a franchise.

Support for the NFL proposal came from some places with teams, and about a third of the members of Congress cosponsored the original legislation. Particularly active was the Oakland-Alameda County Coliseum Commission, which hired a Washington lobbyist who argued that "something is wrong . . . when antitrust theories defeat the legitimate interests of communities, taxpayers and loyal sports fans."[41] The NFL backed these efforts with a hard sell in Washington, replete with expensive lobbyists, generous campaign contributions to key legislators, hints of future expansion franchises, and photo opportunities for members of Congress with gridiron luminaries. Despite these efforts, the exemption stalled in Congress, in sharp contrast to successful NFL efforts to skirt antitrust restrictions in the 1961 broadcasting legislation and 1965 merger law. One basic problem—which would plague all congressional efforts to deal with relocation—was the proposal's lack of appeal for places that wanted teams or for their representatives in Congress. In addition, some cities with teams were not convinced that private league controls were the best way to protect their interests, an understandable concern given the leagues' record of indifference to places in dealing with relocation. After unsuccessful efforts to devise a compromise, the NFL gave up, convinced that Congress could not agree on legislation that advanced league interests.

Baseball, on the other hand, has been able to link its antitrust immunity with protection of the interests of communities with teams. When a congressional task force promoting baseball expansion trundled out the antitrust threat, Commissioner A. Bartlett Giamatti countered by arguing that baseball's antitrust immunity was more important to places than to teams and leagues, since league controls protected places from footloose owners. Baseball sounded the community protection theme loud and clear to counter congressional efforts to end or modify the sport's antitrust immunity in 1990s. Underscoring baseball's point was the pressure from Florida's senators for ending the antitrust exemption; they were infuriated by the National League's refusal to permit the Giants to move to St. Petersburg. As a result, the baseball antitrust legislation also tended to divide Congress and places along lines of haves and have-nots; one vocal defender of the exemption was Senator Dianne Feinstein of California, a former mayor of San Francisco, who reminded legislators from constituencies with teams that league controls kept her city from losing the Giants to St. Petersburg.

Regulating Relocation

Many critics argue that control of franchise locations by unregulated leagues cannot protect community interests. "Taxpayers cannot rely on monopoly sports leagues for adequate protection," notes Stephen F. Ross, who emphasizes that "there is no reason to expect that franchise owners routinely will interfere with the joint-venturers' efforts to make money at the taxpayers' expense."[42] Private controls freed from antitrust scrutiny mean no enforceable relocation standards, league determinations of the adequacy of fan and community support, no explicit protection for public investments in arenas and stadiums, and no judicial review of league decisions. The answer, insist critics, is not to trust leagues to do better, but to protect the interests of fans, places, governments, and taxpayers through public regulation of franchise location. "Restrictive legislation," in the view of Arthur T. Johnson, would "be much more effective than self-regulation in protecting community interests."[43]

Bills introduced in Congress to regulate franchise relocation, primarily during the 1980s, embraced a variety of approaches. One proposed an absolute ban on franchise shifts, another imposed penalties for moving a team, and a third required that investors committed to keeping a team in place be afforded an opportunity to purchase a franchise. Most common were proposals that established federal standards for relocation—dealing with financial conditions, adequacy of facilities, compliance with leases, and fan support—and some means of review and enforcement, either through the courts, arbitration panels, or a national sports commission. For places with teams, the appeal of restrictive federal legislation was the promise of franchise stability and enhanced bargaining power; they would be protected from competing places and would have more leverage with teams. And because of these attractions to places with teams, restrictive bills were anathema to places without teams.

Regulation of relocation faced the same fundamental political barrier as efforts to exempt league controls or end baseball's antitrust immunity. Different places have different interests in the zero-sum game of franchise movement; protecting places with teams means reducing the chances of other places of getting into the big leagues. Political problems inherent in the diverse interests of places in relocation legislation were magnified by the constituency concerns that prompted most of these proposals. Forsaken places wanted their team back or a replacement franchise, which produced legislative proposals with retroactive clauses or incentives to replace relocated teams. Relocation legislation sponsored by Representative Barbara Mikulski in 1985 called for the NFL to add two teams by 1988, one of which had to be in her home town of Baltimore. Such provisions may have salved wounds back home, but did little to win support from places that had attracted teams or were in the hunt, and these locales were also vigorously represented in Congress. Senator Frank Lautenberg of New Jersey, whose state was one of the most aggressive pursuers of major league teams, underscored that he could not "stand by while legislation proceeds that satisfies the haves in baseball and not the have-nots," and ventured the "guess that the Senators who represent the long list of cities that are begging for franchises at the doorstep of baseball and football and the other sports will be there with me."[44]

One way out of the zero-sum trap was to couple relocation and expansion. Senator John Danforth acknowledged that "without some reasonable prospects for expansion, cities without NFL teams have little enthusiasm for a bill making it more difficult for franchises to relocate."[45] Senator Slade Gorton's relocation proposal mandated expansion of the NFL because "every member who represents Phoenix or Louisville and wants to get a franchise is hurt by stability because there is no longer a city they can raid."[46] In the end, these efforts were unable to bridge the gap between haves and have-nots; as one observer of the process noted, the only compromise that probably would have satisfied Congress was "a guaranteed National Football League franchise to each of the 435 congressional districts in the nation."[47]

Relocation legislation was also handicapped by differences between those who wanted league controls and those who insisted on public regulation. Professional sports opposed legislation that restricted league control over franchise location. Federal standards, league officials argued, were an invitation to litigation and wrangling over team accounting practices. Owners protested that governmental regulations and restrictions would limit the market for teams and thus the value of their franchises. Supporters of federal standards rejected these arguments, pointing to the public benefits that teams extracted from communities: "They want a guaranteed stadium, they want guaranteed ticket sales," complained Representative Mikulski in 1985, "then, when we try to protect the fans, they cry, 'Capitalism.' Well, you can't have it both ways."[48] Having it both ways, protecting places and insuring league control over relocation, while satisfying have and have-not places, proved to be a political impossibility in the 1980s; and the same conflicting interests worked against the NFL's efforts to secure a relocation antitrust exemption following the wholesale movement of football teams in the mid-1990s.

Keeping Owners in Town

Owners are the key to relocation; they make the basic decisions to move or stay. Teams are private property, owned by private parties who have the same property rights as other individuals and corporations. Efforts by leagues or government to force teams to operate at a loss, or to prevent owners from moving to more profitable locations, are constrained by the reality of property rights. "No one can keep me in Washington," insisted Robert Short of his baseball team, "I own it and . . . I will move wherever I want."[49] Like almost every other owner who was determined to move or sell his team to buyers who would relocate, Short was able to do what he wanted. Critics of franchise movement deplore the realities of private ownership; for Jonathan Rowe, it is "barbarous and benighted" that the "repository of local identity and loyalty called a baseball team is deemed the exclusive property of a single individual called an 'owner,' who can move it to another city as though it were his body and fender shop."[50] Barbarous, benighted, or whatever, private ownership and property rights are fundamental realities that frame efforts to keep teams in town.

For places, the best kind of owners are those committed to the community where the team plays. But owners, no matter how devoted to the local community, eventually sell their teams to buyers who may be less committed. Strongly rooted local owners usually seek purchasers who will keep the team in town; when Jerry Hoffberger decided to sell the Orioles, he strongly preferred a buyer who would stay in Baltimore, telling Bowie Kuhn that "he would not become involved in the 'rape of Baltimore.' "[51] In selling the San Diego Padres, Joan Kroc promised in 1986 to "take every step legally available to us to assure that the team will not be moved."[52] And she bolstered the pledge by signing a new stadium lease that committed the team to San Diego until 2000.

Political and business leaders often pressure owners to sell to local buyers or purchasers who promise not to move. In some cities, efforts to insure that new owners will not relocate have included public investments in teams. A $20 million loan from the city played a central role in permitting a local consortium to buy the Pirates in 1985. Montreal and the Quebec provincial government provided one-third of the $98 million that local buyers paid for the Expos in 1991. Leagues can reinforce these pressures, with officials in some cases actively participating in efforts to find buyers who will not relocate. Bowie Kuhn met with business leaders in Seattle in the hopes of identifying a local buyer for the Pilots after the disastrous 1969 season; and two years later, "knocked on doors, looked for new owners, looked for people who might suggest owners and gave newspaper interviews that were virtual advertisements for owners in a futile quest to keep the Senators in Washington."[53] In a few instances, leagues have forced owners to sell locally rather than to out-of-towners. Intervention by league officials prevented sale of the San Francisco Giants in 1991 to purchasers who planned to move the franchise to St. Petersburg, leading to the acquisition of the club by local buyers. The NBA in 1994 blocked the sale of the Timberwolves to purchasers who planned to move the team to New Orleans, and then played a central role in finding a buyer who would continue operating in the Twin Cities.

Successful efforts to use ownership to keep teams from being moved have prompted proposals for more formal arrangements to promote or insure local ownership. One possibility would be for leagues or government to force owners to consider buyers who would not relocate a franchise. Another is to provide local buyers with the right to match any bid from outside purchasers. But limitations on the ability of an owner to sell a team raise questions about property rights and compensation for losses incurred as a result of requirements that prevent sale of a team to the highest bidder. Robert Lurie received $15 million less for the Giants from the San Francisco group that purchased the team after the sale to St. Peterburg interests was blocked by the National League; Lurie, who had purchased the Giants in 1976 to prevent the team from being moved to Toronto, accepted the costly outcome, but another owner might well have sued. First refusal rights inevitably dampen interest in a team;

potential owners are reluctant to go through all the trouble and expense of negotiating and financing a purchase only to face the possibility that a local buyer will match their offer. Teams, moreover, often are easier to sell to someone who wants to move to a place that offers a newer facility, more benefits, and better broadcasting deals.

Realistically, local buyer provisions only work when there are purchasers committed to keeping a team in place. In Baltimore, lack of a local alternative led Hoffberger to sell his team to Edward Bennett Williams, which aroused local fears that the Orioles would be moved to Washington, where Williams lived and worked. Efforts by Kuhn to interest Willard Marriott of the hotel Marriotts, local newspaper owners, and other well-heeled Washingtonians in the Senators turned up a possible purchaser, but the group was unable to raise sufficient funds to buy the team before the American League voted on relocation. The availability of local buyers is limited by league rules concerning size of ownership groups, resources of owners, corporate ownership, multiple team ownership, and public ownership, all of which restrict the pool of prospective purchasers. In Winnipeg, a last-ditch campaign by local investors failed to raise an additional $80 million requested by the NHL to cover future losses and help finance a new arena. Efforts to sell the moribund Seattle Pilots locally faltered because the plan called for a nonprofit community-owned franchise, which was opposed by American League owners, ending any hope that the Pilots would be sold to local interests and kept in Seattle.

Leagues, of course, are not always committed to keeping a team in place, especially when an owner in good standing with other owners decides to move. League interests also override local considerations in some instances. Kuhn favored sale of the San Diego Padres to purchasers from Washington who planned to move the team to the nation's capital, and thus solve baseball's "Washington" problem. League officials also saw sale of the Giants or Athletics to outsiders who would relocate as a solution to the problem of too many teams in the Bay Area. And the NHL welcomed sale of the Quebec Nordiques and Winnipeg Jets to outsiders who moved the franchises to more attractive markets in Denver and Phoenix.

New owners may provide no more than a temporary fix for a place seeking to retain a major league team, especially marginal franchises in smaller markets. Acquisition of the Minnesota North Stars by Norman Green in 1990 foreclosed a move to San Jose planned by the previous owners, but Green the savior soon became Green the traitor when he took the team to Dallas three years later. In Seattle, purchase of the Mariners by Jeff Smulyan, an energetic broadcasting entrepreneur, promised stability for a franchise whose previous owner constantly threatened to relocate. Burdened by debts and problems with his broadcasting ventures, Smulyan soon was looking for a way out of Seattle; only an eleventh-hour purchase offer from a local consortium kept the team out of the hands of buyers from St. Petersburg. Three years later, the new local owners were sounding a familiar tune, warning that without public commitments for a new stadium and more revenues they would "sell or move the team."[54]

Increasingly, as in Seattle, places find that new owners committed to keeping a team in town come at a heavy price. Kevin McClatchy's purchase of the Pirates in 1996, and his concomitant pledge to maintain the franchise in Pittsburgh, was predicated on $7.5 million in lease concessions on Three Rivers Stadium and completion of financing arrangements for a new ballpark built largely with public funds within two years. In another relocation showdown in Seattle, a local buyer acquired an exclusive option to purchase the Seahawks, which checked the efforts of the team's owner to move the franchise to Los Angeles. Completion of the deal was conditioned on an agreement to renovate or replace the Kingdome before the expiration of the option in 1997.

Buyer strategies, of course, are only available when an owner wants to sell. Owners that seek to move to greener pastures are not interested in selling to purchasers committed to maintaining teams in their current location. New York's Rockefeller clan tried to buy the Dodgers, but Walter O'Malley wanted to move his team. According to Neil J. Sullivan, the way to insure local buyers is to prohibit relocation by present or prospective owners: "If an owner wants to relocate to another community, he or she should sell the club and buy a new one."[55] Why all teams should be frozen in place is not clear; surely protecting the legitimate interests of communities in their tangible and intangible investments in professional sports does not require that teams must either persist or perish in place. What is clear is that professional sports would never accept a system that locked teams in place, nor are the courts or the political system likely to approve such restrictions.

Moves and Threats

Far more teams threaten to move than actually relocate, both between and within metropolitan areas. Teams expressing an interest in moving generally will not; instead they will be persuaded to stay by market conditions, league interests, and better deals from places eager to keep their teams. Threats often are expressed with assurances that no one is being threatened, or with reluctance—tactics designed to minimize conflict and hard feelings for teams likely to stay in place. In Indianapolis, the Pacers were "not threatening anybody" but were "saying, 'Hey, the community needs a new arena.'"[56] "We'll have to make a decision we don't want to make," warned the owner of the Sabres, but if public funds were not forthcoming for a new arena, "come hell or high water, we'll have to move out of Buffalo."[57]

Threats to move have been increasing in recent years, although the percentage of teams relocating has been dropping. More threats reflect the benefits that result from exploring relocation, as well as the growing number of places competing for teams with ever more lucrative offers. Fewer moves result in part from positive responses to threats by the places that want to keep their teams. Less relocation also reflects the steady reduction in the number of attractive open markets, as a result of earlier franchise moves and league expansion. For places with teams, these trends offer scant comfort. Fewer teams may move, but more threaten to relocate, and places cannot ignore the possibility that a team will carry through on its threat. Moreover, teams play the relocation game with ever greater skill. Throughout the negotiations that provided the Orioles with a magnificent new ballpark on extremely favorable terms loomed the threat that Edward Bennett Williams might move his Orioles down the road to Washington; "it was masterfully done," notes an associate of Williams, "it was always hanging in the air."[58]

Threats to move within metropolitan areas pose distinctive problems. Relocation inside a metropolitan area both increases options for teams and enhances the credibility of threatened moves. Large metropolitan areas offer a variety of possible places to play; the Chicago Bears, for example, have flirted with a phalanx of communities in their quest for a new stadium. Threats to move within metropolitan areas are more plausible for teams in large markets than talk of relocating to marginal markets. The Yankees were never very serious about leaving New York for Denver or New Orleans, neither of which could come close to the television revenues that the team earned in New York; but northern New Jersey was a different story, providing the benefits of a credible bargaining chip and an attractive alternative location without any market risks. Little wonder that New York City responded with anger and frustration at the rising volume of threats to leave in the 1990s, along with ever-grander plans for rebuilding Yankee Stadium, transforming the area around the ballpark, or constructing a new stadium somewhere else in the city. Places contesting an intrametropolitan move have more difficulty mobilizing opposition than they do when teams abandon an area. Fans, major businesses, and the local media still have a home team, while political and economic leaders are likely to be divided in their loyalties, depending on their base of operations. Reinforcing the perils of intrametropolitan moves for places trying to keep a team within their boundaries is the lack of league controls over moves within urban areas and the fact that internal relocations rarely involve a change of ownership, providing team owners with almost complete freedom of action and places with fewer opportunities to protect their interests.

11

The Expanding Realm

IN THE second half of the twentieth century, expansion has been the most common path to the big leagues for places. The addition of new teams has been driven primarily by the forces of urban growth, and by the continuing need of major leagues to place teams in key metropolitan and regional markets. The push of demographic and economic change has been reinforced by the ability of leagues to sell expansion franchises for ever-higher prices, attractive offers from places that want big league teams, political pressures to make professional sports more accessible, and fears that rival leagues will set up business in bypassed markets.

Expansion poses fewer emotional and political perils for major league sports than relocation. It does not leave abandoned cities, stadiums, and arenas in its wake, just unsuccessful competitors for new teams, who arouse less sympathy than places that lose their team, and who rarely threaten political retaliation or court action. Still, expansion is controversial, with winners and losers among places and prospective owners. Expansion is also scorned by many observers of the sporting scene, who see the process as unnecessary, unfortunate, and generally badly done by the greedy monopolists who own professional sports. Expansion, argue critics, breaks with tradition; expanded leagues are bloated with too many teams, subdivisions, and playoff games; expansion dilutes the quality of major league competition, results in pitifully weak teams, and fosters unstable leagues.

Almost half of the major league teams in existence in 1996—fifty-five in all—began as expansion franchises granted since 1960.[1] Expansion has been most important in hockey, largely because the NHL had only six teams until 1967. Sixteen of the NHL's twenty-six teams in 1995 began as expansion franchises granted between 1967 and 1993 (throughout, dates for expansion franchises are for the year the team began playing rather than when a league awarded the franchise). The NBA has granted seventeen expansion franchises since 1960, accounting for almost 60 percent of the league's twenty-nine

Table 11.1   Post-1960 Expansion Teams by League

	MLB[a]	NBA	NFL	NHL	Total
Expansion teams	14	17	8	16	55
Total teams	30	29	30	26	115
Percent beginning as expansion teams	46.7	58.6	26.7	61.5	47.8

[a] Includes two expansion teams scheduled to play in 1998.

teams in 1995. Expansion has been least important in the NFL, with only eight expansion franchises granted since 1960; less reliance on expansion in the NFL reflects the larger role of a merger, with ten teams arriving from the American Football League in 1970. Baseball has been criticized for its allegedly tardy pace of expansion; Andrew W. Zimbalist argues that "baseball has expanded more slowly than the other sports leagues," suggesting that antitrust immunity has reduced the incentive to expand by shielding baseball from rival leagues.[2] The expansion record of major league baseball (MLB), however, is not substantially different from that of basketball or hockey, considering that baseball grew from a larger base, with sixteen teams in 1950 compared with ten in the NBA and six in the NFL (see Table 11.1).

Professional team sports expanded most rapidly in the 1960s, reflecting efforts by all leagues to catch up with the burgeoning growth of western and southern metropolitan areas following World War II. Altogether, twenty-four expansion franchises were granted during the 1960s, almost 44 percent of the new teams added between 1960 and 1998. Expansion tailed off in the following two decades, with fourteen new teams in the 1970s and only five in the 1980s, as professional sports caught up with the backlog of unrepresented metropolitan areas. The slowing pace of expansion also resulted from the difficulties of assimilating a large number of new teams in a relatively short period of time; expansion tripled the size of the NHL between 1967 and 1974, and doubled the NBA between 1961 and 1974. From 1977 to 1988, only one new team was added to any league, the Dallas Mavericks in the NBA in 1980.

Beginning in 1988–1989 with the NBA's admission of four teams, professional sports has recently vigorously pursued expansionary agendas. By 1996, seventeen franchises had been granted, six in the NBA, five in the NHL, four in major league baseball, and two in the NFL. Renewed interest in expansion reflects ongoing development of promising new markets in emerging urban centers, as well as the growing willingness of places to expend public funds to get into the big leagues and an enlarging pool of prospective owners of major league teams. Expansion has also become highly lucrative for professional sports, with the escalating value of franchises making entry fees an increasingly important source of revenue for existing teams and their owners.

Thirty-one metropolitan areas obtained expansion franchises between 1960

Table 11.2   Population of Metropolitan Areas with Expansion Teams: 1990–1991

	Number of Areas	Average Population	Highest Population	Lowest Population
MLB	11	5,761,405	19,342,013 (New York)	1,980,140 (Denver)
NBA	16	2,633,513	8,239,820 (Chicago)	1,162,093 (Charlotte)
NFL	8	2,244,576	4,037,282 (Dallas)	937,891 (Jacksonville)
NHL	15	4,890,971	19,342,013 (New York)	920,857 (Ottawa)

NOTE: Table does not include 1998 expansion franchises.

and 1998. Seattle has had the most expansion teams, four in all, with two in baseball to go along with its NBA and NFL franchises. All three of Tampa-St. Petersburg's major league teams are products of expansion, as are three of Miami's four big league entries. Baseball and hockey, as indicated in Table 11.2, have expanded into areas with larger average populations than those with basketball and football. Denver, the smallest metropolitan area with a baseball expansion team, had a 1990 population only slighter lower than the average 1990 population of the eight areas with NFL expansion franchises. Concerns about market size have also led baseball to stray the least from demographic rankings in expansion, adding teams almost exclusively from among the largest open metropolitan areas. Football concentrated on the biggest available markets in the 1960s and 1970s; expansion and merger with the AFL moved the NFL into twenty-four of the twenty-five largest U.S. metropolitan areas. In 1995, however, the league paid little attention to metropolitan area size, reaching down to attractive growth markets in Charlotte and Jacksonville. The NHL has expanded primarily into large metropolitan areas; five of the six places added in 1967—Los Angeles, Philadelphia, San Francisco, Pittsburgh, and St. Louis—were among the top ten metropolitan areas.[3] Subsequently, the primary emphasis remained on larger metropolitan areas, with new franchises placed in New York, Los Angeles, Washington, and Miami. Basketball has given substantially less weight to metropolitan rank than other leagues throughout the modern expansion era. After Chicago was added, the league jumped over a number of larger areas to put teams in Milwaukee, Seattle, and San Diego, and then bypassed eighteen other markets to tap rapidly growing Phoenix. Subsequent expansions followed the same pattern, combining addition of a large metropolitan area or two with selection of attractive smaller markets such as Portland, Charlotte, and Vancouver (see Figure 11.1).

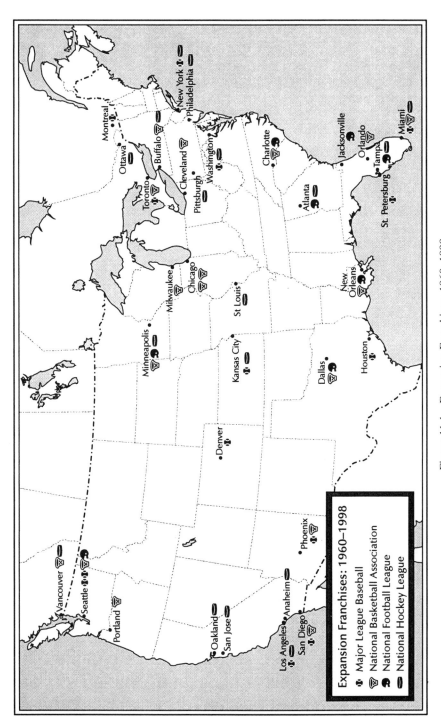

Figure 11.1   Expansion Franchises: 1960–1998

Ambivalence

As rational economic actors, leagues should be strongly attracted to expansion into markets capable of supporting major league sports. "Self-interest of league members," emphasizes James Quirk, "argues for expansion of membership in a league until all cities capable of supporting a franchise in the sport are absorbed into the league."[4] Ignoring attractive markets opens the door to new leagues that would offer alternatives for places and prospective team owners. Organization of the Continental League in the late 1950s resulted from baseball's reluctance to expand beyond sixteen clubs; and the American Football League was formed by entrepreneurs frustrated by the NFL's internal disagreements on expansion. Failure of the NFL to expand after 1976 spurred creation of the United States Football League in 1983. The NHL's refusal to expand in the early 1960s led to threats of a new league by west-coast interests. Expansion left the Continental League stillborn, kept the AFL out of key locations, and more generally greatly reduced the opportunities for rivals as the established leagues extended their web to most major markets in the United States and Canada.

Another attraction of expansion for professional sports is control. Expansion provides far more control than relocation since teams acting collectively, rather than individual owners, determine locations. Expansion also permits the rest of a league to profit from opening new locations; expansion franchises pay for the right to operate in a territory, whereas a relocated team traditionally pays nothing to other clubs for its new venue. Control over expansion is additionally a means of rationing the number of teams, thereby maintaining an increasingly lucrative market for expansion franchises, protecting the value of existing teams, and enhancing the bargaining power of professional sports with places.

Despite all the rational reasons to expand, professional sports has been wary of the risks involved in adding teams in new places. New teams may fail, or jeopardize the economic well being of existing franchises. Rational strategies are not always successful business moves; despite the demographic imperatives of being in Chicago, the NBA's first expansion team in the Windy City failed to win games or attract fans. A 1949 appraisal of baseball concluded that "the majors are afraid to disturb a system that is, on the whole, quite profitable."[5] With its six teams selling 95 percent of their seats, most NHL owners opposed expansion until well into the 1960s; "we're a pretty successful operation," insisted the league president, "we'd only be buying a headache."[6] Expansion itself tends to reinforce concerns about the economic risks of another round of expansion. After adding four teams between 1962 and 1968, the National League did not expand again for twenty-five years; more expansion, explained one club owner in 1982, "may never happen. The league is healthy right now, and I see no reason to make any big changes."[7]

Expansion is often viewed by established teams as a zero-sum game, with more teams meaning less of everything for existing clubs, from revenues to players. Adding teams to a league reduces the number of home games with established teams and traditional rivals, while adding games with new teams that are often poor drawing cards. As the NBA mulled expansion in 1986, an owner cautioned that "each of us would have a lesser franchise coming into our arena."[8] For the owner of the Chicago Blackhawks, adding two teams to the six-team NHL meant "we're gonna lose four games with the Montreal Canadiens and four with the Toronto Maple Leafs."[9] Quality of play also has been viewed in zero-sum terms; expansion would dilute talent by spreading players over more teams, with adverse consequences for the quality of the product and competitive balance, and thus for fan interest, attendance, broadcasting audiences, and revenues. More teams also dilute the influence of owners of existing clubs in leagues in which each franchise has a single vote.

Fear that an increase in the number of teams will jeopardize the value of existing franchises provides owners with another reason to question expansion. The Chicago Cardinals opposed enlarging the NFL in the late 1950s because it would mean that fewer places or prospective buyers would be interested in a team whose days in Chicago were numbered. Commissioner Fay Vincent characterized the National League's 1993 expansion as a "dilution of the equity of baseball."[10] And in every league, concerns about cutting the pie into more pieces have multiplied as national television contracts have grown more lucrative. Montreal and Toronto, for example, blocked admission of Vancouver to the NHL in 1967 because their owners did not want to share Canadian television revenue.

Because of these different perspectives and widespread doubts, expansion is a contentious process within professional sports; owners who prefer the status quo quarrel with those who embrace change as inevitable in a dynamic society. Conservatives have rallied around their individual and collective self-interest in existing schedules, player rosters, broadcasting revenues, and patterns of influence within a league. Expansionists have insisted that growth was the best way to capitalize on change by capturing new markets, foreclosing rival leagues, increasing appeal to broadcasters, and reaping the rewards of a bigger league with more revenues, higher franchises prices, and rising fees for expansion teams. Even owners who favor expansion, however, often differ about timing, number of new teams, and where expansion franchises should be located. Internal conflicts underlie a good deal of the incoherence surrounding expansion; the mix of positive and negative signals—as well as the typically fitful way leagues approach expansion—often reflect disagreement among league members. To be sure, leagues have an interest in uncertainty, particularly when they are fending off pressures from places and politicians that want to get into the big leagues. But deliberate obtuseness is further fuzzed by conflicting statements by opposing parties within leagues.

The Leagues' Game

Leagues control expansion; they determine when to expand, the number of teams to be added, and prices for new franchises; they decide where expansion teams will be located and who will own them; they specify the rules and criteria governing the process. Control provides league members with another product to sell—expansion franchises. By limiting the number of franchises, leagues increase their value; "a professional sports franchise is like a Picasso," explains Commissioner Pete Rozelle, "there are only a limited number of them available."[11] Well, not quite like a Picasso, since unlike the work of a dead master, the supply of teams can be increased if the price is right.

League control has dictated expansion within the context of existing leagues rather than through new organizations. Major league baseball rejected expansion through creation of an associated league despite the fact that baseball was already organized as two semi-autonomous leagues that played independent schedules. Suggestions that major league baseball expand westward by permitting the Pacific Coast League to become a third major league were brushed aside in favor of having existing teams and leagues capture the west-coast markets. Baseball also rejected the entreaties of the Continental League, which hoped to operate as a third major league rather than as a rival league; it preferred to expand into the Continental's planned locations rather than share markets and power with another league.

Decisions on expansion, like rules for relocation, require extraordinary majorities of league members. During the 1950s, unanimous votes were necessary to approve expansion in baseball and football. Challenges from rival leagues, however, prompted procedural modifications to facilitate adding teams. Baseball's change to a three-fourths vote was spurred by the Continental League, and the NFL made a similar change after formation of the AFL. Expansion also requires a three-fourths vote in the NBA and NHL. Requirements for extraordinary majorities for adding teams, as with relocation decisions, increase the influence of individual teams. In the 1967 NHL expansion, St. Louis was awarded a franchise even though no one applied because the owners of the Chicago Blackhawks saw expansion as an opportunity to unload the arena they owned in St. Louis for an inflated price.

League expansion rules are highly sensitive to territorial rights, providing owners with a veto over expansion into their realms. The ability of owners to preserve local monopolies reinforces the preference of leagues for placing expansion franchises in new markets. Overall, all but four expansion franchises granted since 1960 have been for teams in new markets for a league; and each of these four exceptions reflected compelling league interests in having teams in New York or Los Angeles, and in keeping rival leagues out of these key markets. Admission of the New York Mets in 1962 put the National League back in New York after a four-year absence, as well as coopting the key franchise in the stillborn Continental League. Expansion of the American League to Los Angeles was a quid pro quo for permitting the National League back into New York. The NHL put a team on Long Island in 1972 to block the rival World Hockey Association from establishing a base in the New York metropolitan area. The NHL granted another expansion franchise in the Los Angeles region in 1993, primarily as a means of adding the marketing skills and megabucks of the Disney empire to the league's lineup.

Owners also use their influence to block expansion that threatens broader market areas. When the National League decided on expansion franchises for 1969, Bowie Kuhn indicates, "the sentiment of the meeting favored Dallas, but it became clear that Judge Hofheinz of Houston had no charity for that idea."[12] The American League rejected Washington's bid for a 1977 expansion franchise in part because of opposition from the Baltimore Orioles. Asked about the prospects of the chances of Indianapolis for an expansion baseball franchise, Marge Schott, whose Cincinnati Reds played 100 miles from Indianapolis, answered "over my dead body."[13]

Protection of territorial rights in expansion depends importantly on league controls over relocation. Teams in major markets would have much less interest in expansion if franchises in smaller areas, which is where most expansion teams are located, were able to move freely to areas offering more customers and broadcast bucks. Roger G. Noll emphasizes that the NBA in 1988–1989 "would have been reluctant to let in four new teams, all in relatively small cities," if the league had not believed that it had "solved the problem of unauthorized relocations" posed by the Clippers' move to Los Angeles.[14]

The most critical league control over expansion is the determination of whether to expand. Leagues can just say no. Major league baseball refused to expand until 1961, despite considerable interest by cities in California and elsewhere. The NFL resolutely turned its back on expansion during the 1940s and 1950s, leaving a lengthening list of frustrated places and prospective owners, as did the NHL until 1967. Expansion plans have been held hostage to the uncertainties of labor negotiations, television contracts, legal entanglements with rival leagues, and the national economy. Delays have also resulted from disagreements over stocking new teams with players, realignment and playoff formats, and other internal issues. After the NFL admitted Seattle and Tampa for 1976, Rozelle indicated that the league would add two more teams within a "reasonable period of time," which turned out to be almost twenty years.[15] At other times, expansion timetables have been accelerated; the NFL's leisurely approach to adding teams quickened after the formation of the AFL in 1959. The NBA had planned to admit three expansion franchises in 1988–1989, but decided to award teams to all four finalists, Charlotte, Miami, Minneapolis, and Orlando. Amended plans, however, are still league plans; the NBA set both the initial and revised number of expansion teams for 1988–1989.

Leagues determine whether prospective owners of expansion franchises pass muster, employing the same general criteria that are used for buyers of existing teams. For the 1993 expansion, baseball wanted local owners, individuals rather than corporations, and arrangements in which one person was clearly in charge. Prospective owners were expected to be worth at least $100 million, willing to make a long-term commitment to the team and community, and prepared to give priority to the ball club over other business interests. League judgments about prospective owners have become increasingly critical factors in expansion; whatever the attractions of a particular place, leagues want rich owners who have the resources to make a go of an expansion franchise. "This is a business deal," emphasized a baseball official during selection of the teams added to the National League in 1993, "one thing we don't want to do is put in a franchise that's in trouble two years down the road."[16]

Leagues decide where franchises will be located, on the basis of league criteria for places and playing facilities. Over time, these factors have become more explicit and detailed, but they remain flexible, serving at best as guidelines for whatever decisions leagues finally make. Market is obviously a critical factor in any expansion decision, measured by population, wealth, growth potential, and television market. Among other information to be provided in the NFL's most recent expansion application was the number of households with income of $35,000 or more, while baseball wanted an estimate of the projected revenue from local broadcasting contracts. Leagues increasingly have sought evidence that a market will support a team, usually by requiring applicants to secure a sizable number of commitments for the purchase of season tickets. The NBA wanted a guarantee of 10,000 season tickets from its 1995 expansion teams, accounting for half or more of the seats in a typical arena.

The appeal of market size has increasingly been modified by the regional context of prospective expansion franchises. Locations that open new areas for a sport are more appealing than places closer to existing teams; a baseball owner expressed a widely held view in the sporting fraternity when he told reporters in 1990 that "I'm partial to putting teams in areas where there's not a close proximity" to existing clubs.[17] Washington's chances for a baseball team in 1993 were reduced by its nearness to Baltimore, whereas Baltimore's bid for a 1995 NFL expansion franchise was burdened by the presence of the Redskins in Washington. Among the handicaps faced by Buffalo and Columbus in seeking to get into baseball's big leagues in 1993 was being too close to places with teams: Toronto and Cleveland in the case of Buffalo, Cincinnati and Cleveland for Columbus. In hockey, teams in Toronto and Buffalo combined to dim the hopes of Hamilton, Ontario, for an NHL expansion franchise. Enhancing the importance of these considerations is the steady growth of the territorial realm claimed by existing franchises, as highways and cable television extend the market areas of teams.

Demands for bigger and better stadiums and arenas have steadily escalated, largely as a result of the success of teams and leagues in extracting better facilities from places that want to be in the big leagues. When baseball first expanded in 1961, the American League was far more interested in being in Los Angeles than insuring that the Angels had a suitable place to play, so the team wound up playing its first season in an aging minor league park that had only 20,457 seats, then spent four seasons as unwelcome tenants of the Dodgers at Chavez Ravine before moving to a new stadium in Anaheim. By the 1993 expansion, baseball wanted a stadium with at least 40,000 seats, parking for one-quarter of the seating capacity, and control of the stadium and its revenues by the team. A strong preference was articulated for ballparks with a natural grass field, open to the heavens, and used only for baseball. The application also asked for information about luxury seating, video displays, and lease arrangements, presumably to insure that new league members would be playing in facilities with all the modern conveniences at least possible cost. The NHL has been most concerned about control; "If you are in control of your arena," emphasizes an owner, "it will make you a profitable business."[18] Facility standards, however, still take a back seat to other considerations when final decisions are made about expansion franchises. One of the winners for baseball's 1993 expansion, the Florida Marlins, shares a football stadium with an NFL team, and the 1998 entry from Tampa-St. Petersburg will play indoors in a dome.

Expansion procedures, like league criteria, have become more regularized over time. Initially, expansion was an ad hoc process undertaken with little in the way of application procedures, no formal market research, and nothing resembling an overall strategy. Leagues reacted to external stimuli such as rival leagues, political pressures, lawsuits, insider connections, and internal conflicts. The NFL rushed a franchise into Dallas to compete with the AFL in 1960; another expansion franchise went to Minneapolis to preempt the market and prospective owners from the AFL. The NFL next expanded to Atlanta, again to head off the AFL; after efforts to secure an AFL franchise for Atlanta surfaced, recalls the man who wound up with the Falcons, "the NFL came flying down and told us to wait a couple of weeks, that they'd get us a team."[19] The NHL awarded a franchise to Long Island for 1972 with neither an application process nor a prospective owner in order to prevent the rival World Hockey Association from securing a toehold in the New York area. In baseball, the American League sought to keep pace with the National League by putting an expansion franchises in Los Angeles, even though no one had applied for what became the Angels.

By the 1980s, expansion procedures had become considerably more formalized, reflecting both increased competition and rising financial stakes. Leagues now usually create expansion committees, undertake market research, develop substantive criteria, prepare complicated applications, listen to detailed presentations, examine financial records, and inspect the most promising sites.

Applicants for the 1993 baseball expansion franchises initially had to answer a thirty-nine item questionnaire, provide additional information, and enclose a certified check for $100,000. But expansion procedures are controlled by leagues, which means they can be adjusted to serve the interests of teams and leagues. San Jose went to the top of the list for the NHL's 1991–1992 expansion to accommodate the owners of the Minnesota North Stars, who wanted to shift their hockey operation to San Jose.[20] And the NHL had no formal competition for its 1993 expansion, instead awarding franchises in Anaheim and Miami to prospective owners with big bucks. With more formal processes and more intense competition, expansion has attracted increasing attention. The sporting press covers the expansion game as another event, complete with appraisals of competitors' strengths and weaknesses, summaries of vital statistics of various places and prospective owners, predictions about outcomes, and betting odds for those inclined to wager on one more sporting event.

Selling Franchises

What has changed the most about expansion in recent years is the price of expansion franchises. Baseball's first expansion teams cost $2.1 million in 1961; thirty-five years later, the price was $130 million. During the same period, the increase in the price of NFL expansion teams was even more spectacular, rising from $600,000 for the Dallas Cowboys in 1960 to $140 million in 1995. And the NBA was able to charge $125 million per team for its expansion into Canada in 1995. By comparison, the NHL's increase from $2 million to $50 million between 1967 and 1993 was more modest; still, the fees charged by the NHL in 1991–1992 were higher than for any previous expansion in professional sports. Part of the increase in expansion franchises results from inflation, but the rise in prices in real dollars is nonetheless striking. As indicated in Table 11.3, buying a NFL expansion team in 1995 cost almost forty-seven times as much in constant dollars as in 1960. Even more spectacular was the fiftyfold rise in the cost of an expansion franchise in the NBA between 1961 and 1995. For expansion teams in all four leagues, average prices in 1994 dollars rose from almost $16 million in the 1960s to over $91 million in the 1990s. Rising real prices reflect increased demand and monopoly control. Buyers have been willing to pay more for major league teams in general, which has driven up the prices leagues can charge for expansion teams. The market, of course, is skewed upward by control of the supply of franchises by leagues. Delaying expansion in a bull market further increases demand, pushing up prices that can be charged for new teams when a league finally expands.

Prices for expansion franchises are fixed by leagues rather than through market mechanisms such as auction. Expansion fees have generally been based on judgments of what the market will bear in the context of recent selling and asking prices for existing franchises. Leagues also set general prices

Table 11.3   Increase in Expansion Fees by League, in 1994 Dollars

	First Expansion	Most Recent Expansion	Percent Increase
MLB	$10.4 million (1961)	$130 million (1998)	1250
NBA	$2.5 million (1961)	$125 million (1995)	5000
NFL	$3.0 million (1960)	$140 million (1995)	4667
NHL	$8.9 million (1967)	$51 million (1993)	611

for a given expansion, rather than individual prices based on what a franchise would be worth in a particular place. Thus, the National League charged New York and Houston the same $2 million in 1962; and the NHL priced its first expansion franchises at $2 million for markets that ranged in size from Los Angeles to Minneapolis-St. Paul. Leagues, as James Quirk and Rodney D. Fort have shown, tend to sell expansion franchises for less than the prevailing market prices for established teams.[21] These discounts reflect the fact that expansion fees are only part of the cost of a new team; additional startup expenses were estimated to add another $30 million to the $95 million paid for baseball's 1993 expansion teams. Further increasing the real cost of expansion teams is the unwillingness of leagues to share national television revenues fully with their new members; the NFL provided its 1995 cohort with only a half share for three years, which added almost $50 million to the real price of the franchises. Below-market prices also result from considerations other than maximizing fees, including competition with rival leagues, responses to internal and external pressures to expand, and a concern that expansion teams not be too heavily weighted with financial burdens in their early years, when they are likely to encounter little success on the field, court, or ice.

Rising prices increase the appeal of expansion to teams and leagues, despite disclaimers from sports leaders like Fay Vincent, who insisted that expansion was a "non-economic issue," that "despite the common myth, owners in baseball are not expanding because there is money to be made."[22] That selling franchises has become an important source of revenue is not a myth; the attractions of making money from expansion clearly have increased as the costs of professional sports escalate and the prices that can be charged for expansion franchises soar. For baseball, one analyst of the sports business concludes, the "$190 million infusion of franchise fees" from the 1993 expansion was "a life buoy to keep the incumbent owners' heads above water."[23] Of course, the only way to realize more of these revenues is to expand further. The NBA may well have been unable to choose between Miami and Orlando for 1988–1989, but league members also wound up sharing an extra $32.5 million in expansion fees by admitting an additional team. Baseball officials, after emphasizing that no teams would be added for years after the 1993 expansion, began talking seriously about additional growth in the wake of the phenomenal success of teams in Denver and Miami, and the ability of the NFL and NBA to sell teams for considerably more than baseball got for the Rockies and Marlins.

To suggest, however, that money is the driving force in expansion is to endow the process with more coherent goals than in fact have generally existed. A lack of clearly defined objectives and strategies has been characteristic of all four leagues, as each has responded over time in a largely ad hoc fashion to various pressures and opportunities. Expansion plans typically have dealt with numbers and timing rather than particular markets. The NHL's 1989 blueprint proposed adding as many as seven teams before the turn of the century, but provided no specifics about where the league might go beyond a general objective of adding teams in the west and south. Lack of planning reflects owners' wariness about expansion, and their desire to keep their options open. In 1947, Commissioner Happy Chandler proposed an expansion plan that would have added teams in Los Angeles and San Francisco to each baseball league, but the idea was rejected by owners who opposed expansion. Pete Rozelle commissioned a study of twenty-four prospective markets in 1973, but NFL owners never adopted a comprehensive plan for expansion; instead, the league added a team in Seattle to settle a political debt and another in Tampa, which had the advantage of being in Florida where many NFL owners vacationed.

New Arrangements in Space

Expansion not only involves adding teams to leagues, but fitting new franchises into league organizational and spatial structures. More clubs means new scheduling arrangements, which result in teams playing fewer games against most other teams, even though schedules have lengthened for all four sports in the expansion era. During the first sixty years of the twentieth century, baseball teams played twenty-two games against each of the other seven clubs in their league. By the mid-1990s, the sixteen teams that predated expansion were playing 40 percent fewer games against each other than in 1960. Additional teams also necessitate unbalanced scheduling, involving more games with some teams than others, and no contests against a number of teams in the case of the NFL, whose thirty teams play only sixteen games during the regular season.

More teams have prompted the subdivision of leagues into conferences and divisions, which in turn structure postseason arrangements. Baseball's two leagues were split into two divisions after its second wave of expansion in 1969, and then subdivided into three units following the 1993 expansion. Football's east-west division multiplied through expansion and merger of the NFL and AFL to two conferences, each with an east, central, and west division. Through expansion, basketball evolved from an east-west divisional format to two divisions encompassing four conferences. In hockey, expansion changed a six-team league into four divisions in two conferences.

The necessity to change schedules and alignments complicates expansion for leagues and their members. Which teams are played and how often, and which opponents are direct competitors for postseason places, are important for the performance of teams and leagues on the field, at the box office, and with broadcast audiences and advertisers. As a result, an NFL owner emphasizes, "there is nothing minor about realignment. You would have an easier time declaring World War III."[24] Teams understandably want to play as many games as possible with rivals that attract the most customers and viewers. In the NFL, the Dallas Cowboys have resisted a move out of the National Football Conference's eastern division because of spirited rivalries with the Washington Redskins, Philadelphia Eagles, and New York Giants. The Arizona Cardinals, also in the NFC east, has been unwilling to move west organizationally unless the Cowboys, their prime rival, were realigned. Tentative plans by NFL officials to group the 1995 expansion teams in Charlotte and Jacksonville with Atlanta, Miami, and Tampa in a southeastern unit foundered on the insistence by Atlanta and New Orleans, both located in the NFC's west division, that their rivalry be maintained in a revised league structure.

Many of these rivalries, of course, are the result of earlier realignments rather than products of "natural" rivalry between nearby cities or historic antagonists. Dallas and Washington, for example, are only rivals because of the Cowboys and Redskins, and this competition would wither if a more rational geographic alignment ended the annual pair of games between the two teams. By the same token, the Cowboy-Redskins experience suggests that realignments create new rivalries, as teams play other teams more often and battle them for division titles and playoff spots. Realignments that group teams geographically also promise to foster rivalries more readily than those based on ad hoc additions of new teams to existing league units. In the NHL, putting the New York area's three teams into a single division stimulated intense competition among players and fans. More generally, the NHL has used expansion to develop geographically coherent units that encourage natural rivalries; the New York trio are grouped with Philadelphia and Washington; traditional rivals in Toronto, Detroit, and Chicago are slotted with other midwestern teams; and the Los Angeles area clubs are in the same division, as are the two Florida teams. The NBA also has reshuffled existing teams and allocated expansion teams to produce a rational geographic allocation that nourishes rivalries among nearby places; both New York area teams are grouped together, as are the two Florida entries, the Atlanta and Charlotte clubs, and all the west-coast teams.

Baseball and football have taken less advantage of the opportunities provided by expansion to develop more spatially compact units and enhance natural rivalries, largely because of basic structural impediments. Realignment in baseball has been framed by the two-league structure; organizational changes following expansion have been confined to single leagues that played separate schedules until 1997. Although the NFL is a single league with an integrated schedule, its organization into two conferences whose games are televised by different networks limits organizational options. New teams have to be allocated to maintain the relative balance in the television markets represented in each conference, since network contracts reflect these differences; and organizational shifts to enhance natural rivalries, like those between the Giants and Jets in New York or the 49ers and Raiders in the Bay Area are foreclosed by the necessity for each network to have a foothold in major metropolitan and regional markets.

Television has also influenced post-expansion realignments in baseball, basketball, and hockey. Heavy dependence on local broadcast revenues means that teams prefer to play against opponents in the same time zone so fans can watch or listen to games at a standardized time. Broadcast considerations were at the heart of a bitter fight over the proposed restructuring of the National League prompted by admission of the Marlins and Rockies, which sought to correct the geographical anomaly created after the 1969 expansion by switching Chicago and St. Louis to the west and Atlanta and Cincinnati to the east. The Cubs successfully protested the severance of traditional rivalries, emphasizing the adverse effect on Cubs' fans who would have to stay up to watch their heroes because more of the teams' games in an unbalanced schedule would be played on the West Coast. What was not emphasized was the fear of the Chicago Tribune Company, owner of both the Cubs and superstation WGN, that more games from California would reduce audiences and advertising revenues for Cubs' telecasts on WGN.

A year later, baseball teams were reshuffled into three divisions in each league, which pleased the Cubs, who were placed in the National League's central division and would be playing a balanced schedule. Other teams were less happy; the Pittsburgh Pirates grumbled that leaving the National League east to accommodate the expansion Marlins "would negatively impact our gate and our television revenue."[25] Television considerations also led the Texas Rangers to object to being in the American League west, "where most of our games are in the middle of the night and most of our fans are asleep."[26] Neither objection carried the day, but the Detroit Tigers were permitted to stay in the American League east to sustain their traditional rivalries with the Boston Red Sox and New York Yankees.[27]

Post-expansion realignment also has to cope with the reality that most new teams have dreadful records in their initial seasons, which leads to efforts to distribute expansion teams around a league's units in order to reduce the advantages of existing teams. In the process, spatial logic takes a back seat to the objective of spreading around the victories to be won against newly minted teams. In 1972, the expansion Atlanta Flames were assigned to the NHL's western unit to balance the placement of the other new team, the New York Islanders, in the east. Distributing NFL expansion teams put Tampa in the NFC's central division, while Atlanta and New Orleans were assigned to the western division. Three of four new NBA franchises added in 1988–1989 were in the southeast, leading to a complex shuffling of teams among divisions. Orlando played its first season in the Atlantic Division and Miami in the Midwest; Charlotte and Minnesota came aboard the following season and were placed in the Midwest Division, with Orlando going to the Central and Miami to the Atlantic; this game of musical franchises came to an end in 1991, when Miami and Orlando were joined in the Atlantic Division, Charlotte went to the Central, and Minnesota to the Midwest. "This rotating system," the league explained, "will give the fans in all these new franchise cities a chance to see all the NBA stars several times in the first three years."[28] And lessened the impact on divisional outcomes of four expansion teams that lost most of their games over this period.

One constant in efforts to deal with structural issues raised by expansion is the absence of any systematic concern for place interests. The importance of rivalries is determined by teams and leagues, with little reference to the views of the governments that provide most facilities, the general public that underwrites the subsidies, or the fans that support a team. To be sure, teams and leagues seek to maximize their interest in more customers, viewers, and listeners, but leagues make decisions in the interests of their members. Places, as the next chapter examines in detail, are secondary players in the expansion game—players with large stakes and little influence.

12

Making the Cut

FOR PLACES, expansion is a good news-bad news story. The good news is that expansion offers places the best opportunity to get into the big leagues. Forty-six teams playing in 1995 came to their current locations through expansion, accounting for over 54 percent of the eighty-five teams that have been added to the major league roster since 1950. Expansion also is the most respectable way for places to snare a place in the major leagues, involving neither the opprobrium of stealing a team from another city nor the stigma of sneaking into the big time through the back door via a rival league. And franchises that places secure through expansion are their home team, not some other place's former team like the Indianapolis Colts or Dallas Stars.

The bad news is the meager influence of places in the expansion process; cities, suburbs, states, and provinces are supplicants in proceedings controlled by leagues. To secure an expansion team, places have to compete for a limited number of franchises. The NBA, for example, decided to expand for 1995 to Canada; and the only places considered among numerous hopefuls were Toronto and Vancouver. Places have no control over the supply of expansion franchises or their availability; they have to play by rules determined and applied by league members. Expansion is not a process that pays much attention to the interests of places. Leagues and their members pursue their own interests; places are locations, markets, facilities, and sources of subsidies, but not prospective partners who need to be considered on their own terms. In the pungent words of a Denver official, "people in major league baseball didn't give a shit about whether or not we got baseball."[1] To be sure, the pooh-bahs of professional sports periodically proclaim that expansion is really about making their game available to more people and places. "We have cities out there who have waited years," noted an NFL owner who felt "we have to satisfy that appetite."[2] "Cities are spending a lot of money," a baseball man insisted in 1983, "and we can't just keep dragging them along."[3] But cities have been dragged along, for ten years after 1983 in the case of baseball, as leagues have tried to determine what was best for their members.

Leagues call the tune; cities are expected to dance. "Expansion hinges on two cities coming forward with everything in place," Commissioner Bowie Kuhn indicated in 1979, "they would have to have the proper financing, good ownership, a stadium, a lease agreement"; but if they danced to baseball's tune, there were still no guarantees that anything would happen because Kuhn "wouldn't say the prospects are particularly bright right now."[4] The NBA's ability to dominate places, in the view of a league official, was a key factor in the successful expansion of 1988–1989; "the NBA knew it could stop cold the expansion mechanism anytime and not hurt the league, and if prospective cities balked at its terms, the league could reject candidates."[5]

A major objective of league control of expansion is restricting the supply of teams, which reduces the number of franchises available for aspiring places, while increasing the costs of new teams to places and prospective owners. Limiting the supply of teams intensifies competition and enhances the leverage of professional sports with places that seek the few spots that leagues make available. The NBA, for example, drove hard bargains in the 1988–1989 expansion, insisting that 10,000 season tickets be sold and persuading the governments building arenas in Miami and Orlando to add more parking spaces. Baseball emphasized that places that wanted an expansion franchise in 1993 needed a supportive, complaisant government, what Commissioner Peter Ueberroth termed a "commitment for long-term government support."[6] Governments were expected to provide ballparks, eliminate tax disincentives, supply police around and within the stadium, and minimize political pressures on the team; baseball also sought places willing to cede revenues from concessions, parking, signage, pay television, and luxury boxes to the expansion team.

Places may be squeezed and strung along, but they have no alternative to playing the game if they want an expansion team. So mayors, prospective franchise owners, and local leaders seek to please the lords of the leagues; they are humble, supplicative, and responsive as they try to win the favor of league officials, expansion committees, and team owners who guard the gates to the big leagues. Local emissaries who met with Ueberroth in 1984 to discuss expansion were so deferential that, in the words of one participant, it was "almost as if we had been granted an audience with the Pope."[7] Speaking of the NFL owners who controlled expansion, the mayor of Memphis emphasized that the city's "job is to serve them and provide them a partnership that is contributing to the success of the NFL and to the franchise holder in Memphis."[8]

Rationing expansion franchises is also contrary to the interests of places that already have major league teams. A stock of eager cities unable to obtain an expansion team guarantees that leagues and teams have credible places to move to, which increases insecurity in places with teams and enhances the ability of owners to extract concessions in their current location. After the NFL selected its 1995 expansion locales, talk about relocating to the also-ran cities was heard from half a dozen teams. Once Denver and Miami emerged as sites for baseball's 1993 expansion teams, also-rans St. Petersburg and Washington were eyed by a number of teams unhappy with their current locations. For their part, places that fail to land one of the rationed expansion franchises often eagerly turn to luring an established team, since they have no idea when a league may expand again or whether their chances would be any better. When baseball bypassed the nation's capital, Mayor Sharon Pratt Dixon emphasized her readiness to "work with investors and other baseball boosters to pursue teams for sale in order to bring baseball to Washington, D.C."[9] Losing the NFL's 1995 expansion led Baltimore and St. Louis to purloin established NFL teams. More expansion, of course, would have eased both competition for existing teams and threats to places with major league franchises.

Competition among Places

Expansion involves the most structured competition for places seeking major league teams, contests which increasingly resemble the pennant races and playoffs of the professional sports leagues. The expansion game has favorites and long shots, efforts to bolster a contestant's weaknesses with a better stadium deal or more richly endowed prospective owners, elimination of weaker competitors, and a final round among survivors to see who gets to put a team on the field, court, or ice for the real pennant races and playoffs. Expansion is usually played over a longer season than the games themselves, often stretched over a decade for preliminaries and two years for the formal contests, but suspense about the outcome is often maintained until the very end, as when the NFL picked Jacksonville over Baltimore and St. Louis.

Over time, these competitions have tended to attract more contestants. The initial expansions involved relatively few places, with leagues deciding where they wanted to go rather than choosing among a large number of applicants. For the 1969 expansion, baseball attracted nine cities pursuing one of the four new franchises; seven were in the hunt for two spots in 1977, and more than twice that many, seventeen in all, for the two 1993 expansion teams. But the competition was more limited for 1998, with only four places making final bids. Not until 1977 did the NFL consider many places, picking Seattle and Tampa from a field of six serious competitors. For its 1995 expansion, the NFL ran an elaborate sweepstakes that attracted fifteen urban areas, eleven of which formally applied. Competition has been more muted in the NBA, with the league operating a closed process before the 1988–1989 expansion, when seven places vied for what became four openings. The NBA returned to a closed competition for its 1995 expansion, which involved only two Canadian cities, with the league deciding whether to admit one or both places. The NHL selected its initial six expansion locations from among a dozen places, then made a series of closed expansions until 1992, when ten possible locations were narrowed to six which formally applied for the two expansion franchises. But there was no competition for the 1993 expansion franchises, which were awarded to two attractive targets of opportunity, Anaheim and Miami.

Open competitions have increased opportunities for places to get into the big leagues. Long shots like Charlotte in the NBA and Jacksonville in the NFL have a better chance in an open field than when leagues preselect expansion locations. More competition, however, also intensifies bidding among places, thus raising costs for all places that seek to win an expansion franchise. These contests pit places against other places in what are bound to be zero-sum games. As the largest state without major league baseball, Florida was almost certain to get a 1993 expansion franchise, but political and marketing considerations made putting both new teams in Florida unlikely. The result was a three-way competition for one opening, featuring constant jibes among the adversaries. Orlando and St. Petersburg stressed Miami's crime and chaos; Miami and Orlando chuckled about somnolent St. Petersburg with its elderly population; and Miami and St. Petersburg suggested that Orlando was out in the sticks somewhere. Orlando bragged about its plans for "a marvelous park without a dome" in a knock at St. Petersburg's dreary dome, insisting that "to be cooped up in a dome is not baseball."[10] St. Petersburg countered with dire predictions of the health hazards of watching baseball outdoors in Florida's summer heat.

The Right Stuff

Competing for expansion teams has become an increasingly complex and sophisticated activity. Organizations are formed like the Denver Baseball Commission and Touchdown Jacksonville! to spearhead efforts to get this or that place in the big leagues. Glossy reports and snazzy videos are prepared that portray an irresistible opportunity for a league, and stadium and arena models depict gleaming monuments to local endeavor and largess. The result is expansion as a substantial civic activity, a rallying point for a community, and a test of local ability to compete successfully against other places. These frenzied civic efforts underscore that expansion is not primarily about sports. Instead, expansion is about getting a place in the big leagues; winning an expansion team is a means rather than the end.

Chasing an expansion franchise is an inexact science. Leagues make, change, and apply rules as they please. Uncertain about what works, places and prospective owners try everything. Reams of data on demographic trends, broadcasting markets, and the local economy are massaged to persuade a league that a place rests on an irresistible market base regardless of its size, location, or economy. Large metropolitan areas emphasize their scale; Washington's mantra in the 1993 baseball expansion was the 4.2 million inhabitants of a sprawling metropolis.[11] Smaller areas talk about location and growth rates rather than size; Orlando offered baseball Florida's most central location and "the fastest-growing area of America"; the pitch was "guys, have some vision, look to the future, the future of Florida is here."[12]

Regional empires rather than mere metropolitan areas are depicted as natural markets for teams in a particular location; and the smaller the metropolitan area, the more imperative that the net be cast over a wider region. With a small metropolitan population in baseball terms, Denver portrayed its market as the entire Rocky Mountain region, preparing a video on "The Time Zone without a Team," an eight-state area with 8.4 million television viewers and the closest major league team over six hundred miles away in Kansas City. Charlotte refused to be bounded by traditional boundaries when it defined its market for NFL football as extending 150 miles in all directions; "a city limit, county, or MSA is not as relevant to the fundamental question of how many people would come," explained the consultant who transformed a metropolitan area of 1.2 million into a region with almost 10 million inhabitants.[13] Memphis used a similar approach, marketing itself to the NFL as the center of the Mid-South Common Market, whose population of 3.8 million was four times the size of the Memphis metropolitan area. Major league baseball was offered the southern Florida region, with over 4 million residents, rather than merely the Miami metropolitan area. Framing the market in terms of South Florida also was designed to overcome the negatives associated with Miami; the broader region connoted growth, suburbs, and affluence in contrast with Miami's crime, drugs, riots, and poverty.

Places seek to demonstrate that the enticing market they have portrayed will support a major league team. Selling tickets to exhibition games gets boosters involved and kindles public enthusiasm, as well as providing another opportunity to outdo competitors. By selling out a preseason game between the Kansas City Chiefs and New York Jets in 1991, St. Louis hoped to "send a clear signal to . . . NFL owners that we have great football fans who want the NFL back here" as well as to "create ongoing fan excitement and a lasting message that will carry through until we are awarded a franchise."[14] Leagues, however, rarely put much weight on these heavily promoted one-shot events; as an NFL official explained, "I don't think it's that important. How much weight would you put on . . . a preseason game played between teams not from that town?"[15] What leagues put weight on is real money for real games. Charlotte helped overcome the NBA's concerns about market size by taking deposits for 15,000 season tickets. And Jacksonville impressed the NFL by selling more than 10,000 season tickets at $7,500 per seat for five years.

Support for lesser leagues is offered as evidence of a place's readiness to move up to the big leagues, but a successful team in a failed football league or baseball's bush leagues usually does not impress expansion committees. That Jacksonville was admitted to the NFL and Memphis was not had little to do with the strong support in both places for teams in the World Football League and United States Football League. Denver was one of the most successful minor league baseball franchises, but Miami, the other winner of a 1993 expansion team, had no minor league team. Backers of big league baseball in Buffalo, the first minor league city to draw over a million fans two years a row, hoped "to earn our way into the major leagues" by putting "the numbers up on the board" in the form of "fans through the gate."[16] Buffalo lasted longer in the 1993 race than three other highly supportive locales for minor league baseball—Columbus, Indianapolis, and Louisville—but was a distant also-ran when the contest ended, its phalanx of loyal fans unable to overcome the handicaps of a marginal market and a prospective owner unwilling to make the financial commitments demanded by the lords of baseball.

Past support for big league teams is also valued more highly by places than leagues. Oakland heralded its 121 straight sellouts for the Raiders, but failed to make the final cut for a 1995 NFL team. Baltimore emphasized the city's passionate devotion to the Colts before they were stolen away, but other factors were more important when the NFL chose Charlotte and Jacksonville over Baltimore. Charlotte's emphasis on the area's strong support of the NBA Hornets, however, did advance its cause with the NFL, largely because the backing of the Hornets addressed the issue of whether a small metropolitan area like Charlotte could support professional football. A similar argument by Sacramento, whose NBA Kings played before sellout crowds, on the other hand, did not bolster the city's prospects with major league baseball or the NFL.

Places boost whatever else might help. Ottawa was not modest about being Canada's capital in successfully seeking an NHL expansion team. Washington kept reminding baseball that the national pastime belonged in the nation's capital, but could not overcome the liabilities of two failed teams in the past, an aging stadium in a deteriorating neighborhood, and weak prospective owners. Abandonment is another claim that has produced mixed results. New York, Kansas City, and Seattle all persuaded baseball to replace departed teams with expansion franchises, bolstering their cases with threats of rival leagues, political punishment, or ruinous lawsuits. Baltimore, Oakland, and St. Louis played the game according to the NFL's rules, threatening nothing while seeking to convince the league that they deserved a 1995 expansion team because they had lost teams. The NFL was sympathetic but not responsive; Oakland never made the final cut, while Baltimore and St. Louis were edged out by Jacksonville, one of whose attractions was having no other major league teams, past or present.

Emphasizing the positive is accompanied by all sorts of activities designed to impress. Banquets, helicopter tours, and keys to the city are standard fare when league bigwigs come to town. Church bells rang "Take Me Out to the Ball Game" when the National League's expansion committee visited Denver, and 3,000 fans were chanting "Baseball! Baseball! Baseball!" in the atrium of an office building when the group arrived downtown.[17] Washington greeted Commissioner Ueberroth with banners pleading the city's case when he met with members of Congress to discuss expansion in 1986. Complementing the telegenic outside activities is constant work on the inside. Representatives haunt the meetings of the target league, keeping their place in play, wining, dining, and pressing their case with whoever will listen.

Efforts to win expansion teams usually are joint ventures of public officials, local business interests, and prospective owners of the franchise. As competition for teams has intensified, top public officials—mayors, governors, heads of sports agencies—are increasingly the focal points of campaigns. They bring together key actors, recruit prospective owners, mobilize public support, and use whatever influence they have to press their community's cause with league officials and members. They are expected to say the right things about the importance of being in a particular league, attract attention in the local media, pressure companies to buy season's tickets, trek to league meetings, and host visitation committees. And they wait when the league finally anoints the winners, ready to step before the cameras, decked out in a cap or shirt emblazoned with the new team's logo, to claim modest credit for victory, or accept defeat graciously with a promise to continue working to get their city or state or province into the big leagues.

Escalating demands from leagues for playing facilities and other benefits for expansion franchises have reinforced the importance of public officials in expansion campaigns. Mayors and governors typically hold the keys to new and improved arenas and stadiums, public works and services for these facilities, subsidies and tax benefits, sympathetic regulation, and gambling restrictions. Top-level political support is essential in moving measures critical to expansion campaigns through legislative bodies, and in securing public approval of new facilities and expenditures when referendums are required. Failure to provide acceptable facilities, on the other hand, is an increasingly fatal handicap to places. Problems with existing or planned arenas helped eliminate Anaheim, St. Petersburg, and Toronto from the 1988–1989 NBA expansion. Older stadiums damaged the chances of Buffalo and Washington in the 1993 baseball expansion. New facilities, however, do not guarantee success, which further complicates the expansion game for political leaders. Developing a new public stadium on speculation was not enough to put St. Louis over the top in the 1995 NFL expansion: "What do you mean we don't get an expansion team," was the incredulous reaction of a local politician when St. Louis was stiffed, "we're building a stadium!"[18]

Partners in the Hunt

The role of Wayne Huizenga in bringing baseball and hockey to South Florida underscores that places do not obtain expansion teams without an owner. "GREAT CATCH The Marlins Are Florida's Team," read the headline in the *Miami Herald*, but the hat in Huizinga's hand in the accompanying photo was appropriately emblazoned "WAYNE'S TEAM."[19] Expansion franchises go to prospective owners rather than places. "Everyone looks at this as a competition among cities," cautioned Commissioner Fay Vincent as baseball geared up to expand in 1993. "It is not that. It is a competition among ownership groups."[20]

Prospective owners have become steadily more important, as stakes rise and there is more competition for teams. During the 1960s, expansion decisions often were made with no specific owner identified; baseball picked Los Angeles, Washington, and San Diego without having firm commitments from owners; and hockey expanded to St. Louis even though no owner had applied for a franchise. In 1974, the NBA selected Toronto and the NHL picked Seattle, but both expansions were canceled when suitable owners never materialized. By the 1990s, the practice of adding teams without owners seemed as archaic as the flying wedge in football or center jump in basketball. Leagues were selecting places and owners, or more frequently owners and places, or sometimes primarily owners.

As a result of league preoccupation with ownership and the rising cost of new franchises, places find their expansion chances more and more dependent on the strength of prospective owners. Identifying suitable partners is often difficult, given the capital needed and league requirements about financial resources, majority ownership, and local connections. Houston and Seattle withdrew from the NHL's 1992–1993 expansion because prospective owners were not in place; and the same fate befell the efforts of New Orleans and Vancouver to compete for 1993 baseball expansion teams. Washington had people who wanted to own a 1993 expansion team, but none of the wannabes impressed baseball; the size and affluence of the Washington metropolis, along with baseball's desire to be politically correct, carried the nation's capital into the final round, but inadequate ownership was a fatal handicap; "you can't take it seriously," scoffed one of the lawyers involved in the expansion, "there's no money there."[21]

Likely owners often fall by the wayside during the expansion process, victims of changing personal fortunes, rising prices for expansion teams, and shifting economic conditions. Places then either scramble for replacements or withdraw. Toronto fell out of the running for an NBA team in the 1988–1989 expansion when the league raised the price from $25 million to $32.5 million, leading an ownership group to withdraw. Chances of contenders in the 1993 baseball expansion were strongly influenced by second thoughts among financial backers as the time approached for decisions about committing their millions. Phoenix struck out when the prospective owner balked at an expansion fee that he did not believe was "economically viable" given the area's limited potential for local broadcasting revenues.[22] Buffalo's slim hopes evaporated when Robert Rich, the wealthy applicant for the franchise, indicated that he did "not believe in baseball at any cost," expressing doubts about the viability of a small market like Buffalo and indicating that big league baseball might be beyond his financial reach, and thus out of reach of Buffalo, which had no hope without Rich and his riches.[23]

Expansion chances also have been damaged by competition among prospective owners. Baltimore's campaign for an expansion football team was seriously handicapped by the presence of three competing ownership groups. The bid of St. Louis, once a favorite in the 1995 NFL expansion, came unraveled when the original ownership group fractured; a new combine was patched together at the last minute, and it in turn was challenged by a member of the original group. St. Petersburg was harmed throughout the 1993 baseball expansion by internal conflicts. First St. Petersburg and Tampa competed for the team, then three prospective ownership groups sought the blessings of the National League. St. Petersburg's problems were compounded when the National League anointed a contestant with an apparent willingness to spend big bucks but with no local backing; then his commitment waned, leaving considerable bitterness among the locals: "Baseball picked the jockey for our horse," complained a local official, "and then when the jockey failed, we lost."[24]

For places, the best way around these pitfalls is a partnership with a single owner who has substantial resources, which of course is easier said than done. Leagues clearly prefer individuals over complex syndicates and partnerships. Both the 1995 NFL expansion franchises went to places whose teams would be individually owned. Miami was the strongest contestant in the 1993 baseball expansion because of Wayne Huizenga, who offered the irresistible combination of big bucks, no partners, and partial ownership of the stadium in which his team would play. Baseball picked Huizenga over two competing local groups, including the one preferred by city interests that wanted big league baseball played in Miami by a team bearing the city's name.

The fortunes of places also can be affected by noneconomic considerations involving owners. Perhaps most important after all the numbers are tallied for wealth, markets, and facilities is that people rather than places are being admitted to an exclusive club. One of the problems with the competing ownership groups in Baltimore was the NFL's doubts about letting either Baltimore clothing tycoon Leonard "Boogie" Weinglass or Florida investor Malcolm Glazer into the club; team owners told reporters "they were uncomfortable with Weinglass's flamboyance, which includes a gray ponytail," and worried that Glazer was a "corporate raider."[25] Huizenga, on the other hand, had no trouble passing muster with the lords of baseball. "They like Wayne

Huizenga," explained a leader in the campaign to bring baseball to South Florida, "I don't know what it takes to get in their club of owners besides money but they look for certain qualities, and whatever those qualities are, he filled the bill."[26]

Expansion Politics

Expansion is less controversial than relocation. Relocation has victims; expansion is a competition with winners and losers rather than a heist with robbers and robbed. As a result, expansion is a more legitimate process than relocation. Places and prospective owners generally accept league control, not in the least because to challenge the process is to diminish the likelihood of winning an expansion team. Since most participants acknowledge the legitimacy of league control, expansion has attracted less political and legal flak than relocation.

Legitimacy, however, does not foreclose places and prospective owners from seeking to influence the process through political means. Leagues and team owners are lobbied by local and state officials; members of Congress wave the banners of their cities, metropolitan areas, states, and regions; and prospective owners and business leaders throw their political weight around to impress or intimidate league officials. Most of this effort is traditional pressure-group politics; supplicants and their political supporters spread the word, press the flesh, and see what kinds of deals might be done. Political activity has increased as the number of places competing for new teams has grown, both because more places mean additional politicians with a stake and because more contestants lead places and prospective owners to exploit any opportunity that promises an edge over the competition.

Pressures from Washington have attracted more attention from leagues than local and state political efforts. Members of Congress, unlike state and local leaders, can do more than plead the case of their favored locale for a place in the big leagues; in expansion as in relocation, congressional involvement carries the threat or promise of regulatory change, which insures that leagues are sensitive to congressional concerns. For Congress, expansion is a relatively easy issue; most members favor more teams; many because their districts and states are not in the big leagues; others because expansion promises to reduce the threat of relocation for places that have teams.

Congress has pursued expansion on two tracks, one involving general efforts to induce leagues to quicken the pace and widen the scope of expansion, the other entailing specific endeavors to advance the cause of particular places. Football and baseball have been the principal targets of general pressures for expansion. Congress began urging the NFL to expand in the 1960s; and an unsuccessful effort was made following the Raiders' move to require the league to add six teams. The most concerted general congressional effort emerged in 1987 with organization of the Senate Task Force on the Expansion of Major League Baseball, which wanted six new teams by 2000. General efforts, however, primarily attract members of Congress with specific objectives, namely, securing a team for their districts or states. "The driving force behind this task force," explained the organizer of the Senate group, Tim Wirth of Colorado, "is the baseball fever we each see in our home states. Fans are calling and writing to members of Congress, seeking our help."[27] Efforts in the 1980s to force the NFL to add six teams, and later to discuss general expansion plans with interested senators, were led by Senator Albert Gore of Tennessee, whose principal concern was getting Memphis into the league.

Given the primacy of interests in particular places, general alliances like the baseball task force are difficult to maintain in the zero-sum world of expansion. Even six expansion franchises would not have satisfied the twenty-odd members of Wirth's group; with only two baseball teams to be added in 1993, there would be far more losers than winners. As individual members boosted their constituencies for expansion franchises, the task force faded out of the picture, and its principal influence was on the fortunes of individual places. "Not so coincidentally," Andrew W. Zimbalist noted after the franchises went to Miami and Denver, "the two most active members of the congressional task force were Senators Connie Mack of Florida and Tim Wirth of Colorado."[28]

Lurking behind congressional pressures for expansion is the threat of restrictive antitrust legislation or other punitive measures. After baseball indicated that only two teams would be added in 1993, the Senate task force reminded baseball that Congress also could play hard ball, promising "to pursue all available avenues to correct the inequities of the existing expansion procedure."[29] Senators have also hinted that the NFL could lose its right to pool television revenues if more expansion teams were not approved. Professional leagues have stoutly resisted congressional efforts to force expansion. "Don't be threatening us," was Ueberroth's message to Congress, "it's not going to get anybody anywhere. . . . if you want to be political, we won't get anything accomplished."[30] Commissioner Paul J. Tagliabue claimed that politics was irrelevant to the NFL's decision to expand, insisting that "we're doing this on our own."[31]

Ueberroth and Tagliabue, of course, were playing politics by denying the relevance of political factors in expansion. No sport has been able to ignore political pressures for expansion. Before the NHL expanded in 1967, hockey worried with good reason that "some day one of these politicians is gonna say, 'we've got big-league towns out here, you've got to let us in.'"[32] Washington obtained one of the first two American League expansion teams to placate congressional displeasure at the departure of the Senators to the Twin Cities. Kansas City went to the top of the expansion list to fend off Senator Stuart Symington, who promised retaliation against baseball's antitrust exemption unless the Athletics were replaced. While Tagliabue was denying the relevance of politics, an influential team official was talking about the league having "a commitment and an obligation" because "Pete Rozelle made a statement to Congress . . . that we would expand."[33] Vincent acknowledged that baseball's decision to expand in 1993 was influenced by "considerable pressure over the years from political circles."[34] As congressional and other political pressures steadily mounted, owners concluded that continued inaction could be costly in terms of public opinion, political support, and baseball's privileged antitrust status. "Political force," a baseball executive conceded to David Whitford, had "reached sort of a critical mass" that could "not be ignored."[35]

Congress has offered carrots as well as sticks to induce sports leagues to expand. Numerous efforts were made to promote expansion during congressional consideration of the relocation bills discussed in Chapter Ten, with members of Congress emphasizing connections between movement of teams and expansion. Senator Gore argued that the NFL's proposal to exempt league franchise controls from antitrust did "not address the underlying problem, which is the scarcity of teams, which compounds the demand for teams."[36] Gore offered to trade antitrust immunity for six new teams in the NFL. Earlier, Congress had blessed the NFL-AFL merger in return for promises of future expansion.

For their part, leagues use expansion to enhance their political influence. Critical congressional support for the football merger came from Louisiana in exchange for an expansion team for New Orleans. Rozelle told Senator Russell Long and Representative Hale Boggs "that if the merger didn't go through, we wouldn't be able to afford to expand, and that it would be a shame, since New Orleans would be automatic for a new team."[37] Three weeks after the legislation was approved, New Orleans was added to the NFL. In 1975, a similar understanding brought an expansion franchise to Seattle after Washington's Senator Warren Magnuson blocked a bill that extended the ban on television blackouts of NFL games.[38] Expansion, both in general and for specific places, was dangled during consideration of the NFL's relocation proposals in the mid-1980s. Rozelle assured Congress that "if you pass this sports bill, we're ready to expand."[39] The NFL also personalized expansion quid pro quos during the relocation campaign; Howard Baker of Tennessee, the Republican leader in the Senate, was courted with the understanding that Memphis could follow the path of New Orleans and Seattle into the NFL.

For baseball, expansion offered a means of fending off attacks on its antitrust exemption in the 1990s. Senator Dennis DeConcini of Arizona helped kill an antitrust measure in committee after receiving "strong indications that Phoenix is a front runner" from several owners.[40] Assurances that Tampa Bay was in line for an expansion team mollified members of Congress from Florida who had pushed antitrust legislation after the Giants were prevented from moving to St. Petersburg. According to Senator Connie Mack, "a definitive statement" was made by top baseball officials concerning St. Petersburg's expansion prospects, in return for which Mack agreed "that I'd be quiet for a while" on the antitrust issue.[41]

Expansion has been contested in political arenas more frequently than in court. Leagues have faced relatively few legal challenges of their control over expansion, primarily because of the reluctance of places and prospective owners to sue and thus risk their future chances to get in the big leagues. The NBA shied away from expanding to San Diego in 1974 because one set of prospective owners had previously sued the league.[42] Even the hint of lawsuits can be damaging to expansion hopes. The causes of Baltimore and St. Louis in the 1995 NFL expansion were damaged by fears that losers in last-minute reshuffles of ownership groups might sue the league should either city have been awarded a franchise.

When contested in court, league authority over expansion has been upheld in cases involving seekers of NFL teams in Memphis and Los Angeles. At issue in Memphis was the NFL's refusal to consider an application from a group that had operated the Mid-South Grizzlies in the World Football League. Mid-South contended that the NFL had illegally conspired to keep Memphis out of the league. The federal trial and appeals courts disagreed, ruling that the NFL's action did not constitute an antitrust violation since Memphis could play in a rival league, as it had been doing.[43] Another unsuccessful test of league control over expansion arose from the inability of the Los Angeles Memorial Coliseum Commission to secure an expansion franchise to replace the Rams, as the commission failed to persuade a federal judge that the NFL's requirement for unanimous approval to locate a new team within the territory of an existing franchise was an unlawful restraint of trade under the Sherman Act.[44]

Litigation arising from relocation has had more influence on expansion than lawsuits that challenge league authority to add teams. An expansion team was the goal of the lawsuit against baseball by Milwaukee and Wisconsin; the trial judge, notes one of the National League's lawyers, "did his best to persuade us to settle the case by granting Milwaukee an expansion franchise."[45] Although Milwaukee eventually lost in court, the litigation fueled baseball's antitrust fears, which accelerated expansion in 1969. Seattle, King County, and the state of Washington sued the American League for moving the expansion Pilots after a single season in Seattle. Fear of an adverse antitrust ruling, as well as the specter of millions in damages, led baseball to negotiate a settlement; "there was going to be a jury trial in the state of Washington," explained the league president, "and I didn't think we were going to fare very well" so "we gave them an expansion team."[46]

Political and judicial influence on expansion are a mixed blessing. Political pressures, legislative requirements, or court rulings promise more teams, but political and legal actions typically give an advantage to some places at the

expense of others. In the zero-sum game of NFL expansion, the political good
fortune of New Orleans and Seattle meant sharply lessened chances for other
places with hopes of getting into the big leagues. Similarly, the political pressures that put Kansas City back in the American League in 1969 and the legal
settlement that returned major league baseball to Seattle in 1977 reduced prospects for other contenders.

Winners and Losers

Places, according to conventional wisdom, win and lose when they secure an
expansion team; they win a place in the big leagues, but they lose because they
wind up with a lousy team with marginal long-term economic prospects that
probably will move when the going gets tough. One element of the conventional wisdom has been beyond dispute: expansion teams almost always have
been losers on the field, court, and ice. The NHL's expansions, in the words of
a sportswriter, have been "replete with . . . horrible hockey teams."[47] Perhaps
the worst were the Washington Capitals, who lost 67 games, tied 5, and won
only 8 in their first season. The team celebrated its initial (and only) victory
away from the Capital Centre by circling the ice with a trash can held aloft in
a bizarre parody of the triumphant victory lap of winners of the Stanley Cup.
Among other spectacularly inept expansion teams were the New York Mets,
who lost 120 games the first time out, at least 20 more defeats than the typical
baseball tailender, and proceeded to finish last in a ten-team league for the next
three seasons, posting a cumulative record of 154 wins and 332 losses over that
period.

Some expansion teams have done better in their first seasons. The Los Angeles Angels managed to finish ahead of an established team in the franchise's
first year, and vaulted to third place in a ten-team league the following year,
winning 86 of 162 games. The Colorado Rockies qualified for baseball's expanded playoffs in their third year; and the Florida Panthers reached the final
round of the Stanley Cup playoffs four seasons after joining the NHL. One of
the NFL's two 1995 expansion teams, the Carolina Cougars, won 7 of their 16
games in their first year, bettering the performance of five established teams
and matching five more. Most expansion teams, however, have taken a substantial number of seasons to achieve parity with the rest of the league, defining parity as the achievement of a .500 won-loss record. Expansion teams in
baseball have taken the longest, averaging 7.8 seasons to achieve parity; NHL
expansion franchises have needed 5.8 seasons, while NBA and NFL teams
average 5.5 years.

Expansion franchises typically play poorly in their early years because established organizations have been unwilling to make available sufficient talent
to permit new clubs to field competitive teams. Until recently, expansion
teams have been almost totally dependent on existing teams for their players.

League members determine arrangements for stocking new teams, deciding how many players can be protected by existing teams and thus the general quality of players available to expansion teams. Faced with the choice between making an expanded league more competitive and advancing their own interests, established teams usually have chosen the latter; "the new teams will be weaker and they ought to be," insisted Detroit's general manager as the NHL expanded in 1967; "why should the Red Wings spend millions to build up a franchise and then let these new guys move in on the same level?"[48]

Expansion franchises, of course, seek better pools of players, arguing that every team in a league has an interest in the competitiveness of new entries. Owners of expansion teams also have a compelling economic interest in fielding respectable teams. Concern about the competitive and economic consequences of past expansion drafts led to some enrichment of player pools during the round of expansions that began in the late 1980s. Liberalized rules in the NHL reflected what one owner termed a "more market-oriented . . . philosophy" designed "to help the expansion teams become more competitive."[49] Even more important for brightening the prospects of expansion teams has been the liberalization of free agency, which has made skilled players available to new entries like the Colorado Rockies and Carolina Cougars with the resources to outbid established teams for quality performers.

Expansion, many critics insist, not only produces bad teams for the places that obtain franchises, but dilutes the quality of play everywhere by spreading a finite supply of major league performers among a larger number of teams. As a result, the price of bringing the major leagues to more places is to cheapen the big league experience for fans in places that already have teams. Expansion obviously has some effect on performance, since the additional players on big league rosters presumably are less skilled than those already in the big leagues. Quality, however, is affected by the size of player pools as well as by the size of leagues. The same population increases that spurred expansion have bolstered the number of potential major leaguers in the United States and Canada. Ending the exclusion of blacks dramatically enlarged the talent available to basketball, baseball, and football at the dawn of the expansion era. The talent pool in the NHL has steadily expanded from its traditional Canadian base to include more and more players from the United States and Europe; baseball has drawn a growing number of players from Latin America and a few from Asia; and the NBA has reached out to Africa and eastern Europe.

Expansion also troubles critics because places that obtain new teams are in smaller metropolitan areas with fewer people to buy tickets and form broadcast audiences. Gerald W. Scully saw small markets and dismal teams placing baseball's 1993 expansion teams on the road to economic woe, arguing that "a franchise in a smaller place like Buffalo or Denver . . . won't be able to compete financially."[50] Certainly, some expansion teams in small markets have been dubious and even disastrous business ventures. The San Diego Padres

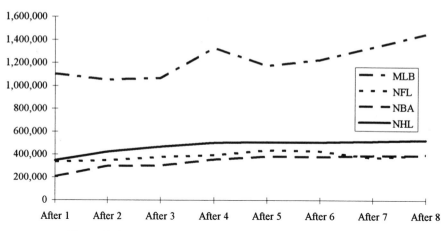

Figure 12.1   Average Attendance of Expansion Teams by League

have struggled from their inception in a metropolitan area hemmed in by the Angels and Dodgers, the Pacific Ocean, the Mexican border, and arid mountains. An NHL expansion team lasted only one season in Kansas City, one of the smallest major league markets in the United States. And baseball's first expansion effort in the relatively small Seattle market failed.

Success stories, however, are more common than business failures among expansion teams in smaller metropolitan areas. Although all of the NBA's 1988–1989 expansion cohort was located in small markets, three of the four have been successful business ventures. Charlotte, in the NBA's smallest market, attracted 950,000 spectators in 1988, the second highest attendance in the league. Despite Scully's worries, Denver's new baseball team in 1993 was a smashing success, drawing 4.48 million customers, by far the largest attendance in major league history, in the fourth smallest metropolitan market in baseball. Skeptics caution that the first few years do not tell the real story for expansion teams that draw well at the outset but then fade as customers lose interest in a poor team. Most expansion franchises, however, have registered steady gains in attendance, as indicated in Figure 12.1.

Expansion is sometimes pictured as a predatory game in which an operator gets a team, cleans up during a honeymoon period when grateful fans flock to see their new major league team, and then moves on when the public stops supporting a loser. Altogether, ten new teams have moved since the beginning of the expansion era in 1960, but expansion teams have been no more likely to move than established franchises during this period. All ten of those who relocated were franchises granted before the most recent round of expansion began in 1988; and the ten accounted for 24 percent of the forty-one new teams added by leagues between 1960 and 1981, which is a bit lower than the relocation rate for all teams.[51] Expansion franchises have been most rooted in the NFL, where none has moved. Baseball's two relocated expansion franchises, Seattle and Washington, were shaky enterprises from the start, rather than cases of shrewd operators exploiting a new territory. Four of the NBA's eleven expansion franchises teams have moved, two of them twice. The quest for a larger market took the current Clippers from Buffalo to San Diego to Los Angeles; the other resulted from the failure of the league's first expansion team in Chicago, which moved to Baltimore and then on to a new suburban arena outside Washington.

Expansion and relocation have been most closely connected in the NHL, where four of the six teams that moved have been expansion franchises, one of which moved twice, from Kansas City to another small market in Denver before winding up in New Jersey. Relocation of new NHL teams reflects in part the greater risks of expansion for hockey. In most of the United States, the game is much less familiar than baseball, basketball, and football, resulting in a smaller fan base and less television coverage than the other sports. The NHL compounded these problems by stumbling badly in its first ventures outside the hockey heartland of the northeast and midwest, resulting in unstable franchises in Oakland and Atlanta.

Despite its many problems, expansion has generally been a success story for places, sports fans, leagues, and players. Expansion has contributed to the greatest period of growth in professional sports. More teams in more places have boosted overall attendance and increased the value of national television contracts. Average attendance has increased during the expansion era, despite the fears of losing customers through the dilution of playing quality and reduction of playing dates against established teams and traditional rivals. Expansion has been accompanied by rising team revenues and franchise values, and demand for major league teams by prospective owners. And most important for places, expansion has strikingly increased the opportunities to be in the big leagues, albeit on terms dictated by the private rulers of professional sports.

13

Back Door Play

NEW LEAGUES offer a way around controls over the supply and location of teams. For potential owners as well as places, new leagues increase opportunities and lower costs of acquiring teams. Additional leagues also bring professional sports to more places and people. For both places and owners, however, new leagues are most valued because they are a means of getting into the real major leagues. All but five of the sixteen baseball teams that emerged in 1903 were products of other leagues. Four of NFL's twelve teams in 1950 began playing in rival leagues; and ten more came from the American Football League in 1970. The NBA resulted from the triumph of a rival league, the Basketball Association of America, over the established National Basketball League; of the eight charter NBA teams that survived, three were from the BAA, three defected to the BAA from the NBL, and two came from the NBL in the 1949 merger. Four more teams joined the NBA in 1976 from the American Basketball Association. In the NHL, the Detroit Red Wings began as the Victoria Cougars of the rival Western Canada Hockey League, and four teams were added in 1979 from the World Hockey Association.

Market Opportunities

Failure of existing leagues to put teams in places large enough to support major league sports encourages organization of new leagues; and the wider the gap between supply and demand, the more likely is formation of rival leagues. Markets left open by the National League helped spur formation of the American Association in 1882 and the America League at the turn of the century. Founding of the All-American Football Conference in 1946 was a direct consequence of the NFL's unwillingness to add more teams; and the tardiness of the NFL in expanding into new markets led to formation of the American Football League in 1960. The Continental League resulted from baseball's reluctance to expand, leading major cities without big league teams to join New York in the venture. Refusal of the NHL to expand led owners in the

Western Hockey League to consider a new major league. As an NHL owner who favored expansion emphasized, "you just can't tell people forever and ever that they're gonna be minor league and there's nothing they can do about it, because there is something they can do about it. They can say, . . . 'We'll just start our own league.' "[1]

Although open markets present opportunities for new leagues, markets served by established leagues constrain the locational choices of rival leagues. Existing teams have considerable advantages over newcomers; they have fans, media coverage, and games against traditional rivals; they play in big league arenas and stadiums; and they bear the stamp of the major leagues. And these advantages grow over time as leagues become more established as *the* major league. As a result, new leagues have become increasingly reluctant to challenge established leagues head-to-head. The exceptions have usually been in the largest markets, especially New York, the nation's biggest metropolis and media center, which is seen as essential for a league to be considered big league, especially by New Yorkers. The All-American Football Conference competed directly with the NFL only in the three largest metropolitan areas in 1946. Baseball's Continental League planned to operate in New York and seven metropolitan areas not served by the existing leagues. Initially, the American Football League expected to challenge the NFL only in New York and Los Angeles. Just three of the American Basketball Association's eleven charter franchises in 1968 were in markets with NBA teams: New York, Los Angeles, and San Francisco.

A few leagues organized after 1960 were more venturesome in locating in markets with teams in established leagues, but none did well in direct competition. The World Hockey Association took the ice in 1972 with half of its twelve teams going head-to-head with NHL franchises, but was unable to sustain a challenge in any of these markets. Two years later, the World Football League arrived with teams in the NFL's five largest markets, and folded after two seasons with few of these franchises in place. The United States Football League operated almost exclusively in markets with NFL teams, including the eight largest metropolitan areas. The USFL, however, did not compete directly for fans or television viewers in these areas, since the league played football in the spring. And when an ill-fated move to the fall was planned, the USFL adopted a more conservative strategy; "the scenario," indicated an owner, "is New York, Chicago and Los Angeles, with nine other cities where the NFL isn't."[2]

Market disparities between new and established leagues are increased by the difficulties rival leagues experience in competing in shared markets. Moving AFL franchises out of markets with NFL teams—from Los Angeles to San Diego and Dallas to Kansas City—further widened the gap between the metropolitan areas served by the leagues. Similar shifts by the ABA, WHA, and WFL took teams from large shared markets to smaller metropolitan areas.

ABA franchises in Los Angeles and San Francisco were moved to Salt Lake City and Norfolk. The WHA retreated from Boston to Hartford, Los Angeles to Baltimore, New York to San Diego, and Philadelphia to Calgary. And the WFL substituted Charlotte for New York and Shreveport for Houston.

Established leagues typically have responded to rival leagues by increasing the supply of franchises, which reduces the number of open markets available to challengers. Formation of the Continental League spurred baseball to add four teams in 1961–1962. Expansion of the NFL was accelerated by creation of the AFL in 1960, with the NFL scrambling to beat the newcomers into open markets. Rival basketball and hockey leagues also pushed the NBA and NHL to add teams. Growth of established leagues, along with the reluctance of new leagues to compete directly in any but the largest markets, pushes fledgling leagues into ever-smaller metropolitan areas. As a result, unshared markets for new leagues tend to be substantially smaller than for established leagues. The average unshared AFL market in 1960 was only 58 percent of the NFL average, while the ABA's unshared markets were 62 percent of the NBA average. In the case of the WHA, the disparity was even greater: the new league's unshared markets were only 43 percent of the NHL average, primarily because one-third of the WHA's franchises were in open markets in Canada with small populations.

A limited presence in large metropolitan areas inevitably reduced the customer base of new leagues, with adverse effects on gate and television revenues. Credibility was harmed by the absence of teams in major urban centers; real big leagues are supposed to be in the largest metropolitan areas. And of critical importance, new leagues usually have not operated in enough major media markets to attract network television. "Significant television revenues have always escaped the ABA," the league's president emphasized in 1973, because, except "for New York, the franchised teams are located outside the large television markets."[3] Of leagues organized during the television era, only the AFL sustained support from major networks. In addition to offering fairly substantial markets, the AFL was in the right sport at the right time, benefiting at the outset from the desire of ABC to get a foothold in professional football, and then from NBC's need for sports programming on Sunday afternoon after being outbid by CBS for NFL games in 1964.

Supply and Demand

After World War II, demand from potential owners far outpaced the supply of existing teams for sale or expansion franchises made available by leagues. The NFL's success attracted well-heeled businessmen who bankrolled the All-American Football Conference in 1946. A few years later, enough people were interested in owning professional football teams to provide owners for two NFL expansion teams, the eight teams that formed the AFL, and expressions of interest in AFL franchises from potential buyers in sixteen other urban centers.[4] By the 1970s, dozens of wealthy people wanted a piece of the action; their money underwrote the American Basketball Association, World Hockey Association, World Football League, and United States Football League, bringing what was advertised as big league sports to dozens of places. Many of these investors turned to new leagues after their efforts to buy major league teams or secure expansion franchises were frustrated.

New leagues not only increase the supply of teams, they do so at bargain prices, which widens the circle of potential buyers, particularly as the cost of established teams and expansion franchises mounts. Original AFL owners paid $25,000 for a franchise, compared with $600,000 for a NFL expansion team in the same year. Charter ABA teams were priced at $30,000 at a time when the NBA charged $1.75 million for expansion franchises. Investors in the WHA only paid $25,000 when the NHL was selling expansion teams for $6 million. Even with an escrow payment of $545,000 along with a $75,000 entry fee, WFL teams in 1974 cost far less than NFL expansion franchises, which went for $16 million two years later. Increasing the attraction of teams at these bargain prices is the hope of most owners of parlaying their franchises into a place in the real big leagues, as did almost all of the original AFL owners.

The AFL experience, however, was exceptional; rarely are there many winners in what is an extremely risky business. The odds of joining a successful league, operating a profitable team, winning recognition as a major league, or using the new league as a means of getting into an established league are low. The AFL was the only league since the American League to put all its franchises in the big leagues. Very few of the many owners and franchises that carried the tattered banners of the ABA and WHA slipped through the back door into the NBA and NHL. And the WFL and USFL were complete failures, unable to survive financially or win recognition or put any teams into the NFL.

Critical to survival and success of all new leagues are owners with sufficient resources to survive the tide of red ink that washes over these ventures at the outset, as well as to supply the cash needed to compete with established leagues. New leagues also need owners willing to take on collective responsibility for underfinanced franchises. The fortunes of the upstart American League depended heavily on Charles W. Somers, a coal baron who financed teams in his native Cleveland as well as Boston, Chicago, and Philadelphia. New leagues, however, have rarely been able to muster enough wealthy backers to avoid serious financial problems. Despite a substantial set of owners, the Federal League was on the financial ropes after two seasons of costly competition with the baseball establishment. The Baseball League, which planned to open in 1990, was shelved when prospective owners had second thoughts about the economic viability of the enterprise. Compounding the financial problems of many new leagues have been bargain prices, which inevitably attract owners with limited resources who cannot afford to suffer initial losses, resulting in under-financed teams and less collective capability to sustain a league. Seven of the twelve charter ownerships bailed out during the WFL's inaugural season, undermining the league's credibility and its prospects for merger with the NFL.

Credibility

To survive, new leagues have to put on a big league show. Proclaiming a new major league is far easier than producing games and championships that rival the quality of an established league. Credibility requires big league facilities and players as well as franchises in major metropolitan areas. New leagues have to be sufficiently entertaining to attract customers, and teams have to offer a reasonable facsimile of major league play to justify charging big league prices. In addition, the whole package has to pass muster with the media, in terms of both how a league is judged by journalists and whether broadcasters are willing to invest in the enterprise. By the 1960s, television had become essential to the credibility of new leagues. Winning acceptance is very difficult without television coverage, and television revenues are necessary in competing with established leagues for players.

To be viable, a rival league needs performers of sufficient skill that people will pay to watch them play. Lower prices, more amenities, different rules, and other innovations cannot be substituted for the quality of the basic product. Two-point conversions did not appreciably enhance the AFL's ability to compete with the NFL, whose superior product could be examined comparatively by any football fan flipping the dial between CBS and ABC on Sunday afternoons in the early 1960s. Assembling teams of major league quality is difficult because most players with big league ability are under contract with existing teams. Some players will move to a new league for more pay or a chance to play, but established players usually are reluctant to move to new leagues and teams with uncertain futures. Players also want to perform in the major leagues; they want to play in big league arenas and stadiums before major league crowds; they want to travel first class and get paid regularly with checks that do not bounce; they want to play in the World Series and skate for the Stanley Cup; in short, they want to be big leaguers.

Credibility of new leagues also is affected by playing facilities, which usually have been inferior to the arenas and stadiums used by teams in established leagues. Availability is a problem in competitive markets, since urban areas with teams rarely have unused major league facilities; and existing teams usually control the arenas and stadiums that they use. Places with major league franchises are reluctant to antagonize their teams by opening their facilities to rival leagues. Even in open markets, local officials have been wary of making public sports facilities available to new leagues, fearful that support for a rival league will jeopardize chances for a place in an established major league. Operators of arenas and stadiums have been cautious because of the dubious financial prospects of teams in new leagues. In some cases, failure to secure adequate facilities has forced new leagues to relocate franchises. Inability to rent the Orange Bowl led the AFL's organizers to substitute Buffalo for Miami. Arena problems in Kansas City caused the ABA to shift one of its charter franchises to Denver. Failure of the Washington Capitals of the WFL to secure playing dates at Robert F. Kennedy Stadium put the team in Orlando.

Because of these constraints, some teams usually wind up in facilities that undermine the credibility of new leagues. The Jersey Knights of the WHA played at a 5,500-seat arena in suburban Cherry Hill with an irregular surface. The AFL Oilers brought major league football to Houston in a 24,000-seat school stadium, and the Raiders, unable to find a place in Oakland, played their first season at a high school field across the bay in hated San Francisco. The Boston nomads, as the Patriots might have been called, played their first "home" game in Birmingham, Alabama, then moved from Boston University to Fenway Park to Boston College to Harvard Stadium, where only the visiting team had a dressing room. And the WFL's Honolulu Hawaiians played in an old wooden stadium known as the "Termite Palace."[5]

Competition

The fate of new leagues is shaped largely by their ability to compete with established leagues. Rivals that mount a credible challenge win acceptance as equals or are merged into an existing league; those that cannot compete disappear. New leagues understandably prefer peace to war. The AAFC wanted an agreement with the NFL that would structure professional football along the lines of baseball, with two cooperating major leagues whose champions would play in a football equivalent of the World Series. AFL founder Lamar Hunt explored a similar arrangement with the NFL, with two leagues under a single commissioner holding a common draft of college players and blacking out television coverage of home games. Branch Rickey envisaged his Continental League coexisting with the American and National Leagues within the organizational structure of professional baseball. Established leagues, however, have little interest in cooperating with new leagues. Major leagues invariably see new leagues as rivals rather than partners, a perception enhanced by the warnings that usually accompany olive branches proffered by newcomers. Ban Johnson wished "to work in harmony with the major league," but warned that his American League would "choose our own grounds and infringe on National League territory, even without its consent, if our wishes are not respected."[6]

Existing leagues have few incentives to embrace new leagues that challenge their control over markets, compete for players and customers, dilute their dominance of a professional sport, and promise higher costs and lower profits. Established leagues want to control the number of teams and markets in their sport; they want to determine the timing of adding teams and prices of new franchises. "When we expand," explained Pete Rozelle in brushing aside rumors that some USFL teams would be taken by the NFL, "we'd want to pick our own cities and our own owners."[7] And pocket the expansion fees rather than enrich USFL owners like Donald Trump, who stood to parlay a $6 million investment in the New Jersey Generals into an NFL franchise worth $100 million or more if he was able to slip through the back door.

Existing leagues do not want to cede valuable markets to rival leagues, or share customers in established markets, or lose television viewers to a new league. NFL fears of being shut out of California's largest markets by the All-American Football Conference was a factor in the move of the Rams from Cleveland to Los Angeles. The Continental League planned to move into the most attractive open markets, which would have constrained expansion and relocation by the existing baseball leagues. By and large, however, rival leagues have not posed serious competition to most established teams in their home markets. The AAFC was routed by the NFL in New York and Chicago, and AFL owners threw in the towel in Dallas and Los Angeles. Market competition between teams of different leagues has been most intense when neither team was established in the given metropolitan area. The battle between the AAFC's Dons and the NFL's relocated Rams was especially bitter and expensive, with each side bankrolled by heavy hitters intent on winning sole possession of Los Angeles. In Dallas, the AFL's Texans and the NFL's expansion Cowboys battled for supremacy in a market that had failed to support a single professional football team a decade earlier; the fight was costly in terms of fan support, community backing, and financial losses.

Competition for players has been more troublesome for established leagues than market contests with rivals. To have any chance of being a credible major league, new leagues have to compete with existing leagues for players. The better financed the new league, the more intense the competition for quality players and the higher the costs for both leagues. Nonetheless, competition has been preferable to established leagues than cooperation, at least at the outset of a new league. The National League refused to recognize the American League as an equal, setting off a spirited battle for markets and players. Coexistence or cooperative arrangements of any kind that conferred legitimacy on the AFL were anathema to the NFL, which repeatedly rebuffed proposals for a common draft and a championship game.

Established leagues have fought new leagues with every means at their command, including efforts to lure away key franchises and owners. The National League hastened the demise of Union Association in 1884 by inducing the league's founder, who owned its best team, to jump to the established league. The American Association was fatally weakened by the shift of the Brooklyn,

Cleveland, and Pittsburgh franchises to the stronger league between 1887 and 1890. The Federal League challenge was ended by letting its most powerful owners buy into the established leagues. Once the AAFC was established, the NFL tried to end the threat by offering to admit Cleveland and San Francisco, the new league's solidest operations. Efforts were made to prevent the AFL from getting off the ground in 1960 by bringing potential AFL owners into the NFL, but the NFL was unwilling to add enough franchises to satisfy all the prospective AFL owners.

Expansion offers existing leagues another potent means of checking rivals. Creation of the AFL accelerated the NFL's planned expansion to Dallas in order to prevent the rival league from sewing up the market; and the NFL wrested Minneapolis-St. Paul from the AFL by awarding an expansion franchise to an ownership group that had already joined the upstart league. Speaking of these moves, an NFL owner claimed that "the only reason for expansion that I have heard from other owners is that we would destroy the new league."[8] In 1966, the NFL struck again, adding Atlanta after the AFL had awarded an expansion franchise to an Atlanta group. The NFL's successful gambits in Minneapolis and Atlanta underscore the advantage of existing leagues over rivals in the franchise game. The Twin Cities ownership had joined the AFL because they were unable to secure commitments for an NFL expansion team; but they strongly preferred doing business in the established NFL over the problematic AFL, and jumped at the chance to be in the real major league. For Atlantans there also was no contest between the AFL and NFL, although by 1966 the rival league was fairly well established and merger talk was in the air. Expansion has also been used by the NHL to neutralize rival leagues. The addition of six metropolitan areas in 1967 was motivated in part by the threatened challenge of the Western Hockey League, a threat made more ominous by indications that U.S. television networks were interested in the WHA's plans; and the NHL expanded to Long Island in 1972 to preempt a location coveted by the World Hockey Association.

Exclusive leases provide another weapon in the uneven wars between established and new leagues. The AFL's plans for an expansion franchise in the nation's capital were checked by the Washington Redskins, whose lease provided for a veto over the use of Robert F. Kennedy Stadium by another professional football team. A few years later, the Redskins kept the WFL out of Washington by refusing to permit the rival league to use the stadium. In New Orleans, the Saints threatened to move to Jacksonville when the Breakers of the USFL obtained a more favorable lease for the Superdome. Protests from the Chargers persuaded San Diego to deny Jack Murphy Stadium to the USFL, and opposition from the Vikings kept the USFL from playing in Minneapolis' Metrodome.

New leagues have typically responded with cries of foul play and headed for the courts, charging established leagues with violating the Sherman Act.

Judges, however, have not been very receptive to the claims of new leagues. The AFL failed to convince federal courts that the NFL exercised monopoly power by expanding into cities where the AFL planned to operate. For Judge Roszel Thomsen, the central issue was the power of the NFL to monopolize professional football, not its dominance in particular local or regional markets. He ruled that the NFL had neither prevented creation of the AFL nor expanded into markets merely to block the AFL, in the process concluding that the NFL's moves to Dallas and Minneapolis were undertaken primarily for "business" reasons rather than "an intent to destroy the new league."[9] New leagues have also had little luck in court with allegations that established teams have monopolized local markets through their control over access to arenas and stadiums.

Even when new leagues have bested their established rivals in court, victory has not guaranteed the success of these ventures. The USFL won an antitrust suit against the NFL but the outcome proved to be a mocking footnote to the history of a defunct league. The jury agreed that the NFL had operated a monopoly, but concluded that the demise of the USFL resulted from the league's failings rather than the monopolistic practices of the NFL and its television partners; instead of the $1.32 billion in damages sought by the USFL, the league was awarded $3, barely enough to buy a soft drink at an NFL game.[10] The WHA fared better in court, persuading a federal judge to enjoin the NHL from enforcing the lifetime reserve clause in players' contracts.[11] The two leagues then negotiated a settlement that paid the WHA $1.75 million, permitted the rival league to use NHL arenas, provided for exhibition games between the two leagues, and required each league to honor the other's labor contracts. But winning in court did not save the WHA, most of whose franchises were insolvent when the league was folded into the NHL in 1979.

With the notable exceptions of the American League and the Basketball Association of America, new leagues either fail or are absorbed by existing leagues. Coexistence once was the goal of new leagues; from the American Association to the American Football League, new leagues hoped to win acceptance as a second or third major league. More recently, and more realistically, merger has been the goal of new leagues and their franchise owners. The ABA, for example, was organized in 1967 as a means of securing places in the NBA. "From the outset," writes the league's president, "a strategy of conflict was conceived and designed to force a merger with the more powerful and established NBA."[12] Such strategies usually take a heavier toll on new leagues than their rivals, hastening their demise or absorption by an established league.

Existing leagues almost always determine the fate of new leagues and their teams and owners. The NFL's superior product, resources, and markets produced unconditional triumphs over the WFL and USFL. Despite strong backing in major cities and Congress, the Continental League never played a game, as baseball used its resources and staying power to prevail. Half a century earlier, the Federal League was bought out by its established rivals. In 1926, the NHL acquired the rival Western Canada Hockey League, moving one team to Detroit and distributing the rest of the defunct league's players among expansion teams in New York and Chicago. Established leagues typically dictate terms of settlement when rival leagues are merged. The AAFC, ABA, and WHA disappeared without a trace into the NFL, NBA, and NHL, as did the American Association into the National League in 1891. The AFL dealt with its established rival with a stronger hand; the league had a lucrative television contract with NBC, a growing fan base that had substantially narrowed the attendance gap between the two leagues, and a growing corps of stars led by Joe Namath, who played in New York where he attracted enormous media attention. These strengths led to the best modern merger deal, with all the AFL teams surviving, player contracts honored, and television money equally shared. Still, the AFL vanished into the National Football League, which retained its constitution, bylaws, and Commissioner Pete Rozelle.

Typically, only some teams or owners in rival leagues survive merger with an established league, usually the strongest franchises with the most powerful owners. Three of the seven surviving AAFC franchises were accepted into the NFL in 1949; a fourth team, the Buffalo Bills, was combined with the Cleveland Browns, with the Bills' owner given a 25 percent interest in the Browns. Four of the six remaining teams in the ABA were incorporated into the NBA; four of the six teams left in the WHA found spots in the NHL; and only three of eight prospective Continental League cities got teams in baseball's 1961–1962 expansion.

Surviving teams from rival leagues usually have to pay for the right to join the establishment, leaving no doubt as to who is calling the shots. AFL teams were obliged to pay $18 million to join the NFL, primarily to compensate the Giants and 49ers for infringement of their territories by the Jets and Raiders. Each ABA team shelled out $3.2 million to get into the NBA , plus compensation for the two ABA franchises that disbanded; the merged teams were also frozen out of the NBA's national television revenues for five seasons. The WHA survivors paid $7.5 million in expansion fees and indemnities to get into the NHL, as well as $1.5 million to the teams that were not included in the merger. The four clubs additionally were forced to relinquish players who had been under contract to NHL teams; and the Canadian franchises from the WHA were prohibited from sharing Canadian television money for five years.

The merger of the BAA and NBL that produced the NBA was more even-handed and involved no financial penalties. Still, the BAA was the winner, and exacted a price for its superior markets, arenas, and financial resources. Eleven of the twelve BAA teams continued into the new league, compared with only six of the ten NBL franchises. In addition, BAA owners insisted on a divisional structure and schedule that minimized the number of contests against former NBL teams, which played in small arenas and were uncertain drawing cards compared to rivals from the BAA. One team from the NBL, the Syracuse Nationals, played only ten games against eastern division rivals, while BAA teams were scheduled for twenty-six divisional games.

Risky Route to the Big Leagues

New leagues have limited appeal to places, primarily because these risky ventures provide no guarantee that a city or metropolitan area will get into the real major leagues. Rival leagues are inherently unstable; two-thirds of the new leagues organized in the twentieth century failed in two seasons or less. Even when new leagues persevere, they are usually not firmly rooted in places; teams fold or move as owners come and go, fans fail to materialize, and arenas and stadiums become available and unavailable. Over its nine seasons, the ABA had franchises in twenty locales; the league failed in metropolitan areas large and small in all parts of the country; and only four of its original eleven franchises remained in business in the same metropolitan area when the league was folded into the NBA in 1976.[13] The World Hockey Association also presented an ever-changing lineup of places during its seven seasons—twenty-five in all, with only Edmonton, Quebec, and Winnipeg staying the course. Leagues with shorter life spans, like the World Football League, were even more unstable; four of the original WFL franchises moved before the league began play in 1974; and four other charter locales were abandoned during or after the first season. In the USFL's third and last year, only one team remained in its original location with the same owner

Of the various post-World War II new leagues, the AAFC and AFL offered the most stability to places, reflecting the superior financial resources of both these leagues and the strong place connections of many owners. Only one of the AAFC's nine charter teams relocated, from Miami to Baltimore, and another in Brooklyn merged with the New York club. All eight of the charter AFL franchises survived, six in the metropolitan areas where they began; Dallas shifted to Kansas City and Los Angeles to San Diego. Still, teams in both of these leagues were tenuous residents in a number of places. The AAFC kept franchises in Chicago and Baltimore only through ownership changes and league intervention. The AFL barely managed to survive in New York, and came close to moving the Oakland Raiders to Atlanta or New Orleans.

Another problem for places is the weak local connections of many owners. Place connections are usually less important than financial resources when prospective owners are being recruited by organizers of new leagues. After plans to play in Miami fell through, the AFL gave Ralph Wilson, a wealthy native of Detroit, his pick of five cities; as he recalls, "they were Cincinnati, Buffalo, St. Louis, Louisville, and one other, I've forgotten which."[14] League promoters frequently have peddled franchises to buyers with no concern for links between owners and places where teams would play. In leagues like the WFL and WHA, weak place connections combined with underfinanced owners to increase instability, as leagues scrambled to find new owners willing to operate a team somewhere, which often was not where the team had been located under the previous owners.

Place interests are likely to be sacrificed when rival leagues make peace with the established competition. Four cities wound up without major league baseball when the National League swallowed the American Association in 1892. Peace with the Federal League sent Baltimore, Buffalo, Milwaukee, and Newark back to the minor leagues. Five of the Continental League's eight prospective locales were left waiting for big league baseball by the deals that ended the Continental threat and produced baseball's initial expansion. In return for solid fan support of the AAFC Bills, Buffalo got nothing, while the team's owner obtained a quarter interest in the Cleveland Browns.

New leagues also offer an uncertain means for places to boost their prospects for securing a team in an established league. Memphis and Birmingham hoped to translate their success in the WFL into membership in the NFL, but the NFL responded with a meaningless promise that in some indefinite future "Memphis and Birmingham . . . will be among the cities receiving strongest consideration for NFL franchises."[15] When the NFL finally expanded, Jacksonville's cause was helped by its backing of WFL and USFL teams, but Memphis lost out despite an even stronger record of support for teams in these leagues, and Birmingham never was in contention.

Liabilities and limited appeal mean new leagues attract much less political attention than franchise shifts, expansion, or existing major league teams. Places generally have not competed for franchises in new leagues, nor have they been willing to build arenas and stadiums, or offer other inducements to teams with shaky claims to major league status. Teams in new leagues have much less leverage with local officials than do established franchises, and little is heard about the economic benefits that these teams will bring to a particular city. Local politicians would much rather have a franchise in an established than an unproved league, playing against real major league opponents rather than unknown teams. In both Minneapolis-St. Paul and Atlanta, stadium officials helped insure that the NFL rather than the AFL would be playing in new public facilities.

Public involvement is most likely in places without major league teams where leaders are eager to demonstrate their readiness for the big time. Birmingham loaned $1 million to keep the USFL Stallions in business in 1985 and sustain the city's hopes for a future NFL franchise. Officials in places without teams also may decide that a team in a new league is better than nothing. Memphis agonized over embracing the WFL Southmen in 1974; the initial bid of the team to lease the city's stadium was rejected, but politicians relented after Memphis's chances for a place in the NFL appeared to fade: "We couldn't stand it any longer," explained Mayor Wyeth Chandler, "there was no assurance we wouldn't still be waiting for a team in 1990."[16]

The political attractions of teams in new leagues also depend on the league's prospects. The AAFC gained access to municipal stadiums because the league was considered a good risk due to its strong financial backing and the widespread feeling that two professional football leagues were viable and desirable. Support for the Continental League was bolstered by the strong backing of New York City, the track record of Branch Rickey who organized the league, and the seeming willingness of the baseball establishment to accept the new league and thus its member cities into the big leagues. The improving prospects of the American Football League in 1963 led Kansas City to offer a two-year rent-free stadium deal and a guarantee of 25,000 season tickets, which turned the Dallas Texans into the Kansas City Chiefs and put Kansas City on the road to a place in the NFL.

Limited local and state interest in new leagues has been reflected in Washington. New leagues have attracted less congressional attention than relocation or expansion, in substantial part because of the lack of constituency pressures to secure or save teams in most of these problematic ventures. Congress, however, has responded when concerns about new leagues have been strongly expressed. Backing for the Continental League in New York and other cities across the country was echoed in Congress, with members emphasizing the desirability of making major league baseball available to more people. Constituency concerns were also an important factor in 1966, when Congress was asked to bless the proposed merger of the AFL and NFL. Professional football emphasized that AFL cities with weak franchises such as Boston and Denver would probably lose their teams if the war between the leagues continued, with only the strongest surviving teams to be merged eventually into the NFL. In return for blessing the merger, Congress protected place interests, providing in the legislation that no areas would lose their teams, including New York and San Francisco-Oakland, which had franchises in both leagues.

Four years later basketball owners sought the same kind of antitrust protection for the merger of the ABA into the NBA in return for a promise of no reduction in the number of places with basketball franchises. But a basketball deal was less attractive to Congress, in part because place issues were less important. Professional basketball franchises were not as highly valued as football teams, resulting in relatively little constituency pressure to protect places with ABA teams. Basketball owners also had less political clout in Washington than the football barons and their network allies; and they faced determined opposition by players who had been the prime beneficiaries of interleague rivalry. Basketball legislation never was enacted, and the leagues did not merge until an agreement was hammered out with the players. Only six of the eleven cities with teams in 1970 still had franchises when the leagues merged in 1976, and two of these were left out of the eventual merger; thus, the net result of the political and legal maneuvering was to keep seven places out of the NBA.[17]

Political and legal considerations also influenced the merger of the WHA into the NHL in 1979. Antitrust scrutiny from the U.S. Department of Justice and fears of being taken to court by players in a reprise of the basketball scenario delayed the merger, as did opposition within the NHL. An agreement almost consummated in 1977 would have included all eight surviving WHA teams; two years later only four were taken.[18] Political considerations in Canada also loomed large in determining the winners among the WHA franchises; including Edmonton, Quebec, and Winnipeg among the four WHA survivors foreclosed adverse political reaction to the merger by substantially increasing the number of Canadian cities in the NHL.

Payoffs for Places

Despite the high risks, joining new leagues usually has paid off for some places and team owners. Of the 113 major league teams in 1995, 40 came from new leagues, beginning with Pittsburgh's move from the American Association to the National League in 1887. Eighteen of the 40 have been added since 1969, 10 in football, 4 in basketball, and 4 in hockey; this set of teams accounted for 16 percent of major league franchises in 1996. Fifteen metropolitan areas currently have teams that began in the AFL, ABA, and WHA. San Antonio in the NBA and Edmonton and Hartford secured their only major league team through mergers. Three of Denver's four teams came from new leagues; and one of the two major league franchises in Buffalo, Cincinnati, Indianapolis, Kansas City, and San Diego began in the AFL or ABA.

Payoffs for places have always depended heavily on the credibility and financial strength of new leagues. Places win with new leagues when an existing league recognizes that peace is preferable to continued conflict. Favorable outcomes for places have also been influenced since 1960 by the success of rival leagues in securing political backing. Places with AFL teams were the biggest winners because the political price for congressional approval of the merger was the inclusion of all the AFL teams. Conversely, political discord cost a number of places a chance to use the ABA as a back door into the NBA. And minimal political interest left the WFL and USFL with no political champions in their unequal contests with the NFL.

In addition to being back doors into the big leagues, new leagues help provide places with more front doors by stimulating expansion of established leagues. Organization of the Continental League forced baseball to face up to expansion, with the commitment to add four teams in the early 1960s resulting from an agreement with the Continentals. Support for expansion in the NFL solidified following creation of the AFL in 1959, and the pace was accelerated to claim markets targeted by the rival league. Rumblings from the Western Hockey League helped persuade the reluctant lords of the NHL to expand in 1967, and the formation of the WHA shaped expansion strategy in the 1970s. Once the ABA was in business, the NBA began to expand more rapidly, adding seven expansion franchises during the ABA's first three seasons.

This much expansion may well have occurred without new leagues, but both the pace and places would have been different. Without question, places obtained expansion franchises more quickly because of the threat of new leagues. Just when baseball would have gotten around to expanding into new markets, rather than relocating teams as was done in the 1950s, is not clear, given the reluctance of many owners to share their game with additional partners. What is certain is that the Continental League provided the essential stimulus to put expansion in motion, and thus brought major league baseball to places sooner than would otherwise have been the case. The initial locales were not the only beneficiaries of the quickened pace of expansion brought on by rivals, since other places moved into contention for future expansions more quickly than would have been the case without the spur of new leagues.

New leagues have also influenced the chances of certain individual places for expansion franchises. Minneapolis and Atlanta got inside tracks to the NFL when the league moved quickly to claim markets coveted by the AFL; and Long Island received an expansion team in a preemptive strike by the NHL against the WHA. The Continental League was promised the first four baseball expansion franchises, and priority consideration for the other four cities in future expansions. This agreement was only partially honored; the National League followed through by adding Houston and New York from the Continental's proposed lineup, but the American League took only one Continental venue. Once the Continental threat dissipated, promises of priority consideration in future expansion were worthless; none of the places on the Continental list was tapped when four teams were added in 1969.

On the other side of the coin are places whose expansion prospects have been dimmed by new leagues. Putting Minneapolis at the top of the list to check the AFL blocked other areas eager to get into the NFL, as did grabbing Atlanta ahead of the AFL in 1966. Mergers with rival leagues substantially reduce the expansion prospects of other places. After the NFL took Baltimore, Cleveland, and San Francisco from the AAFC, the league closed the door on franchise seekers in other cities, with Commissioner Bert Bell indicating that he did "not believe there will be any action on any new teams until the owners have had a chance to see how the thirteen-team league operates in 1950."[19] Nothing happened until 1960, when the NFL's hand was forced by another new league. Adding all ten AFL teams so filled the NFL that only two expansion franchises were granted between 1970 and 1993. Hosting teams in new leagues has also reduced the expansion prospects of some places. Memphis lost its chance for an NFL expansion team when the WFL moved to town in

1974, because the NFL did not want to risk a direct confrontation that could provoke a costly legal showdown with the WFL. A decade later, the NFL delayed considering expansion until the USFL case was officially closed because, as Pete Rozelle explained, "a lot of the cities we will consider are currently USFL cities" and "we don't want to give them grounds to take us back to court."[20]

Most places that entered the major leagues through the back door have held onto their teams, despite being smaller than average markets in most cases. Only two of the fourteen teams from the ABA and AFL have moved between metropolitan areas, and one of them, the Raiders, returned home to Oakland in 1995.[21] Small markets, however, have posed the most severe problems for the WHA alumni in the NHL; Hartford has been a problematic franchise in one of the smallest metropolitan areas with a major league team in the United States; and limited market size increasingly troubled the three Canadian franchises that came over from the WHA, with the league finally abandoning Quebec and Winnipeg in the mid-1990s for Denver and Phoenix.

In competition, teams from the three leagues have performed considerably better than expansion franchises, as would be expected considering the superior talent available over longer periods of time to these teams. Of the four ABA teams that joined the NBA in 1976, the Denver Nuggets won a division title and tied for the second best record in the league. The following season, San Antonio and Denver won division titles, with the Spurs posting the third best record in the NBA. Among the four WHA franchises admitted to the NHL was the Edmonton Oilers, which became one of the dominant teams in sports history. The AFL alumni in the NFL included the Miami Dolphins, winner of two of three Super Bowls and arguably the best team in professional football in the years immediately after the merger. And the earlier merger with the AAFC brought the Cleveland Browns into the NFL, winners of three league championships in their first six seasons.

New leagues thus provide some happy endings along with many sad tales of unmet payrolls, bush league facilities, teams vanishing in the night, and poorer but wiser owners of would-be major league teams. Whether more happy endings for places and players and owners are to be found in the future is less clear. Far more places are in the major leagues in 1996 than in the years when the Continental League, American Football League, American Basketball Association, and World Hockey Association were founded, which means fewer markets are available. In 1960, the AFL squared off against a twelve-team league and one network; any future competitor of the NFL faces a monolith with thirty teams in twenty-eight metropolitan markets and national contracts with five television networks worth more than a billion dollars.

14

Ballpark Figures

$\mathbf{A}$RENAS and stadiums are the focal point of the relationship between places and major league teams. Providing a major league arena or stadium is the way places demonstrate they are ready for the big time. New buildings and attractive deals are the means by which places tempt teams to relocate and compete for expansion franchises. Better facilities and deals also are at the center of efforts by places to keep teams. Arenas and stadiums consume most public investments in professional sports. And leases on playing facilities are the principal formal connection between places and major league teams, setting forth the terms under which the home team stays in town.

For teams and leagues, arenas and stadiums determine whether a metropolitan market is a suitable place to play. Seating capacity rather than size of a metropolitan area fixes the number of tickets that can be sold for any single contest. Ticket sales and revenues are further influenced by the nature of the seating—luxury boxes, good seats for season ticket buyers, closeness to the action. Attendance and revenues are affected by the amenities offered by arenas and stadiums, as well as by their accessibility and the nature of the surrounding area. Better deals reduce operating costs of teams, boost revenues, and increase profits. And the age, size, lease arrangements, and revenue potential of arenas and stadiums affect the value of franchises, as well as their appeal to potential buyers.

Arenas and stadiums, of course, are not just buildings that house the home team. They are the sites of a community's past glories and disappointments, hallowed ground where heroes wore the home team's colors, buildings redolent with memories of shared triumphs and defeats, festooned with championship banners and relics of yesterday's stars. And they play a wide range of roles beyond major league sports. Baseball parks have historically been the largest gathering place in most American cities, where people came for political rallies, religious revivals, circuses, wild west shows, boxing matches, and football games. Arenas have played a similar role, hosting political conventions, civic functions, trade shows, and charity events, as well as a wide variety of sporting contests and other entertainment. Along with these community functions, contemporary arenas and stadiums serve as dramatic instruments to renew cities, energize local economies, attract tourists, demonstrate civic cohesion, and underscore confidence in the future.

Arenas and stadiums are also symbols and civic monuments; "a city needs a big public stadium," writes James A. Michener, "because that's one of the things that distinguish a city."[1] Sports facilities reflect the desires of their builders to erect testaments to the greatness of their cities, their teams, and themselves. Ben Shibe's ballpark in Philadelphia was as an expression of the "culture, taste, and manners" of the City of Brotherly Love.[2] The Coliseum in Rome was the model for Comiskey Park in Chicago, and Jack Kent Cooke outfitted his Forum in Los Angeles with attendants in togas. "A stadium," notes Peter Richmond, "is a project to stoke the most insanely inflated egos. . . . Future generations will gauge the culture by our ballparks—which is something of a disconcerting thought."[3] Especially, one might add, when stadiums turn out to be monuments to egos run amuck, as in the case of Montreal's Olympic Stadium, locally dubbed the Big O or the Big Owe, given its huge cost overruns, repair bills, and interest burdens.

City Ballparks and Arenas

From the earliest ballparks, location, design, and size of playing facilities have reflected the interplay of urban development, technology, and the economics of professional sports. Ballparks were originally built in peripheral locations because land costs were high at the center of the booming cities with major league teams; and as these cities grew, ballpark sites moved outward. Making ballparks accessible to large numbers of spectators required locations convenient to transit lines; horsecars, then trolleys, elevated trains, and subways opened more distant locations for ballpark builders. Ballparks were typically fitted into the pattern of urban streets and land uses, which usually meant working within rectangular blocks. Field dimensions were dictated by a site's size and shape. These constraints imposed by the existing urban grid produced the unique configuration and irregular shapes of ballparks built through the first decades of the twentieth century. Short fences and high walls at Ebbets Field and Fenway Park were the consequence of city streets that had to be accommodated, and the fence at Griffiths Park in Washington jagged around five houses whose owners refused to sell to the ballpark's builders.

Before the turn of the century, ballparks were built of wood, resulting in relatively small and inexpensive facilities. Oriole Park in Baltimore, for example, was constructed in 1883 for $5,000. Low capital costs provided team owners with locational flexibility; limited investments facilitated moves as the city spread outward. The attraction of cheap construction and flexibility made baseball reluctant to build with steel and other new materials that were changing the face of the American city. But what made wooden parks attractive to owners in an era of rapid urban change marked them for extinction, as concerns for public safety mounted in the wake of fires and other disasters. One-third of the National League's parks burned in 1894 alone, and flimsy grandstands collapsed in a number of cities, leading cities to enact building and fire codes that required use of safer materials in new construction.

Beginning with Shibe Park in Philadelphia, ten fields were built with steel girders and reinforced concrete between 1909 and 1915. The new ballparks were more comfortable, with better seats, modern restrooms, and ramps instead of stairways. Nicer facilities increased the appeal of baseball to a wider audience, including more women. The new facilities were much more expensive than their predecessors; Shibe Park, with a capacity of twenty thousand, cost $500,000, compared to the $75,000 investment a few years earlier for the last big league wooden field, the sixteen thousand-seat Highlander Park in New York. All of the new parks were bigger than the wooden fields they replaced, seating twenty thousand or more, which increased revenues for heavily attended games on weekends, holidays, and during pennant races. Larger capacities also put more fans farther from the action on the field; and in comments similar to those that would greet successive changes in stadium architecture, critics complained that "the new parks 'depersonalized' the game, separated players from fans, and destroyed much of the previous era's informality when customers and athletes were cheek-by-jowl."[4] Bigger and more luxurious ballparks also divided spectators along economic and class lines, with better-off customers in box and reserved sections, while poorer fans wound up in the distant cheap seats.

From the places' point of view, the most important feature of the new ballparks was their permanence: they fixed the location of major league teams within their cities for half a century. Steel and concrete parks were too costly to abandon for better locations and newer facilities; owners would improve their fields rather than move on as they had in the past. Various additions turned Detroit's Navin Field with twenty-three thousand seats in 1912 into Briggs Stadium with a capacity of fifty-three thousand in 1938. Beginning in Cincinnati, lights were installed in all but one of the major league fields between 1935 and 1950; this was the last major improvement for most of the city ballparks.

Unlike baseball, professional football built no stadiums during its first half century. NFL teams neither needed nor could afford to construct their own facilities. They played only six home games; and no team was sufficiently profitable to provide capital for playing facilities. Unlike baseball teams, which had no alternatives to building ballparks, NFL franchises could play on someone else's field. Most performed in baseball parks; a few used college or municipal stadiums. Playing football on baseball fields, however, had many drawbacks. Ballparks were often too small for the crowds professional football attracted as the game became more popular. Spectators often had bad seats because football and baseball are strange bedfellows, difficult to accommodate in the same stadium due to differences in the shape and size of their playing areas.

Arenas, in contrast with ballparks, usually were located downtown. Arenas needed less land than ballparks, so land prices were not as significant a deterrent to central locations; and they booked more dates than baseball fields, generating revenues to offset higher land costs. Sites at the center were also desirable because most events were staged at night; patrons were drawn from the same groups that crowded downtown theaters, restaurants, and nightclubs; and downtown offered the safety of numbers and transit connections to speed customers home after a night at the arena. Boston Garden was built over a busy railroad station, and the incarnation of Madison Square Garden built in 1925 was located a few blocks from the entertainment and transit hub of Times Square.

By the end of the 1920s, when arenas were in place in most major cities, professional sport facilities were locked into urban locations—arenas downtown and ballparks along the transit lines that radiated from the center. Over the next half century, cities would change rapidly and metropolitan areas would spread people and businesses farther from ballparks and arenas. Like so much else in older cities, sports facilities became increasingly obsolete, particularly the ballparks built before World War I. Seating capacities were limited, narrow wooden seats were uncomfortable, and sightlines were restricted by the steel pillars that supported upper decks and roofs. Aging facilities were hard to clean and maintain; and maintenance and modernization were widely deferred during the lean years of the Depression and World War II.

Located to be accessible by public transportation, arenas and stadiums were poorly adapted to the automobile. Parking was inadequate in the vicinity of sports facilities in every city; and efforts to increase the supply were defeated by the lack of space in crowded city neighborhoods and the limited resources of the private companies that owned ballparks and arenas. Ebbets Field provided only seven hundred parking spaces for crowds that averaged over twenty thousand per game between 1946 and 1957. Arenas and ballparks were often inconvenient to the expressway networks that began to spread across metropolitan areas in the 1960s, forcing fans to battle traffic jams on crowded city streets in search of scarce parking spaces.

Adding to the problems of many ballparks and some arenas were locations in areas undergoing rapid physical and demographic change. Deteriorating neighborhoods with growing numbers of minority groups were not attractive places for most sports fans, more and more of whom lived in the suburbs. Lack of parking increased security concerns, forcing customers to walk long distances from their cars, as well as causing anxiety about theft or damage to vehicles. Racial change intensified these worries. By 1950, cities with major league teams were in the midst of profound changes in the racial composition of their populations. White fans became increasingly reluctant to attend games in areas with growing black populations. Riots and racial violence in the 1960s underscored the dangers of areas like the black neighborhoods surrounding Connie Mack Stadium in Philadelphia.[5] Like many other urban businesses, sports operators were sensitive to the racial concerns of their customers. Calvin Griffith made no secret of his desire to relocate out of Washington, with its large black population that he felt kept whites away from Senators' games.[6] The Dolphins left the Orange Bowl for the suburbs north of Miami in part to escape a black inner-city neighborhood.

Studies of the effect of urban racial change on professional sports have had difficulty extracting racial factors from the complex set of changes occurring concomitantly with the migration of blacks to cities. Examining baseball and basketball attendance data in the early 1970s, Roger G. Noll found black populations were associated with lower attendance. But, as Noll notes, "cities with large black population also tend to be the largest oldest cities in which the baseball stadium has inadequate parking facilities and is located in an unattractive, perhaps even dangerous, slum" and such cities are "more likely to have arenas located in downtown neighborhoods that are less attractive to fans."[7] A study of factors affecting baseball attendance from 1967 to 1987, however, did not observe the relationship reported by Noll, finding "that as the fraction of a city's total population represented by blacks increases, everything else equal, attendance at baseball games increases as well."[8] The connection between race and team relocation rather than attendance has been analyzed by Alan Sager and Arthur Culbert, who conclude that neighborhood racial composition was more important than team performance, stadium age, or attendance in predicting whether teams would relocate between 1950 and 1970.[9]

Assessing the relative influence of specific factors such as race is perhaps less important than understanding that urban change continually alters the attractiveness of professional sports facilities and their locations. Neil J. Sullivan argues that location and accessibility were more important than neighborhood decline and racial change in marginalizing Ebbets Field. For Sullivan, the survival of Yankee Stadium in an area with more deterioration but better road connections than Ebbets Field "suggests that the racial factor has been overemphasized as a threat to the stability of the Dodgers. More important was the inconvenience of getting to the park and the discomfort inside."[10] Race, accessibility, and comfort, however, were part of a larger problem for all the ballparks and arenas that succumbed to the wrecking ball. Ebbets Field was worn out and obsolete; so were Connie Mack Stadium and the Polo Grounds, which were located in or near heavily black areas, as well as Braves Field and Forbes Field, which were not. In Dallas, the Cowboys left for the suburbs because they no longer wanted to play in the Cotton Bowl for the same complex of reasons that took major league teams out of most older buildings—a deteriorating location with a growing black population where limited parking and crowded city streets produced monumental traffic jams on game days, and an aging stadium with uncomfortable seats, spartan restrooms, and outmoded facilities for teams and the press.

Urban change, racial transition, and the corrosive effects of age are usually ignored by those who decry the passing of the ballparks built early in the century. Baseball parks have a greater hold on loyalties and emotions than football arenas and stadiums, reflecting both their place in the urban firmament and the distinctiveness of the old parks. Baseball, moreover, is strongly influenced by the size and shape of its fields; teams have been built around the dimensions of ballparks; great plays could only have occurred in particular fields, such as Bobby Thomson's home run that won the 1951 pennant, which would have been an easily caught fly ball almost anywhere but in the oddly shaped Polo Grounds. Devotees of the classic parks insist that greed underlies the abandoning of the old fields, or that they "fell victim . . . to footloose teams or to the 1960s mania for round multipurpose stadiums."[11] But most of them just wore out; old ballparks, emphasizes an executive of the Detroit Tigers, who play in baseball's oldest field, are "wonderful . . . but that doesn't mean they are meant to last forever or that they can be economically feasible."[12]

From Private to Public Development

Prior to the Great Depression, big league playing facilities were private enterprises. Entrepreneurs acquired land, built ballparks and arenas, and operated them. In baseball, teams shifted from grounds rented from other private parties to building their own fields, with all clubs playing in team-owned parks by World War I. Ownership provided teams with control and security, without which they would not have been willing to invest large sums in new facilities. Private building involved acquiring substantial amounts of land, often with help from local politicians who facilitated street closings. Buying land at acceptable prices from existing owners was no simple task; Charles Ebbets quietly purchased property for his new ballpark through intermediaries, a process that took three years but kept sellers in the dark about the project and thus held down costs. Funding for privately developed ballparks and arenas came from owners, other investors, and financial institutions. Connie Smythe built Maple Leaf Gardens in downtown Toronto in 1931; he bought the land for $350,000, with the seller taking a $300,000 mortgage and $25,000 in stock in Smythe's hockey team, and borrowed $1.8 million from a bank and insurance company to build the arena.[13] Expansion and modernization also were private undertakings, which usually required additional borrowing.

The era of private development of ballparks ended with the opening of Yankee Stadium in 1923. Baseball's boom in the 1920s did not produce additional new stadiums; most parks were relatively new and represented substantial sunk costs, and land and construction prices were on the rise. Depression and war drained the resources of major league baseball, leaving no money to build new stadiums or refurbish aging ballparks. After World War II, private stadium development became more daunting, as urban land prices rose rapidly, large parcels became more difficult to assemble, and land requirements increased because of the need to provide parking.

Private unwillingness to invest in new stadiums opened the door to growing public involvement after 1950. The few existing public stadiums in large cities had been built for the Olympics rather than professional sports. Los Angeles constructed the Coliseum in a futile bid for the 1924 Olympics, but won the games in 1932, besting Cleveland and Chicago and their new stadiums.[14] Neither the Los Angeles Coliseum nor Soldier Field in Chicago would be used by professional teams until after World War II, but Cleveland's Municipal Stadium became home for the Indians in 1933, marking the first regular use of a public facility by a major league baseball team. Fans, however, were few and far between in the seventy-eight thousand-seat stadium at the depth of the Depression; and, in a harbinger of things to come, the team was dissatisfied with the city's terms for using its stadium. By 1934, the Indians were back in their private ballpark for most games, playing in the city stadium only on Sundays and holidays. Not until 1947 did the Indians again play a full schedule in Municipal Stadium, where the pennant-winning team drew a record 2.6 million customers the following year.

Cleveland's Municipal Stadium remained an anomaly until baseball's game of musical chairs was set in motion by the Braves in 1953, a series of moves prodded by construction of new stadiums by local governments. A prime attraction of Milwaukee for the Braves was a public stadium built expressly for major league sports and located on a site with substantial parking. The Braves attracted 1.8 million fans in their first season in Milwaukee, underscoring the appeal of new publicly financed facilities to other owners whose teams were playing in aging ballparks in increasingly unattractive neighborhoods with inadequate parking. A year later, the Browns moved to Baltimore and a stadium built by the city; in 1955 the Athletics went to Kansas City, where the city had turned a minor league ballpark into Municipal Stadium; and the Senators were lured to the Twin Cities in 1960 by the construction of a public stadium. Also in 1960, Candlestick Park opened in San Francisco, built by the city for the relocated Giants; it was the first of a new generation of sports facilities with no supporting posts blocking views of the action.

Successful use of public stadium development to attract teams on the move was followed by a wave of building by local governments to replace aging private parks, provide facilities for expansion teams, and modernize older stadiums. The coming of age of professional football intensified demands on governments for new stadiums, with football seeking larger facilities more suitable to the gridiron than the old ballparks. Cities also got into the arena

Table 14.1   Public and Private Facilities by League and Type: 1995

	Public	Private	Total	Percent Public
MLB	24	4	28	82.1
NFL[a]	26	3	29	90.0
NBA	20	9	29	69.0
NHL	19	7	26	73.1
Total	89	23	112	79.5
Stadiums	40	6	46	87.0
Arenas	34	11	45	75.6
Total	74	17	91	81.3

[a] Two NFL teams, the Giants and Jets, play in the same public stadium.

business, often in connection with urban renewal programs that in the United States were financed by the federal government. By 1970, close to 70 percent of the arenas and stadiums used by big league teams were publicly developed.[15] Twenty-five years later, as indicated in Table 14.1, almost 80 percent of all major league facilities had been built by government, ranging from 90 percent of all stadiums used by the NFL to more than two-thirds of NBA arenas.

For professional sports, the basic attraction of public facilities has been economic. "Build your own stadium?" exclaimed Edward Bennett Williams when he was president of the Washington Redskins; "we would never do that. The economics of stadium operation are impossible unless you have an assurance of subsidies from the city or state government."[16] Reinforcing the lure of public money has been the mounting costs of arenas and stadiums with luxury seating, spectacular scoreboards, and other state-of-the-art features, and the eagerness of governments to make public facilities available to teams on highly favorable terms in order to secure a place in the big leagues.

Public money has been particularly appealing to baseball and football, reflecting the unfavorable economics of modern stadiums with their high construction costs and limited utilization for other events. Between 1950 and 1995, only one privately financed baseball park was built, Dodger Stadium in 1962. During the same period, two private football stadiums were undertaken, for the New England Patriots in 1971 and Miami Dolphins in 1987, and another was under construction by the Carolina Cougars. Public development has been less pervasive in the case of arenas, largely because arenas are utilized more than stadiums; private arenas have been built since 1950 in Boston, Chicago, Cleveland, Detroit, Los Angeles, Minneapolis, New York, Sacramento, and Washington. Almost all of these projects, however, have been less private than the ballparks and arenas of an earlier era, as governments have acquired land, built infrastructure, subsidized loans, and provided tax concessions.

Public development of arenas and stadiums fundamentally changed relations between professional sports and places. What had been private property operated by private parties became public facilities planned, financed, built, and often managed by public agencies. Teams became tenants of governments that owned arenas and stadiums, creating a new set of relationships affecting everything from scheduling of games to relocation of teams. Inevitably, public arenas and stadiums increased the politicization of professional sports, involving teams, leagues, and their business allies with public officials and government agencies, and entangling the sports business in conflicts over spending priorities, bond issues, subsidies, and location of facilities.

Despite these fundamental changes in the connections between places and teams, the movement of government into the stadium and arena business was accomplished relatively smoothly. Although the extent and cost of governmental involvement has been contentious in many jurisdictions, the general appropriateness of public involvement has been widely accepted, most significantly by courts, which have repeatedly turned away legal challenges to public development of arenas and stadiums. Construction of Cleveland's Municipal Stadium was upheld by a state appeals court in 1930, which emphasized the widening range of facilities provided by cities for their residents.[17] The Ohio Supreme Court rejected the contention that Riverfront Stadium in Cincinnati benefited private parties rather than the public, emphasizing that because professional baseball and football were "national pastimes providing the public with a great source of relaxation and entertainment, no one could question the extent of public interest in . . . professional baseball and football teams."[18] In Colorado, Denver's purchase of Mile High Stadium was upheld by a court that was impressed by the fact that Denver was following in the footsteps of other cities that had developed professional sports facilities.[19]

Public development has been accompanied by significant changes in the location of professional sports facilities, particularly in siting of stadiums. In part, these shifts reflected the sweeping urban changes that occurred during the surge of public stadium development after 1950. The new stadium builders sought locations with space for parking and easy access to the metropolitan highway network, which put many new facilities in peripheral locations within cities or at suburban sites astride the expressway system. With governments in the picture, however, local boundaries mattered more than would have been the case if professional teams had continued to develop their facilities privately. Cities built stadiums within city limits, while other jurisdictions were only interested in sites inside their boundaries.

Location has been further affected by the widespread desire of local governments to use arenas and stadiums to stimulate economic development. The logic of land costs and space needs had steadily moved ballparks away from the center of cities, and the spreading metropolis of the automotive age should have accelerated this process. New public arenas and stadiums in many cities, however, have been coupled to downtown development plans, resulting in locations that primarily advance a city's political and economic development ends rather than sports facility needs. Baltimore insisted that its new stadiums be downtown, despite consultants' studies that recommended peripheral locations with better highway connections and more space for parking. Buffalo's Crossroads Arena was sited to serve as a centerpiece in the rebirth of the Lake Erie waterfront adjacent to downtown. Without public development, there would be hardly any stadiums downtown, fewer arenas in the center of the city, and a smaller number of professional sports facilities within the city limits.

Financing Public Sports Facilities

Like other large public works, arenas and stadiums are funded with long-term borrowing. Bonds for public sports facilities are backed by the general tax base of the borrowing jurisdiction, specific taxes dedicated to pay off the loans, or revenues generated by a stadium or arena. Revenue bonds have been more commonly used than general obligation borrowing because they have no direct impact on local budgets and taxes, and because they usually do not require voter approval. Most public sports projects in the United States have been financed by tax-exempt bonds, which offer lower interest rates than private borrowing since dividends are exempt from federal taxes.

The first wave of public stadium building in the 1950s was based on a relatively simple model featuring tax-exempt revenue or general obligation bonds. By the 1990s, nothing was simple about financing public sports facilities. Tax exemptions for state and local borrowing for activities that primarily benefited private industry have come under increasing attack in Washington; and the Tax Reform Act of 1986 restricted exemptions for the type of bonds used to finance many sports facilities. Just the threat of an absolute ban on the use of tax-exempt securities for professional sports facilities in 1996 was sufficient to cause Nashville to postpone a $60-million bond issue for a new stadium for the relocating Houston Oilers because buyers could not be assured of tax-exempt income.[20] General obligation bonds have been used infrequently for public arenas or stadiums since the 1970s because of opposition to government spending in general and sports projects in particular. Borrowing backed by rent and other stadium income has been squeezed by insistent demands by teams for more favorable deals that reduce the revenues available to underwrite bonds.

The need for additional funds to finance public sports facilities has caused government to turn to a wide range of taxes and other revenue sources. Taxes on hotels, restaurants, and bars have been most popular because purveyors of lodging, food, and drink presumably are prime beneficiaries of professional sports; and these taxes have the added political benefit of being borne in part by visitors rather than local taxpayers. The Louisiana Superdome is partially financed by a 4 percent hotel-motel tax; borrowing for the Metrodome in Minneapolis was backed by taxes on lodgings and liquor by the drink; a 1 percent tax on restaurant and bar bills provided funding for the Hoosier Dome in Indianapolis; half the cost of the Orlando Arena came from a resort tax; and Phoenix increased its hotel levy and added a tax on rental cars to finance the city's share of the America West Arena. Hotel guests and restaurant patrons throughout Illinois were taxed to underwrite state bonds for the White Sox's new park. In Cleveland, special taxes on cigarettes and alcohol are dedicated to financing Jacobs Field and Gund Arena.

Other jurisdictions, mindful of the political problems in any increased tax. burdens, have looked to alternative revenue sources. Lotteries appeal to sports builders, as to governments more generally, because they offer revenues without increasing taxes. Maryland underwrote bonds for stadiums in Baltimore with proceeds of a special state lottery that was raising almost $27 million by 1994. Another way of avoiding the pain of increased taxes is to couple stadium and arena building to public activities that generate surplus revenues. In New Jersey, construction of Giants Stadium was financed by revenues from a race track developed as part of the state's sports complex.

Escalating costs and mounting political opposition to public spending in recent years has turned the search for funds to nongovernmental sources. Foundations with strong local connections and communal commitments were key elements in the financing of sports facilities in Indianapolis and Milwaukee. The Lilly Foundation contributed $25 million to help launch the Hoosier Dome, and the Bradley Foundation underwrote a new arena in Milwaukee. Direct private investment in public sports facilities has become increasingly common, usually with funds invested by private parties that secure a direct benefit from a stadium or arena. Anheuser-Busch provided $5 million for the stadium built by St. Louis in 1966 for the company's baseball team. Increasingly, teams are participating in joint ventures with government; the Phoenix Suns, for example, took a sizable equity share in the America West Arena, which it operates under a forty-year lease with the city.

Part of what Anheuser-Busch got for $5 million in St. Louis was its name on Busch Stadium, a practice which has become an important source of private revenues for public sports facilities. In Cleveland, Richard Jacobs, the owner of the Indians, anted up $13.8 million for the privilege of having his name on the city's new ballpark. The naming of Busch Stadium and Jacobs Field underscores the transformation of professional sports facilities; once owners like Charles Ebbets and Ben Shibe put their names on ballparks they built, now owners buy naming rights from public agencies that develop their stadiums. Other companies have invested in public arenas and stadiums in return for concessions, advertising space, and exclusive marketing rights. In Toronto, $75 million was raised from fifteen corporations that paid $5 million each for a piece of the action at the SkyDome; and additional private funds came from sale of $15 million worth of sponsorship tiles on a "Wall of Fame."

Private funds can also be tapped by selling rights to seats in advance of construction or dedicating these revenues to underwrite borrowing for a stadium or arena. Seats first were sold to finance Texas Stadium, built for the Dallas Cowboys in 1971; purchasers of season tickets had to buy a $250 revenue bond issued by the local government, with those acquiring seats between the thirty-yard lines required to buy four bonds; the scheme raised $15 million for the $25 million stadium.[21] As other revenue sources have become politically more difficult to tap, selling seats has become an increasingly attractive means of underwriting both public and private sports projects.

More private funding and other innovative financing has not been sufficient to make most public sports facilities profitable operations. Some do not generate enough revenue to pay their operating costs, much less contribute to payments on interest and principal. Those public arenas and stadiums whose revenue exceeds operating expenses often fall short of covering amortization of their debt.[22] Deficits increase the public burdens of sports facilities; someone has to make up the difference, typically taxpayers in the jurisdiction that took on the risk of a stadium or arena. Similarly, when special taxes or lottery proceeds or other income sources do not close gaps between revenues and total costs, additional public funds have to be found, usually in the form of higher taxes of one kind or another.

Public arenas and stadiums require subsidies for a number of reasons. Major league sports facilities are expensive to build and difficult to utilize sufficiently to cover full costs. A stadium with both baseball and football teams has games on fewer than ninety dates; additional tenants are hard to attract to most stadiums, and often are limited by team controls over use during the playing season. Unprofitable operations also result from the superior bargaining position of teams, which reduces revenues and leads to increasingly expensive public investments to keep or attract teams. Competition among places for teams further reduces income and drives up the costs of major league facilities. Using arenas and stadiums to promote the local economy or downtown renewal often boosts costs by dictating sites that are expensive to acquire and develop. Edifice complexes and monumental desires can mean additional millions so that a particular city can boast the biggest or best arena or dome or whatever. Costs are also driven up by inefficient public management of sports facilities, padding sports agencies with patronage jobs, and inflated payments to politically connected suppliers of goods and services to public arenas and stadiums.

Precarious finances reinforce the dependence of places on teams that use their arenas and stadiums. Professional teams provide the lion's share of revenue for stadiums and a sizable portion of arena income; replacing teams with tenants who can generate comparable income from rent and concessions is almost impossible, especially for stadiums. As a result, losing these primary tenants risks substantial increases in the financial burdens on places and their taxpayers. The Rams' move to Anaheim, for example, cost the Los Angeles Coliseum over $700,000 in rent and concession revenues. This imperative need for teams to generate revenues further weakens the bargaining position of places with teams, and the outcome of these unequal contests typically increases the shortfall between revenues and costs for public sports facilities.

Not So Binding Ties

Leases on playing facilities are the principal legal ties between teams and places. Wide variations exist in leases among places and from sport to sport, reflecting differences among facilities in age, size, cost, and financing arrangements, as well as when the lease was negotiated and the bargaining skills of the contracting parties. Leases have become increasingly complicated, a consequence of the widening range of connections between teams and places.

Basically, leases set the price a team will pay to use a facility over a specified period. The simplest arrangements are straight rentals, with the lease specifying a fixed rent to be paid for a stadium or arena, either per game or for a season. Few sports facilities, however, are leased in this manner any longer; instead, leases combine rental arrangements with allocation of revenues from concessions, parking, advertising, and special seating. Most contemporary rental agreements involve a percentage of gate revenues rather than fixed payments. Stadium rents are often conditioned on attendance, particularly in baseball leases. Rents also can vary over the life of a lease, with rates increasing or decreasing over time. Duration and attendance variables can be combined, as in the White Sox's agreement with the Illinois Sports Facilities Authority. For half of the twenty-year lease on Comiskey Park, the team retained all ticket revenues for the first 1.2 million in attendance, and paid the authority $2.50 for each additional seat sold up to 2 million and $1.50 for each seat over 2 million; during the remainder of the lease, the team will pay $4.00 for each ticket between 1.5 and 2 million, and the same $1.50 for each seat over 2 million. Similar variations and complications govern sharing of concessions, luxury seating, and other stadium and arena revenues. Additional variations in financial relationships result from the division of responsibilities for maintaining and operating facilities, which can significantly affect the balance sheets for both parties. Leases that provide for team operation of an arena or stadium usually increase team revenues from concessions, as well as provide additional income from other events.

Leases bind a team to an arena or stadium for a fixed number of years, anywhere from year-to-year arrangements to as much as ninety-nine years in the Penguins' contract for the Pittsburgh Civic Center, although no other recent lease exceeds forty years.[23] Leases often have shorter lives than their formal duration. Renegotiations leading to new leases are common, as the result of renovations of existing buildings, construction of new facilities, and demands from teams for better deals. Many leases include buyout clauses, which free a team from an agreement if it pays whatever amounts are specified in the lease—in effect, setting a fee that a team has to pay its landlord to move. Duration of leases also may be conditioned, with a team being released from its commitment if specified attendance levels are not met or promised improvements in the facility not undertaken by the landlord. The Twins' lease on the Metrodome permitted the team to opt out of the agreement if attendance fell below 1.4 million during three straight seasons, a provision that triggered a serious effort to move the franchise to Tampa in 1984.

Terms for leases are determined by negotiations rather than set by market forces. Typically there is one seller, the owner of a arena or stadium, and one purchaser, a major league team with a franchise to operate in a particular territory. Given the circumstances in which leases are typically negotiated, Benjamin A. Okner concludes that "there are few guidelines for what the resulting price will or should be."[24] Teams and places, however, do not negotiate in a vacuum; instead they bargain within the context of what other teams are paying for their facilities and what other places are charging for their arenas and stadiums. Teams argue that their outlays for playing facilities have to be comparable with prices that other teams in their league are paying. "Something has to be done about the Bills' lease," the team's owner insisted in 1989, or the franchise would "not be able to compete financially with others in the league."[25] The result is an approximation of a market, in which lease terms reflect the scarcity of teams, interdependence of teams in a league, control over the supply of teams by leagues, and competition among places for major league franchises, all of which tend to drive prices down.

In this competitive context, places seek leases that provide the most revenues for the longest period of time. The minimal goal for most public sports facilities is to cover operating costs. For places, a better lease would underwrite debt service as well as operating costs, and an optimal deal would cover all governmental outlays for arenas or stadiums, including infrastructure investments and tax revenues forfeited by public use of the site. In practice, places rarely try to recover full costs, and most accept the need to subsidize all or part of their outlays for debt service. Governments are willing to subsidize arenas and stadiums to be competitive with other places, and because they desire the benefits commonly associated with major league teams and want to advance development goals.

Duration of leases is often more important for places than the rental price. In 1995, New Jersey's stadium authority offered the Giants and Jets $1 million cuts in annual rental payments in exchange for ten-year lease extensions. Long leases offer the best means of keeping a team, which is the prime reason why governments build arenas and stadiums; they also provide assurance that revenues from a major league tenant will be available over much or all of the life of the bonds that financed the facility. Extensive leases cannot provide absolute protection, given the use of buyout clauses and other escape hatches, as well as the possibility of teams successfully contesting leases in court.

Nonetheless, long leases clearly offer more protection than short ones. In Oakland, a long-term lease kept the Athletics from being moved to Denver in 1977; Charles O. Finley, as Bowie Kuhn notes, "was not . . . able to sell the club to anybody away from Oakland without the consent of his landlord, the Oakland-Alameda Coliseum."[26] Insistence on a long lease, however, can be risky, particularly with footloose owners or teams with attractive alternatives. Officials in Kansas City were unwilling to begin construction of a new stadium without a long-term contract with the Athletics, which was unacceptable to Finley and contributed to his move to Oakland. Al Davis' refusal to sign a long-term lease, which Oakland officials demanded in return for stadium improvements, helped propel the Raiders to Los Angeles.

Teams increasingly bargain for short-term leases as protection against uncertainties in the rapidly changing world of professional sports. A long lease like the Washington Redskins' thirty-year commitment to Robert F. Kennedy Stadium, for example, bound the team to one of the smallest stadiums in the league, no share of concessions, and no luxury boxes. Commissioner Peter Ueberroth wanted leases no longer than seven years because of the difficulty of knowing what baseball's financial conditions would be in the future. Such league concerns provide teams with a weapon to use in bargaining for short leases; in declining to sign a thirty-year extension in 1987 in return for additional city investments in Yankee Stadium and its surroundings, George Steinbrenner indicated that Ueberroth "told us he would not approve any extraordinarily long leases, and certainly thirty years is a long lease."[27] Shorter leases also offer teams a means of taking advantage of opportunities to move elsewhere, or improve facilities, or lower arena or stadium costs. The more frequent the expiration of a lease, the more options and choices for a team. "When you have that situation," explains the owner of the Atlanta Falcons, "you hear from all kinds of people" in cities that "would like to have NFL teams."[28] And since shorter commitments increase a team's bargaining leverage, either in its present location or a greener pasture, such leases boost the selling price of a franchise should an owner decide to sell.

Teams also press for low rents and as much arena or stadium revenue as possible. Better deals on facilities reduce operating costs, increase the prospects for profits, and enhance the value of franchises. Noll questioned the importance of arena and stadium costs to teams in 1974, emphasizing that "rents are a relatively small part of expenses for most teams."[29] Rents remain a fairly minor element in team finances, but facility revenues have become increasingly important, particularly revenues from luxury seating, concessions, and state-of-the-art advertising. "As the cost of new or purchased franchises rises," notes a 1991 appraisal of the sports business, "owners are coming to realize that it's not whether you win or lose, but how you raise cash flow per seat that counts."[30]

Negotiations increasingly tend to result in leases in which teams achieve more of their objectives than places. The threat to move is a key element in bargaining over stadiums and leases, and enough teams have moved to make the threat real. League control over the supply of teams reinforces the advantage of mobility, since arenas or stadiums cannot easily replace a footloose team. Competition among places further enhances the bargaining leverage of teams by providing lower-cost alternatives, particularly among places that compete for expansion franchises. In Denver, prospective owners of an expansion team successfully argued that a favorable lease was critical to their ability to finance the team, and thus to Denver's chances to get in major league baseball. The result was a rent-free deal on Mile High Stadium for the owners, as well as almost all of the concessions income and a new stadium built by taxpayers to be leased under even more generous terms.

Over time, the cumulative effect of these negotiating advantages has produced leases of shorter duration that give teams control over more revenues. Stadium leases executed in the 1960s averaged 34.0 years for NFL teams and 30.8 years for baseball teams, compared with 13.5 and 10.2 years in the 1980s.[31] Rental and revenue sharing arrangements have become more and more favorable to teams, with gate revenues shared only if teams reach ever higher attendance thresholds, if at all. Teams have also successfully bargained for more concessions, parking, and other revenues generated by their home arena or stadium, as well as complete control over use and operation of public sports facilities.

The bargaining advantage of teams over places makes almost anything negotiable, rendering both the terms and length of leases less durable than they might appear. Leases are routinely renegotiated when teams seek improved facilities or more advantageous deals, often under real or implied threats of relocation. New owners frequently press for revised leases, arguing that more public help is needed given the high price that was paid for a team, and suggesting that they will have no choice but to look elsewhere unless they get a better deal. After purchasing the New York Yankees in 1973, George Steinbrenner insisted on a new lease with New York City for Yankee Stadium that permitted the team to maintain the ballpark, essentially without city supervision, and then deduct the maintenance costs from the rent due the city—an arrangement that resulted in the city owing the Yankees money in some years. When Mayor Edward Koch complained that the arrangement was unfair, Steinbrenner responded that "a lease is a lease."[32] Until a team demands a new lease.

Leases inevitably cause friction as parties with sharply different objectives bargain over substantial sums of money and control of public facilities in negotiations whose outcome may determine whether a place remains in the big leagues. Conflict is exacerbated by the superior bargaining position of teams in most negotiations, which increases the pressure on public officials and animosity toward team owners. Friction also results from the increasingly complex provisions of leases, involving joint operations, revenue-sharing formulas, and detailed conditions. In Cincinnati, both the Bengals and the Reds have sued the city in lease disputes over maintenance, luxury boxes, and improvements for Riverfront Stadium. Conflict has also been frequent in Pittsburgh, where the city and the Steelers have sued each other over lease differences, and the Pirates went to court in 1993 because of dissatisfaction with the maintenance of Three Rivers Stadium, in a move designed to pressure the city to agree to a more favorable lease.

Open conflict, however, is a risky path for places dealing with restless teams backed by sympathetic leagues. The Bengals responded to Cincinnati's refusal to renegotiate or enlarge or replace Riverfront Stadium by making serious noises about moving. Caught between footloose teams and competition from other places, officials who control sports facilities usually make concessions to keep their teams. After agreeing to spend $73 million to rebuild the Seattle Center Coliseum under a new fifteen-year lease highly favorable to the Super-Sonics, Mayor Norman Rice bravely heralded the outcome as "a great deal for the city, and a great deal for the taxpayers."[33] The really great deal was for the SuperSonics, and such deals are becoming ever more costly as teams seek newer, bigger, and better playing facilities.

15

Newer, Bigger, Better

THE RELATIONSHIP between places and professional sports is increasingly driven by the desire of teams and leagues for new arenas and stadiums. Underlying these demands is the accelerating obsolescence of existing facilities. Larger arenas and football stadiums, reinvention of the ballpark, premium seating and luxury boxes, better food, more bathrooms, and state-of-art technology have steadily widened the gap between old and new buildings, shortened the life span of facilities, and increased pressures on places to build new sports palaces. Decisions about adequacy of arenas and stadiums are made by teams and leagues. Places with teams respond to these decisions, devising plans that they hope will satisfy the home team; places without teams seek to provide the newer, bigger, and better facilities desired by teams and leagues.

Rapid Obsolescence

Economic obsolescence is more important than physical aging to teams and leagues. New arenas and football stadiums are bigger, which means larger sellouts and more gate revenues; premium seating generates more income, as do fancy stadium clubs, restaurants, better concessions, more parking, and ancillary facilities like amusement areas and shopping arcades. Twenty years after Atlanta-Fulton County Stadium was built in 1965, the Falcons' owner insisted the stadium was economically outmoded; "we're playing in the second-oldest stadium in the NFC in a division against teams that can generate $5 million to $6 million more per year in gate revenues than we can. We can't compete on that basis."[1] New arenas and stadiums are also seen as necessary in the competition with other sports; "baseball and basketball have been very aggressive with stadiums and have created new levels of expectations among fans," noted NFL Commissioner Paul J. Tagliabue in 1995, "we have to be responsive to that."[2] Comfortable seats in place of wooden benches, concessionaires peddling crab cakes as well as hot dogs, electronic razzle dazzle in place of minimal score boards—all are part of a total package in new wrappings designed to increase team and league revenues.

New facilities are strongly preferred because modernization of aging arenas and stadiums is difficult and costly, and the final product is rarely comparable with the newest state-of-the-art building. A renovated facility remains in its original location, which often means inadequate parking and poor highway connections, as well as a less desirable locale than can be had by starting anew. Yankee Stadium was rebuilt in the 1970s with bigger seats, unobstructed views, luxury boxes, nicer concessions and a stadium club, ramps and elevators, new press facilities, and a lowered field to improve sight lines. The result was a modernized stadium and preservation of a physical link with a glorious past, but the project cost New York City over $100 million, the stadium still lacked parking, and the surrounding neighborhood remained unappealing to most customers. The Yankees continued to want a new stadium in a better location with more premium seats, lots of parking, and better highway connections.

Over half of the major league facilities in use in 1995 were constructed in the 1960s and 1970s. Development of new arenas and stadiums slacked a bit in the 1980s, a decade of limited expansion and a time when most teams were in relatively new facilities. The pace picked up in the 1990s, as most of the remaining pre-1960 facilities were replaced, expansion accelerated, and demands escalated for state-of-the-art arenas and stadiums. The effect of new construction, along with expansion and relocation, is shown in Figure 15.1, which tracks the median age of playing facilities between 1950 and 1995. The building boom and growth of leagues sharply reduced the median age of facilities during the 1960s and early 1970s; thereafter, median age crept upward. The advancing age of the typical major league building, combined with accelerating economic obsolescence, underlies the rising demand for new facilities in all four sports in the 1990s, a demand that between 1993 and 1995 resulted in almost $7 billion in investments and commitments for sports facilities.[3]

More Seats

Bigger arenas and stadiums generally are a prime attraction for teams and leagues. A larger building with higher seating capacity means more revenue, especially for the substantial number of teams that sell out all or most of their games. Teams that play at or near capacity in smaller arenas and stadiums chafe at the revenue disadvantage imposed by the size of their buildings. The Miami Heat pressed for a bigger facility soon after joining the NBA, claiming that Miami Arena, opened in 1988 with 15,200 seats, was too small to generate sufficient revenues for the team to be competitive with franchises in larger buildings. In the NFL, small facilities have a substantial effect on the revenues of all teams, since visitors get 40 percent of the gate. The collective interest in

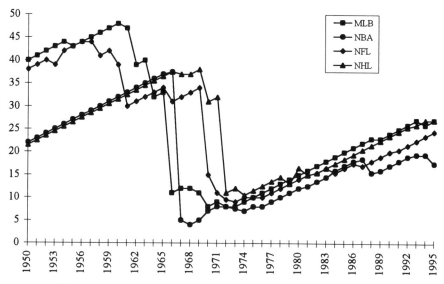

Figure 15.1   Median Age of Playing Facilities by League: 1950–1995

larger capacities was reflected in the NFL's boosting its minimum stadium size to 55,000 after the merger with the AFL in 1970 and to 70,000 in the mid-1980s.

The desire for more seats has been a key factor in the quest of most NFL teams for new stadiums, as well as an important consideration in relocation. All stadiums built since 1970 have substantially increased seating capacities, which has intensified pressures for bigger facilities in those places that have stood pat. The Washington Redskins doggedly sought a new stadium to replace Robert F. Kennedy Stadium, ruing the lost revenues from thousands of would-be customers who could not be accommodated in the NFL's smallest facility. The Cardinals justified moving to Phoenix on the unwillingness of St. Louis to replace Busch Stadium with a larger building, although the woeful Cardinals were barely filling half the 54,392 seats in their last years in St. Louis. More seats in a new stadium helped move the Giants and Jets from New York City to New Jersey, and the increased capacity of the Georgia Dome over Atlanta-Fulton County Stadium kept the Falcons in Atlanta.

Stadium size is less important in baseball, where full houses are infrequent. Smaller stadiums also get more people close to the action, which is concentrated at home plate, and place fewer people in less desirable seats in the distant reaches of the outfield. Smaller parks also increase demand for season tickets and advance sales by customers who want to insure that they will be able to go to games and have good seats. The preference of baseball for smaller stadiums is strikingly underscored by the new wave of ballparks built in the 1990s, whose average capacity is nine thousand less than those constructed in the 1960s. New football stadiums, on the other hand, are larger than those built in the previous three decades and new arenas have steadily increased seating capacities for basketball and hockey games.

A Home of Our Own

All twelve public stadiums built for major league teams between 1960 and 1971 were developed for use by baseball and football. Multi-use designs were dictated by public considerations rather than the desires of baseball or football teams. Dual-purpose stadiums generate more revenue than single-purpose facilities, and a single structure costs less to build and operate than a pair of stadiums. In Philadelphia, the Phillies pressed the city for a new ballpark rather than a multipurpose stadium, offering to share in financing the field, but city officials insisted on a facility that would house the Phillies and Eagles at less public cost than separate baseball and football fields.

Joint use of stadiums is an inherently unstable arrangement laden with potential conflict. Differences arise over leases, shares of concessions, premium seating, scheduling, and control over the playing field. Historically, baseball teams controlled the use of shared ballparks, which limited the dates available to NFL teams at the start of the football season. They also drove hard bargains with respect to ancillary revenues; the Detroit Tigers, for example, took all the concessions income when the Lions played in their ballpark. As prime tenants in the new public multipurpose stadiums, baseball usually had better deals on leases and concessions, as well as control over scheduling. In New York, the Mets did not permit the Jets to play in Shea Stadium until the end of the baseball season, which forced the football team on the road for its first three to five games and required it to schedule most home games in the latter part of the season, when bad weather was more likely.

Co-tenancy has been just as problematic when football teams control stadiums. In Cleveland, where the Browns operated Municipal Stadium, the Indians were unhappy tenants whose pressures for a better deal created what the Browns' owner decried as "an adversary relationship between our two organizations" in which "mutual trust and understanding is nonexistent."[4] The Indians responded in 1983 by suing the Browns, claiming that the team had been shortchanged on concessions revenues to the tune of $1.25 million over ten years. Concerns over control have mounted with lengthening seasons and rising financial stakes. The Colts moved in part to get out of co-tenancy with the Orioles; and the Falcons secured a new football stadium after threatening to leave Atlanta unless they had a place to play that did not have to be shared with the Braves.

Multipurpose stadiums also pose intractable design problems because of the different sizes, shapes, and focal points of baseball and football fields. Circular or square buildings placed too many seats for baseball in the outfield, or too far from the foul lines, or with poor sight lines to action concentrated at home plate. Round stadiums left NFL fans with midfield seats, normally the choice location for football, at a considerable distance from the playing field. Multiuse stadiums large enough for football were too big for baseball, resulting in much less intimate settings than the old ballparks. Most of these compromises were artistic failures—bland, poured concrete structures lacking distinctiveness or sense of place; the stadiums in Cincinnati, Philadelphia, Pittsburgh, and St. Louis create the impression that almost identical flying saucers landed in the middle of a parking lot in each city.

Another problem with dual-purpose stadiums for baseball has been the widespread use of artificial turf following its introduction in the Astrodome in 1965. Artificial turf has strong appeal for operators of multipurpose facilities, increasing utilization and reducing maintenance costs. But baseball is a different game on a rug, with less bunting, more ground ball singles, and more balls hit between the outfielders or over the fence on a bounce. By the 1990s, baseball was expressing a strong preference for grass fields, and governments responded by building new ballparks with natural playing surfaces. The NFL has been more comfortable with artificial turf despite the higher risk of injury on fake fields; every new NFL stadium since 1970, except for the privately developed Joe Robbie Stadium, was built with an artificial playing surface.

Dissatisfaction with shared facilities has generated demands for new stadiums used exclusively for one sport. Teams want stadiums built to their specifications, with control over the building and its revenues. Leagues have added to the pressures for exclusive stadiums; Commissioner Peter Ueberroth declared in 1985 that baseball's objective was that "we not share stadiums any more, with anybody. I'd convert all the baseball stadiums in major league cities. . . . They would not be multipurpose stadiums."[5] Teams have resisted plans for new shared facilities; in Chicago, neither baseball team wanted to play in a multipurpose dome promoted by the city. Despite the understandable preference of public officials for multipurpose stadiums, places generally have been responsive to the growing pressures for exclusive stadiums. Kansas City was first with separate public stadiums, constructing Arrowhead Stadium and Royals Stadium in 1972–1973. By 1995, only ten public stadiums were jointly used by baseball and football, and pressures for separate facilities were pushing most of these places toward construction of new ballparks or football stadiums or both.

The most striking consequence of the desire for exclusive use has been the reinvention of the ballpark. No longer required to accommodate football, architects have designed baseball stadiums inspired by the old ballparks. Smaller than multipurpose stadiums, with grass fields and irregular dimensions and seats closer to the field, the new parks have the feel of the old, with all the conveniences and revenue producers of the new. The breakthrough came with Baltimore's Camden Yards in 1992, a modern stadium with luxury boxes, premium seating, and spiffy concessions, but reeking in nostalgia for Ebbets Field and Wrigley Field. The new facility for the Texas Rangers lacked Camden Yard's dramatic backdrop of downtown Baltimore, but the Ballpark in Arlington was another pleasing blend of old and new, with an odd-shaped playing area, right-field bleachers modeled on Tiger Stadium, and roof trusses suggestive of Yankee Stadium. Cleveland's Jacobs Field was a more modern rendition of these nostalgic themes, with the downtown skyline beyond the bleachers. Coors Field in Denver presented a western version of the old brick ballpark in modern guise, with spectators looking over the field at the Rocky Mountains looming through the urban haze. And similar combinations of the old and new were in the works by 1996 in Atlanta, Cincinnati, Detroit, Phoenix, San Francisco, and Seattle.

Camden Yards and its progeny marked a new age for the ballpark, as sharp a break from the past as the steel and concrete parks of the first decades of the century and the concrete multipurpose stadiums of the 1960s and 1970s. One architectural critic saw the new stadiums as a rebirth of the ballpark as monument, "a place in which baseball and the idea of civic architecture come together."[6] The new ballparks also reflected the ability of teams to get what they wanted from government: exclusive use of new public stadiums built to their specifications, typically controlled by the team, and leased under highly favorable terms. And the success of these new stadiums insured that other places would face strong pressures to build even better ballparks for their teams, or risk losing them to places that would.

Basketball and hockey coexist more comfortably than baseball and football in the same building. Playing areas are the same general shape, which means that most seats in arenas afford similar sight lines for basketball and hockey. To be sure, a basketball court is smaller than the playing surface for hockey, but the design compromises needed to accommodate the two sports are minor compared to fitting baseball and football in one structure. In 1995, ten of the fourteen locales with teams in the NBA and NHL shared arenas, and three of the four with separate arenas involved teams that played in different parts of large metropolitan areas. By contrast, only eleven of the twenty-two possible pairs of baseball and football teams shared a stadium in 1996, and most of these teams would be in separate facilities by the turn of the century.

State-of-the-Art Facilities

The Astrodome in Houston, opened in 1965 as the self-styled eighth wonder of the world, was the first of a new kind of sports facility in which the building was as much of an attraction as the team—or perhaps more, in light of the mediocre teams that often performed in Houston's dome. The Astrodome set off a wave of dome fever in its wake, as city after city unveiled plans for their own version of a domed wonder. For a time, scale models of domed stadiums were part of the decoration of many mayoral offices, symbols of a city being reborn or bound for the big leagues. For places without teams, domes were promoted as a sure ticket to the big time; "you have to start with a dome," advised a booster of the Hoosier Dome, "that's the key."[7] In addition to their monumental appeal, domes offered cities all-weather facilities that could be utilized more frequently than open-air stadiums. Playing inside air-conditioned or heated buildings meant protection from Seattle's rain, the heat and humidity of New Orleans, and cold and snow in Minneapolis. More like arenas than stadiums, domes could also be used for trade shows, conventions, concerts, tractor pulls, and other events.

Despite these attractions, far more domes have been discussed than completed; only one of eleven domes reported under consideration in 1984 was built, the Suncoast Dome in St. Petersburg.[8] In 1996, only ten domed stadiums housed baseball or football teams; the teams playing in these facilities accounted for fewer than 20 percent of all baseball and football franchises. Domes compounded design problems for dual-use facilities because of the size constraints imposed by a closed stadium. Multipurpose domes have also been victims of the preference of baseball and football for exclusive facilities. Only two domes—the Kingdome and the Metrodome—sheltered baseball and football teams in 1996, and both were going to lose one or both tenants before the end of the century. Domed stadiums have also lost favor because baseball is a different game inside, one that few would argue is better than the outdoor variety. Lighting and air currents detract from the game, as do roof trusses and loudspeakers that intrude on the playing field. Limited playing area in Minneapolis and Seattle made both stadiums hitters' paradises, with the Metrodome earning the dubious sobriquet of the Homer Dome. "The park should be banned from baseball," was the succinct verdict of a manager of the Minnesota Twins.[9]

Domes have had more than their share of design and construction problems. Roofs that leak, blow away, or collapse have not enhanced the appeal or reliability of domed stadiums. Problems with roofs have led to cancellation of baseball games in Montreal and Seattle, and relocation of the entire home schedule of the Seattle Seahawks in 1994. The Kingdome's flaws also provided an opening for the team's owner to terminate the club's lease in order to move the Seahawks. Kenneth Behring claimed that the threat of earthquake invalidated his lease, although his planned move to Los Angeles, hardly the place to go to lessen earthquake risks, did not enhance his credibility. Behring was kept in town by legal action and opposition within the NFL, leading him to sell the team to a local buyer; the purchase was conditional on a satisfactory solution of stadium issues. In all likelihood, the result would be a new facility for the Seahawks in addition to the one already in the works for the Mariners, and the doom of another drab dome.

Retractable roofs added the promise of flexibility to the allure of domes, permitting games to be played inside or out depending on the weather. But the first retractable dome used by a major league team, Montreal's Olympic Stadium, was both extremely expensive and impractical, resulting rather in an intractable dome. More successful has been Toronto's SkyDome, which opened in 1989 as the centerpiece of a $300 million entertainment complex featuring a luxury hotel with suites overlooking the field, a three-tiered restaurant with views of the playing area, health club, miniature golf, multiplex movie theater, and shopping mall. Retractable roofs were incorporated in the retro ballparks designed for Seattle and Phoenix's 1998 expansion team, and were featured in proposals for new ballparks in a number of other cities.

The SkyDome also ushered in a new era of megastadiums, with major league sports facilities designed to provide diversified amusements in attractive settings while serving as the focal point for entertainment, tourism, shopping, and business development. The Ballpark in Arlington opened in 1994, complete with restaurants, a hall of fame, a youth park, a learning center, and an amphitheater. Jacksonville built a new stadium in 1995 as part of a riverfront entertainment complex, while the Dallas Cowboys were planning to enlarge Texas Stadium to over a hundred thousand seats, enclose it with a retractable dome, and add a theme park featuring a sports museum, team hall of fame, and virtual reality displays.[10] As buildings and development schemes become ever grander, the game often gets lost in the shuffle; in Toronto, notes a journalist, "the SkyDome became a monument to itself, with baseball reduced to a minor sideline."[11]

For team owners, luxury seating is the most important element of state-of-the-art sports facilities. Modern luxury seating was introduced in 1965 in the Astrodome, which included fifty-five luxury boxes; and private suites quickly became an essential feature of arenas and stadiums. Luxury accommodations come in a variety of sizes and shapes, ranging from premium seating to ornate suites. Premium seating expands the concept of box seats, providing comfortable seats in desirable locations, often with more privacy, better food service, and reserved parking. Money has been the principal appeal of luxury seating to team owners. Luxury boxes are cash cows, renting from $10,000 to over $200,000 a season; Toronto's SkyDome leases 161 luxury suites for $100,000 to $225,000, which does not include game tickets, interior decorating, or use for special events or postseason games. Luxury seating revenues have the added attraction, like season tickets, of being collected in advance. Selling rather than leasing luxury seating further increases up-front revenues, as well as providing capital for building arenas and stadiums.

Eager to squeeze more from the luxury cash cow, owners have pressed hard for more sky boxes and premium seating in existing facilities, new arenas and stadiums with more space devoted to luxury accommodations, and deals that put these revenues in team coffers. Owners insist that their teams cannot remain economically competitive without more luxury revenues. New buildings are the best way to increase income from premium seating, since they provide the opportunity to incorporate large numbers of posh accommodations in the basic design, along with more sumptuous supplementary facilities for box holders, and thus to charge higher prices. The revenue potential of luxury seating increases the importance of arenas and stadiums to teams, and in the process often restructures relationships between teams and the places where they play. Places come under strong pressures to build new facilities and cede luxury revenues to teams; negotiations are often accompanied by threats to move to a place offering more luxury seating in a newer building, with the team getting all the money.

For football and baseball teams, luxury boxes have the added attraction of generating revenues that do not have to be shared with other league members. The appeal is particularly strong in the NFL, where 40 percent of gate revenues go to the visiting team, but none of the income derived from luxury seating is shared aside from the price of game tickets. Moving to the Georgia Dome in 1992 gave the Atlanta Falcons 183 luxury boxes to lease for an average of $65,000 per season, which generated close to $12 million in unshared revenues, about the same as total ticket receipts in the 70,500-seat stadium. To reap even larger riches, the Washington Redskins' planned stadium in suburban Maryland featured 331 sky boxes, six times as many as the Astrodome three decades earlier.

Luxury seating, of course, has its risks; not all prospective gold mines tap rich veins. The market for expensive sky boxes is greater in some cities and metropolitan areas than others. Major urban areas usually have a substantial supply of businesses interesting in forking out large sums of money for luxury suites to entertain customers and reward executives. But although prices in some cities exceeded $200,000 in the late 1980s, luxury boxes in Green Bay, Indianapolis, and Pontiac were renting for as little as $10,000. Teams, particularly in smaller metropolitan areas, have worried about their ability to sell luxury suites in competition with two or three other major league franchises in the same market. Construction of a new arena and the outfitting of the Suncoast Dome for baseball added more than 140 luxury boxes to the Tampa-St. Petersburg market, more than tripling the number of suites available in the metropolitan area, and the Buccaneers were pressing for renovations or a new stadium that would substantially increase the 57 luxury units at Tampa Stadium. Worries about overbidding and saturated markets, however, are not limited to smaller metropolitan areas. Almost 600 luxury boxes will be competing for corporate dollars in the Washington-Baltimore area with the construction of new stadiums for the Redskins and Ravens and an arena in downtown Washington, and even more would be on the market if major league baseball returned to the nation's capital in a new ballpark.[12] Symptomatic of these concerns was the New Jersey Devils' insistence that the agreement which kept the team from moving to Nashville include a promise that no additional major league teams were to play in the Meadowlands sports complex; "this area cannot sustain more competition," explained a Devils' executive, "there's just· so much the fans and corporate sponsors can sustain."[13] And luxury-box revenues in metropolitan areas large and small, for teams and the governments that build stadiums, assume a buoyant economy in which corporations are able to cough up tens of thousands of dollars for a very pricey frill.

Premium seating raises hackles as public arenas and stadiums are designed or refurbished around posh facilities at the expense of ordinary customers. Accommodating three tiers of luxury boxes required raising the upper deck of the new Comiskey Park, which pushed the regular seats farther away from the field. Additions of luxury suites to existing arenas and stadiums have often eliminated regular seats; in the Boston Garden, complains a Bruins' fan, "people who had supported the franchise for generations [were] dispossessed . . . so that a few wealthy people, corporations and politicians could have some bragging rights in their fancy special boxes."[14] And the newest designs put luxury seating close to the action—premium luxury suites at Cleveland's Gund Arena are only fifteen rows back from the court—which shift other seats further from the playing surface. Critics have also been troubled by the exclusivity that lies at the heart of the appeal of luxury seating. John Underwood, a longtime sports writer and editor, sees luxury seating as "death on the synergism and the shared appreciation that has traditionally tied sports fans together."[15] For Robert A. Baade, an economist whose work questions the benefits of public sports facilities, government financing of elite seating "smacks of inequity," as "something that could potentially create social tensions."[16]

Team owners and stadium operators respond that premium seating benefits rather than harms fans because revenues from luxury boxes help keep prices of ordinary seats within reach of the average customer. "You have to underwrite the average fan," insists the owner of the Hartford Whalers in defense of high-priced luxury seating; "how much can you keep raising ticket prices? There has to be a subsidy."[17] The owner of the Philadelphia Flyers was hopeful that "corporate revenues will give us enough revenue" in a new arena "to reduce ticket prices . . . for the average Joe."[18] Whether cross-subsidization is a pricing reality or a public relations gimmick designed to keep critics at bay is hard to know, given the creative and secretive accounting practices of professional sports teams. What is clear is that luxury seats and their revenues have become a dominant consideration in the stadium and arena game.

Building state-of-the-art facilities with the latest bells and whistles increases the costs of arenas and stadiums, costs borne largely by governments. Domed stadiums have generally been more expensive to build than open structures; the Astrodome cost $38 million, compared to $24 million for similar open stadiums built in New York and Atlanta. The Super Dome in New Orleans cost three times as much as any previous stadium; and the $600 million retractable domes in Montreal and Toronto pushed construction costs off the charts. Construction costs, of course, are boosted by inflation, and are also affected by the capacity of the stadium. Average costs in 1992 dollars rose about 65 percent for stadiums built between 1960 and 1997, from under $3,000 to almost $5,000 per seat. Increases have been particularly sharp for the new generation of state-of-the-art ballparks, with all but one exceeding the 1960–1989 constant-dollar average by 80 percent.

Arena construction costs have been rising more rapidly than those for stadiums, reflecting substantial increases in the size of arenas, ever grander facilities, multi-use projects, and the high costs of sites in the central business district, where most arenas continue to be located. The most expensive arenas involve multipurpose developments like New York's Madison Square Garden, a 1968 project that combined an arena, auditorium, office building, and reconstruction of a railroad station, and cost three and one-half times as much as the Astrodome, the most expensive stadium constructed in the 1960s. More recently, the Rose Garden in Portland, completed in 1995 and combining sports facilities with hotel, office, and retail development, cost almost $100 million more to build than any previous arena. Costs per seat in constant 1992 dollars increased from $4,000 in the early 1960s to over $7,000 in the middle 1990s.

Costs are further magnified by the downtown locations favored by city political and business leaders, and increasingly desired by team owners seeking to sell luxury suites and other premium seating to the major businesses that cluster in the central business district. Downtown sites typically involve higher land and site development costs, bigger transportation investments, and more expensive construction, as well as additional expenditures necessitated by multipurpose projects such as the SkyDome and Rose Garden. A replacement for Yankee Stadium in mid-Manhattan, to be built on a platform over a railroad yard, was estimated to cost $1.04 billion in 1996, twice the projected expense of a new ballpark for the Yankees in New Jersey or the Mets in Queens.

Reconsidering Private Development

Until recently, the rising costs of building new arenas and stadiums were almost universally borne by public agencies. Interest in private sports facilities rekindled in the 1980s, largely as a result of the revenues promised by premium seating. The first to take the plunge was Joe Robbie, who financed a private stadium for his Miami Dolphins by raising $90 million from luxury boxes and other premium seating. A year after Joe Robbie Stadium opened in 1987, the Detroit Pistons built the Palace at Auburn Hills, using $12 million generated annually from 180 luxury boxes to cover the arena's debt service. With these models in hand, private development of arenas and stadiums had a new lease on life. Team owners, real estate developers, and their financial consultants rushed to put together plans for private sports palaces underwritten by premium seating; "in our deal," emphasized an investment banker for the United Center in Chicago, "the skybox sales are really the engine pulling the whole train."[19] A new wrinkle was developed in Charlotte, where the NFL expansion franchise sold lifetime rights to buy tickets to particular seats for $600 to $5,400, which were valid only as long as the purchaser continued to buy season tickets; "in effect," declared Jerry Richardson, the principal owner, "the fans will own the stadium."[20] In fact, of course, Richardson and his partners owned a stadium paid for by fans and other customers.

Part of the appeal of private facilities is financial; the opportunity to capture all of the growing revenues generated by arenas and stadiums. "We have to find new revenue streams that aren't related to the game," noted a Pistons' official of the team's move to its suburban Palace, "that's why we are seeing a lot of teams building their own arenas."[21] The control over revenues provided by ownership also enhances the value of professional sports franchises; "the more control a team has over its stadium or arena and other real estate, the more valuable the franchise" in *Financial World's* annual estimates of the worth of major league teams.[22] Arenas and stadiums, moreover, are assets that can increase the value of a team or be sold independently. And private development can put teams directly into the real estate business, offering possibilities for substantial additional profits.

Private arenas and stadiums provide teams with control over their facilities. In building the only private stadium developed for almost half a century, Walter O'Malley was determined to control his new ballpark. "The new park," he insisted, "will not be a municipal stadium. That would mean a political landlord, which isn't desirable."[23] Teams that own their facilities have control over the playing surface, scheduling, mix of seats, and other matters that must be negotiated in public arenas and stadiums. Private development promises freedom from the political hurdles that any public project must overcome; frustrated in a series of attempts to secure a public stadium, the Washington Redskins acquired a site and proposed to build privately; "every step" in the process, noted a reporter, seemed "calculated to limit interference from politicians and government officials."[24]

The quest of teams for control over their playing facilities, as well as the desire to enhance their profits, has spurred privatization of existing arenas and stadiums as well as private development of new buildings. Busch Stadium, built in 1965 with public funds, was acquired by Anheuser-Busch in 1980 and sold with the team in 1995. Another variation is virtual privatization—essentially, public financing of a stadium developed and operated privately. Irving underwrote the financing of Texas Stadium through bonds backed by the suburb's tax base, but the stadium was designed by the Dallas Cowboys, constructed by a company belonging to the team's owners, and managed by a subsidiary of the Cowboys.

The rebirth of interest in private sports facilities has been heralded as highly desirable. "Quit trying to soak the voters to build a ballpark," is John Feinstein's advice to owners, "build it yourself."[25] Neil J. Sullivan strongly prefers private stadiums because public development is a costly and contentious way to build arenas and stadiums for private sports franchises; Candlestick Park, he notes, "was rushed to completion for the 1960 season amid every aggravation associated with public construction projects. Strikes, lawsuits, allegations of corruption, and grand jury probes threatened the stadium."[26] Public arenas and stadiums, critics emphasize, have rarely been financial successes; instead, most constitute a perpetual drain on public treasuries because of problems inherent in governmental enterprises, including underestimating costs, overestimating revenues, additional investments to satisfy political interests, and concessions to teams. Compounding the consequences of public development is subsidization of the rich; for Sullivan, "the municipal stadium is a most pernicious form of welfare awarded to millionaire sports owners."[27] The appropriate model for stadium development, he contends, is Dodger Stadium because "it puts the burden to produce where it belongs—on the club owner. . . . Walter O'Malley, rather than the community, was on the hook."[28]

Private development has also been warmly embraced by advocates of privatization of governmental functions, who extol the virtues of private planning and design, professional management, the rigors of private financing, and the discipline imposed by bottom lines. Dean Baim, in a volume on *Entrepreneurship and the Privatizing of Government*, concludes that private sports facilities cost less to build and operate than public projects. He found that construction costs for public stadiums averaged 71 percent more per seat than private facilities, and public arenas 46 percent more.[29] For arenas built since Baim's study, however, the average cost per seat has been 4.5 percent higher for private than public projects. Convergence of the costs of public and private arenas probably reflects the desire of teams for state-of-the-art facilities, as well as the availability of revenues from premium seating to underwrite expensive private buildings.

Advocates of private arenas and stadiums argue that privately owned facilities strengthen ties between teams and the places where they play. Teams that own their playing facility have a fixed physical asset connecting them to a particular place; as a result, argues Baim, "one way of ensuring an economic stake in the community is to have team ownership of playing facilities."[30] Privately owned arenas and stadiums are seen as decreasing the prospects that new owners will move teams; "owners who wanted to move their franchises would have to sell the stadium," suggests Sullivan, "which would be of interest only to another ball club. Dissatisfied owners would probably sell the team rather than move it."[31] Private ballparks, however, did not keep the Braves in Boston, Athletics in Philadelphia, Browns in St. Louis, Dodgers in Brooklyn, Giants in New York, or Senators in Washington. In none of these cases did owners want to spend the money to fix up their old parks, most of which were located in declining areas; nor were any except O'Malley prepared to invest in new private stadiums. So they departed to play somewhere else in new public stadiums that they rented under attractive terms or, in the case of the Dodgers, in a private one developed with considerable public assistance.

The relationship between relocation and public or private ownership is difficult to distinguish from other factors that influence franchise movement. In making his case for private development, Baim emphasizes that only one of twenty franchise moves between 1971 and 1984 involved leaving a private facility—the relocation of the Cincinnati Royals to Kansas City. Whether this reflects the greater hold of private facilities on franchises or the fact that most teams were playing in public facilities by 1970 is not clear. From 1953, when most teams played in privately owned buildings, to 1961, 80 percent of franchise moves were from private to public facilities, as were 38.5 percent from 1961 to 1970. Nor do very clear trends emerge from relocations within metropolitan areas; teams have moved from public facilities in Cleveland, Detroit, Los Angeles, and Miami to private ones in the suburbs, and in Cleveland back to a new public arena in the city.

Proponents see private development as enhancing the economic calculus that figures so prominently in discussions of professional sports in cities and metropolitan areas. Sullivan suggests that "whatever economic benefits may be produced by a public stadium would also result from one that is privately financed"; the difference between public and private development is that under the private alternative "the community would receive these benefits without the obligation of stadium ownership."[32] Perhaps, but private development places decisions about where to build in private hands, which conflicts with the desire of places to determine specific locations for arenas and stadiums to maximize or target local economic benefits. Cities and suburbs want sports facilities located within their jurisdiction, and their ability to insure that sports facilities are built in favored locations is substantially less with private than public development. Of particular importance to cities is the likelihood that private enterprise would build fewer arenas and stadiums in central business districts, with their higher development costs and problematic parking, than have governments, which view sports facilities as a means of stimulating downtown growth.

Supporters of private development usually assume that teams want to own their playing facilities. Most owners, in fact, continue to prefer public to private investment, for the obvious reason that arenas and stadiums generally are bad investments. "The Denver Broncos," insisted the team's owner in 1994, "are not in the stadium-building business."[33] The year before, the owner of the New England Patriots emphasized that "these days governments help teams instead of the other way around, like by asking the teams to pay."[34] Places, suggest the proponents of privatization, should not want teams whose owners are unwilling to invest in playing facilities. Few places, however, are likely to risk losing a team by demanding that a reluctant owner invest in a stadium or arena for which private financing may well not be available. Similarly, places in the hunt for major league sports are understandably reluctant to rely on private enterprise to build the facilities necessary to snare a team.

Places, moreover, do not have uniform interests in franchise stability or private development. Suitors want to enhance rather than reduce their opportunities to get into the big leagues, and are not very interested in changes like privatization that might reduce their chances. For places with teams, privately developed facilities threaten to compete with existing public arenas and stadiums, resulting in reduced revenues and larger deficits to be shouldered by governments and their taxpayers. Teams playing in private arenas and stadiums also have fewer formal obligations than those bound by leases to a public facility; local officials may well see the resulting risks as outweighing the benefits of teams owning the building where they play.

Illustrative of the hazards to places posed by private facilities are the problems of the Target Center, built in 1990 by the owners of the Minnesota Timberwolves. Relocation of the NHL's North Stars to Dallas in 1993, in part because of dissatisfaction with lease arrangements with the arena's owners, cut off a vital source of revenue for entrepreneurs who were already hard-pressed because cost overruns doubled the price of the building. To escape financial ruin, the owners put the Timberwolves on the market, and were prepared to sell to buyers who planned to move the franchise to New Orleans until the NBA intervened to keep the team in Minneapolis. For the Twin Cities, the lessened control inherent in private sports facilities contributed to the loss of one team. And government wound up spending millions to acquire the arena and keep the basketball team in town, an outcome likely to be repeated when other places have to choose between bailing out private facilities or losing a major league team.

Further complicating the issue of private sports development for places is the reality that almost all private arenas and stadiums built since World War II have involved significant governmental participation. Private sports facilities, in reality, are public-private ventures whose development is possible only through governmental assistance. From the start of his efforts to replace Ebbets Field, Walter O'Malley sought public help to develop a private stadium, unsuccessfully in New York with a plan to build on land assembled under the federal urban renewal program, then triumphantly in Los Angeles where the city provided a site worth $18 million and the city and county invested $4.7 million in public works for the stadium project.[35] O'Malley rarely mentioned the critical public role in the project when he "boasted that Dodger Stadium was the only privately owned park."[36]

Joe Robbie Stadium was a product of substantially more public help than Dodger Stadium. Robbie turned to private development after failing to secure a commitment from Miami to replace the Orange Bowl; "we didn't do this out of choice," he told a reporter, "we did it because the community defaulted on building a stadium."[37] Dade County proved more responsive than the city government, supporting Robbie's private venture by leasing the 160-acre site, providing $30 million in public improvements, and permitting the use of tax-exempt bonds, which lowered interest costs. Robbie, like O'Malley, tended to ignore the critical role of government in building his field of dreams, which he extolled as "a monument to a free, competitive enterprise system" that "showed that anything government can do, we can do better."[38]

Elsewhere, governments have supplied land, built roads, lent money, and provided tax breaks for private arenas and stadiums. The private Capital Centre in Landover, Maryland, was built in 1973 on sixty acres of public park land, and serviced by $2 million in access roads and other infrastructure provided by Prince George's County. Land was purchased for Charlotte's new private football stadium by city and state government at a cost of $57 million. More and more public arenas and stadiums are also partnerships involving complex mixes of participants and financing. One of the first such ventures was the Astrodome, promoted by two influential Houstonians who put up $6 million for the $38 million stadium, with most of the rest coming from Harris County and smaller shares from the city, state, and federal governments. In a typical contemporary deal, the arena built in Buffalo in the mid-1990s combined city, county, and state funds with capital from the team, a concessionaire, and cable television interests.

Whether private or public enterprises or some mixture of the two, arenas and stadiums are expensive and problematic undertakings. Private facilities, like their public cousins, face the daunting challenge of securing sufficient utilization to pay operating costs and capital charges, a task more difficult for stadiums than arenas, and particularly challenging for football stadiums. Joe Robbie Stadium was not a viable enterprise when it operated primarily as the home of the Dolphins, who play eight regular season home dates and a couple of exhibition games; "without baseball," acknowledged Robbie's son, "this stadium would never be much more than a break-even proposition."[39] The stadium was designed to accommodate baseball but Robbie, financially drained by his private stadium venture and constrained by his bankers, was unable to get in the hunt for a baseball franchise. Shortly after Robbie's death in 1989, a half interest in the stadium was sold to Wayne Huizenga, who had the means to secure a baseball team for it.

Joe Robbie Stadium underscores the risks inherent in private stadium building. Despite premium seating revenues, tax-exempt bonds, free land, and substantial public infrastructure investment, the Robbies did not survive building their private stadium. Huizenga acquired 15 percent of the Dolphins in the stadium deal; four years later he bought the rest of the team and the stadium from the Robbie family, which had been financially crippled by the demands of private stadium building. The last vestiges of the Robbies disappeared in

1996 when the stadium became Pro Player Park in return for a hefty naming fee. Toronto's SkyDome, a public-private partnership involving twenty companies that invested more than $300 million through the Stadium Corporation of Ontario, struggled under the burden of $26.4 million in annual interest payments, incurring an operating loss of $15.8 million in 1991, even though the Blue Jays broke the four million mark in attendance for the first time in baseball history. Private development also does not guarantee stability, good management, or nice facilities. Unable to secure a public stadium in Boston, the Patriots settled for a bargain-basement private facility built in 1971 in a distant suburb. A decade later, the financially pressed owners of the Patriots bought the stadium from the realty trust created to finance the project, which led to more than a decade of turmoil, with ownership changes, conflicts between the owners of the stadium and team, lawsuits, threats to relocate, and intervention by the NFL to keep the troubled franchise afloat.

Private ownership is inevitably shadowed by the pervasive competition for teams among places, competition in which public subsidies of playing facilities are the principal means of outbidding other places. Teams with private arenas and stadiums have to compete with teams playing in public facilities who reap the benefits of lower prices as places offer better deals. "Municipal competition," as Robert A. Baade and Richard F. Dye note, "serves as a strong disincentive for private team involvement in stadium projects. . . . Since league teams compete in publicly and privately financed facilities, the teams playing in publicly owned facilities have a clear economic advantage."[40] One answer for teams that own their playing facilities is to seek more public help, in the form of loans or tax abatements or public investments in improvements or other subsidies, perhaps accompanied by threats to move if some kind of rescue mission is not launched.

Both demands for more public investments and threats to relocate are likely to increase as private arenas and stadiums age and become obsolete, requiring renovation or replacement. When an earlier generation of private ballparks aged, government wound up building new stadiums or rebuilding old ones, or faced the probable loss of a team. That places may well wind up facing similar dilemmas as more recent facilities age and demands escalate reinforces the attractions of the control offered by public development, even at the cost of more substantial public subsidies. Sullivan sees such public development as the fatal flaw in the relationship between places and professional team sports, arguing that "when the politics of stadium financing are confused, communities become hostage to club owners. Having committed the capital to build or to renovate a stadium, the city is in a position to be pressured by the franchise for future concessions."[41] But the pressures that Sullivan sees resulting from public development are rooted in the mismatch between the supply and demand for major league teams rather than in public-private considerations.

Competition among places for scarce major league franchises underlies the politics of professional sports. Both teams and places seek to maximize their control in a game with high stakes for both parties; teams want to make as much money as possible, while places want to keep their teams with as little political and financial risk as possible. Given these objectives and the substantial costs of major league arenas and stadiums, privately developed facilities remain the exception rather than the rule. Despite the enthusiasm for private development and the proliferation of grand plans, only two of the fourteen arenas and stadiums completed during the early 1990s were predominantly private.

16

Political Players

AT FIRST glance, the politics of professional sports appear quite simple. Because demand for big league teams substantially exceeds the supply, professional sports have great political leverage with places. "When it comes to striking deals between the cities which build the stadiums and the sports industry which uses them," concludes Amy Klobuchar in her study of the Metrodome in Minneapolis, "the industry is blessed with all of the negotiating advantages."[1] From their weak competitive position, places seem to have little choice but to give teams what they want. "Cities desperate to be 'big league' and politicians desperate to avert civic catastrophe," insists John Helyar, are "putty in owners' hands."[2]

Without question, professional sports frequently prevail in contests with places that want or have teams. Public arenas and stadiums in metropolitan areas across the United States and Canada are testaments to how often sports win, as are the ever-sweeter deals that deliver subsidies, tax breaks, and favored treatment to teams and leagues. Sports interests, however, lose as well as win. Walter O'Malley failed to secure a new stadium in Brooklyn because he "lacked the influence in New York to exert his will."[3] In Dallas, city officials preferred to refurbish the Cotton Bowl rather than build the new stadium desired by the Cowboys. When teams win, moreover, they frequently settle for less than originally sought and wait considerably longer than anticipated for their plans to be realized. The Phillies wanted a baseball park in northeastern Philadelphia, but wound up in a multipurpose stadium south of downtown. O'Malley settled for half of the publicly owned land that he originally sought. In Baltimore, city officials and the Orioles first talked about a downtown stadium more than twenty years before Camden Yards opened in 1992.

These varied results underscore the fact that sports teams do not decide most place issues unilaterally. They also suggest that government is not as helpless, nor outcomes as predictable, as suggested by commentators who emphasize the more spectacular political successes of professional sports. Neil J. Sullivan, for example, points to governors William Schaefer and Jim Thompson, who "jumped through the hoops in Maryland and Illinois to give stadiums to the Orioles and White Sox."[4] Both of Sullivan's examples, however, underscore the complexity of political relationships between places and teams. Camden Yards was built only after years of political controversy in which politicians rebuffed demands by the Orioles and Colts; location of the stadium was fixed by political leaders determined to bolster downtown Baltimore rather than by team officials, who preferred a location more accessible to suburban fans. And to portray Schaefer as merely doing the Orioles' bidding is to ignore the magnitude of his commitment to building a downtown stadium and keeping Baltimore in the big leagues. In Chicago, the White Sox were successful in squeezing the political system for a sweetheart deal, but the new Comiskey Park was built astride a heavily black area, which was not the team's preferred location; sites favored by the team, a study of sports politics in Chicago emphasizes, "were opposed by the federal government, . . . by suburban voters, and by Chicago's governing coalition."[5]

Baltimore and Chicago, like every other place with big league teams and aspirations, are distinctive political arenas with complex sets of participants. The politics of professional sports inevitably reflects the diversity of local and state government in the United States, as well as the particular settings of Canadian metropolitan areas with major league teams. Formal arrangements vary among and within governments. Mayors in some cities have considerably more authority than in others; counties are important players in sports issues in some places and insignificant in others; powerful sports agencies have central roles in some urban areas and are nonexistent in others; state and provincial governments are critical arenas for sports politics in many places, but not all. Differences in local economies shape the structure, involvement, and influence of business elites on issues such as professional sports. The influence of labor, political parties, grass roots groups, and other interests varies considerably among cities and metropolitan areas.

Within this diverse set of places, professional sport is typically a complicated game, involving numerous players with different interests. "Walter O'Malley," notes Sullivan in his study of the Dodgers' move to California, "was but one actor in two distinct political games played in New York and Los Angeles."[6] In New York, the game involved the mayor, board of estimate, city council, state government, a public authority created to build a new stadium in Brooklyn, and the public works empire controlled by Robert Moses. The game in Los Angeles was different, but no less complex as played by local officials, various supporters and opponents, the public in a referendum on the issue, and litigants seeking to block the deal in court. In neither place did O'Malley control the outcome; he lost in New York, while in Los Angeles he had little direct influence on the vote in the city council, or the referendum, or the lawsuit—in any one of which an adverse outcome would have killed the deal that brought the Dodgers to Los Angeles.

As in New York and Los Angeles, professional sports issues usually involve a multiplicity of governmental players. Rare indeed is the team that deals with one official or agency or single governmental unit. Within individual jurisdictions, authority is shared between executive and legislative branches, often parceled out to independent agencies of one kind or another, sometimes cannot be exercised unless approved by the public, and usually is challenged in court by those who lose in the more public arenas. Involvement of additional governments results from the multiplicity of local jurisdictions in metropolitan areas, as well as from the superior political, legal, and financial resources of state and provincial governments. Complex and expensive sports deals tend to bring more governmental players into the game, increasing the number of parties that have to be satisfied and necessitating that additional formal consents be secured. Cities, suburbs, counties, metropolitan agencies, and states, moreover, are generically different political arenas, as are their Canadian counterparts, each with its own rules, resources, and influential players. State or provincial involvement in professional sports, for example, inevitably broadens the range of players and interests. In Maryland, consideration of Schaefer's proposals were affected by the sports geography of the state: "Representatives from Prince Georges and Montgomery counties were Redskins fans, while representatives from the western part of the state, out near Hagerstown, were Pirates fans. Neither group was disposed to aid the Orioles or their city."[7]

Political Clout of Professional Sports

Teams, to be sure, are the central players in the politics of professional sports. They typically are initiators of demands; thus they set agendas and determine timing in most places. As Charles C. Euchner emphasizes in his analysis of sports politics in Baltimore, "the sports franchises had the advantage in talks with the city because they could initiate action whenever and wherever they wanted in the long process of negotiations."[8] Teams have the most intense interest in outcomes because they are the principal beneficiaries of sports deals that pump millions of public dollars into their private businesses. Their financial stakes are the most clearly perceived, even though total costs to other parties usually are larger than the benefits received by teams. As a result, teams are the most focused players in the politics of professional sports, which adds to the advantages that flow from their control of a scarce good highly desired by places.

Owners also benefit from having shared interests with top political and business leaders in most places. Getting and staying in the big leagues and winning accolades for bringing or keeping a major league team in town usually make local political and economic elites close allies of teams. Downtown redevelopment goals have been particularly important in cementing alliances among professional sports, public officials, and business leaders, which have paved the way for new arenas and stadiums at the heart of many cities. Teams and their business allies typically have more money than their adversaries to spend for lobbyists, lawyers, and public relations specialists, as well as for campaign contributions and other rewards for responsive politicians.

Political influence is further enhanced when teams are owned by individuals or corporations with substantial local clout. Roy Hofheinz, who brought major league baseball to Texas and built the Astrodome, was a well-connected former mayor of Houston with a web of local business interests. Hofheinz crafted a deal in which the Astrodome was built primarily with public funds but controlled by his private Houston Sports Association. Politicians who bowed to the demands of the Chicago Cubs to install lights at Wrigley Field were dealing with the Chicago Tribune Company, which owned the city's leading newspaper and a local television station as well as the Cubs. Team ownership and local political power often are synergetic. Disney, already a major player in Anaheim, bolstered its influence by acquiring an NHL expansion franchise for Anaheim and then by securing a substantial interest in the California Angels. Bringing NBA basketball to Sacramento helped a group of real estate promoters secure zoning changes for 1,400 acres of land they planned to develop around the arena they built for their team. In St. Louis, purchase of the Cardinals in 1953 by August A. Busch Jr. enhanced the already formidable local influence of the Anheuser-Busch brewing empire. Busch used his economic clout and political connections to advance the intertwined interests of his team and brewery. He played a central role in building a new stadium in downtown St. Louis, as part of the more general urban renewal efforts spearheaded by Civic Progress, a business alliance that he headed. Later, Anheuser-Busch employed its muscle to take control of the stadium, in the process hinting that the Cardinals might move if the brewery did not get what it wanted.

Although major league teams generally pursue their political goals unilaterally rather than in concert with other franchises in a city, occasionally they have come together to pursue common interests, as with the organization of the Philadelphia Professional Sports Consortium, which promoted the teams' economic benefits to the metropolitan area.[9] But competition is more common than cooperation in the politics of professional sports. Teams have conflicting interests in the design of arenas and stadiums, use of these facilities, provisions of leases, and control of concessions, luxury boxes, and other revenues. Conflict between the Colts and Orioles reduced the ability of either team to advance its stadium interests in Baltimore. Disagreements between the White Sox and Bears over design, location, and control killed plans for a multipurpose dome favored by Chicago officials and business leaders. And the incidence of conflict has increased as more and more metropolitan areas have franchises in three or four sports, with each team chasing the same corporate customers and government dollars.

Basketball and hockey teams have been more likely to cooperate than baseball and football clubs. Because basketball and hockey teams are more easily accommodated in the same building than baseball and football, the likelihood is greater that they will join forces to seek new facilities. Basketball and hockey are also more willing to cooperate because they tend to have less influence than baseball or football teams. Their owners are generally neither as rich nor as powerful as those who control baseball and football franchises. And basketball and hockey teams are less valued by places, which means they have less individual political opportunities. Increasingly, however, the quest for additional arena revenues, particularly from luxury seating, makes basketball and hockey teams uneasy bedfellows in a number of places.

Regardless of whether teams compete or cooperate, multiple franchises in a place provide professional sports with political opportunities. Concessions to one team fuel demands by others for new leases, more subsidies, and other benefits. In Baltimore, "the city was buffeted by a protracted game of 'metooism' by the Colts and Orioles" which started with the Orioles securing a more favorable lease in 1972, triggering successful demands from the Colts first for parity and then for lower payments than the Orioles.[10] The biggest prize for teams that ratchet up demands are separate facilities; the Braves won a new ballpark after the Falcons got the Georgia Dome. And calls for parity can be coupled with threats to leave or actual departure. One of the factors that led Arthur Modell to move his NFL team to Baltimore was Cleveland's new baseball and basketball facilities; as Modell explained, "I wanted and was promised equal treatment and it wasn't forthcoming."[11] Similarly, a new ballpark for the Mariners and nothing for the Seahawks was one of the factors prompting the abortive effort to move the franchise to Los Angeles. "The experiences in Cleveland and Seattle," warned a sportswriter, "should serve as a red flag for other cities. Like it or not, they can't cater to one pro team while doing less for another in the same town. . . . If they think they are being slighted, they can find plenty of suitors elsewhere who are willing to treat them better."[12]

Some teams are much better at levering up demands than others, or at using relocation threats to win concessions, or at employing their local political influence. Considering that over one hundred professional sports teams operate in more than forty metropolitan areas, substantial variations in political effectiveness are not surprising. Differences in political styles and skills, and their appropriateness to particular political settings, inevitably shape both the political objectives of teams and their success in pursuing their goals. Led by Jerry Reinsdorf, the White Sox coolly orchestrated a bidding war between Chicago and St. Petersburg that maximized the team's political leverage in both places. Contrast the skilled maneuvering of Reinsdorf with the passivity of Robert Carpenter when he owned the Philadelphia Phillies. Carpenter wound up waiting years for a new stadium, and the one that resulted was neither in the location preferred by the Phillies nor designed for baseball.

Charles O. Finley was a controversialist far more successful at alienating local officials than influencing them. "Finley," notes Bowie Kuhn, "had a knack for stirring up petty problems. One year he invited Mayor Joe Alioto of San Francisco to throw out the first ball at a World Series game in Oakland. That was an obvious insult to Oakland and part of his continuing war with that community and its leaders."[13]

For teams, like any political interest, the political bottom line is whether sufficient influence and skill can be mustered to secure its objectives in a particular setting. The Washington Redskins have been one of the most successful operations in professional sports, with a rich and powerful owner as well as numerous influential politicians among its legions of devoted fans in a vast and prosperous metropolitan area. Yet the Redskins had great difficulty overcoming the political obstacles to building a new stadium. "For almost five years, I have planned and struggled to obtain permission to build the new Redskins Stadium in the District of Columbia," complained owner Jack Kent Cooke in 1993, "I now know I cannot overcome the forces against me."[14] The year before, local opposition had killed a new stadium in Alexandria across the Potomac from Washington. Cooke then turned to the Maryland suburbs, where his initial proposals ran into the formidable opposition of Governor William A. Schaefer, who accused Cooke of undermining Baltimore's bid for a NFL franchise; "he worked against us . . . by saying he was going to build a stadium in Maryland," charged Schaefer, "he'll need roads to get in there and other things. I'm not going to approve that."[15] Winning in politics, as in sports, often depends on who you are playing and where; and in Cooke's case, he eventually won approval from Schaefer's successor for a stadium in a location that aroused less opposition and made fewer demands on the public purse.

Business Elites and Big League Sports

In both the United States and Canada, far more often than not efforts to attract, retain, and house major league teams are backed by powerful economic interests. They support professional sports because of civic pride and the prestige of being in the big leagues; they want to enhance the desirability of their city or metropolitan area, or state or province, improve its competitive position, and stimulate economic development and growth; and in so doing, they seek to advance their own business interests. Businesses with strong local roots and interests tend to be more involved with professional sports than national and international firms. Among such businesses, the press plays a particularly important role on sports issues through its ability to mobilize public support for proposals. Big league sports are attractive to metropolitan dailies because they enhance local prestige and development, and because home teams sell newspapers. The publisher of the *St. Petersburg Times* was a passionate advocate of major league baseball for his city, and his newspaper a tireless cheerleader as St. Petersburg competed with Tampa, developed a stadium, and sought to snare a team.[16] In Minneapolis, the *Star & Tribune* played a key role in organizing the private effort to acquire land for the Metrodome, and made the largest cash contribution of all the private parties involved.

Common interests in downtown development have allied major businesses with professional sports in many cities. Business groups like the Chicago Central Area Committee, Civic Progress in St. Louis, the Gateway Economic Development Corporation in Cleveland, the Greater Indianapolis Progress Committee, and New Detroit have been prominent and influential advocates of professional sports projects in central business districts. Individual businesses are frequently intimately tied into sports development; in Atlanta, a leading developer wanted the city to build an arena to generate business for his downtown parking decks, and lured the Hawks to Atlanta to play in what became the Omni.[17] Outside the city, economic interests rally around sports proposals that promise to spur growth in suburban areas in which they have a stake. Particular projects attract clusters of business interests composed of land owners, lenders, lawyers, insurers, designers, contractors, and suppliers who seek a piece of the millions that are spent building arenas and stadiums.

For most economic interests concerned with sports, being in the major leagues or stimulating development of an area or building a stadium is more important than the fortunes of a particular team. As a result, interests of teams and many businesses overlap but are not identical, and often differ on questions of timing, location of facilities, and magnitude of subsidies. Siting is a particularly sensitive issue, since major businesses often have different locational priorities than teams. Economic elites want arenas and stadiums in favored locations, usually downtown, where benefits will spill over to adjacent businesses and real estate. Teams are more concerned about the size, accessibility, and safety of a site, all of which may be sacrificed in the central business district. Lack of parking at downtown arenas and stadiums, for example, increases inconvenience for customers and reduces team revenues from parking lots. Teams, of course, may share locational interests with other businesses; in Cleveland the Indians, owned by a leading local real estate developer, enthusiastically supported the sports complex promoted by downtown business interests.

Businesses with connections to teams—broadcasters, sponsors, concessionaires, and operators of arenas and stadiums—have a wider range of shared interests with professional sports. Close ties between businesses and teams also result from financing arrangements that put corporate names on sports facilities, as with Arco in Sacramento and Coors in Denver. Business and team interests are most intertwined when powerful firms own a team. In Toronto, the SkyDome brought a bevy of companies into a close relationship with the

Blue Jays, which an envious owner of a baseball team saw as "an economic juggernaut . . . the ultimate marriage between government, which builds these facilities, and the corporations and the people who tie into them."[18]

Juggernaut or not, business support of professional sports often contributes significantly to favorable outcomes for teams. Economic elites have substantial influence with public officials in all urban areas, an inevitable result of their control over jobs and capital, as well as their preeminent role in financing political campaigns. Informal alliances of business and political leaders dominate substantial areas of public policy in most cities; these urban regimes tend to be particularly influential in policy areas that most affect professional sports such as economic development, downtown revitalization, and large-scale public works. Business leaders usually play leading roles in organizations that promote business development and tourism, as well as in groups formed to boost sports projects. Major economic interests are well represented on the public agencies that propose, build, and operate arenas and stadiums. The magnitude of contemporary sports projects further increases their appeal to economic interests. Big stakes attract more players, and to those with the economic and political clout to secure a piece of the action, they promise hefty rewards in terms of contracts, enhanced land values, and more business activity.

As in other political arenas, money is a major advantage of business in the politics of professional sports. Business interests have often financed studies of the economic impact of professional sports and preliminary planning for arenas and stadiums. Business supplies most of the money for groups like Citizens for San Antonio's Future, which far outspend opponents in sports referendum campaigns. Business pumped more than $400,000 into Yes for Nashville, more than twenty times the funds raised by Concerned Citizens for Nashville, in the battle over a new stadium in 1996. The biggest bucks often come from the most interested businesses; the largest contributor in an unsuccessful campaign for a baseball stadium in New Jersey was Harry M. Stevens, Inc., a concessionaire with a close relationship to the state sports agency promoting the new stadium. Business money can spell the difference between success and failure in financing sports projects. Corporate pledges to buy season tickets, advertising, and luxury boxes have been critical components of numerous arena and stadium deals. Businesses committed to a downtown stadium in Minneapolis put up $14.75 million to acquire land; and local financial institutions bought the stadium bonds that were not attractively priced for the national market, insuring that the stadium was located in central Minneapolis. To build Kiel Center in downtown St. Louis, leading companies invested $30 million and guaranteed $99 million in public and private borrowing, as well as putting up $3.8 million for deposits on suites and other premium seating at the arena.

Business involvement and influence in the politics of professional sports vary widely from place to place. Economic interests tend to be most influential in places trying to break into the big leagues, often providing leadership and financing for efforts to lure teams, win expansion franchises, build sports facilities, and recruit potential owners for expansion teams. Most of these aspiring places are newer metropolitan areas in the south and west, where economic interests generally are more influential than in the older and more pluralist urban centers of the northeast and midwest. Business cohesion and mobilization on professional sports also varies because economic interests often differ over priorities and development plans. Locating a stadium in the central business district is more attractive to some economic interests than others, and downtown business leaders are unlikely to mobilize behind an effort to build a new arena or stadium in the suburbs. Financial arrangements for arenas and stadiums can adversely affect some businesses more than others; taxing hotels and restaurants to pay for sports, for example, rarely is welcomed by these businesses.

Economic interests have had their most influence on downtown sports projects. Despite the dispersal of commerce and industry in every metropolitan area, downtown remains the most important economic concentration, with the largest and most influential firms. Downtown business interests typically are closely allied with mayors and other top city officials on development issues. In most metropolitan areas downtown businesses are also the prime market for season tickets and luxury suites, which both increases the interest of these firms in sport facilities in the central business district and reinforces the appeal of downtown locations for sports teams, thus fueling the synergy of professional sports and major urban firms.

Business influence in sports politics, as on any issue, depends in part on the interests and political resources of other parties. In places without teams, business leadership has been relatively painless because of widespread public approval for getting into the big leagues, at least until costs and other details become known. Demands of existing teams for new facilities and other benefits are more likely to be controversial, increasing the likelihood that some economic interests will decline to become involved. Political leaders may defer to business on sports issues or work in close partnership; or they may insist on playing leading roles, or resist business pressures for public commitments to sports projects. Business generally adapts to these variations in political roles because support from political leaders is critical to the success of sports ventures. In the process, business usually settles for less than its original goals in terms of specifics like location, finance, and timing; in Minnesota, securing public commitment to a new stadium took three years of legislative struggles, where "in spite of all the maneuvering and meddling of the Minneapolis business corps, the outcome of the controversy was only partially favorable to its interest."[19]

Whatever the influence and cohesion of local economic interests, support from professional sports is essential for business to be successful in bringing or keeping teams, or building arenas or stadiums. Leagues have to approve expansion franchises and relocation, which among other things means choosing among business interests from the cities involved in the zero-sum games of professional sports. Owners have to approve deals designed to induce their teams to move or stay, and few are as committed to a particular place as the local business interests that promote a favored location. In St. Louis, backing for a planned domed football stadium by the city's economic leaders failed to dissuade the Cardinals from moving to Phoenix. After business and political leaders capitalized on the loss of the Cardinals to secure approval for the new stadium, the ultimate success of the venture was outside the control of local elites, depending instead on actions by the National Football League, prospective investors in an expansion franchise, and, once the expansion bid had failed, owners of teams that might be interested in moving to St. Louis.

Playing with the Pros

Governments make the final choices about public involvement in professional sports. Governments are authoritative; they are empowered to regulate private development, condemn land for public purposes, tax and borrow money, build public facilities, operate or lease these facilities, and engage in other official acts that affect the attractiveness of particular places to professional sports. Few of these decisions are made unilaterally by public officials, particularly when the stakes are high, as is the case with many public determinations involving major league teams—public decisions are influenced by a variety of interested parties outside of government, of whom the most important usually are teams, businesses with direct stakes, and other economic interests. Nonetheless, decisions have to be made by public officials; they are not self-executing, regardless of how powerful the forces pressing for approval of a sports project.

Government, moreover, is not merely a means of registering the preferences of various interests. Individual jurisdictions, elected officials, and public agencies have their own stakes on most sports issues, which often overlap with those of other parties but rarely are identical. Political leaders have frequently joined teams and economic elites in supporting development of new stadiums, but have differed with sports backers over sites, financing, and design. Formal control over decisions that authorize public actions provides officials with leverage that usually affects outcomes. Sites that are unacceptable to political leaders cannot be developed. Public financing schemes cannot underwrite new arenas or stadiums unless officially approved. Multipurpose stadiums were built over the objections of baseball teams because city officials insisted on the most cost-effective designs. Public officials, despite the appeal of big league sports and the power of sports backers, can always say no, concluding that costs outweigh benefits. Support for major league sports is neither universal nor cost-free; expensive projects, public subsidies for private firms, and locational disputes involve political risks and costs, as do securing favorable votes in legislative bodies and public referendums when required.

The result is the primacy of political choices ultimately based on political calculations. These political costs and benefits differ from place to place, as does the calculus used by different public officials. Some will be highly responsive to economic elites and sports teams; others will give greater weight to financial costs, constituency concerns, and locational complications. More often than not, the political appeal of professional sports outweighs costs and risks, but proposals must still pass political muster, a process that shapes outcomes to political realities. "We wanted desperately to get the team," acknowledges the mayor of Los Angeles who dealt with Walter O'Malley, "but made it clear we would have to come up with a plan that wouldn't get all of us run out of the city."[20]

In most places, elected executives have been the key political players in the politics of professional sports. Mayors and governors have more authority and power than city councils and state legislatures; they command the resources to negotiate with teams, plan new facilities, and devise financing schemes. Elected executives also have bigger stakes in professional sports issues than legislators. As the most visible local political players, they are primary targets for teams and their business supporters, as well as for opponents of sports projects. They are positioned to reap most of the political benefits that come from successful sports projects, as well as to bear the blame when teams depart or sports deals go awry. But legislators as well have been both strong advocates and spirited opponents of sports projects. Sports plans normally have to be approved by legislative bodies, a requirement that affects the shape of proposals and their fate. When legislative opposition cannot be overcome, sports plans are abandoned or revised. Legislators in Massachusetts killed a proposed arena-stadium project for downtown Boston in 1962; in Illinois, the first proposal for state action on a new stadium for the White Sox died in the state legislature. Nonetheless, legislators tend to be secondary players, rarely determining agendas, devising proposals, building coalitions, or otherwise displacing political executives as the primary political actors on sports issues.

Mayors and governors have generally been advocates of professional sports; most have supported, and many have taken the lead, in attracting teams, keeping franchises, and building arenas and stadiums. Support for professional sports by elected executives, however, typically reflects more than responsiveness to the political influence of teams and business interests. Politicians also are drawn to sports endeavors by a desire to enhance their jurisdiction's prestige, boost the local economy, reap the political benefits of large-scale public works, advance development goals, and appeal to voters who want big league sports. Concern about possible political consequences of losing a team reinforces the predisposition of elected officials, particularly highly visible mayors and governors, to support professional sports. Pondering the possible loss of the Yankees to New Jersey when the team's lease with the city was to expire in 2002, Mayor Rudolph Giuliani defined his "responsibility" as doing "the best I can to make certain the Yankees stay in New York City."[21]

Despite these attractions, professional sports have had little appeal for some political executives. Faced with the threatened departure of the Philadelphia Athletics in 1953, Mayor Joseph Clark chose inaction; Clark, as Bruce Kuklick emphasizes, "was not interested in baseball. Professional sports in the city were a low priority" for the mayor, who opposed public subsidies for sports teams.[22] Mayor Robert Wagner in New York gave little attention to the city's fitful efforts to meet the Dodgers' demand for a new stadium or to resolving internal conflicts among officials that prevented New York from offering O'Malley viable alternatives. Worries about costs and public support have deterred a number of politicians from embracing ambitious sports proposals. In Dallas, city officials resisted pressures from the Cowboys and business interests for construction of a new downtown stadium, preferring the less expensive alternative of fixing up the Cotton Bowl. In Minneapolis, polls indicating that two out of three voters opposed a new stadium, along with a torrent of negative testimony at a public hearing, dissuaded Mayor Charles Stenvig from backing the proposal to build one in 1972.

In recent years, inaction or opposition on the part of elected leaders has become less common than in the first decades of public involvement in professional sports. Once sports facilities are built by government, public investments need to be protected; and past actions create future expectations on the part of professional sports and other interested parties. Officials may harbor doubts, but are more likely to go along in the face of ever more insistent pressures from teams, business interests, and fans. In Sacramento, Mayor Ann Rudin was dubious about using $50 million in public funds to lure the Raiders, but reluctantly supported the measure because "everybody wants the Raiders here."[23] Still, there are always limits; an effort to lure the Philadelphia 76ers across the Delaware River to Camden was shelved because the financing of the proposed deal was deemed too risky by Governor-Elect Christine Whitman. "I'd love to have the 76ers in New Jersey," explained Whitman, "but we can't do it."[24]

Among mayors and governors who support professional sports, roles and effectiveness vary enormously, including the critical ability to orchestrate support from legislators, diverse governmental units, financiers, and other interested parties. A few have made sports projects a central objective of their administrations. Mayor Jean Drapeau was the driving force behind the building of Montreal's domed stadium, the promise of which enabled Drapeau to snare an expansion baseball team and the 1976 Olympics for his city. Like Drapeau, Governor John McKeithen of Louisiana was bitten by the dome bug;

he joined forces with private promoters, rammed the project through the legis-lature, and pressured banks to buy stadium bonds. In San Antonio, Mayor Henry Cisneros hitched his political fortunes to the Alamodome. Strong sup-port from business, which raised $500,000 to promote the project, was impor-tant. But Cisneros' leadership was critical in moving the stadium to the top of the political agenda, crafting development and financial plans, and winning support from a skeptical city council and dubious voters.

First as mayor of Baltimore and then as Maryland's governor, William A. Schaefer pursued with skill and determination his goals of keeping Baltimore in the big leagues and building a new stadium downtown. Schaefer succeeded despite considerable conflict with the Orioles, and without much business or public support. He never lost sight of his goals as he negotiated with the Ori-oles, waded through consultants' studies, haggled with the legislature, crafted a state stadium authority, devised a financing scheme, and avoided a statewide public referendum that promised to doom his plans. To be sure, the Orioles did very well by Schaefer, winding up with a beautiful ballpark under highly fa-vorable terms. But Schaefer also did well by Schaefer, and without Schaefer the outcome would have been different for the Orioles and Baltimore, in terms of the kind of stadium that was built, its location, and financing.

Drapeau, Cisneros, and Schaefer represent exceptional commitment to pro-fessional sports projects, but political executives can have substantial impact even when sports has a lower priority in their overall schemes. Mayor Norris Poulson skillfully put together the agreement that brought the Dodgers to Los Angeles at far less cost to the public than most sports' deals. In Pittsburgh, Mayor Richard Caliguiri organized the amalgam of private investors and pub-lic funds that kept the Pirates from leaving town in 1985. Governor James R. Thompson used his political skill and muscle to push the stadium deal that kept the White Sox in Chicago through both houses of the Illinois legislature in a single evening, and Chicago's Mayor Harold Washington defused black opposition to the stadium project with promises of generous relocation pay-ments and substantial minority contracting by the stadium agency.

For many political executives, however, support for professional sports is more rhetorical than active. Mayors and governors often provide general back-ing for efforts to get into the major leagues, keep teams in town, and provide new facilities, without making substantial commitments. Sometimes elected officials play lesser roles by choice, preferring to let others take the political risks inherent in professional sports ventures. In other instances, political exec-utives lack the resources or authority to play influential roles, as in the case of mayors who do not control the public agencies that deal with professional sports. In Los Angeles, the principal public player during the controversies over the Rams and Raiders was the Los Angeles Memorial Coliseum Commis-sion, rather than the mayor. Similarly, the stadium agency in Oakland rather than city hall had the final say in any deal with the Raiders, and the Oakland-Alameda County Coliseum Commission ultimately rejected a tentative agreement supported by the mayor, ending any hope of keeping the team from moving to Los Angeles.

Agencies and Their Interests

Expanding public involvement in professional sports has spurred development of specialized governmental agencies like the coliseum commissions in Los Angeles and Oakland. Organizations are needed to build and operate public arenas and stadiums, and these agencies in most places have primary responsibilities for teams and sports issues. Sports agencies locate and finance arenas and stadiums, design and build facilities, negotiate leases with teams, and manage their buildings. These agencies come in a wide variety of packages, reflecting the diversity of the decentralized political systems of the United States and Canada, as well as the increasing complexity and magnitude of public involvement in professional sports. Special agencies are used more frequently than regular government departments, and most have more freedom of action than line agencies. Sports commissions, districts, and authorities usually have policy boards whose members serve fixed terms, making them less subject to control by elected officials than regular agencies. Special sports agencies often operate with dedicated revenues—from special taxes, lotteries, rent, and concessions income—that insulate them from general budgetary processes. Agencies responsible for sports also vary widely in the scope of their activities, which in turn affects their role in sports politics. Many are responsible for a single arena or stadium, others for all major sports facilities in a city, metropolitan area, or state. As a result of these variations, agencies may deal with one or more teams, coexist with other agencies within the same jurisdiction, and compete with other agencies in the same metropolitan area.

Specialized sports organizations often begin as development rather than operating agencies. Typically, they are created to prepare plans and to build the facilities if their proposals are acceptable. Sports agencies whose proposals fail usually do not survive; the Greater Boston Stadium Authority wound up with nothing to build or operate after the state legislature rejected its plans for a domed stadium and adjacent arena. The New Jersey Sports and Exposition Authority, on the other hand, moved from planning to building to operating Giants Stadium and other facilities. In the process, the New Jersey authority became a principal player in the politics of professional sports in the New York and Philadelphia metropolitan areas, as well as a formidable power in state politics through its control over jobs, contracts, and other goodies.

Sports agencies, like most governmental organizations that work closely with particular activities, have strong vested interests in their turf. Success and often survival of these agencies depend on professional sports; they need teams to build and sustain arenas and stadiums. As a result, sports agencies are strong boosters of major league sports; they usually trumpet the benefits of being in the big leagues and typically are in the forefront of activities to attract and retain teams. Closeness with professional sports is reinforced by the people who direct sports agencies. Business supporters of major league sports tend to be well represented on policy boards. Agency officials and board members are often chosen because of their experience or interest in sports; the result, says one critical official, is too many "jock types . . . enthralled with professional sports. They are willing to build at any cost."[25]

Sports agencies also develop close relations with businesses eager for a piece of the action. Businesses are drawn by the growing amounts of public funds involved in sports facilities, money that moves through sports agencies, and often is exempt from requirements for competitive bidding and other contracting and purchasing restrictions. Almost all of this money goes to private firms, which compete vigorously for the favor of officials who decide on architects, consultants, bond counsels, underwriters, insurers, contractors, concessionaires, and management companies. Business clienteles of sports agencies typically comprise a mix of politically connected local businesses and politically sophisticated national firms. Among the later, sports management companies, concessionaires, financial specialists, and stadium architects market their services heavily and lobby creatively, cultivating close relationships with sports agencies and other key players in the arena and stadium game.

Operating in a highly politicized atmosphere involving big money, competition for contracts, and considerable discretion, sports agencies have been plagued by favoritism, lack of accountability, conflict of interest, and corruption. By their nature, sports agencies are attractive sources of patronage and favors for politicians, and in turn many of these agencies have doled out tickets, jobs, and contracts to build political support. Cost overruns have been common, often encouraged by inadequate fiscal controls and exacerbated by corruption. Montreal's Olympic Stadium, whose original estimated cost of $120 million ballooned to perhaps $900 million in the wake of inflation, waste, fraud, and bribery, resulted in what one provincial official charitably termed "a monument to incompetence."[26] Close relations with teams and contractors have resulted in complex tangles of interests on many sports agencies. In Denver, the chairman of the metropolitan stadium board negotiated a deal that was far more favorable to the Colorado Rockies than what had been promised to voters, then left the stadium agency to become the team's executive vice president, setting off a furor over favoritism and conflict of interest.

Sports agencies have divergent as well as common interests with teams, however, on everything from provisions of leases to design of new stadiums. Landlord-tenant relationships often produce tensions over arena and stadium management. Renegotiating leases frequently leads to disputes over rents, concessions, and duration of agreements. Demands by teams for new facilities are not welcomed by agencies that may be bypassed by development of a new arena or stadium. And everywhere the relationship with teams is shadowed by the possibility of relocation, which would drastically reduce an agency's income, prestige, and prospects.

The ability of sports agencies to deal effectively with teams also varies widely. Some are highly sophisticated political actors, building durable relationships with teams and other influential players and operating their facilities effectively. On the other end of the political scale are inept organizations like the Los Angeles Memorial Coliseum Commission. Hobbled by weak leadership, internal disagreements, and poor management, the commission stumbled from one crisis to another, eventually losing all of its major league teams. Conflicts with the commission led Jack Kent Cook to build the Forum and move his Lakers out of the Los Angeles Sports Arena. The commission's inability to modernize the Coliseum was an important factor in the decision of the Rams to move to Anaheim and the Raiders' return to Oakland.

Whatever their political successes and failures, sports agencies have become institutions in transition in recent years. They have been a product of the expanding public role in professional sports, a role that is changing as more arenas and stadiums are built by the private sector, or developed as business-government partnerships under private management, or are privately operated. To be sure, some sports authorities, particularly state agencies like those in Maryland and New Jersey, have emerged in recent years as powerful players in the politics of professional sports. Still, a growing number of public arenas and stadiums are managed by teams and other private firms that essentially control all aspects of operations, matters that once were in the hands of public officials. These changes enhance private influence in the politics of professional sports as they exchange public for private control and substitute private for public priorities; they also seem likely to reduce the ability of places to protect their particular sports interests, which is the reason why most public sports agencies were created.

Skeptical Voters

Serving the public, boosters insist, is why government gets involved with professional sports. Political and business leaders emphasize that everyone benefits from major league teams and facilities. Elected officials claim they are responding to the public's desire to have big league sports, and fear retaliation by voters should a team be lost on their watch. Backers build on the popularity of professional sports and home teams, seeking to translate sports loyalties into political support for building larger facilities, promoting economic development, and subsidizing private industry. Opponents, on the other hand, dismiss the image of an irresistible tide of public support; "the real people do not want the stadium," argued a Maryland legislator critical of Camden Yards, "the only ones who want it are the fat cats."[27]

In reality, some people support sports proposals and some do not; backing is neither as widespread as boosters claim nor confined to fat cats. Supporters often equate the public in general with specific publics that favor professional sports, particularly fans. Sports fans usually provide a base of public support for efforts to make a place more attractive to major league teams. Fans obviously have more intense interests in professional sports teams than the rest of the general population, which often makes them vocal and visible supporters of sports proposals. Over 1,200 people packed a city council session in Sacramento in 1989, most to support a $50-million offer to the Raiders, some clad in Raiders' silver and black, others carrying "Go Raiders" balloons. Because fans value major league sports, they tend to be less interested than others in the costs of attracting and retaining teams. Raucous fans at the Sacramento council session "booed suggestions that the city's money might better be spent on housing the homeless, helping drug addicts or building libraries."[28]

Fans, however, are not a monolithic political interest; the intensity of their sports attachments vary, and they often have cross-cutting interests, particularly when higher taxes are part of a sports package. Of the respondents in a 1978 survey of fans, 53 percent opposed the use of tax dollars by local governments "to build sports facilities, even as a way to attract pro teams."[29] Fans, moreover, are not synonymous with the public. Lots of people in metropolitan areas are neither fans nor customers of major league teams, do not feel strongly attached to local professional sports teams, and are not interested in public subsidies for private games. Fans that attend games tend to be a small portion of the population of a metropolitan area, especially in the largest urban complexes. Roger G. Noll estimates that major league baseball teams attract fewer than 10 percent of the residents of their metropolitan markets, with football drawing substantially fewer because most seats are held by season ticket holders, and basketball and hockey an even smaller proportion of the public because of the limited capacity of arenas and heavy season ticket sales.[30]

Whether fans or not, people bring all sorts of concerns to sports issues. Many are primarily interested in the costs of professional sports, in terms of taxes, priorities, and implications for other public activities. Poll after poll underscores hostility to public financing of sports facilities; in 1995, only 19 percent of those polled in Cincinnati supported a tax increase to pay for a new stadium, and only 21 percent in a New Jersey poll favored using tax dollars to keep the Devils from leaving the state.[31] Some people worry about the impact of sports facilities on particular communities, traffic congestion, property values, and other locational issues. For others, sports issues are entangled in larger questions, such as the appropriate activities of local or state government or the allocation of public resources between downtown and other sections. And many people do not care much one way or another about sports issues; a poll taken during one of the efforts to snare the Raiders from Los Angeles indicated that two-thirds of the respondents in southern California were indifferent as to whether the team departed or remained.[32]

How public views on sports issues affect outcomes varies widely from place to place, depending significantly on the opportunities for public participation in sports decisions. Obviously, the public always matters in democracies to some degree. But connections between elections for public office and sports issues are usually blurred; personalities, parties, and taxes generally are far more important in voters' minds than complicated sports deals. Despite a good deal of folklore about voters punishing politicians for losing teams or building stadiums, few if any elections for public office have been fought on sports issues. And, as noted earlier, there is little evidence that elected executives have suffered adverse political consequences because of sports failures, or gained much politically as a result of triumphs.

Votes definitely matter, however, when the public participates directly in sports questions, as when referendums are required or citizens can petition for a public vote on issues. Since 1950, voters have had an opportunity to make basic decisions about public sports facilities in a substantial number of places. Results have varied widely; sports measures have passed easily in some places, narrowly in others, and been defeated in many jurisdictions. Outcomes in these votes obviously depend on all sorts of local factors. Sports projects are distinctive in their magnitude, financial implications, and locational impact; and ballot proposals ask voters particular questions, which may be framed in terms of borrowing money, levying new taxes, creating a sports agency, or expanding the authority of an existing government to undertake sports projects. Supporters and opponents of sports proposals differ in numbers, resources, cohesion, and effectiveness in mobilizing voters. Timing of sports referendums and other issues on the ballot affect who votes and in what numbers. Outcomes are decided by the distinctive electorates of cities, counties, metropolitan areas, and states, depending on whose approval is required. In the Denver area, establishing a stadium district that encompassed suburban counties provided the margin for victory in a 1990 referendum, since a majority of voters in Denver itself opposed the proposed stadium tax. During the same year, new sports facilities for Cleveland were approved in a countywide referendum, although only 45.4 percent of city voters were in favor.

A local factor that does not have a consistent effect is whether teams are doing well or poorly when their fate is decided at the polls. Despite frequent speculation on the sports pages about the connections between the performance of teams on the field and at the ballot box, voters have voted for and against both winning and losing teams. An upturn in the fortunes of the Texas Rangers contributed to the landslide victory in the referendum that launched the Ballpark in Arlington, but votes in Seattle capped the Mariners' march to the playoffs in 1995 by turning down a new stadium. In Cleveland, voters first rejected a new stadium and then approved a different plan during a period in which the Indians were consistent losers.

Amidst all these variations, what emerges most clearly from sports referendums is considerable voter skepticism about spending public funds on major league sports. Although trends are difficult to assess because of the variations among elections, the available evidence suggests that sports proposals have become more difficult to sell to the public. Voters rejected thirteen of fifteen proposals in the 1970s and 1980s, compared with only two of nine in the 1950s and 1960s. A particularly bad year for sports boosters was 1987, when stadium proposals were defeated at the polls in Miami, New Jersey, and San Francisco. Sports projects, however, have done better at the polls in the 1990s, with victories in twelve of seventeen elections held between 1990 and 1996, including a clean sweep in 1996 in Cincinnati, Detroit, Houston, Miami, Nashville, San Franciso, and Tampa. Whether these recent results indicate declining voter resistance is not clear, given the variations in how sports questions are framed, what is being voted on, and the scope of the electoral district. In San Francisco, for example, voters approved a new stadium for the Giants in 1996 after four previous efforts had been rejected at the polls; but the last referendum, unlike earlier ones, did not involve public financing, only an exemption from building restrictions for the privately funded ballpark.

Whatever the general trend, negative outcomes in referendums underscore the fact that voters matter, and neither teams nor political and economic elites always get what they want. At a minimum, defeats at the polls delay sport development; in addition, they usually kill a particular proposal, whether for financing, creation of an agency, or locating a facility. Concern about general public support looms over most sports contests, shaping the strategies and tactics of the players with the greatest stakes in outcomes. The next chapter examines the interplay of these interests in contests that determine how professional sports facilities are financed and where they are located, the most contentious aspects of sports politics in most places.

17

Political Contests

MAJOR SPORTS facilities are complex undertakings. Disagreements tend to multiply as proposals move to the specifics of organizational responsibilities, financing arrangements, siting, and agreements with teams. In Minnesota, the overall issue was clearly framed: "A new stadium would insure that the teams remained in Minnesota. If the legislators failed to provide them with a new or vastly remodeled facility, there was a chance they would leave the area"; but there was considerable disagreement over the details: "Legislators argued over who should bear the support costs. . . . They questioned which locality would benefit more from a stadium."[1]

Insiders vs. Outsiders

Most public contests over arenas and stadiums match insiders who support sports proposals against outsiders who are opposed. Political and business leaders, teams, sports agencies, and associated interests usually are insiders. They develop and promote proposals; they provide most of the expertise and political muscle in sports campaigns. Political leaders usually have been out front favoring projects, while business money has underwritten campaigns and newspapers have run favorable stories and editorials. Opposition typically comes from interests that have not been involved in the development of sports proposals. Among these outsiders are taxpayer interests, neighborhood groups, preservationists, environmental organizations, and champions of the disadvantaged, few of whom can match the influence and resources of sports insiders.

Insiders have enormous advantages in sports contests. They control agendas, occupy key decision-making positions, and generally set the timing for consideration of sports proposals. Sports insiders have a near monopoly over specialized information and advice from experts inside and outside government. Insiders command campaign funds, endorsements, jobs, contracts, and other resources to influence political outcomes. They frame laws, referendum questions, and other rules of the game, and almost always prevail when sports projects are challenged in court. Superior resources, however, do not guarantee favorable outcomes; in San Jose, stadium proponents spent $1.1 million, including $240,000 from the San Francisco Giants, enrolled 15,000 new voters, and mailed a forty-page "Voter Information Guide" extolling the project to 120,000 households, all in a losing cause.[2]

Opponents typically lack access and resources; they react rather than propose, and are usually forced to contest sports proposals under procedures and timing controlled by advocates. Collective action is handicapped by the tenuous common interests among opponents. Some are activated by concerns about the financing of a particular project or its location; others are against higher taxes, or oppose public involvement in sports, or are political adversaries of proponents. Foes also have to contend with an adversary that does not have many enemies; as Charles Euchner points out, "since a franchise's demands do not directly affect many interests, opponents of stadium projects have difficulty developing coalitions to oppose them."[3] Opponents are most likely to overcome these obstacles when public approval is needed for tax-financed sports proposals. But referendums also pose formidable hurdles for challengers, since sports supporters command substantial campaign resources and frame the terms of the debate. In Detroit, the Tiger Stadium Fan Club, even though it mustered 10,000 supporters who wanted to preserve the existing ballpark and fought a tenacious battle against the $240 million stadium supported by the city's political and economic establishment, was overwhelmed in a 1996 referendum.

Insiders seek to enhance their advantages by limiting public participation in sports decisions. Supporters of Minneapolis' downtown dome reacted to surveys indicating widespread public opposition by insuring that voters never had an opportunity to pass judgment on the plan. As an advocate explained, "I don't think that there was any question in anybody's mind that if there had been a referendum on the stadium it would have been defeated."[4] Champions of the St. Petersburg dome secured state authorization for creation of a sports agency empowered to issue bonds without voter approval. Unsuccessful referendums spur efforts to devise plans that bypass tests at the polls; after a stadium proposal had been voted down in Phoenix in 1989, a new financing scheme was devised that did not require voter approval. In Maryland, avoiding a referendum was a critical element in Governor William A. Schaefer's successful stadium campaign. A proposed stadium in downtown Baltimore had been decisively rejected by city voters once, and public opinion polls indicated substantial opposition across the state to Schaefer's plan. Opponents organized under the banner of Marylanders for Sports Sanity collected enough signatures to force a referendum, but Schaefer was able to block a public vote in a contest eventually decided by Maryland's highest court.[5]

Along with sidestepping referenda, political and business leaders have sought to reduce other opportunities for public participation in sports decisions. Authority can be concentrated in the executive branch, and legislative responsibilities for financing, site selection, and other controversial aspects of arena and stadium building thereby reduced or eliminated. Limiting public involvement is one of the attractions of authorities and commissions for sports proponents; these bodies typically do not have to secure approval from legislatures, usually avoid referendums, frequently have broad powers to select sites and acquire land with little or no participation by other parties, and generally are less responsive to public opinion than regular government agencies. Public-private ventures can further reduce public roles in sports ventures by creating corporate entities that function more like private enterprises than governmental agencies.

Proponents have the added advantage of staying power. They can use their resources to return to the fray after a setback, either by trying again for a favorable vote or seeking a way around the need for public approval. As a result of these second efforts, defeats in sports referendums or legislative votes have less impact on outcomes than victories. Six years after voters defeated a stadium proposal, political and business leaders in Cleveland crafted a new proposal with different funding and subject to approval by a broader electorate, and this time they carried the day. Voters rejected raising taxes to pay for a new ballpark in Seattle in 1995, but the state government stepped in with an alternative plan that did not have to pass muster at the polls.

Insiders are most successful when internal differences are resolved before specific proposals are the subject of hearings and other actions that attract attention and public involvement. A united front on the part of political and economic elites is often sufficient to move sports measures to approval, particularly in places where business interests are powerful and cohesive and public participation in sports decisions is limited. Lack of elite cohesion, on the other hand, reduces or negates the advantages of insiders in sports contests. In New York City, where politics are fragmented and contentious, political and business leaders have never presented a united front on professional sports issues, in the process losing four teams and facing an ongoing threat from the Yankees to depart. Outcomes in Los Angeles have been shaped by tensions between the stadium commission and other public officials, and by the limited involvement in sports issues of a downtown business elite that has assigned higher priority to other interests.

Teams pose special problems to insider cohesion; they have interests different from those of political and economic elites, and these differences are often difficult or impossible to resolve. In Dallas, disagreements between city leaders and the Cowboys over a new downtown stadium were never resolved, and the team moved to the suburbs. A similar dispute in Miami led the owner of the Dolphins to oppose city efforts to refurbish the Orange Bowl. Joe Robbie urged "all season ticket holders, all fans, and all supporters of the Miami Dolphins to join with all other oppressed taxpayers to vote no" on a 1982 bond issue.[6] The referendum went down to defeat, and Robbie built his stadium beyond the city limits. Controversial owners are particularly difficult to bring into the fold. In Baltimore, Robert Irsay's bombast, threats to leave, and criticisms of city and state leaders severely handicapped efforts to develop politically acceptable sports proposals. Unpopular owners also intensify concerns about who benefits from sports projects, by providing an easy target for critics of public spending on private teams.

Proponents often mute these concerns by having owners on the sidelines during public consideration of sports proposals; supporters seek to frame the issues in terms of the general attractions of professional sports rather than the specific benefits accruing to team owners. As a result, teams tend to be most active politically in initiating action, making demands, playing the exit option, and negotiating deals with government, and typically become less visible as contests unfold in the public arena. Privatization, however, puts owners in more prominent public roles, both in soliciting governmental assistance and selecting sites for their arenas and stadiums. Owners, whether in the background or forefront, also are available to provide strategic reminders that failure to approve a sports project may cost a place its home team. Early in the game to secure a new stadium for the White Sox, Governor James R. Thompson told the team's owners: "You'll never get one built . . . unless people think you're going to leave if you don't get one."[7]

Who Pays?

Conflicts over sports projects are rooted in disagreements over costs and benefits, particularly the differences between those who bear the costs of sports facilities and those who reap the benefits. Costs in the form of taxes and lost opportunities for alternative uses of public funds are shouldered by relatively large groups of people. Tangible benefits go to a much smaller group, composed mostly of successful firms and affluent individuals. Teams and their rich owners are the most direct beneficiaries of public sports subsidies. Affluent players share in these benefits as increased team revenues underwrite higher salaries for performers. Customers, most of whom are relatively well off, also benefit from larger and more attractive facilities. And wealthy businesses get subsidized luxury boxes, perhaps the most potent symbol of public funds underwriting the rich and powerful. "Taxpayers," complains an Indianapolis politician, "have paid for a domed stadium that's a frill for the rich."[8]

Tying sports projects to downtown development goals reinforces concerns about who benefits. Major landowners, large developers, and big businesses typically promote arenas and stadiums in order to enhance real estate values and bring more customers into central business districts. "The poor people will pay for it," argued the leader of an alliance of community groups that opposed increasing taxes to finance the Alamodome in downtown San Antonio, "but the wealthy businessmen will benefit."[9] In bolstering their downtown investments with sports facilities, business interests usually try to stick the public with most of the bill; in crafting a 1994 proposal for an arena in the heart of Washington, a development corporation supported by "the city's business elite . . . bargained away local property taxes on the facility, offered no rent guarantees for the publicly owned land, exempted the arena from future sales tax increases, and obligated the city to police the arena on event nights" along with "asking the city to raise $92 million for construction."[10] Public outcry over this deal led to modifications that lowered the overall cost to the city, but similar proposals are constantly being hatched by the business beneficiaries of big league sports schemes.

Conflicts over costs are intensified because most sports projects are planned for cities with serious financial problems and social needs. For Sacramento's mayor, "major league status is worth the financial outlays if you have that kind of money laying around. But when you have other things going begging, it's not."[11] Scarce public resources, opponents argue, should be spent on schools, police, housing, parks, and other things that people really need. "What in the name of heaven are we doing," asked an Illinois legislator during consideration of a new stadium for the White Sox, "when we can't take care of the children, we can't take care of the poor and we can't take care of the people who need our help?"[12] Spending money on downtown sports projects, critics insist, means that fewer public funds are available to spend on neighborhood improvements. Sports facilities also involve additional costs that have to borne by taxpayers; attracting more people means more traffic and more crime. "We can't control the crime we have now," complained a law enforcement official in opposing public subsidies to lure the Raiders to Sacramento.[13] Another concern of opponents is the financial consequences of public investments in professional sports facilities. Public development of arenas and stadiums often removes large amounts of land from the tax rolls. Borrowing for sports facilities reduces the bonding capacity available for other projects. Financing a new stadium in Jacksonville delayed a planned expansion of port facilities which, in the view of a critic on the city council, meant trading an investment in "10,000 very high-paying longshoreman-type jobs" for a sports project that would create "3,000 seasonal minimum-wage jobs."[14]

Arguments based on lost opportunities to house the poor or improve schools or create high-paying jobs usually are not very effective weapons against sports projects. More often than not, choices between sports projects and alternatives are rhetorical rather than real. Arenas and stadiums normally are built with capital funds not readily transferable to the needs emphasized by opponents of sports facilities. Even if funds could be used for other programs, there is no reason to believe that this would happen in particular cases. Legislators in Illinois, for example, were not likely to have spent the money earmarked for Comiskey Park on children and the poor unless there were strong pressures for such expenditures, and the presence or absence of such pressures had little or no relation to the stadium issue.

Direct connections to the costs of sports projects are most readily made in the case of taxes that underwrite arenas and stadiums. Any tax to finance sports facilities spurs opposition from those who bear the particular burden. The more general the tax for sports projects, the broader the potential opposition and the more vulnerable on grounds of unfairness to those least likely to benefit from professional sports. Opponents of a stadium for the San Francisco Giants in Santa Clara County focused on the burdens of a proposed 1 percent utility tax; "it just wasn't reasonable," emphasized a leader in the successful campaign against the plan, "the elderly in this county cannot afford to pay any more taxes."[15] Poorer people, who are most dependent on public transportation, were understandably troubled by using a tax on transit fares to finance San Antonio's Alamodome. Mayor Bob Lanier of Houston opposed tax-based financing for a new stadium for the Oilers because he had "this terrific hard time with the idea that the average guys . . . are called on to pay for this out of the taxes on their house and then can't afford to buy a ticket."[16]

Targeted taxes have the obvious appeal to sports proponents of reducing the scope of taxpayer opposition. Most attractive politically are taxes that will be paid by someone else. Speaking of the hotel tax that underwrote a new ballpark in Chicago, Governor Thompson emphasized that "it's financed largely by out-of-towners. You can't get a better deal than that."[17] Some special taxes, such as those on lodgings or admissions, can be marketed politically as being borne substantially by those who benefit from sports facilities, although these connections are tenuous in the case of taxes that indiscriminately fall on all hotel rooms, restaurant meals, entertainment tickets, or car rentals.

Despite their political attractions, special taxes risk alienating business interests that otherwise support professional sports. Hotels and restaurants rarely welcome additional taxes on their services, despite their interest in more visitors and additional people downtown in the evening; nor does the passion for sports among some of their clientele make bar owners receptive to financing stadiums with liquor taxes. Special taxes for sports facilities have been opposed by the Hotel Association of Greater Detroit, the Indiana Restaurant Association, bar owners in St. Paul, and motels in St. Petersburg. Opera, ballet, symphony, and theater companies in Denver and Sacramento understandably objected to admission taxes earmarked for sports projects. Surcharges on sports tickets, which place the tax burden directly on those who attend sports facilities, have been strenuously opposed by teams, whose owners, like every other economic interest, prefer taxes that do not adversely affect their businesses.

The political acceptability of taxes to support sports projects is affected by the nature and scope of the proposed taxing jurisdiction. Central cities with their high tax rates, beleaguered budgets, and concentrations of poorer people are increasingly tough sells for tax-financed sports facilities. Use of a broader political or tax base has increased political acceptability in some cases; opposition to sports tax proposals in Cleveland and Denver in 1990 was offset by support from beyond the city limits; and Illinois financed a new baseball stadium in Chicago with state taxes because local tax financing was unacceptable to the city government. But wider taxing jurisdictions are often even more resistant to sports taxes, especially for facilities located in the central city. Efforts in 1995 by Cincinnati's political and business leaders to involve a broader area in financing new stadiums for the Bengals and Reds were rebuffed by outlying suburban counties that wanted nothing to do with having their tax dollars spent in downtown Cincinnati.

Proposals for sports facilities in the suburbs also face substantial tax hurdles, intensified by the often limited tax bases of smaller jurisdictions, local tax revolts, and widespread use of referendums. Threats by the Chicago Bears to move to Arlington Heights in 1975 evaporated when the suburb was unwilling to shoulder the costs of building a stadium. Voters turned out in record numbers in suburban Lewisville to reject a proposed arena for the Dallas Mavericks to be financed by an increase in local sales taxes; "the one thing that hurt," emphasized a council member who favored the plan, was "hammering of the tax" by opponents.[18]

The political risks inherent in tax-financed sports facilities increase the appeal of alternative revenue sources such as lotteries, luxury boxes, premium seating, concessions, and private payments for naming rights and other privileges. Lotteries have attracted increasing favor from sports proponents in the wake of the successful use of gaming revenues to underwrite Baltimore's new stadiums. Lotteries, however, raise the same kind of priority issues as taxes for arenas and stadiums. An opponent of stadium development in the Maryland legislature emphasized that using lottery proceeds foreclosed use of these revenues for other public purposes: "When you dedicate lottery money to that purpose it precludes you from dedicating it to areas like low- and middle-income housing."[19]

Tax concerns are usually the best rallying point for opponents of sports projects. Opponents of sports projects are best able to capitalize on these concerns when voter approval is required. Financial considerations, however, generally are not fatal to public development of arenas and stadiums. Proponents have an expanding range of funding options; and they rather than opponents make the choices about whether taxes will be used, what kinds of taxes and rates, and what other revenues may be tapped. Advocates normally have considerable control over the political arenas in which financing proposals are judged and the timing of such consideration; sometimes they can avoid referendums, or if unsuccessful try again with a revised proposal that may involve different sources of funds, an enlarged jurisdiction, or new institutional arrangements.

Contests over financing of sports projects also are influenced by the relatively small amounts involved. To be sure, two or three hundred million for an arena or stadium is a lot of money, especially since it will primarily benefit rich team owners. And a billion or more for a ballpark in mid-Manhattan is an enormous sum, even by New York's profligate norms. But the direct costs of most sports projects are small in comparison with overall city or state or provincial budgets. And the political impact of sports spending is further reduced because projects are financed by long-term borrowing, which spreads the cost over an extended period of time and requires relatively modest annual subsidies to finance the bonds. Small average costs increase political acceptability, particularly when what is being bought is something as desirable as major league sports. "We re not talking about big dollars," emphasized an insider in connection with the financing of Denver's new ballpark; "it's a twelve-pack of Coca-Cola per taxpayer in the district, it's not a big deal. Is that worth the price of having major league baseball in Denver? I think your average person would say yes, that's worth it."[20]

Costs of sports projects also frequently appear smaller than the burdens that taxpayers wind up bearing. Because lower price tags increase political acceptability, supporters often overestimate revenues and understate public financial obligations for arenas and stadiums. "There will be no cost to the taxpayer," voters were assured on the eve of the 1990 stadium referendum in St. Louis by backers who emphasized that "bonds for the project will be paid off by stadium events, and the rest will come from a hotel tax."[21] Perhaps, but only if revenue and utilization projections were realistic, and often they are wildly optimistic in order to dampen opposition. Optimistic cost estimates tilt the decision-making process in favor of proposals while increasing public burdens once the bills come due. Rebuilding Yankee Stadium and associated improvements were supposed to cost $24 million, but New York wound up spending over $100 million in city, state, and federal funds. The Louisiana Superdome was sold to voters in 1966 as a $35 million project; the stadium eventually cost $163 million, saddling taxpayers with annual deficits that grew to more than $13 million. The promise of New Jersey officials that a proposed arena in Camden would be financed by revenues rather than tax dollars prompted a Philadelphia sportswriter to note that "somehow, they are able to say this and still fall into undisturbed sleep."[22]

Deficits and cost overruns fuel political opposition, which is reinforced in some places by legal legerdemain, conflicts of interest, and corruption in connection with sports projects. The Superdome proposal approved by voters was supposed to protect taxpayers by prohibiting use of the state's general credit to back the bonds; newspaper advertisements urging voters to support the proposal promised that "neither the state nor the city backs the construction bonds."[23] As costs escalated, the prohibition was sidestepped through state rental payments in the amount of the deficit, a trick play that passed muster with the Louisiana supreme court.[24] Sweetheart deals, kickbacks, and payoffs increase public distaste for sports facilities. Opponents, however, cannot easily capitalize on public discontent with particular sports projects on their home turf. Most information about cost overruns, additional financial burdens, legal sleight of hand, political deals, and dubious undertakings reaches the public after basic decisions have been made by legislatures or voters. Once these decisions have been taken, citizens normally do not get a second chance at bat against sports proposals. And future determinations by legislatures and other officials tend to be preordained by the initial approval of an arena or stadium, leading to additional commitments of public funds to insure that the project is completed and the facility sustained.

Conflicts over the costs of sports facilities are settled primarily by place factors—the influence of the various players, the nature of the proposal, and the rules of a particular political setting that determine which parties make what kinds of decisions. More often than not, supporters of sports development prevail; still, what works in one place for proponents or opponents may be irrelevant in some other urban political setting. "Cities are different," emphasizes a former member of the Los Angeles Memorial Coliseum Commission, "Indianapolis built a stadium just in hopes of getting a team. They spent millions in taxpayers' money. In Los Angeles, it seems politically out of the question."[25]

Where to Play?

Arenas and stadiums are not easy to locate. Land needs have steadily increased as arenas and stadiums have become larger, with higher capacities, bigger concessions areas, and ancillary developments such as restaurants, hotels, and amusement parks. Additional land is needed for parking lots, access roads, and expressway connections to accommodate the automobiles that bring most customers to games. Their size and nature make sports facilities unwelcome neighbors for most urban dwellers. Arenas and stadiums bring crowds, litter, noise, and crime to an area, along with more traffic, air pollution, and parking problems. Residents fear that sports facilities, like other large developments, will inalterably change the character of their communities and reduce their property values, worries that are reinforced by the scheduling of most sporting events at night.

Site problems tend to be greater for stadiums than arenas because they require more land, draw more people and cars, and have a bigger impact on surrounding areas. Traditionally, ballpark builders sought to minimize opposition, as well as keep land costs down, by seeking sites in outlying sections of cities. Similar considerations led government to select peripheral locations for the first stadiums built after 1950. County Stadium was located in an industrial area several miles south of downtown Milwaukee. Candlestick Park sits on an isolated parcel of waterfront land at the southern edge of San Francisco. Shea Stadium was built on reclaimed land in an industrial wasteland on the outskirts of New York City. After a long search for a politically acceptable site, Philadelphia placed its new stadium and arena in a warehousing district well south of downtown.[26]

Locating stadiums became more difficult when cities shifted their sights to downtown areas in the 1960s. Large parcels are hard to assemble in the urban core, which limits locational choices and reduces the amount of parking that can be provided. In Philadelphia, plans for developing a stadium near the center were abandoned because federal funds could not be secured to acquire the site. A barrier to downtown construction in Dallas was the resistance of city officials who felt the proposed site was too small to accommodate a 70,000-seat stadium and its associated parking lots and access roads. Sites in or near the central business district also involve intensively settled areas, which increases the likelihood of opposition from those adversely affected by sports development. A proposed stadium to replace Soldier Field on Chicago's lakefront was opposed by a variety of business, cultural, and environmental interests. Another plan called for locating a stadium immediately south of Chicago's Loop, but this too failed in the face of opposition from residents and developers in the gentrifying area. Worries about traffic congestion and the costs of road construction to serve a downtown stadium added to the political liabilities of these ill-fated Chicago projects. Putting a new stadium for the Yankees in mid-Manhattan, critics argued, would worsen conditions on already overloaded streets, tunnels, buses, and subways. Inner-city locations also raise concerns about crime and personal safety, particularly when on-site parking is inadequate.

Opposition to the location of sports facilities comes primarily from those who object to a particular site. Their concerns often are intense, and their determination to protect their turf formidable. "People will stop traffic, lay down in front of bulldozers, whatever they have to do to preserve their neighborhood," warned a politician as South Boston mobilized against a two-stadium "megaplex" favored by city leaders.[27] Grass-roots foes of stadiums, however, usually are no match for the political and business elites that select sites. Those who locate sports facilities are drawn to sites where local inhabitants, often poor or members of minority groups, lack political influence; and they seek to avoid areas where residents and businesses have the political wherewithal to protect their turf. Local opponents have difficulty rallying others to their specific cause since sports facilities do not have wide areal impact, unlike airports or nuclear generating plants, which are seen as adversely affecting large areas. Allies also are harder to find for singular projects such as a sports facility that jeopardizes one location than for unwanted developments that come in multiples such as public housing complexes or drug rehabilitation centers. In effect, location of major sports facilities is a zero-sum game for those who do not want the project in their community; one place's loss is a win for all the rest who were spared, and thus have little incentive to join forces with the loser.

Lacking allies and political influence, most grass-roots opposition to arenas and stadiums has been brushed aside by the beneficiaries of new facilities. "Here you are, trying to build your own community," complained a local opponent of the Metrodome in Minneapolis, "suddenly outside forces with enormous resources and power try to build this vast project—ironically underwritten with public money."[28] Homeowner objections to locating Joe Robbie Stadium next to a black suburban neighborhood carried little weight with officials and economic interests eager to have the Dolphins and sensitive to the team's threats to leave the Miami area. Residents of the largely black South Armour Square neighborhood in Chicago lost their fight to spare five hundred households from displacement by construction of the new Comiskey Park, despite intensive community mobilization that included negotiations, demonstrations, and threats of legal action, although these efforts did secure concessions for those forced to resettle.

Political opportunities for opponents of arena and stadium locations are significantly shaped by the rules that govern site selection and land use regulation. In recent years, locational decision making has been opened to a wider range of interests through requirements for public hearings, open meetings, and disclosure of site studies. Selection processes also have to take into account environmental considerations, community impact, and historic preservation, requirements that usually bring governmental agencies into the process that are less likely to favor sports development than the official promoters of arenas and stadiums. All of these changes have increased the capabilities of local interests to contest unwanted land uses, and have provided community groups with potential allies among those interested in protecting the environment or historic areas. More participants and regulatory requirements offer more opportunities for opponents to delay projects, thus driving up costs and raising stakes for proponents.

Despite these changes, the initiative in selecting sites for arenas and stadiums remains with teams, sports agencies, and other proponents. They set agendas, determine criteria, and select among alternatives. What you get usually depends on what you want. A study prepared for a stadium task force created by William Schaefer when he was mayor of Baltimore favored Camden Yards over twenty-one other sites in the area, hardly a surprising outcome considering Schaefer's downtown agenda. Control over these critical phases provides advocates with enormous advantages in determining where arenas and stadiums are located. Proponents can pick sites to maximize their locational objectives and political prospects, whereas opponents have to react to whatever choices are made. Backers of sports projects also have sought with considerable success to insulate site selection from more open political processes. Locational decisions are less likely to be subject to legislative or popular approval than financing proposals.

Use of special sports agencies for locating public facilities further insulate site selection from local political pressures. In explaining the ineffectiveness of neighborhood interests in contesting the location of Baltimore's new ballpark, Euchner emphasizes that the Maryland Stadium Authority "had the power to select a stadium site and condemn property in the area without negotiations"; the authority's "extensive powers liberated it from the inconvenience of arguing with local interests."[29] Stadium agencies may also command the resources and flexibility to overcome resistance by funding local improvements or providing generous resettlement allowances. In Chicago, the Illinois Sports Facility Authority spent $10 million to compensate displaced residents of South Armour Square, considerably more than was legally required, to forestall a lawsuit that would have delayed and might have blocked construction of the stadium on the authority's proposed site.

Local opponents of large public projects are more likely to influence site selection in smaller than larger political jurisdictions. In big cities like Baltimore or Chicago, individual communities inevitably comprise a small part of the overall electorate, and thus have limited influence on singular locational issues. Suburbs, on the other hand, offer more opportunities for successful efforts against sports facilities, which are likely to affect a substantial proportion of the local electorate. In these smaller political systems, government is more sensitive to the interests of affected areas. Many residents of Addison, where the Chicago White Sox and DuPage County officials floated a stadium proposal, strenuously objected to the adverse effects of the 150-acre project on their quiet suburban community. Their case was bolstered when critics persuaded the U.S. Environmental Protection Agency to restrict the size of the site to protect adjacent wetlands. Opponents then forced an advisory referendum in which Addison residents rejected the stadium, leading local officials and state legislators to abandon the project. Alexandria successfully fought off a proposed stadium for the Washington Redskins, which the suburb's mayor condemned as "an end run around our land-use goals" that makes us "angry because land use is a very important part of what we're about."[30] Voters in suburban Lewisville decided in 1995 that the costs in terms of congestion, crime, and higher taxes outweighed the promised benefits of a new arena for the Dallas Mavericks; "do we want to trade what we have here in the community for the money?" asked a local opponent before the vote, "it's gonna change the culture of this city."[31]

Sports facilities usually wind up in locations that are most acceptable politically. The desirability of suburban sites—in terms of accessibility to the affluent customers of professional sports, availability of vacant and, relatively inexpensive land, space for parking, and connections to metropolitan highway grids—often are offset by the power of local opponents and the limited financial capabilities of most suburban governments to undertake large-scale projects. Support for downtown sites from powerful political and economic interests, on the other hand, has overcome high development costs, limited parking capacity, displacement of residents and businesses, and locations that are close to inner city areas that sports patrons prefer to avoid.

Political Infighting

Conflicts within and among governments influence whether, when, how, and where professional sports facilities are developed. Some of these result from competition for teams among jurisdictions in the same metropolitan area. These competitions involve city against city, as in the fight between St. Petersburg and Tampa for major league baseball, city against suburb, as with suburban efforts to lure the Raiders from Los Angeles, and state against city, as in New Jersey's battles with New York and Philadelphia. Contests among cities and suburbs have been fought with limited involvement of state government in California and Florida, in contrast with critical interventions by state officials in Illinois, Maryland, and Minnesota, which resulted in state decisions about the financing and location of sports facilities.

Whether governments compete or not within a metropolitan market, expanding public involvement in sports facilities has increased the number of officials, agencies, and jurisdictions with a stake in sports development, with concomitant growth in political relationships and potential conflicts. Increasingly complex and expensive sports projects involve a widening range of government players. These officials and agencies typically pursue their own interests in sports projects, which affect the financing, location, and prospects of proposals. Robert Moses, New York City's urban renewal czar and parks commissioner, successfully checked development of a new baseball stadium in Brooklyn by a rival agency; Moses' opposition undercut city efforts to keep the Dodgers, but opened the way for building Shea Stadium on land controlled by his Parks Department. Internal sectional conflicts also plagued efforts to keep the Dodgers, with Brooklyn politicians resisting Moses' plan to move the team to Queens from its namesake borough. Forty years later, political leaders in the Bronx bitterly opposed a stadium proposal designed to keep the Yankees in New York City, but not in the Bronx.

Sports projects frequently involve the creation of new agencies that adversely affect the interests of established organizations and their leaders. Plans for a new football stadium for the Bears bypassed the Chicago Park District, which operated Soldier Field. Baltimore's Department of Recreation and Parks, whose responsibilities included Memorial Stadium, was supplanted by the Maryland Stadium Authority when the state assumed the principal role in developing new stadiums. State control and financing of stadium development also diminished the involvement of Baltimore's mayor in sports politics. Similarly in Colorado, creation of a six-county metropolitan stadium district by the state diluted city hall's role in developing a ballpark in Denver for an expansion franchise that had been zealously pursued by top city officials.

Involvement of state governments and metropolitan agencies increases the potential for political conflicts over sports projects. Disagreements between Chicago's mayor and the governor of Illinois over appointments to a state sports authority and control over the agency's contracts delayed implementation of the city's original stadium agreement with the White Sox. Developing the Metrodome in Minneapolis was greatly complicated by the earlier establishment of a metropolitan agency that built the area's first big-league stadium in suburban Bloomington. The Metropolitan Stadium Commission favored modernizing the existing stadium, while Minneapolis wanted a new stadium located downtown; Minneapolis' plans were opposed by Bloomington, which wanted to stay in the big leagues, as well as by St. Paul, which wanted a piece of the sports action. Sorting out these conflicts involved long delays, complicated negotiations, repeated intervention by the state legislature, and creation of a state agency that built the Metrodome.

Politics Matter

Politics have always been a factor in where and under what conditions major league teams have played, but political considerations were relatively muted as long as playing facilities were privately provided by teams. The success of professional sports in shifting responsibility for arenas and stadiums to government has increased the importance of politics. Governments rather than teams largely determine whether sports facilities will be built and where, and public funds have underwritten the lion's share of investments in arenas and stadiums in the second half of the twentieth century. To be sure, governments have responded to the demands of teams, leagues, and powerful economic interests in making decisions concerning big league facilities. Still, politics constantly shape outcomes because public officials have to assign priorities, make choices, assess political opportunities and risks, worry about their jurisdictions and constituencies, find funding, select sites, mediate conflicts, and patch together compromises. In Chicago, a new stadium emerged from a series of compromises involving city hall, state leaders, business interests, and the White Sox. Mayor Washington and his allies, as John P. Pelissero, Beth M. Henschen, and Edward I. Sidlow emphasize, were "able to get state support for a Chicago stadium for the Sox only after engaging in logrolling that produced public financing for a suburban racetrack"; and the final obstacles were overcome when "the Chicago regime compromised with the Sox and the neighborhood residents on a more costly stadium and development policy that would keep the Sox from moving to Florida and end organized resistance to the project."[32]

Politics also means sports projects are riskier when voter approval is required than not, and in more jeopardy when legislative consent is needed than not. Political considerations make sports projects funded by general taxes and borrowing poorer bets than those financed by other means, and proposals underwritten by special taxes less attractive than those that do not involve taxation. Large governmental jurisdictions are better bets politically for sports projects than smaller ones, especially when locational controversies are involved. Politics also fosters exaggerated claims of economic benefits for sports projects, as politicians seek to win public support by promises to harvest fabulous riches from their fields of dreams. And politics almost always lengthen and complicate development of sports facilities, and in the process increase the cost of the final product to taxpayers.

Perhaps the most striking effect of politics is the continued location of most professional sports facilities within the boundaries of central cities, and the siting of a sizable portion of these projects in central business districts or their immediate environs. More often not, political considerations have prevailed over economic and social forces that push activities like professional sports out of cities to the suburbs. To be sure, economic factors have increased the appeal of downtown sites for major league teams, particularly the growing dependence on revenues from luxury boxes. But the economic appeal of downtown locations rarely offset the business negatives of expensive land, high construction costs, and inadequate parking, considerations that are particularly punishing in the case of stadiums, with their low utilization rates.

Determined efforts by political and business leaders in cities have tipped the balance in favor of downtown sites for sports facilities, efforts that have been rooted in the desire to spur downtown development and underwritten by public funds. Thus, politics rather than economics has cast arenas and stadiums as leading players in downtown schemes. The political muscle of political and economic elites has mustered the resources needed to turn plans into the realities of the Alamodome, Camden Yards, Gund Arena, SkyDome, and other downtown sports palaces. "Central cities," notes John F. Rooney Jr., a sports geographer, "are basically becoming recreational and tourist centers. They're essentially playgrounds, and that's where a sports team belongs."[33] Politics rather than economics, however, has been the driving force behind this trend; very few of the expensive playgrounds being built in central business districts would be where they are if arenas and stadiums were purely private enterprises. Most downtown sports facilities—like aquariums, convention centers, and other hallmarks of the revitalized center city—are enduring monuments to the importance of politics—public projects built largely with tax dollars and located primarily by political rather than market forces.

18

Private Games and Public Stakes

P ROFESSIONAL team sports in the United States and Canada have always been rooted in places. Major league teams have fostered close identification with the urban areas where they played, and sports fans are primarily interested in the fortunes of their home team. Public development of big league playing facilities has turned professional sports into a joint venture of private teams and the governmental jurisdictions that build and provide arenas and stadiums. The close identification of major league teams with local prestige and civic self esteem raises the public stakes in professional sports, spurring spirited competition for a limited number of places in the big leagues and escalating public commitments to secure and retain home teams.

Distinctive public interests in professional sports are largely defined by these place-based connections with major league teams and their leagues. Professional sports are not an essential activity that fulfills critical public needs. Teams and leagues provide entertainment; "it's just a game," writes Richard Ford of baseball, "an amusement, a marginal thing, not an art, not a consequential metaphor for life, not a public trust."[1] Public interest is magnified in this segment of the amusement business because of the linkages to places and hometown fans. In business terms, professional sport is a middling-sized industry of relatively minor importance to the national economies of the United States and Canada, and a modest element in the local economies of the forty-odd metropolitan areas with major league teams. The inflated economic claims advanced by sports advocates reflect the intensity of place concerns about being in the big leagues—as well as the self-interest of teams and their powerful allies—rather than the intrinsic economic importance of professional sports. Threats to relocate arouse public concern largely because of the emotional and symbolic connections between teams, places, and people.

Public interests in where big league teams play revolve around two basic concerns: the overall geographical scope of professional sports leagues and the permanence of the location of teams in particular places. The public interest is usually defined in terms of making professional sports available to greater numbers of people, which means having more teams playing in more places. Congress has pushed professional sports to serve more people by adding teams, and has tried to insure that mergers put more places in the big leagues. Maximizing access to major league sports, of course, is limited by a number of constraining factors, including market size, suitable playing facilities, league controls over expansion, and owners who are willing to invest in marginal locations.

The public interest in keeping teams in places derives in part from the goal of making professional sports as widely available as possible; relocation reduces access unless a league has more than one team in a metropolitan area. Public interests also are served by franchise stability because of the identification of teams with places, connections reinforced by the prestige value and other benefits of major league teams for places. Public stakes in locational stability are raised by government development of sports facilities. Public investments in arenas and stadiums are best protected by insuring that teams stay in town; and the growth in direct governmental involvement in professional sports has fueled demands for more public controls over franchise movement and greater accountability on the part of teams and leagues.

Availability and stability are not always complementary objectives. Places with teams are more interested in stability, in keeping a team in town and protecting public investments in arenas and stadiums. Places seeking to get into the big leagues are primarily concerned with availability, either through expansion or by inducing a team to relocate. Tensions between these goals, and between places with teams and those without, have been most pronounced with respect to relocation, but also arise in discussions of expansion, new leagues, and public investments in sports facilities.

Opening Up the Big Leagues

One way to make professional team sports more widely available is to lower the barriers that control entry into the major leagues. Roger G. Noll suggests that "government could insist that leagues expand whenever someone is willing to put up a reasonable amount of money for a franchise."[2] With leagues no longer restricting admission, owners rather than leagues would select the markets in which they wanted to field major league teams, with economic considerations rather than a cartel determining which metropolitan areas had teams and how many teams played in a particular market.

Eased entry presumably would mean more teams playing in a larger number of metropolitan areas, and thus would bring the tangible and intangible benefits of big league sports to more places. With leagues unable to limit the supply of franchises, competition among places for teams would be expected to ease, relocation would be less attractive, and professional sports would have less leverage on places. More bargaining power for places in dealing with teams should lessen the need for public investments in arenas and stadiums; "with unlimited entry," Arthur T. Johnson thinks "a city could quickly replace a relocating team, and therefore not be subject to having to escalate public subsidies to retain a franchise."[3] Eased entry should enhance franchise stability by reducing the effects of market size on the fortunes of teams—more teams would locate in the largest markets. As a result, intermarket differences would narrow, producing less inequality among teams. Healthier teams in smaller markets, goes the argument, would be more attractive investments and less likely to relocate. And with market size declining in importance, sports entrepreneurs would be attracted to lesser urban areas, further increasing the number of places with major league teams.

To what degree these predicted benefits of eased entry would be realized is not clear. With or without league controls, the number of metropolitan areas with teams is not likely to increase dramatically because professional sports have claimed most markets that are large enough to support major league sports. To compensate for their limited size, smaller urban areas seeking franchises would probably continue to compete with one another to offer teams facilities and other subsidies. Lesser areas also might well face increased pressures to provide greater benefits to keep teams from moving to larger markets in the absence of league constraints on relocation. Bidding among places for teams presumably would be less restrained if leagues no longer controlled entry or territorial rights, since places seeking a franchise would only have to satisfy a particular owner rather than an entire league.

Eased entry has less attraction for cities with teams than for places seeking to get into the big leagues. More cities building facilities and offering subsidies in hopes of securing teams might well continue to bid up prices for places with teams. Some cities seeking a spot in the big leagues are sure to prefer an established team, which would be easier to secure in the absence of league controls on team movement. A sizable increase in the number of teams in the major leagues also would magnify the adverse effects of expansion on places with teams, diluting the quality of play and reducing games with traditional rivals. Uncertainties for places with teams would increase if eased entry reduced league stability. And the value of major league status might be lowered if scores of places were able to join the club, although the addition of seventy-three teams since 1950 does not seem to have lessened the desirability of being in the big leagues—witness the willingness of places to spend hundreds of millions of dollars for a home team.

Despite these uncertainties, places and the public have more to gain than lose from eased entry. Additional metropolitan areas would have teams, which would increase the availability of big league sports, albeit at some cost in terms of the stability of major league franchises and their connections to places. Increasing the number of teams would reduce competition among places because the supply of teams would be more in balance with demand. Eased entry also would substantially enhance the influence of places, since an increased supply of teams would strengthen the hand of most jurisdictions in their bargaining with professional sports.

Whatever the benefits for places, less control over entry and market areas clearly is anathema to professional sports. Proposals to open up the major leagues are rejected as impractical and unfair. Existing teams, argue defenders of the status quo, have a collective interest in the viability of new teams, which means they need to insure that new members of leagues meet minimum financial and competence standards. Free entry, critics contend, would produce instability, with a changing set of teams and places in leagues that would adversely affect schedules, rivalries, records, and championships. Not incidentally, free entry also threatens the economic interests of established teams and leagues, which understandably resist giving away membership in a successful league, a share of its collective revenues, and control over the supply of teams.

Proponents of eased entry respond by conceding the need for collective controls on admission and compensation for existing teams. Henry G. Demmert suggests that applicants be required to accept league rules and meet minimal playing quality criteria.[4] Entrants would be expected to compensate existing teams for players and lost revenues. Noll additionally would have new teams post an indemnity to protect the rest of a league should a new team be unable to complete a season.[5] Applicants could also be required to meet minimum standards regarding population, arenas and stadiums, and the financial resources of owners. Johnson would add restrictions on reentry, proposing that "cities in which franchises fail financially might be required to wait five years or longer before reentry into the league."[6] Such entry standards would decrease the availability of major league teams while increasing stability. Minimum population requirements would limit the number of places eligible for a place in the major leagues, while reducing the prospects for unstable franchises in marginal markets. Similarly, financial standards would restrict the pool of potential owners, and thus the number of teams and places with teams, while increasing the likelihood that new franchises will be relatively stable. Restrictions on reentry and indemnities likewise would limit the availability of big league sports in the interests of stability and protecting established teams and the places where they play.

Leagues, of course, have already developed a variety of standards for expansion teams. But current standards are determined and applied by leagues, and qualifying under these requirements guarantees nothing to places and prospective owners. With open entry, places and prospective owners that met minimal standards would presumptively be eligible to join a league. Members of a league would no longer be able to decide whether to expand, or to ration the number of expansion franchises, or to protect territories of established teams, or to determine who could join the clubs of major league team owners. These consequences make eased entry unacceptable to professional sports, even with standards designed to protect the interests of existing teams and their leagues. Public standards would dilute self-regulation, and automatic entry for qualified applicants would end internal control over the size, locations, and membership of major leagues.

Given the resistance of professional sports to easing entry, changes in major league admissions procedures would have to come from government, presumably through the courts or legislation establishing national standards and a regulatory mechanism for sports leagues. Substituting public for private governance of professional sports, however, is highly unlikely. Courts have accepted league controls over entry in cases involving expansion, prospective owners, and rival leagues. Congress has shown little interest in federal sports regulation. Nothing came of legislation introduced in 1972 to establish a Federal Sports Commission empowered to regulate the sale of teams, transfer of franchises, territorial restrictions, and broadcast rights, or the work of the House Select Committee on Professional Sports, which was established in 1976 to determine whether federal legislative controls were needed.[7] Federal controls over professional sports would fly in the face of widespread doubts about the effectiveness or desirability of government regulation in the United States. Developing and applying standards would be difficult, leading in all probability to protracted proceedings, conflicting expert testimony, and challenges to regulations in court. Regulatory agencies, moreover, tend to be most responsive to the regulated industry and other well-organized interests—teams, leagues, broadcasters, and players in the case of professional sports. The concerns of publics and places surely would get short shrift in any regulatory process unless these fragmented interests were better organized than has been the case to date.

Any effort to substitute public for private control over entry also faces formidable obstacles posed by the political clout of teams, leagues, and their allies. Political influence has enabled the sports industry to deflect demands for more public regulation and greater accountability despite rising governmental investments in sports facilities and other subsidies. Bolstering its political influence has been the industry's success in framing the terms of the debate over professional sports. Public interests, sports argue and many agree, are best served by existing arrangements that provide for self-regulation by private teams organized into leagues. This system, proponents contend, has greatly expanded the scope of major league sports while providing relatively high levels of franchise stability; and in the process has produced games, seasons, and championships that have attracted steadily increasing numbers of customers and television viewers. As Michael Roberts notes, professional sports have capitalized on public wariness of government rules and the image of sports as special and private "to make the public believe that regulation would wreck sports as we know it."[8]

More Places to Play

Expansion controlled by leagues rather than eased entry regulated by government almost certainly will determine where new major league teams play in the foreseeable future. Despite its shortcomings, the existing system has substantially increased the availability of major league sports. Expansion under league rules has been the principal factor in the spread of major league sports from twenty-two metropolitan areas in 1950 to forty-three in 1995. Some observers question whether this expansion can continue. Concerns about the availability of markets led Anthony Baldo to conclude in 1991 that the NFL's expansion for the 1995 season "will be it, unless the leagues want to start franchises in third-tier American cities."[9] Negative assessments of the prospects of remaining markets, it should be noted, have followed almost every expansion; in 1973, for example, James Quirk and Mohamed El Hodiri emphasized that "expansion in baseball and in the other major sports has pretty well blanketed the country. . . . Perhaps the era will end because there isn't any place to go."[10] The expansion era, of course, did not end in the early 1970s; since 1973, baseball has added six teams, basketball eight, hockey seven, and football four.

Expansion has continued because urban growth increases the number of places that want to be in the big leagues, are willing to invest in major league facilities, and offer sufficient prospects of success to attract prospective owners willing to pay $100 million or more for an expansion team. Within the United States, eleven metropolitan areas without teams in 1995 were larger than Jacksonville, the second smallest area with a big league team (Green Bay, the smallest, does not provide a useful benchmark for future expansion any more than it has in the past). Metropolitan areas that rank just below those with teams also are likely to continue to attract future expansion franchises, as underscored by the NFL's reaching down to tab Jacksonville. Some potential locations are more attractive to major leagues than others. New markets for a league usually are preferred over places where teams have failed in the past. Metropolitan areas with extensive drawing areas are preferable to locations relatively close to existing teams in the same sport. Rapidly growing areas are much better bets than stable or declining metropolitan markets; and future expansion is likely to be even more growth-oriented given the need of major leagues to pick among relatively small markets. The attractions of growth and extensive market areas means that expansion teams will continue to be placed primarily in urban centers in the Sunbelt.

Demography, of course, is not the only factor that affects the willingness of leagues to expand. Each expansion raises anew questions about the future enthusiasm of established teams for sharing revenues with newcomers, especially in the wake of the rapid growth of broadcast revenues. Noll argued in

1991 that "NBA owners are likely to face a declining incentive to expand if national broadcasting revenues continue to climb."[11] But the NBA expanded for 1995 after negotiating a record television contract, as did the NFL. Expansion will continue to override these concerns as long as benefits exceed costs for teams and leagues. The principal benefit is the price at which expansion franchises can be sold; the secondary benefits are adding new markets for major league sports, bidding up the inducements that places offer teams, and bolstering political support by increasing the availability of big league games. Expansion teams are part of what the business of professional sports has to sell, and presumably leagues will continue to expand as long as demand exceeds supply at prices acceptable to existing teams.

Future expansion also depends on whether leagues continue to locate teams only in the United States and Canada. Growth of professional sports has steadily reduced the number of attractive markets for expansion in the United States. Adding teams in Canada is limited by the paucity of large metropolitan markets. Only Toronto, Montreal, and Vancouver entered the 1990s with populations greater than one million, and these three metropolitan areas had seven teams by 1995. Europe, Latin America, and the Pacific rim, on the other hand, offer huge urban areas, vast television audiences, and large markets for merchandise, as well as plenty of corporate advertisers and sponsors. Penetration of these markets becomes more attractive with the growth of multinational corporations, creation of regional trading zones in Europe and North America, and freer flow of capital across national boundaries. Increases in the number of television channels, introduction of pay television, and rapid advances in communications technology add to the appeal of internationalizing the reach of American professional team sports. Expansion beyond Canada, however, would complicate the economic, political, and competitive world of professional team sports. Different national interests, political realities, legal responsibilities, business practices, and social conditions would have to be accommodated by leagues that strongly prefer to control their own destinies with minimal outside interference.

Canada illustrates some of these complications. The NHL's failure to include Vancouver and Quebec in its initial expansion in 1967 spurred efforts to subject the league to the provisions of Canada's Combines Act; and the NHL subsequently sought to mollify critics by maintaining a substantial presence in Canada. Teams in Canada complain about the competitive disadvantages imposed by a weak Canadian dollar and higher tax rates. Canadian nationalists see professional sports as another example of the dominance of Canada by the United States and its voracious business interests. For Richard Gruneau, "modern hockey and baseball . . . represent a classic dramatization of the . . . exploitative nature of Canada's association with the American metropole."[12] And protection of the Canadian Football League—and its distinctive variant of the game—has blocked the NFL from joining the other three leagues in Toronto, the tenth largest market area served by major league sports in North America.

To date, the risks in expanding abroad have carried more weight than the benefits; professional sports have preferred to concentrate on selling products in foreign markets while producing their game in the United States and Canada. Illustrative is the approach of the NBA, which has the most exportable product, since basketball is played everywhere. Expanding the NBA abroad would build on the burgeoning popularity of the American professional game in Europe, perhaps with existing professional teams in Italy, Spain, and France providing the basis for a trans-Atlantic division of the league. The NBA, however, has preferred to market itself worldwide rather than expand abroad. NBA games are telecast in a growing number of countries; a preseason tournament matches leading European teams and an NBA club; teams play regular season openers in foreign cities; and the Dream Teams demonstrated the awesome skills of the league's superstars in the Olympics. All of this sells more merchandise, sponsorships, joint promotions, and television broadcasts around the world, while keeping the NBA out of the clutches of foreign entanglements bound to accompany the location of teams in Madrid or Milan.

Marketing also has been the principal emphasis of the National Football League, which labors under the burdens of selling a uniquely American game and competing with the immensely popular sport that the rest of the world calls football. To build interest, the NFL has played exhibition games overseas, while steadily expanding the telecasting of games in foreign markets. In addition, the NFL sought to promote its game by creating the World League of American Football, which initially included teams in Europe and North America, then reappeared as a purely European league. Interest in expansion abroad, never strong within the NFL, was further dampened by the World League's financial losses and other difficulties. Europe might be expected to have more appeal to the NHL than the NFL, given hockey's popularity in a number of countries and the growing corps of NHL players from Russia, Sweden, Finland, and the Czech Republic who could provide local teams with home-grown stars. Trying to maintain a presence in Canada's smaller metropolitan markets, however, has been a more pressing international concern for the NHL in recent years than expanding to Moscow or Stockholm.

Baseball has been most intrigued by the possibilities of expansion abroad, with talk of teams in Mexico, the Caribbean, and Japan. Moving from talk to action is the difficult step, one that confronts baseball with the same realities as face other sports. Japan's baseball leagues are just as likely to defend their turf against American baseball as Canada has been in protecting the Canadian Football League. Mexico looked promising with the enactment of the North American Free Trade Agreement in 1994, but the collapse of the Mexican economy at the beginning of 1995 clouded the immediate future prospects of

Mexico City and Monterey. Other possibilities in Latin America that combine a passion for *beisbol* with large urban areas—such as Caracas, Havana, San Juan, and Santo Domingo—also are shadowed by political complications and shaky economies that seem unlikely to generate the revenues required to support a major league team. Clearly, the best bets should baseball turn to the south are Mexico City and Monterey, with the latter getting an opportunity to market its wares in 1996 when the Padres scheduled three games at Monterey Stadium to avoid conflicts with the Republican National Convention in San Diego. Both cities, however, remain long shots; speaking of baseball's next expansion, an official tempers enthusiasm based on "the population down there and the interest in the game" with the reality that "the economic and governmental situations may be such a handicap over the next ten years that we may not be able to get there at this time."[13]

More Leagues

For some critics, additional leagues rather than more teams are necessary to increase the availability of professional sports and protect public investments in arenas and stadiums. New leagues would break the monopoly of the existing cartels, ending their control over the supply of franchises and lessening their bargaining power with places. Stephen F. Ross advocates the divestiture of existing leagues, arguing that "competing leagues would vie against each other for the right to play in public stadiums, driving rents up and tax subsidies down," while "leagues would be more eager to add new expansion markets, lest those markets fall into the hands of a rival league."[14] Noll sees multiple leagues as increasing the availability of major league sports, noting that "only when an entire league can be formed does competition work in favor of the fan by increasing his access to sporting events."[15] More generally, advocates contend, competitive leagues would substitute market forces for monopoly control, leading to a more efficient allocation of resources in the sports industry.

Competitive leagues would not be painless for places; some teams would fail and some metropolitan areas would be unable to sustain major league sports. And marginal markets would still seek to make themselves attractive by offering generous public incentives to teams, as places do to attract businesses in industries more competitive than professional sports. Competitive leagues also are questioned by those who doubt that "big league" is a divisible concept. Leonard Koppett argues that "a major league sports structure *must* be a monopoly, by definition: an ultimate champion can emerge only from a common set of operating rules"[16] "Major league" implies the best performers playing each other. Spectators, an economic analysis of professional sports suggests, "may be unwilling to give support to two independent leagues, each of which claims to be major perhaps because, with a limited number of star players with innate abilities spread around a larger number of clubs, quality declines."[17] Ross seeks to deal with these concerns by providing for interleague play and championships among his competitive leagues, but would "prohibit any interleague agreement concerning the number and location of franchises, rules for allocating players among teams, and (except for games involving teams from rival leagues) the sale of broadcast rights."[18] But such restrictions might well lead to one league besting its rivals, emerging as the *real* major league with the better players, teams in the strongest markets, the most lucrative broadcast contracts, and places competing to be represented in *the* major league.

Nonetheless, for places and the public, the attractions of truly competitive leagues outweigh the potential drawbacks. More metropolitan areas would have an opportunity to get into the big leagues, and large urban complexes certainly would have more teams. Places would be able to drive harder bargains with teams for the provision and use of public playing facilities. In some places at least, economic and political elites would have less leverage in local considerations of sports investments if more major league opportunities were available. And reduced public funding would shift more of the burden of financing major league facilities to teams, where it belongs. Fans also would benefit from the greater availability of professional sports at the lower prices that should result from competition among leagues.

The real problem with competitive leagues is political; government action to break up existing leagues is highly improbable given the political influence of professional sports and the lack of any sustained public pressure to end sports monopolies. Baseball retains its antitrust exemption despite periodic calls for congressional action to end its special status. When Congress has legislated on professional sports, the usual result has been less rather than more competition, as in the broadcasting and football merger bills. Court rulings in antitrust cases brought by rival leagues have not altered the dominant position of the established circuits. And the trust busters in Washington and Ottawa have shown minimal interest in challenging the professional sports cartels in recent years. That so little enthusiasm is expressed outside academic circles in ending monopoly sports leagues underscores the political success of the sports business in securing acceptance of their cartels as indispensable to major league sports.

Given these political realities, rival leagues seem likely to continue to be the exception rather than the norm in professional sports, at best secondary players that provide some places and owners opportunities to get into established leagues. As such, new leagues play a useful role in increasing the availability of professional sports, permitting both places and entrepreneurs to take advantage of easier entry requirements to seek a spot in the big leagues. Rival leagues also function as a desirable check on established leagues. New leagues typically are organized because an established league's entry procedures are not responsive to market and place demands. And new leagues have often accelerated the spread of major league sports, by spurring existing leagues to expand or add teams through merger with the rival league.

Prospects for new leagues continuing to play these roles depend in part on the availability of franchises in established leagues. Expansion has steadily reduced the number of substantial metropolitan areas without teams that are the prime targets of new leagues. And the prospect of future expansion or of luring an existing franchise makes the most attractive places without teams, as well as the most capable prospective owners, wary of taking risks with new leagues. Organization of rival leagues also depends on the availability of broadcast revenues, especially in light of the rising labor costs of major league sports. Television money and exposure do not guarantee success for new leagues, but are essential for a rival to compete with established leagues for players, corporate sponsors, and customers. Broadcasting contracts, however, are harder to come by as existing leagues have forged extensive webs of network arrangements and placed teams in almost every major media market.

Even if rival leagues overcome the odds and open for business, they are likely to be passing rather than permanent elements under the present system. Places and owners are interested in new leagues chiefly as a means of getting into the real big leagues. For places, the primary benefits of big-time sports come from being in the American or National League, or the NBA, NFL, or NHL; membership in a rival league, after all, is usually a mark of a place's failure to win a spot in an established league. For owners, single leagues are far preferable to multiple leagues; to secure the benefits of monopoly, owners of teams in new leagues typically seek mergers rather than rivalry, and existing leagues usually choose accommodation over continued competition. And whatever the endgame, established leagues normally prevail because they have more prestige, customers, and quality players, as well as better markets and more substantial owners.

In the absence of government action to require multiple leagues, competing leagues promise to continue to be periodic rather than permanent features of professional team sports. New leagues seem destined either to fail or provide alternative routes to the big leagues for a relatively small number of franchises. Successful new leagues can open the way for additional metropolitan areas to win places in established leagues, although these opportunities clearly have narrowed as more markets have major league teams. Rival leagues also provide the most probable means of breaching the territorial rights of established teams in large metropolitan areas, as occurred with the Mets, Jets and Nets in the New York area.

Protecting Place Interests

The stakes of places in professional sports have expanded far more rapidly than the ability of cities, states, and provinces to protect their interests. Places deal from a position of weakness because the sports industry controls the supply of teams, location of franchises, and ownership of clubs. Major league sports urge ever greater governmental investments, but refuse to allow public ownership of teams that play in arenas and stadiums built with tax dollars. Reducing private control over entry and location is one way to enhance the ability of places to protect their interests in professional sports, but as already indicated changes in franchise controls are unlikely in the present political climate in the United States. Breaking up monopoly leagues would increase local bargaining power, but competitive leagues, alas, are another political long shot. Federal regulation of relocation would provide leverage to places with teams in dealing with major league sports. Here, too, the political prospects are daunting because of skepticism about government regulation, opposition of leagues to losing control over relocation, and resistance from places without teams.

More likely politically than any of these reforms is congressional action to extend antitrust exemptions to league controls over relocation. Such legislation would strengthen leagues over teams, but would not necessarily benefit places, whose interests have never been a major consideration in league decisions about the location of franchises. Congress should insure that any antitrust exemption for relocation includes minimal protections for places. To be eligible for an exemption, a league should have to adopt explicit criteria for relocation that deal with playing facilities, local support, and revenues; an exempt league should also be obliged to regularize expansion procedures so as to provide clear guidelines for places that seek teams. Exemption legislation also should require leagues to specify procedures that provide for sale of teams to owners committed to keeping a franchise in town. These measures would not right the balance between places and professional sports, but they would provide places with additional leverage in dealing with teams and leagues, in negotiations, in political contests, and in court.

Places would benefit if professional sports leagues shared all revenues; and Congress should require that leagues share revenues in any legislation extending antitrust protection, whether an exemption for relocation or a measure to provide uniform treatment for all four sports. Revenue sharing serves the common interests of places represented in a league by reducing the market differences that underlie the locational instability of many sports franchises. Smaller places obviously benefit more than larger ones, but not at the expense of big metropolitan areas; unshared revenues generated by populous urban areas, after all, are reaped by teams rather places. Critics question whether revenue sharing promotes franchise stability; the owner of the Dallas Cowboys insists that places would benefit if NFL teams shared less "so they can produce the revenue where they wouldn't have to look for deals elsewhere to finance their operations."[19] But less sharing is bound to increase the economic disparities between teams, differences rooted in market size. Certainly the growth of unshared stadium revenues from luxury seating, concessions, and exclusive marketing arrangements has widened revenue differences—the Cowboys collected $40 million in 1996 while the Seahawks took in only $3 million—and contributed to the NFL's epidemic of franchise relocation in recent years.

Place and public interests would also be served by insuring that leagues permitted public ownership of teams. Some observers see public ownership as the best means of protecting place and fan interests in professional sports; Peter S. Canellos argues that "teams should be owned by the people of the cities that adopt them; they should be operated as public, nonprofit corporations."[20] Public ownership, however, is too problematic to offer as a replacement for privately owned teams. Many places would not want to own teams, or could not under existing law, or would be unable to afford to purchase and operate a major league team. Public ownership, like government development of arenas and stadiums, risks political interference, patronage, and insider dealings, while not guaranteeing increased public access to sporting events. Although Green Bay has developed a mechanism that works quite smoothly, more complex urban settings could turn publicly owned teams into political footballs, with public officials taking the heat for losing seasons, soaring salaries, bad trades, and poor attendance. Public ownership also will be stoutly resisted by the rulers of professional sports, who do not want public owners admitted to their private clubs.

Despite these uncertainties and obstacles, public ownership should be available as an option, with teams fully or partially owned by nonprofit corporations or stadium authorities or public enterprises. Given the escalation of prices for major league franchises, relatively few places are likely to be interested in buying a team, but it is worth noting that public investments in sports facilities often exceed the market value of the team that plays in an arena or stadium, and the same creative public financing devices that have funded these buildings could underwrite purchase of a team. With public ownership a possibility, places could decide whether they were willing to pay the market price to remain in the big leagues, thus providing an endgame that might moderate conflict over relocation. Public ownership also would permit places to seek an expansion franchise without the necessity of having an owner in place, which would offer a way around a critical obstacle to the big league aspirations of some otherwise qualified metropolitan areas. And full or partial public ownership of a team could provide an insurance policy against relocation; "the idea," argues an advocate, "is to buy the wheels off the team."[21]

Differences among urban areas with stakes in major league sports complicate the protection of place interests. Size divides places into metropolitan markets that are more or less likely to attract and support major league teams. Places with teams have interests fundamentally different from those that seek teams. Metropolitan areas without teams compete with each other for expansion teams and for franchises that might relocate. Among urban areas with teams, interests vary depending on whether arenas and stadiums are publicly or privately owned, on which governmental entity is responsible for public sports facilities, on the duration and terms of leases, and on the commitment of team owners to a particular locale. Place interests are further divided when cities, suburbs, and states compete within metropolitan areas for teams.

Bridging these differences through collective action offers places a means of increasing public influence on major league sports. More effective representation of places also would serve the interests of fans, who have even less influence on professional sports than places. The natural basis for cooperation among places is having teams in the same league. Places represented in a league have shared interests in keeping their teams and controlling public spending for facilities and other subsidies, as well as in league rules concerning ownership, relocation, revenues, and playing facilities. They additionally have a common interest in fostering expansion, since more spots in the big leagues reduces competitive pressures on places with teams. Places with teams are also the most important locales for professional sports; generally they are the largest metropolitan areas and best markets, places where teams want to play and leagues need to be represented. Governments in these places supply most of the arenas and stadiums in which teams play and on which they depend for ever larger amounts of revenue. An organization of places with teams in a league could share information, develop uniform approaches to leases and subsidies, advance collective legislative concerns, and lobby professional sports when decisions affecting place interests are made.

Collective action through league associations would not be easily achieved; Johnson thinks that "a union of sports cities . . . is unlikely to be effective since it could not exercise control over members or non-members who desired a sports franchise."[22] Members would have diverse interests and prospects; some would value their teams more highly than others, or be more susceptible to pressures for new facilities, or be more willing to invest in sports facilities because of other development goals. Places without teams would continue to have interests different from those of cities in leagues, although strong support for expansion from the haves is a way of making common cause with have-nots. The question, of course, is whether league associations could overcome these differences sufficiently to increase the influence of places in dealing with teams, leagues, and national governments. Certainly associations of governments have been successful in advancing common place interests in a variety of policy areas, including activities that involve competition among places, such as airports, seaports, and convention centers, which have some similarity to professional sports. Places will never know whether cooperation will enhance their ability to protect their growing stakes in professional sports unless they join forces, creating organizations with considerable political potential considering the size and influence of major league cities, metropolitan areas, states, and provinces.

Cooperation among places is further complicated by differences within metropolitan areas. Teams are located in particular places in politically decentralized metropolitan areas, most in central cities but some in suburbs; and public sports facilities belong to city, county, metropolitan, state, and provincial agencies, and are paid for by taxpayers in particular jurisdictions. Further muddying the waters is competition for teams within metropolitan areas. Internal competition for major league teams, however, has eased somewhat in recent years, as a result of suburban opposition to sports facilities, as well as the need for broadly based financing of increasingly expensive arenas and stadiums. Central cities, in contrast to most suburbs, want arenas and stadiums, and their economic and political elites are willing to invest considerable resources to create organizations, obtain financing, and secure sites for sports facilities. Professional teams, moreover, are a particularly metropolitan institution, supported by fans through a broad urban region rather than within a particular governmental jurisdiction. Whatever general economic benefits are generated by major league teams tend to be widely distributed spatially, as is the prestige of being in the big leagues and other intangibles. And state governments, increasingly the key players in the politics of professional sports facilities in the United States, typically foster metropolitan approaches, and are able to dictate areawide outcomes through their control over financial resources.

Whatever the prospects for more cooperative action—and they unfortunately are not very promising given the cutthroat competition for teams—individual localities need to play a tougher game with professional sports. "Officials must learn to negotiate better and more aggressively," counsels Johnson, "to be willing to take risks, and to seek alternatives to sports as economic projects and objects of city pride."[23] Those who negotiate with teams need a clear and realistic view of costs and benefits, including the often ignored burdens of additional public services and infrastructure. Intelligent decisions require realistic information rather than the wishful thinking and public relations pap that often passes for analysis on sports issues, particularly with respect to economic benefits. Places should seek leases of long duration, preferably for the life of the bonds that finance an arena or stadium, as well as punitive buyout clauses and rental payments that cover a team's share of capital and operating costs. To be sure, places will not necessarily achieve these objectives, but stronger bargaining positions are essential to producing outcomes that are more protective of public interests and investments.

In driving harder bargains, places with teams have advantages that too often are underestimated; professional sports have to be in most of the markets that already have franchises. Teams and leagues need these metropolitan areas with their large populations, substantial economic bases, and existing web of fans, ticket holders, advertisers, and broadcasters. When push comes to shove, teams and leagues will rarely abandon an attractive metropolitan market, even if they are unable to extract all they want in terms of facilities and other subsidies. Smaller metropolitan areas are more vulnerable to relocation threats than larger markets, which is why their interests need to be bolstered by revenue sharing and public ownership options. And although teams are less likely to abandon large markets, internal competition can weaken the bargaining position of the particular place that houses a team, usually the central city, which is why state or metropolitan arrangements to manage such competition are desirable.

Places also need limits in dealing with teams and leagues, which implies both a willingness to go to the brink and acceptance of the possibility of losing a team. Limits strengthen rather than weaken the hand of officials in dealing with teams and leagues. Bounded rather than open-ended commitments reflect the economic and political realities of professional sports. None of these games is an economic necessity, and the actual economic benefits are quite modest. Sport investments are optional rather than mandatory activities for cities, suburbs, states, and provinces. Public clamor to use tax dollars for professional sports generally has been muted; voters frequently have rejected sports projects when public approval has been required; and the political risks to elected officials should a team depart are greatly exaggerated.

The point is not that major league sports are unimportant or even unworthy of government support; instead, the need is for public sports investments to be put in perspective, for reality to be substituted for fantasy, and for officials and publics to understand what they are buying and why. A new Yankee Stadium will not be an economic gold mine, nor a critical stimulus to growth in the nation's largest business center and urban tourist attraction. To be sure, a strong case can be made that the proud banners of New York's most successful team should be kept within the city limits; without question, mid-Manhattan would provide a magnificent visual backdrop for another retro ballpark. But whether these benefits are worth a billion or more dollars is very dubious, particularly when a move to New Jersey would keep the Yankees in the relevant New York for most of the team's customers, fans, and business associates—the New York metropolitan area.

The biggest obstacle to more realism and hard-nosed bargaining is the political influence of local interests that strongly support sports development. The desire of economic and political elites to use arenas and stadiums to advance business interests and political careers fosters symbiotic relationships in which city leaders get public investment in favored locations while a team secures a sweetheart deal. Public officials and their business allies are unlikely to abandon sports development objectives, especially since these goals can be coupled to the fate of the home team or securing a place in the big leagues, matters of considerable concern to sports fans, the press, and others. If anything, claims about economic bonanzas and growth miracles escalate as the scale and price of sports projects rise. The best reality check is to provide voters with an opportunity to pass direct judgment on sports proposals. The necessity to secure voter approval forces elites to craft proposals that are politically acceptable, while offering a lever for securing a better deal in negotiations with teams. Referendums guarantee nothing; proposals sometimes can be misleading and defeats increasingly are sidestepped by proponents. Still, as Neil J. Sullivan suggests, the record on stadium votes indicates that "voters can examine the merits of this issue with a clearer eye than most public officials in America."[24]

Places also have an interest in encouraging private development of arenas and stadiums. Private development reduces public investment in sports facilities, although public funds often are required for land acquisition or site improvements or roads and other infrastructure. Teams probably are less likely to relocate if they own their own facilities. Pressing for private development, of course, runs the risk of weakening a city's competitive position if other places offer a team more attractive public deals, but so do setting limits to sports investments or driving hard bargains with teams or requiring voter approval of sports projects. Another problem with private development is less public control over locations. Here, locational goals have to be balanced against the lower costs of private development, while bearing in mind that public investments in land or infrastructure provide considerable leverage over the location of private sports facilities.

Public rather than private investment, however, is likely to continue to provide most of the capital for big league arenas and stadiums. In addition to bargaining hard to limit their share and protect their investment, governments should insist that as much of the public contribution as possible be financed by user taxes on professional sporting events. Taxes on tickets, luxury boxes, concessions, and parking are the fairest way to raise public revenues for arenas and stadiums. Insistence on sports user taxes, of course, would put a place at a competitive disadvantage. Congress could ease the competitive disincentive by enacting a national sports facilities excise tax, which would be rebated to jurisdictions that owned arenas and stadiums used by major league teams, and Canada could take similar action. And pegging the rate of the sports tax to the share of the facility underwritten by the public could provide an incentive for private development and ownership.

Limited Partners

Professional team sports have always been a partnership between teams and the places where they play. Major leagues have needed cities from their earliest years to provide identification, rivalries, and customers, and have increasingly depended on places to underwrite facilities and other public benefits for the home team. Places remain a critical part of the professional sports business despite sweeping changes that have vastly increased the economic stakes for all the participants. Teams continue to be rooted in particular places, although broadcasting has fundamentally altered the connections between games and their audiences. Strong place identifications have also survived the nationalization of much of professional sports through the increasing importance of broadcast networks, major corporations, and national markets for the buying and selling of teams.

Professional sports, by and large, have exploited this relationship, seeking to extract as much as possible from places where teams play and giving relatively little in return. Devotion to the home team and the appeal of the big leagues are seen by most owners as opportunities to demand better deals, play places off against each other, and fatten the balance sheet. Growing public investments in major league sports have increased the appetites of teams and leagues, which shamelessly use their control over the supply and location of franchises to bid up prices for a place in the big leagues. Professional sports answer that they are private businesses, subject to the imperatives of market forces and bottom lines. Big league sports, however, are curious private enterprises, claiming to be civic tokens and emotional necessities, and demanding ever larger public investments in their playing facilities. Teams and leagues will also argue that they care about their communities, pointing to support for charities, youth programs, and other good causes by owners and players. Certainly these activities are important, and professional sports are both to be commended for their community activities and urged to do more. But the heart of the relationship between a team and its community is commitment, by the team to the place as well as by the place to the team.

Places have a strong interest in bolstering the commitment of their home teams. Johnson believes that a team's "psychological attachment to the city is as important as the fans' identity with the team."[25] Intangible attachments are enhanced by local owners and by teams that own their playing facilities. Political and business leaders can further increase attachments by treating team owners as highly valued members of the community, deserving of places on boards and committees. The trick, of course, is to foster commitment while protecting the public's stakes; all too often, closer relations between teams and local elites have produced an alliance for picking the public's pocket. Good relations and serious negotiations, however, need not be incompatible; after all, teams constantly claim that they want to be good citizens while pressing their demands. Local leaders should follow the same course, seeking to strengthen commitments with teams while driving hard bargains.

Teams and leagues also have an interest in improving their relationship with places. Most teams are going to remain in their present metropolitan markets, and the bulk of these will continue to be located in the jurisdiction where they presently are playing. Good relations are better for business, resulting in more support from fans, business, the media, and local officials. Leagues, moreover, pay a price for fostering competition for teams. In the NFL, the mad scramble for a better deal has reduced league authority and cohesion, widened the gap between rich and poor teams, and left major metropolitan markets like Los Angeles, Cleveland, and Houston without home teams. Teams, to be sure, continue to secure ever larger benefits from their superior bargaining position, and these benefits translate into higher revenues and franchise values. Pressing this advantage, however, inevitably risks resentment and retribution that can be costly to a team and its league. Professional sport, in its arrogance, forgets that things constantly change; politicians, businesses, voters, and fans all have their limits, especially when dealing with a nonessential activity with a voracious appetite for public largess. To dismiss public officials who ask tough questions about new facilities, as a baseball official did in 1996, as "posturing politicians ... making themselves look good to voters who don't want to spend money" is to trivialize the serious concerns that large numbers of Americans and Canadians have about what big league sports demand of places and the public in return for bestowing its conditional blessings on this or that city or metropolitan area.[26] What makes the home team special needs to be nurtured rather than abused by professional sports; big league sports, as two business analysts emphasize, "is a very special business, one that survives and prospers because of the relentless attachment—even love—of fans."[27]

More balanced relationships between places and teams are both desirable and possible, but the prospects for change unfortunately are minimal. Teams and leagues control the supply of franchises and their location, and government action to regulate or eliminate the power of league cartels is extremely unlikely in the foreseeable future. Places could organize to advance their common interests, but differences among places and the desire of political and business elites in particular places to pursue their sports interests unilaterally pose daunting obstacles to effective collective action.

Places could set limits, promote private facilities, drive harder bargains, be realistic about the benefits of professional sports, and insure that voters had to approve sports projects. But just the opposite is the rule in most places; governments increase spending, give away more revenues, inflate benefits, and avoid or ignore referenda on sports proposals. In an era of less government, professional sports is a glaring exception; cities with decrepit schools and crumbling infrastructure compete to build glittering new arenas and stadiums; governors who slash taxes and cut welfare rolls commit millions of public dollars to sports ventures. Privatization has become a favored solution for many public problems, but privatization in professional team sports has meant more private profits and greater public liabilities. Almost everywhere, the increasingly aggressive behavior of teams and leagues has enhanced the influence of local political and business leaders who seek sports at any price. And the public costs are bound to mount. Each new deal ratchets up the going price while every innovation speeds the financial and physical obsolescence of existing buildings and their leases. The classic ballparks lasted half a century or more, the initial public stadiums thirty or so years, and more recent facilities only a decade or two. The treadmill is speeding up; today's state-of-the-art palaces and sweetheart deals will soon be tomorrow's liabilities; and governments will have to scramble for even more scarce public resources to satisfy the voracious gatekeepers to the big leagues.

For the foreseeable future, teams and their leagues will continue to make private decisions about the number and location of franchises, the adequacy of facilities, and when a team can relocate to another place and a better deal.

Cities, some suburbs, a few counties and states, and a Canadian province or two will remain very limited partners of professional sports, building most of the arenas and stadiums, paying more and more of the capital costs, and being frozen out of the decisions, profits, and equity shares. Someone once said "there's nothing so limited as being a limited partner of George Steinbrenner."[28] Associates of the owner of the New York Yankees, however, are no match for the places that are the pathetically limited partners of big league sports in the United States and Canada.

Appendix
Places and Team Names

Place Name and Location[a] (if different from place name or not specific)	Team Name	League	Years
Akron, Ohio	Firestones	NBL	1937–1940
	Goodyears	NBL	1937–1941
	Indians	NFL	1923–1926
	Pros	APFA-NFL	1920–1922
Alberta (Edmonton)	Oilers	WHA	1972–1973
Altoona, Pa.	Unions	UA	1884
Anaheim, Cal.	Amigos	ABA	1967
	Mighty Ducks	NHL	1993–present
Anderson, Ind.	Chiefs	NBL	1946
	Packers	NBL-NBA	1947–1949
Arizona (Phoenix)	Cardinals	NFL	1994–present
(Phoenix)	Diamondbacks	NL	to begin play 1998
(Phoenix)	Wranglers	USFL	1983–1985
Atlanta, Ga.	Braves	NL	1966–present
	Falcons	NFL	1966–present
	Flames	NHL	1972–1979
	Hawks	NBA	1968–present
Baltimore, Md.	Blades	WHA	1974
	Bullets	NBL-BAA-NBA	1944–1954
	Bullets	NBA	1963–1972
	Colts	AAFC-NFL	1947–1950
	Colts	NFL	1952–1983
	Lord Baltimores	NA	1872
	Lord Baltimores	AA	1882
	Monumentals	UA	1884
	Orioles	AA	1883–1889
	Orioles	NL	1892–1899

Place Name and Location[a] (if different from place name or not specific)	Team Name	League	Years
Baltimore, Md. (*cont.*)	Orioles	AL	1901–1902
	Orioles	AL	1953–present
	Ravens	NFL	1996–present
	Stars	USFL	1984–1985
Birmingham, Ala.	Americans	WFL	1974
	Bulls	WHA	1976–1977
	Stallions	USFL	1983–1985
	Vulcans	WFL	1975
Boston, Mass.	Beaneaters	NL	1883–1906
	Beaneaters	PL	1890
	Bears	AFL3	1940
	Bees	NL	1936–1940
	Braves	NL	1912–1935, 1941–1952
	Braves	NFL	1932
	Breakers	USFL	1983
	Bruins	NHL	1924–present
	Bulldogs	AFL1	1926
	Bulldogs	NFL	1929
	Celtics	BAA-NBA	1946–present
	Doves	NL	1907–1911
	Patriots	AFL4-NFL	1960–1970
	Pilgrims	AL	1903–1906
	Red Caps	NL	1876–1882
	Red Sox	AL	1907–present
	Red Stockings	NA	1871, 1873–1875
	Reds	UA	1884
	Redskins	NFL	1933–1936
	Rustlers	NL	1911
	Shamrocks	AFL2	1936–1937
	Somersets	AL	1901–1902
	Yank(ee)s	NFL	1944–1948
Brooklyn, N.Y.	Americans	NHL	1941
	Atlantics	NA	1873–1875
	Bridegrooms	AA	1889
	Bridegrooms	NL	1890–1898
	Dodgers	NL	1897–1898, 1911–1913, 1932–1957
	Dodgers	NFL	1930–1943
	Dodgers	AAFC	1946–1947
	Eckfords	NA	1871–1872
	Gladiators	AA	1890
	Horsemen	AFL1	1926
	Lions	NFL	1926
	Robins	NL	1914–1931

Place Name and Location[a] (if different from place name or not specific)	Team Name	League	Years
	Superbas	NL	1899–1910
	Tigers	AFL2	1936
	Tigers	NFL	1944
	Tip-Tops	FL	1914
	Trolley-Dodgers	AA	1884–1888
	Wonders	PL	1890
Buffalo, N.Y.	All Americans	APFA-NFL	1920–1923
	Bills	AAFC	1949
(Orchard Park, N.Y.)	Bills	AFL4-NFL	1960–present
	Bisons	PL	1890
	Bisons	NFL	1924–1925
	Bisons	NBL	1937, 1946
	Bisons	AAFC	1946–1948
	Blues	FL	1915
	Braves	NBA	1970–1977
	Buffeds	FL	1914
	Indians	AFL3	1940
	Rangers	NFL	1926–1927, 1928
	Sabres	NHL	1970–present
	Tigers	AFL3	1941
Calgary, Alberta	Cowboys	WHA	1975–1976
	Flames	NHL	1980–present
California (Anaheim)	Angels	AL	1965–present
(Oakland)	(Golden) Seals	NHL	1970–1975
Canton, Ohio	Bulldogs	APFA-NFL	1920–1923, 1925
Capital (Landover, Md.)	Bullets	NBA	1973
Carolina (Charlotte)	Cougars	ABA	1969–1972
(Charlotte)	Panthers	NFL	1995–present
Charlotte, N.C.	Hornets	WFL	1974–1975
	Hornets	NBA	1988–present
	Stars	WFL	1974
Chicago, Ill.	Bears	NFL	1922–present
	Blackhawks	NHL	1926–present
	Blitz	USFL	1983–1984
	Browns	UA	1884
	Bruins	NBL	1939–1941
	Bulls	AFL1	1926
	Bulls	NBA	1966–present
	Cardinals	APFA-NFL	1920–1943, 1945–1959
	Chifeds	FL	1914
	Colts	NL	1890–1897
	Cougars	WHA	1972–1974

Place Name and Location[a] (if different from place name or not specific)	Team Name	League	Years
Chicago, Ill. (*cont.*)	Cubs	NL	1899–present
	Fire	WFL	1974
	Gears	NBL	1944–1946
	Hornets	AAFC	1949
	Majors	ABL2	1961–1962
	Orphans	NL	1898
	Packers	NBA	1961
	Pirates	PL	1890
	Rockets	AAFC	1946–1948
	Stags	BAA-NBA	1946–1949
	Staleys	APFA	1921
	Studebakers	NBL	1942
	Tigers	APFA	1920
	Whales	FL	1915
	White Sox	AL	1904–present
	White Stockings	NA-NL	1871, 1874–1889
	White Stockings	AL	1900–1903
	Wind	WFL	1975
	Zephyrs	NBA	1962
Chicago-Pittsburgh	Card-Pitts	NFL	1944
Cincinnati, Ohio	Bengals	AFL2	1937
	Bengals	AFL3	1940–1941
	Bengals	AFL4-NFL	1968–present
	Bobbies	NBL	1937
	Celts	APFA	1921
	Kellys	NL	1890–1891
	Outlaw Reds	UA	1884
	Royals	NBA	1957–1971
	Red Stockings	NA	1869–1870
	Red Stockings	NL-AA	1876–1889
	Redlegs	NL	1944–1945, 1954–1960
	Reds	NL	1890–1943, 1946–1953, 1961–present
	Reds	NFL	1933–1934
	Stingers	WHA	1975–1978
Cleveland, Ohio	Barons	NHL	1976–1977
	Bluebirds	AL	1901
	Blues	NL	1879–1884
	Blues	AA	1887–1888
	Broncos	AL	1902
	Browns	AAFC-NFL	1946–1995
	Bulldogs	NFL	1924–1925
	Cavaliers	NBA	1970–present

Place Name and Location[a] (if different from place name or not specific)	Team Name	League	Years
	Chase Brassmen	NBL	1943
	Crusaders	WHA	1972–1975
	Forest City of	NA	1871–1872
	Indians	AL	1915–present
	Indians	NFL	1923
	Infants	PL	1890
	Lake Shores	AL	1900
	Molly Maguires	AL	1912–1914
	Naps	AL	1903–1911
	Panthers	AFL1	1926
	Pipers	ABL2	1961–1962
	Rams	AFL2-NFL	1936–1942, 1944–1945
	Rebels	BAA	1946
	Spiders	NL	1889–1899
	Tigers	APFA	1920–1921
	Transfers	NBL	1944–1945
	Warren Penns	NBL	1937
	White Horses	NBL	1938
Colorado (Denver)	Rockies	NHL	1976–1981
(Denver)	Rockies	NL	1993–present
(Denver)	Avalanche	NHL	1995–present
Columbus, Ohio	Athletic Supplies	NBL	1937
	Bullies	AFL3	1940–1941
	Colts	AA	1889–1891
	Panhandles	APFA-NFL	1920–1922
	Senators	AA	1883–1884
	Tigers	NFL	1923–1926
Dallas, Texas	Chaparrals	ABA	1967–1969, 1971–1972
(Irving)	Cowboys	NFL	1960–present
	Mavericks	NBA	1980–present
	Stars	NHL	1993–present
	Texans	NFL	1952
	Texans	AFL4	1960–1962
Dayton, Ohio	Metropolitans	NBL	1937
	Renaissance	NBL	1948
	Triangles	APFA-NFL	1920–1929
Decatur, Ill.	Staleys	APFA	1920
Denver, Col.	Broncos	AFL4-NFL	1960–present
	Gold	USFL	1983–1985
	Nuggets	NBL-NBA	1948–1949
	Nuggets	ABA-NBA	1972–present

Place Name and Location[a] (if different from place name or not specific)	Team Name	League	Years
Denver, Col. (*cont.*)	Rockets	ABA	1967–1971
	Spurs	WHA	1975
Detroit, Mich.	Cougars	NHL	1926–1929
	Eagles	NBL	1939–1940
	Falcons	NHL	1930–1932
	Falcons	BAA	1946
	Gems	NBL	1946
	Heralds	APFA	1920
	Lions	NFL	1934–present
	Panthers	APFA	1921
	Panthers	NFL	1925–1926
	Pistons	NBA	1957–present
	Red Wings	NHL	1933–present
	Tigers	AL	1901–present
	Vagabond Kings	NBL	1948
	Wheels	WFL	1974
	Wolverines	NL	1881–1888
	Wolverines	AL	1900
	Wolverines	NFL	1928
Duluth, Minn.	Eskimos	NFL	1926–1927
	Kellys	NFL	1923–1925
Edmonton, Alberta	Oilers	WHA-NHL	1973–present
Elizabeth, N.J.	Resolutes	NA	1873
Evansville, Ind.	Crimson Giants	APFA-NFL	1921–1922
Flint, Mich.	Dow Chemicals	NBL	1947
Florida (Orlando)	Blazers	WFL	1974
(Miami)	Marlins	NL	1993–present
(Miami)	Panthers	NHL	1993–present
Fort Wayne, Ind.	General Electrics	NBL	1937
	Kekiongas	NA	1871
	Pistons	BAA-NBA	1949–1956
	Zollner-Pistons	NBL	1941–1948
Frankford, Pa. (Philadelphia)	Yellow Jackets	NFL	1924–1931
Golden State (Oakland)	Warriors	NBA	1971–present
Green Bay, Wis.	Packers	APFA-NFL	1921–present
Hamilton, Ont.	Tigers	NHL	1920–1924
Hammond, Ind.	Buccaneers	NBL	1948
	Ciesars	NBL	1938–1940
	Pros	APFA-NFL	1920–1926
	Whiting Ciesars	NBL	1937

Place Name and Location[a] (if different from place name or not specific)	Team Name	League	Years
Hartford, Conn.	Blues	NFL	1926
	Dark Blues	NA-NL	1874–1877
	Whalers	WHA-NHL	1974–present
Hawaii (Honolulu)	Chiefs	ABL2	1961
Honolulu, Hawaii	Hawaiians	WFL	1974–1975
Houston, Texas	Aeros	WHA	1972–1977
	Astros	NL	1965–present
	Colt 45s	NL	1962–1964
	Gamblers	USFL	1984–1985
	Mavericks	ABA	1967–1968
	Oilers	AFL4-NFL	1960–present
	Rockets	NBA	1971–present
	Texans	WFL	1974
Indiana (Indianapolis)	Pacers	ABA-NBA	1967–present
Indianapolis, Ind.	Colts	NFL	1984–present
	Hoosiers	NL	1878, 1887–1889
	Hoosiers	AA	1884
	Hoosiers	FL	1914
	Jets	BAA	1948
	Kautskys	NBL	1937–1939, 1941, 1945–1947
	Olympians	NBA	1949–1952
	Racers	WHA	1974–1978
Jacksonville, Fla.	Bulls	USFL	1984–1985
	Express	WFL	1975
	Jaguars	NFL	1995–present
	Sharks	WFL	1974
Kankakee, Ill.	Gallaghers	NBL	1937
Kansas City, Kan.	A's	AL	1962–1967
	Athletics	AL	1955–1961
	Blues	NFL	1924
	Chiefs	AFL4-NFL	1963–present
	Cowboys	UA	1884
	Cowboys	NL	1886
	Cowboys	AA	1888–1889
	Cowboys	AL	1900
	Cowboys	NFL	1925–1926
	Kings	NBA	1975–1983
	Packers	FL	1914–1915
	Royals	AL	1969–present
	Scouts	NHL	1974–1975
	Steers	ABL2	1961–1962

Place Name and Location[a] (if different from place name or not specific)		Team Name	League	Years
Kansas City-Omaha		Kings	NBA	1972–1974
Kenosha, Wis.		Maroons	NFL	1924
Kentucky (Louisville)		Colonels	ABA	1967–1975
Keokuk, Iowa		Western of	NA	1885
Lancaster, Pa.		Ironsides	UA	1884
Long Beach, Cal.		Chiefs	ABL2	1962
Los Angeles, Cal.		Angels	AL	1961–1964
	(no home games)	Buccaneers	NFL	1926
		Bulldogs	AFL2	1937
		Chargers	AFL4	1960
		Clippers	NBA	1984–present
		Dodgers	NL	1958–present
		Dons	AAFC	1946–1949
		Express	USFL	1983–1985
		Jets	ABL2	1961
	(Inglewood)	Kings	NHL	1967–present
	(Inglewood)	Lakers	NBA	1960–present
		Raiders	NFL	1982–1995
	(Anaheim)	Rams	NFL	1946–1995
		Sharks	WHA	1972–1973
		Stars	ABA	1968–1969
	(Rock Island, Ill.)	Wildcats	AFL1	1926
Louisville, Ky. (Chicago, Ill.)		Brecks	APFA-NFL	1921–1923
		Colonels	AA-NL	1885–1899
		Colonels	NFL	1926
		Eclipse	AA	1882–1884
		Grays	NL	1876–1877
Marion, Ohio		Oorang Indians	NFL	1922–1923
Maryland (Baltimore)		of Baltimore	NA	1873–1874
Memphis, Tenn.		Grizzlies	WFL	1974
		Pros	ABA	1970–1971
		Showboat	USFL	1984–1985
		Sounds	ABA	1974
		Southmen	WFL	1975
		Tams	ABA	1972–1973
Miami, Fla.		Dolphins	AFL4-NFL	1966–present
		Floridians	ABA	1968–1971
		Heat	NBA	1988–present
		Seahawks	AAFC	1946

Place Name and Location[a] (if different from place name or not specific)	Team Name	League	Years
Michigan (Ypsilanti)	Panthers	USFL	1983–1984
(Detroit)	Stags	WHA	1974
Milwaukee, Wis.	Badgers	NFL	1922–1926
	Braves	NL	1953–1965
	Brewers	NL	1878
	Brewers	UA	1884
	Brewers	AA	1891
	Brewer	AL	1901
	Brewers	AL	1970–present
	Bucks	NBA	1968–present
	Chiefs	AFL3	1940
	Hawks	NBA	1951–1954
Minneapolis, Minn.	Lakers	NBL-BAA-NBA	1947–1959
	Marines	APFA-NFL	1921–1924
	Red Jackets	NFL	1929–1930
Minnesota	Fighting Saints	WHA	1972–1976
	Muskies	ABA	1967
(Minneapolis)	North Stars	NHL	1967–1992
	Pipers	ABA	1968
(Minneapolis)	Timberwolves	NBA	1989
(Minneapolis)	Twins	AL	1961–present
(Minneapolis)	Vikings	NFL	1961–present
Montreal, Que.	Canadiens	NHL	1917–present
	Expos	NL	1969–present
	Maroons	NHL	1924–1937
Muncie, Ind.	Flyers	APFA	1920–1921
New England (Foxboro, Mass.)	Patriots	NFL	1971–present
(Boston)	Whalers	WHA	1972–1973
(Springfield, Mass.)	Whalers	WHA	1974
(Hartford)	Whalers	WHA-NHL	1974–present
New Haven, Conn.	Elm Citys	NA	1875
New Jersey	Americans	ABA	1967–1968
(E. Rutherford)	Generals	USFL	1983–1985
(E. Rutherford)	Devils	NHL	1981–present
(Cherry Hill)	Knights	WHA	1973–1974
(E. Rutherford)	Nets	NBA	1977–present
New Orleans, La.	Breakers	USFL	1984
	Buccaneers	ABA	1967–1969
	Jazz	NBA	1974–1978
	Saints	NFL	1967–present

Place Name and Location[a] (if different from place name or not specific)	*Team Name*	*League*	*Years*
New York, N.Y.	Americans	NHL	1925–1940
	Americans	AFL3	1940
	Bulldogs	NFL	1949
	Giants	NL	1885–1957
	Giants	APFA	1921
(E. Rutherford, NJ)	Giants	NFL	1925–present
	Golden Blades	WHA	1973
	Gothams	NL	1883–1884
	Highlanders	AL	1903–1912
(Uniondale, NY)	Islanders	NHL	1972–present
(E. Rutherford, NJ)	Jets	AFL4-NFL	1964–present
	Knicks	BAA-NBA	1946–present
	Metropolitans	AA	1883–1885
	Mets	NL	1962–present
	Mutuals	NA-NL	1871–1876
	Nets	ABA-NBA	1968–1977
	Raiders	WHA	1972
	Rangers	NHL	1926–present
	Stars	WFL	1974
	Tapers	ABL2	1961
	Titans	AFL4	1960–1963
	Yankees	AL	1912–present
	Yankees	AFL1-NFL	1926–1928
	Yankees	AFL2	1936–1937
	Yankees	AFL3	1941
	Yankees	AAFC-NFL	1946–1951
Newark, N.J.	Bears	AFL1	1926
	Peppers	FL	1915
	Tornadoes	NFL	1930
Oakland, Cal.	A's	AL	1968–1986
	Athletics	AL	1987–present
	Invaders	USFL	1983–1985
	Oaks	ABA	1967–1968
	Oaks	ABL2	1962
	Raiders	AFL4-NFL	1960–1981, 1995-present
	Seals	NHL	1967–1969
Oklahoma (Tulsa)	Outlaws	USFL	1984–1985
Orange, N.J.	Tornadoes	NFL	1929
Orlando, Fla.	Magic	NBA	1989
	Renegades	USFL	1985
Oshkosh, Wis.	All-Stars	NBL	1937–1948
Ottawa, Ont.	Civics	WHA	1975
	Eagles	NHL	1917–1930, 1931–1933

Place Name and Location[a] (if different from place name or not specific)	Team Name	League	Years
	Nationals	WHA	1972
	Senators	NHL	1992–present
Philadelphia, Pa	Athletics of	NA	1871–1875
	Athletics	AL	1901–1954
	Athletics	NL	1876
	Bell	WFL	1974–1975
	Blazers	WHA	1972
	Blue Jays	NL	1943–1944
	Centennial of	NA	1875
	Eagles	NFL	1933–1942, 1944–present
	Flyers	NHL	1967–present
	Keystones	UA	1884
	Philadelphias	NA	1872
	Phillies	NL	1890–1942, 1945–present
	Quakers	NL	1883–1889
	Quakers	PL	1890
	Quakers	AFL1	1926
	Quakers	NHL	1930
	76ers	NBA	1963–present
	Stars	USFL	1983
	Tapers	ABL2	1962
	Warriors	BAA-NBA	1946–1961
	Whites	NA	1873–1875
Philadelphia-Pittsburgh	Steagles	NFL	1943
Phoenix, Ariz. (Tempe)	Cardinals	NFL	1988–1993
	Coyotes	NHL	1996–present
	Roadrunners	WHA	1974–1976
	Suns	NBA	1968–present
Pittsburgh, Pa.	Alleghenies	AA	1882–1886
	Alleghenies	NL	1887–1889
	Americans	AFL2	1936–1937
	Burghers	PL	1890
	Condors	ABA	1970
	Innocents	NL	1890
	Ironmen	BAA	1946
	Maulers	USFL	1984
	Penguins	NHL	1967–present
	Pipers	ABA	1967, 1969
	Pirates	NL	1891–present
	Pirates	NHL	1925–1929
	Pirates	NFL	1933–1940
	Pirates	NBL	1937–1938
	Raiders	NBL	1945

Place Name and Location[a] (if different from place name or not specific)	Team Name	League	Years
Pittsburgh, Pa. (*cont.*)	Renaissance	ABL2	1961–1962
	Sheriffs	NBL	1944
	Steelers	NFL	1941–1942, 1945-present
	Stogies	UA	1884
	Stogies	FL	1914–1915
Portland, Ore.	Breakers	USFL	1985
	Trail Blazers	NBA	1970–present
	Storm	WFL	1974
	Thunder	WFL	1975
Portsmouth, Ohio	Spartans	NFL	1930–1933
Pottsville, Pa.	Maroons	NFL	1925–1928
Providence, R.I.	Grays	NL	1879–1885
	Rhode Islanders	NL	1878
	Steam Roller	NFL	1925–1931
	Steamrollers	BAA	1946–1948
Quebec, Que.	Bulldogs	NHL	1919
	Nordiques	WHA-NHL	1972–1994
Racine, Wis.	Legion	NFL	1922–1924
	Tornadoes	NFL	1926
Richmond, Ind.	Bobbies	NBL	1937
Rochester, N.Y.	Braves	AFL2	1936
	Hop-Bitters	AA	1890
	Royals	NBL-BAA-NBA	1945–1957
	Tigers	AFL2	1937
	Jeffersons	APFA-NFL	1920–1925
Rockford, Ill.	Forest City of	NA	1871
Rock Island, Ill.	Independents	APFA-NFL-AFL	1920–1926
Sacramento, Cal.	Kings	NBA	1984–present
San Antonio, Texas	Gunslingers	USFL	1984–1985
	Spurs	ABA-NBA	1973–present
	Wings	WFL	1975
San Diego, Cal.	Chargers	AFL4-NFL	1961–present
	Clippers	NBA	1978–1983
	Conquistadors	ABA	1972–1974
	Mariners	WHA	1975–1976
	Padres	NL	1969–present
	Rockets	NBA	1967–1970
	Sails	ABA	1975

Place Name and Location[a] (if different from place name or not specific)	Team Name	League	Years
San Francisco, Cal.	49ers	AAFC-NFL	1946–present
	Giants	NL	1958–present
	Saints	ABL2	1961
	Warriors	NBA	1962–1970
San Jose, Cal.	Sharks	NHL	1991–present
Seattle, Wash.	Mariners	AL	1977–present
	Pilots	AL	1969
	Seahawks	NFL	1976–present
	SuperSonics	NBA	1967–present
Sheboygan, Wis.	Redskins	NBL-NBA	1938–1949
Shreveport, La.	Steamer	WFL	1974–1975
Southern California	Sun	WFL	1974–1975
St. Louis, Mo.	All-Stars	NFL	1923
	Blues	NHL	1967–present
	Bombers	BAA-NBA	1946–1949
	Brown Stockings	NA	1875
	Brown Stockings	AA	1882
	Browns	AA	1883–1891
	Browns	AL	1902–1953
	Cardinals	NL	1900–present
	Cardinals	NFL	1960–1987
	Eagles	NHL	1934
	Gunners	NFL	1934
	Hawks	NBA	1955–1967
	Maroons	UA	1884
	Perfectors	NL	1899
	Rams	NFL	1995–present
	Spirits	ABA	1972–1974
	Terriers	FL	1914–1915
St. Paul, Minn.	Saints	UA	1884
Staten Island, N.Y.	Stapletons	NFL	1929–1932
Syracuse, N.Y.	Braves	AFL2	1936
	Nationals	NBL-NBA	1946–1962
Tampa Bay, Fla. (Tampa)	Bandits	USFL	1983–1985
(Tampa)	Buccaneers	NFL	1976–present
(St. Petersburg)	Devil Rays		to begin play 1998
(St. Petersburg)	Lightning	NHL	1991–present
Texas (Arlington)	Rangers	AL	1972–present
(Dallas)	Chaparrals	ABA	1970
Toledo, Ohio	Chevvies	NBL	1941–1942

Place Name and Location[a] (if different from place name or not specific)	*Team Name*	*League*	*Years*
Toledo, Ohio (*cont.*)	Jeeps	NBL	1946–1947
	Maroons	NFL	1924
Tonawanda, Pa.	Cardex	APFA	1921
Toronto, Ont.	Arenas	NHL	1917–1918
	Blue Jays	AL	1977–present
	Huskies	BAA	1946
	Maple Leafs	NHL	1926–present
	Raptors	NBA	1995–present
	St. Patricks	NHL	1919–1925
	Toros	WHA	1973–1975
Tri-Cities (Moline, Ill.)	Blackhawks	NBL-NBA	1946–1950
Troy, N.Y.	Haymakers of	NA	1871–1872
	Trojans	NL	1879–1882
Utah (Salt Lake City)	Jazz	NBA	1979–present
(Salt Lake City)	Stars	ABA	1970–1975
Vancouver, B.C.	Blazers	WHA	1973–1974
	Canucks	NHL	1970–present
	Grizzlies	NBA	1995–present
Virginia (Norfolk)	Squires	ABA	1970–1975
Washington, D.C. (Landover, Md.)	Bullets	NBA	1974–present
(Landover, Md.)	Capitals	NHL	1975–present
	Capitols	BAA-NBA	1946–1950
	Capitols	ABA	1969
	Capitols	ABL2	1961
	Federals	USFL	1983–1984
	Nationals	NA	1872
	Nationals	NA	1875
	Nationals	AA	1884
	Nationals	UA	1884
	Nationals	AL	1905–1956
	Olympics	NA	1871
	Redskins	NFL	1937–present
	Ruby Legs	NL	1880–1882
	Senators	NL	1892–1899
	Senators	AL	1901–1904, 1957–1971
	Senators	APFA	1921
	Statesmen	NL	1886–1889
	Statesmen	AA	1891
Waterloo, Iowa	Hawks	NBL-NBA	1948–1949
Winnipeg, Manitoba	Jets	WHA-NHL	1972–1995
Youngstown, Ohio	Bears	NBL	1946

SOURCES: Joseph Cuniglio, *The Names in the Game: A History of the Movement of Sports Franchises* (New York: Vantage Press, 1978); and Peter Filichia, *Professional Baseball Franchises: From the Abbeville Athletics to the Zanesville Indians* (New York: Facts On File, 1993).

NOTES:

[a]Last or most recent location.

League abbreviations:

AA - American Association
AAFC - All-American Football Conference
ABA - American Basketball Association
ABL1 - American Basketball League (1925–1930)
ABL2 - American Basketball League (1961–1962)
AFL1 - American Football League (1926)
AFL2 - American Football League (1936–1937)
AFL3 - American Football League (1940–1941)
AFL4 - American Football League (1960–1969)
AL - American League
APFA - American Professional Football Association
BAA - Basketball Association of America

FL - Federal League
NA - National Association
NBA - National Basketball Association
NBL - National Basketball League
NHL - National Hockey League
NL - National League
PL - Players League
UA - Union Association
USFL - U.S. Football League
WFL - World Football League
WHA - World Hockey Association

Notes

Chapter One
Places to Play

1. The absolute increase was 429 percent; even when adjusted for population, the growth rate was a striking 300 percent (from one admission for each 6.45 Americans in 1960 to one for each 2.15 in 1994).

2. *Sports Geography* (London: E. & F. N. Spon, 1989), 2.

3. "Team" is used interchangeably throughout this book with "franchise" and "club" for the private firms that are the basic units of professional team sports.

4. See Tustar Atre et al., "Sports: The High Stakes Game of Team Ownership," *Financial World*, May 20, 1996, 53–65. *Financial World* first estimated franchise values for major league teams in 1991, and has reported annually since.

5. Harold Seymour, *Baseball: The Early Years* (New York: Oxford University Press, 1960), 347.

6. The total of 113 teams refers to the number that played in the major leagues in 1996; the total will rise to 115 in 1998, when baseball's newest expansion franchises in Phoenix and Tampa-St. Petersburg take the field.

7. "City" is used throughout this volume to refer to the central cities of metropolitan areas as defined by the United States and Canadian governments; suburbs are the adjacent urban areas that compose the remainder of a metropolitan area. "Metropolitan area" refers to the most inclusive governmental definitions—Consolidated Metropolitan Statistical Areas in the case of the largest areas in the United States, Metropolitan Statistical Areas for other U.S. areas, and Census Metropolitan Areas in Canada. Washington and Baltimore, which were not classified as a single consolidated area until the 1990 census, are treated as separate metropolitan areas before 1990, and as one area afterward.

8. Gunther Barth, *City People: The Rise of Modern City Culture in Nineteenth-Century America* (New York: Oxford University Press, 1980), 171.

9. "Sport as a Community Representation," in Gunther R. F. Luschen and George H. Sage, eds., *Handbook of Social Science of Sport* (Champaign, Ill.: Stipes Publishing, 1981), 220.

10. Bale, *Sports Geography*, 14.

11. Neil J. Sullivan, *The Dodgers Move West* (New York: Oxford University Press, 1987), 18.

12. *American Sports: From the Age of Folk Games to the Age of Spectators* (Englewood, N.J.: Prentice-Hall, 1983), 111.

13. "The Baseball Season," editorial, April 12, 1907.

14. *Sports Spectators* (New York: Columbia University Press, 1986), 182.

15. *Soccer Madness* (Chicago: University of Chicago Press, 1983), 14.

16. *To Every Thing a Season: Shibe Park and Urban Philadelphia 1909–1976* (Princeton: Princeton University Press, 1991), 47.

17. *In Its Own Image: How Television Has Transformed Professional Sports* (New York: Free Press, 1984), 199.

18. John F. Rooney, Jr., "Sports from a Geographic Perspective," in Donald W. Ball and John W. Loy, eds., *Sport and Social Order: Contributions to the Sociology of Sport* (Reading, Mass.: Addison-Wesley, 1975), 61; William Baker, *Sports in the Western World* (Totowa, N.J.: Rowan and Littlefield, 1982), 319; and David A. Karp and William C. Yoels, "Sport and Urban Life," *Journal of Sport and Social Issues* 14 (Fall 1990), 93.

19. *In Its Own Image*, 198.

20. "The Home Advantage," *Social Forces* 55 (March 1977), 642–43. Ties are excluded from these calculations.

21. Baseball alternates home advantage in postseason play; and the home advantage operates in NFL only through the penultimate playoff games, with the Super Bowl contested on a neutral field.

22. Tom Jackson, "Home Court Edge Too Often Tips NBA Playoffs off Balance," *Los Angeles Times*, June 6, 1990.

23. "The Home Advantage," 652.

24. "Local Sports Teams and Celebration of Community: A Comparative Analysis of the Home Advantage," *Sociological Quarterly* 26 (Winter 1985), 507–18.

25. U.S. Congress, Senate, Committee on Commerce, *Blackout of Sporting Events on TV*, Hearings before the Subcommittee on Communications, 92d Cong., 2nd sess. (Washington, D.C.: U.S. Government Printing Office, 1973), 73.

26. Quoted in Bob Oates, "Boom-town Days," *Los Angeles Times*, October 6, 1985.

27. E. J. Junior, quoted in Dale Hofmann and Martin J. Greenberg, *Sport$biz : An Irreverent Look at Big Business in Pro Sports* (Champaign, Ill.: Leisure Press, 1989), 158.

28. "Sports from a Geographic Perspective," 58.

29. *Touching Base: Professional Baseball and American Culture in the Progressive Era* (Westport, Conn.: Greenwood Press, 1980), 7.

30. For a discussion of these perspectives, see Alex G. Ingham, Jeremy W. Howell, and Todd S. Schilperoort, "Professional Sports and Community: A Review and Exegesis," *Exercise and Sports Sciences Review* 15 (1987), 427–65.

31. See, for example, Susan S. Fainstein et al., *Restructuring the City: The Politics of Urban Development* (New York: Longman, 1983); John R. Logan and Harvey L. Molotch, *Urban Fortunes: The Political Economy of Place* (Berkeley and Los Angeles: University of California Press, 1987); Michael Peter Smith, *City, State and Market: The Political Economy of Urban America* (New York: Blackwell, 1988); and David Harvey, *The Urbanization of Capital: Studies in the History and Theory of Capitalist Urbanization* (Baltimore: Johns Hopkins University Press, 1985).

32. For a general discussion of urban regimes, see Stephen L. Elkins, *City and Re-*

gime in the American Republic (Chicago: University of Chicago Press, 1987) and Clarence N. Stone, *Regime Politics: Governing Atlanta, 1946–1988* (Lawrence: University of Kansas Press, 1989). Urban regime theory is applied to sports politics in John P. Pelissero, Beth M. Henschen, and Edward I. Sidlow, "Urban Regimes, Sports Stadiums, and the Politics of Economic Development Agendas in Chicago," *Policy Studies Review* 10 (Spring/Summer 1991), 117–29.

Chapter Two
Urban Games

1. *City Games: The Evolution of American Urban Society and the Rise of Sports* (Urbana and Chicago: University of Illinois Press, 1989), 1.

2. The term "industrial city" refers to cities that emerged in the middle of the nineteenth century as the United States rapidly industrialized; some industrial cities were more commercial than industrial, but all were shaped by industrialization; see Stephen Hardy, "The City and the Rise of American Sport: 1820–1920," *Exercise and Sports Sciences* 9 (1981), 184.

3. See John Rickards Betts, "The Technological Revolution and the Rise of Sport, 1850–1900," *Mississippi Valley Historical Review* 40 (September 1953), 231–56; see also Betts, "Sporting Journalism in Nineteenth-Century America," *American Quarterly* 5 (Spring 1953), 39–56.

4. See *The Private City: Philadelphia in Three Periods of Its Growth* (Philadelphia: University of Pennsylvania Press, 1968).

5. See Melvin A. Adelman, *A Sporting Time: New York City and the Rise of Modern Athletics* (Urbana and Chicago: University of Illinois Press, 1986) for a detailed discussion of these developments.

6. St. Louis, the nation's fourth largest city in 1900, with a population of 575,000, was more than twice the size of Milwaukee, with 285,000 inhabitants. The newly consolidated New York City had over 3.4 million residents compared with 509,000 in Baltimore.

7. J. Thomas Jable, "The Birth of Professional Football: Pittsburgh Athletic Clubs Ring in Professionals in 1892," *Western Pennsylvania Historical Magazine* 62 (April 1979), 145.

8. The charter teams represented Akron, Canton, Columbus, Dayton, and Rochester. The NFL dates its beginning to 1920, when the league added teams from Chicago, Cleveland, Decatur, Hammond, Massillon, Muncie, and Rock Island.

9. The Philadelphia entry played in suburban Frankford from 1924 to 1931; the New York Giants joined the league in 1925.

10. *Class, Sports, and Social Development* (Amherst: University of Massachusetts Press, 1983), 120.

11. See John Barnes, *Sports and the Law in Canada* (Toronto: Butterworth's, 1983), 208–9, for a discussion of the early development of professional hockey.

12. *City Games*, 232.

13. Norris Poulson, quoted in Cary Henderson, "Los Angeles and the Dodger War, 1957–1962," *Southern California Quarterly* 62 (Fall 1980), 262.

14. Vincent X. Flaherty to Emanuel Celler, October 24, 1951, in U.S. Congress, House of Representatives, Committee on the Judiciary, Subcommittee on the Study of

Monopoly Power, *Study of Monopoly Power: Organized Baseball*, 82d Cong., 1st sess. (Washington, D.C.: U.S. Government Printing Office, 1952), 702. Flaherty wrote for the *Los Angeles Examiner*.

15. The other new teams were located in Minneapolis-St. Paul, Philadelphia, Pittsburgh, and St. Louis.

16. *In Its Own Image: How Television Has Transformed Professional Sports* (New York: Free Press, 1984), 197.

17. *A Geography of American Sport: From Cabin Creek to Anaheim* (Reading, Mass.: Addison-Wesley, 1974), 36.

18. *American Baseball, vol. 3: From Postwar Expansion to the Electronic Age* (University Park: Pennsylvania State University Press, 1983), 118.

Chapter Three
Market Tests

1. Claire Smith, "State of Game? Not the Same Everywhere," *New York Times*, December 10, 1991.

2. Joel Bierig and Bruce Levine, "Market Driven," *Sporting* News, August 24, 1992, 10.

3. *The Business of Professional Baseball* (Chicago: University of Chicago Press, 1989), 145.

4. See ibid., 119; Henry G. Demmert, *The Economics of Professional Team Sports* (Lexington, Mass.: Lexington Books, 1973), 68; and Roger G. Noll, "Attendance and Price Setting," in Roger G. Noll, ed., *Government and the Sports Business* (Washington, D.C.: Brookings Institution, 1974), 127.

5. "Collusive Competition in Major League Baseball," *American Economist* 14 (Fall 1969), 7.

6. Demmert, *The Economics of Professional Team Sports*, 77, and James Quirk and Mohamed El Hodiri, "The Economic Theory of a Professional Sports League," in Noll, *Government and the Sports Business*, 45.

7. "Professional Basketball: Economic and Business Perspectives," in Paul D. Staudohar and James A. Mangan, eds., *The Business of Professional Sports* (Urbana and Chicago: University of Illinois Press, 1991), 33.

8. Quirk and El Hodiri, "The Economic Theory of a Professional Sports League," 49.

9. *The Business of Professional Baseball*, 78.

10. Quoted in John Merwin, "Dumb Like Foxes," *Forbes*, October 24, 1988, 45.

11. Mike Brown of the Cincinnati Bengals, quoted in Peter King, *The Season after: Are Sports Dynasties Dead?* (New York: Warner Books, 1989), 30.

12. *The Economics of Professional Team Sports*, 19.

13. Noll, "Professional Basketball," 30.

14. Bud Selig, quoted in Bob Verdi, "TV Deal May Allow King George to Rule Game," *Sporting News*, January 2, 1989.

15. Robert Harlan, quoted in Richard Sandomir, "America's Small-Town," *New York Times*, January 13, 1996.

16. Home teams are permitted to deduct 15 percent of the gross revenues to cover stadium and game expenses, with the remaining net revenue shared sixty-forty.

17. Bill Giles, quoted in "Baseball's Future: What Can Fans Expect," *U.S. News & World Report*, April 12, 1982, 55.

18. "The Economic Theory of a Professional Sports League," 57–58.

19. The period 1984–1987 was selected to reduce the effect of expansion teams, which would be expected to have poorer records than established teams; the most recent expansion team operating during these years was the Dallas Mavericks, who were playing their fifth NBA season in 1984.

20. Steven Matt of Arthur Andersen & Company, quoted in Merwin, "Dumb Like Foxes," 46.

21. "Professional Basketball," 30.

22. *The Business of Professional Baseball*, 193.

23. "Sports' Integral Role with a Community," *New York Times*, February 2, 1986.

24. "Sports Broadcasting," in Noll, *Government and the Sports Business*, 303.

25. "Self-Regulation in Baseball, 1909–71," in Noll, *Government and the Sports Business*, 384.

26. Benjamin Rader, *American Sports: From the Age of Folk Games to the Age of Spectators* (Englewood, N.J.: Prentice-Hall, 1983), 208.

27. Jacob Ruppert, quoted in David Q. Voigt, *American Baseball*, vol. 2: *From the Commissioners to Continental Expansion* (University Park: Pennsylvania State University Press, 1983), 251.

28. Harry Sinden, quoted in Michael Farber, "Giant Sucking Sound," *Sports Illustrated*, March 20, 1995, 110.

29. Quoted in Bierig and Levine, "Market Driven," 10.

30. "Professional Basketball," 39.

31. Carl Pohlad, quoted in Bierig and Levine, "Market Driven," 10.

32. See James B. Dworkin, "Salary Arbitration in Baseball: An Impartial Assessment after Ten Years," *Arbitration Journal* 41 (March 1986), 63–69.

33. Stephen Greenberg, quoted in Richard Hoffer, "The Buck Stops Here," *Sports Illustrated*, July 29, 1991, 46.

34. Michael H. Stone of the Texas Rangers, quoted in William C. Symonds et al., "Baseball's Big Leagues Blues," *Business Week,* August 12, 1985, 40.

35. Quoted in Smith, "State of Game? Not the Same Everywhere."

36. "Baseball Impasse: Locking out for No. 1," *New York Times*, March 11, 1990.

37. "Professional Basketball," 38.

38. Todd Vogel, "The NBA Is Paying out Like There's No Tomorrow," *Business Week,* February 5, 1990, 64.

39. Tom Farrey, "The Bottom Line—Television Pays the Bills," *Seattle Times*, July 28, 1991.

40. *American Sports*, 291, 296.

41. *Hardball: The Education of a Baseball Commissioner* (New York: Times Books, 1987), 226.

42. The NFL's Carolina Cougars were based in Charlotte, N.C., but played their home games 122 miles away in Clemson, S.C., pending the completion of a new stadium in Charlotte.

43. "Attendance and Price Setting," 134.

44. Marie Fioramonte of Prudential Power Funding Associates, quoted in Michael K. Ozanian et al., "Suite Deals," *Financial World*, May 9, 1995, 47.

Chapter Four
Private Business

1. "Sports' Integral Role with a Community," *New York Times*, February 2, 1986.

2. Public ownership here refers to ownership by government or a nonprofit institution as in Green Bay, not ownership of a team through public offerings of stock; for a discussion of publicly held, privately owned professional sports teams, see Jerry Gorman and Kirk Calhoun, *The Name of the Game: The Business of Sports* (New York: John Wiley & Sons, 1994), 198–201.

3. David Sarasohn, "Toys of the Rich; Pro Sports Franchises," *Trenton Times*, June 7, 1988.

4. *Winning Is the Only Thing: Sports in America Since 1945* (Baltimore: Johns Hopkins University Press, 1989), 148.

5. Quoted ibid., 71.

6. Quoted in Bob Oates, "The NFL Owners: The AFC Central," *Los Angeles Times*, January 25, 1987.

7. *Hardball: The Education of a Baseball Commissioner* (New York: Times Books, 1987), 93.

8. Sarasohn, "Toys of the Rich."

9. Dale Hofmann and Martin J. Greenberg, *Sport$biz : An Irreverent Look at Big Business in Pro Sports* (Champaign, Ill.: Leisure Press, 1989), 150.

10. Joseph Durso, *The All-American Dollar: The Big Business of Sports* (Boston: Houghton Mifflin, 1971), 29.

11. Richard Beddoes, Stan Fischler, and Ira Gitler, *Hockey: The Story of the World's Fastest Sport* (New York: Macmillan, 1969), 293.

12. Quoted in John Merwin, "Big League Baseball's New Cash Lineup," *Forbes*, March 28, 1983, 168.

13. Quoted in William C. Symonds et al., "Baseball's Big Leagues Blues," *Business Week*, August 12, 1985, 40.

14. *Hardball*, 7.

15. James Quirk and Mohamed El Hodiri, "The Economic Theory of a Professional Sports League," in Roger G. Noll, ed., *Government and the Sports Business* (Washington, D.C.: Brookings Institution, 1974), 42.

16. *Hardball*, 210.

17. See, for example, David Q. Voigt, *American Baseball*, vol. 2: *From the Commissioners to Continental Expansion* (University Park: Pennsylvania State University Press, 1983), 274.

18. *No Joy in Mudville: The Dilemma of Major League Baseball* (Cambridge, Mass.: Schenkman, 1965), 163.

19. "The Political Economy of Professional Sport," in Jean Harvey and Hart Cantelon, eds., *Not Just a Game: Essays in Canadian Sport Sociology* (Ottawa: Ottawa University Press, 1988), 149.

20. *American Baseball*, vol. 3: *From Postwar Expansion to the Electronic Age* (University Park: Pennsylvania State University Press, 1983), 306.

21. J. H. England, quoted in "Monopoly Pays off in the Business of Sports," *Business Week*, October 13, 1980, 148.

22. Charlie Lyons, quoted in Eric Conrad et al., "The Future of Sports: Labor Strife,

Angry Fans, Soaring Salaries and Ticket Prices Muddle Picture," *Houston Chronicle*, January 8, 1995.

23. Margo Vignola of Salomon Brothers, quoted in Calvin Sims, "In Disney's Hockey Venture, the Real Action Is off the Ice," *New York Times*, December 14, 1992.

24. Quoted in David Mills, "The Blue Line and the Bottom Line: Entrepreneurs and the Business of Hockey in Canada, 1927–90," in Paul D. Staudohar and James A. Mangan, eds., *The Business of Professional Sports* (Urbana and Chicago: University of Illinois Press, 1991), 189.

25. Quoted in Brenton R. Schlender, "Take Me out to the Gold Mine," *Fortune*, August 13, 1990, 93.

26. Quoted in Frederick C. Klein, "Owning a Sports Team Looks Like Fun," *Wall Street Journal*, September 9, 1969.

27. *American Baseball*, vol. 3: 304.

28. Quoted in Durso, *The All-American Dollar*, 1.

29. The value of the shelter has varied as tax rules have been adjusted; prior to the Tax Reform Act of 1976, purchasers were permitted to allocate as much as 95 percent of the price of a team, which could be depreciated over five years. After 1976, no more than 50 percent of the purchase price could be depreciated, and the reforms in 1988 further restricted the tax benefits of buying a professional sports team. See Michael L. Lewis, "Professional Sports Franchising and the IRS," *Washburn Law Review* 14 (Spring 1975), 321–29; Valerie Nelson Strandell, "The Impact of the 1976 Tax Reform Act on the Owners of Professional Sports Teams," *Journal of Contemporary Law* 4 (Spring 1978), 219–32; and Howard Zaritsky, "Taxation of Professional Sports Teams after 1976: A Whole New Ball Game," *William & Mary Law Review* 18 (Summer 1977), 679–702.

30. "Alternatives in Sports Policy," in Noll, *Government and the Sports Business*, 413.

31. "Taxation and Sports Enterprises," ibid., 183.

32. *Pay Dirt: The Business of Professional Team Sports* (Princeton: Princeton University Press, 1992), 120–22.

33. *Law and Business of the Sports Industries* (Dover, Mass.: Auburn House, 1986), 6.

34. See James Quirk, "An Economic Analysis of Team Movements in Professional Sports," *Law and Contemporary Problems* 38 (Winter/Spring 1973), 51.

35. Quoted in Peter Richmond, *Ballpark: Camden Yards and the Building of an American Dream* (New York: Simon & Schuster, 1993), 91.

36. "Alternatives in Sports Policy," 415.

37. Quoted in David Whitford, *Playing Hardball: The High-Stakes Battle for Baseball's New Franchises* (New York: Doubleday, 1993), 157.

38. *The Business of Professional Baseball* (Chicago: University of Chicago Press, 1989), 143.

39. Bud Selig, quoted in Bob Finnigan, "Selig: Small-Market Teams Need Help from Communities," *Seattle Times*, June 24, 1991.

40. Quoted in Dave Nightingale, "The Poison Apple," *Sporting News*, March 8, 1993.

41. "So Much of the Joy Is Gone," *Forbes*, September 14, 1992, 88.

42. Quoted in Peter King, *The Season after: Are Sports Dynasties Dead?* (New York: Warner Books, 1989), 155.

43. Andrew Dolich, quoted in Schlender, "Take Me out to the Gold Mine."

44. *The Name of the Game: The Business of Sports*, 247.

45. See Will Dunham, "Reagan's Tax Proposal Alarms Sports Leaders," *United Press International*, June 8, 1985. The share in baseball was 46 percent, in the NBA 51 percent, and in the NHL 60 percent; no data were available for the NFL.

46. Clint Murchison, quoted in Anthony Lucas, "Wanta Buy Two Seats for the Dallas Cowboys?" *Esquire*, September 1972, 122.

47. Nicholas F. Filla, "'Sports Management' Actually Means Fan Manipulation," *Sporting News*, July 13, 1992. Filla was president of the National Sports Fan Association.

48. Quoted by Kenneth Reich, "Baseball Talks Snagged over Salary Arbitration," *Los Angeles Times*, August 5, 1985.

49. October 11, 1987.

50. Bud Selig of the Milwaukee Brewers, quoted in Finnigan, "Selig: Small-Market Teams Need Help from Communities."

51. *Hardball*, 347.

52. Phil Elderkin, "If Players Strike, Will Fans Walk Out?" *Christian Science Monitor*, May 21, 1980.

53. Filla, "'Sports Management' Actually Means Fan Manipulation."

54. "Is the Base-Ball Player a Chattel?" *Lippincott's Magazine* 40 (August 1887), 319.

55. Quoted in Roberts and Olson, *Winning Is the Only Thing: Sports in America Since 1945*, 150.

56. Quoted in David Harris, *The League: The Rise and Decline of the NFL* (New York: Bantam, 1986), 607.

Chapter Five
Business Partners

1. Jerry Colangelo of the Phoenix Suns, quoted in James Flanigan, "Raider's Departure Has Old-fashioned Ring to It," *Los Angeles Times*, June 25, 1995.

2. Brian Weber, "Pepsi Pours $68 Million into Arena," *Rocky Mountain News*, March 17, 1995.

3. *American Baseball*, vol. 2: *From the Commissioners to Continental Expansion* (University Park: Pennsylvania State University Press, 1983), 231.

4. *Pittsburgh Athletic Co. v. KQV Broadcasting Co.*, 24 F. Supp. 490, 492 (W.D. Pa. 1938).

5. *In Its Own Image: How Television Has Transformed Professional Sports* (New York: Free Press, 1984), 55.

6. Clarence Campbell, quoted in Richard Beddoes, Stan Fischler, and Ira Gitler, *Hockey: The Story of the World's Fastest Sport* (New York: Macmillan, 1969), 83.

7. Quoted in Roone Arledge and Gilbert Rogin, "It's Sports, It's Money . . . It's TV," *Sports Illustrated*, April 25, 1966, 100.

8. See David Q. Voigt, *American Baseball*, vol. 3: *From Postwar Expansion to the Electronic Age* (University Park: Pennsylvania State University Press, 1983), 107.

9. Donald E. Parente, "The Interdependence of Sports and Television," *Journal of Communication* 27 (Summer 1977), 129.

10. See Atre et al., "Sports: The High-Stakes Game of Team Ownership," *Financial World*, May 20, 1996, 53–65.

11. "Television Made It All a New Game," *Sports Illustrated*, December 22, 1969, 88.

12. Quoted in David Harris, *The League: The Rise and Decline of the NFL* (New York: Bantam, 1986), 433.

13. "The Growth of American Spectator Sport: A Technological Perspective," in Richard Carhman and Michael McKernan, *Sport in History: The Making of Modern Sporting History* (St. Lucia, Australia: University of Queensland Press, 1979), 38.

14. *Supertube: The Rise of Television Sports* (New York: Coward-McCann, 1984), 275.

15. "It's Sports, It's Money . . . It's TV," 100.

16. See William Oscar Johnson, "For Sale: the National Pastime," *Sports Illustrated*, May 17, 1993, 39.

17. Eddie Einhorn of the Chicago Bulls, quoted in Steve Nidetz, "Einhorn's Game: the Business of TV Baseball," *Chicago Tribune*, April 2, 1989.

18. See Paul Brown with Jack Clary, *PB: The Paul Brown Story* (New York: New American Library, 1981), 330–34.

19. Roger Piantadosi and Bart Barnes, "At Whose-ier Dome and Elsewhere, the Stakes Keep Getting Higher," *Washington Post*, July 11, 1983.

20. "Professional Basketball: Economic and Business Perspectives," in Paul D. Staudohar and James A. Mangan, eds., *The Business of Professional Sports* (Urbana and Chicago: University of Illinois Press, 1991), 22.

21. J. C. H. Jones, "The Economics of the National Hockey League," *Canadian Journal of Economics* 2 (February 1969), 19.

22. Abe Pollin, Washington Capitals, quoted in Paul Attner, "The Big Bang and Its Effect," *Sporting News*, March 18, 1991.

23. Commissioner Gary Bettman, quoted in Joe Lapointe, "N.H.L.'s Northern Lights Starting to Dim," *New York Times*, February 21, 1993.

24. *Sports for Sale: Television, Money, and the Fans* (New York: Oxford University Press, 1988), 19.

25. *American Sports: From the Age of Folk Games to the Age of Spectators* (Englewood, N.J.: Prentice-Hall, 1983), 287.

26. *Supertube*, 153.

27. "Sports Broadcasting," in Roger G. Noll, ed., *Government and the Sports Business* (Washington, D.C.: Brookings Institution, 1974), 275.

28. Thomas Bennett, quoted in William O. Johnson, *Super Spectator and the Electric Lilliputians* (Boston: Little, Brown, 1971), 102.

29. The Atlanta metropolitan area grew from 1.17 million in 1960 to 1.60 million in 1970, an increase of 36.5 percent; the Milwaukee area increased from 1.28 million to 1.40 million, a increase of 9.8 percent.

30. Ira Horowitz, "Sports Telecasts—Rights and Regulations," *Journal of Communication* 27 (Summer 1977), 161.

31. Quoted in Thomas Boswell, "Ueberroth on Offensive in Baseball's TV Wars," *Washington Post*, December 6, 1984.

32. *Hardball: The Education of a Baseball Commissioner* (New York: Times Books, 1987), 289.

33. John Madigan, quoted in Randy Minkoff, "The Baseball Page: Superstation Issue Is Still Bubbling," *Los Angeles Times*, April 19, 1987.

34. *Sports for Sale*, 60.

35. Quoted in *Hardball*, 5.

36. *Chicago Professional Sports L.P. v. National Basketball Association*, 754 F. Supp. 1336, 1364 (N.D. Ill. 1991).

37. John R. McCambridge, attorney for WGN Continental Broadcasting, quoted in Arthur S. Hayes, "Federal Judge Upsets Plan of NBA to Curb Superstation Broadcasts," *Wall Street Journal*, January 25, 1991.

38. Quoted in William D. Murray, "Rozelle Rides Again," *United Press International*, March 20, 1987.

39. Al Harazin, quoted in Claire Smith, "Baseball Owners Approve Joint Venture with ABC and NBC," *New York Times*, May 29, 1993.

Chapter Six
Teams in Leagues

1. Quoted in Ross Atkins, "With Super Bowl Settled, Comes Another Showdown," *Christian Science Monitor*, January 26, 1981.

2. John Fetzer of the Detroit Tigers, quoted in Thomas Boswell, "Baseball: Riches or Ruin?" *Washington Post*, December 21, 1980.

3. Wellington Mara of the New York Giants, quoted in Thomas George, "Rams Given Green Light for St. Louis Move," *New York Times*, April 13, 1995.

4. Quoted in "Stern Testifies in NBA Trial," *United Press International*, December 20, 1990.

5. "The Owners' New Game Is Managing," *Fortune*, July 1, 1991, 86.

6. George Young of the New York Giants, quoted in Peter King, *The Season after: Are Sports Dynasties Dead?* (New York: Warner Books, 1989), xviii.

7. "The Economic Theory of a Professional Sports League," in Roger G. Noll, ed., *Government and the Sports Business* (Washington, D.C.: Brookings Institution, 1974), 37.

8. *The Economics of Professional Team Sports* (Lexington, Mass.: Lexington Books, 1973), 28.

9. Ibid., 29.

10. Commissioner Fay Vincent, quoted in Hal Bodley, "Baseball's Top Concern: Economics," *USA Today*, October 8, 1991.

11. *In Its Own Image: How Television Has Transformed Professional Sports* (New York: Free Press, 1984), 207, 208.

12. See Stephen Taub, "The Puck Stops Here," *Financial World*, July 9, 1991, 41.

13. *Levin v. NBA*, 385 F. Supp. 149, 152 (S.D.N.Y. 1974).

14. See *Mid-South Grizzlies v. National Football League*, 550 F. Supp. 558 (E.D. Pa. 1982).

15. Pete Rozelle, quoted in David Harris, *The League: The Rise and Decline of the NFL* (New York: Bantam, 1986), 91.

16. Bowie Kuhn, *Hardball: The Education of a Baseball Commissioner* (New York: Times Books, 1987), 215.

17. Ibid.

18. Jim Francis, quoted in Gerald Eskenazi, "U.S. Sports Prominent on Japanese Shopping Lists," *New York Times*, October 10, 1990.

19. Commissioner Fay Vincent, quoted in George Vecsey, "Baseball Is Saved Once Again," *New York Times*, June 10, 1993.

20. National Football League, *Constitution* (1970), §4.2.

21. Donald Chipman, Randolph Campbell, and Robert Cavert, *The Dallas Cowboys and the NFL* (Norman: University of Oklahoma Press, 1970), 74.

22. Al LoCasale, quoted in Mark Heisler, "Tis the Season for a Nice, Neighborly Battle," *Los Angeles Times*, December 22, 1985.

23. U.S. Congress, House of Representatives, Committee on the Judiciary, *Organized Professional Team Sports*, Hearings before the Antitrust Subcommittee, 85th Cong., 1st sess. (Washington, D.C.: U.S. Government Printing Office, 1957), 162.

24. Samuel R. Pierce, Jr., "Organized Professional Team Sports and the Antitrust Laws," *Cornell Law Quarterly* 43 (Summer 1958), 593.

25. Robert Moore, quoted in Calvin Sims, "In Disney's Hockey Venture, the Real Action Is off the Ice," *New York Times*, December 14, 1992.

26. *Hardball*, 188.

27. *Baseball Economics and Public Policy* (Lexington, Mass.: Lexington Books, 1981), 70.

28. "Major League Team Sports," in Walter Adams, *The Structure of American Industry*, 5th ed. (New York: Macmillan, 1977), 386.

29. *Los Angeles Memorial Coliseum Commission v. National Football League*, 726 F.2d 1381, 1397 (9th Cir. 1984).

30. "Attendance and Price Setting," in Noll, *Government and the Sports Business*, 154.

31. *Baseball Economics and Public Policy*, 109.

32. "Professional Basketball: Economic and Business Perspectives," in Paul D. Staudohar and James A. Mangan, eds., *The Business of Professional Sports* (Urbana and Chicago: University of Illinois Press, 1991), 35.

33. *Federal Baseball Club of Baltimore v. National League*, 259 U.S. 200, 208 (1922).

34. See *Toolson v. New York Yankees, Inc.*, 346 U.S. 356 (1953).

35. See *Flood v. Kuhn*, 407 U.S. 258 (1972).

36. See *Radovich v. National Football League*, 352 U.S. 445 (1957).

37. See *Philadelphia World Hockey Club v. Philadelphia Hockey Club, Inc.*, 351 F. Supp. 462 (E.D. Pa. 1972); and *Robertson v. National Basketball Association*, 389 F. Supp. 867 (S.D.N.Y. 1975).

38. *United States v. National Football League*, 116 F. Supp. 319, 327 (E.D. Pa. 1953).

39. See *United States v. National Football League*, 196 F. Supp. 445 (E.D. Pa. 1961).

40. See U.S. Congress, House of Representatives, 85th Congress, 2d sess., H.R. 10358, 1958.

41. See 75 Stat. 732.

42. Commissioner Pete Rozelle, quoted in Rader, *In Its Own Image*, 90.

43. U.S. Congress, Senate, *Telecasting of Professional Sports Contests*, Senate Re-

port 1087, 87th Congress, 1st sess. (Washington, D.C.: U.S. Government Printing Office, 1961), 2.

44. Richard Gruneau, *Class, Sports, and Social Development* (Amherst: University of Massachusetts Press, 1983), 124.

45. For a detailed discussion of the legislative history of the anti-blackout legislation, see Harry M. Shooshan III, "Confrontation with Congress: Professional Sports and the Television Antiblackout Law," *Syracuse Law Review* 25 (Summer 1974), 713–45. See also Philip R. Hochberg, "Second and Goal to Go: The Legislative Attack in the 92nd Congress on Sports Broadcasting Practices," *New York Law Forum* 18 (Spring 1973), 841–96; and Philip R. Hochberg, "Congress Kicks a Field Goal: The Legislative Attack in the 93rd Congress on Sports Broadcasting Practices," *Federal Communications Bar Journal* 27 (1974), 27–79.

46. Quoted in Joseph Tybor, "Lawmakers Ready to Block Big-Time Sports from Moving to Pay TV," *Chicago Tribune*, October 28, 1991.

47. See U.S. Congress, Senate, Committee on the Judiciary, *Authorizing the Merger of Two or More Professional Basketball Leagues*, Senate Report 92–1151, 92d Cong., 2d sess. (Washington, D.C.: U.S. Government Printing Office, 1972), 1.

48. The legislation was introduced by Senator Slade Gorton and Representative Rod Chandler.

49. Robert S. Carlson, "The Business of Professional Sports: A Reexamination in Progress," *New York Law Forum* 18 (Spring 1973), 931.

50. "Baseball Jurisprudence," *American Law Review* 44 (May-June 1910), 376.

Chapter Seven
Big League Cities

1. Quoted in Eric Allen Mitnick, "Anticipating an Instant Replay: *City of Oakland v. Oakland Raiders* [646 P.2d 835 (Cal.)]" *U.C. Davis Law Review* 17 (Spring 1984), 984.

2. Quoted in Dale Hofmann and Martin J. Greenberg, *Sport$biz: An Irreverent Look at Big Business in Pro Sports* (Champaign, Ill.: Leisure Press, 1989), 154.

3. Quoted in Ron Word, "Touchdown!" *Island Packet* (Hilton Head Island, S.C.), January 1, 1993.

4. Quoted in "Brewers Have $250M Deal for Stadium," *Newark Star-Ledger*, August 20, 1995.

5. Walter Council, quoted in Dale Gibson, "Sporting Chances: Pro Teams Proliferate on an Expanding Field of Economic Dreams," *Triangle Business* [on line], April 22, 1991. Available: LEXIS Library: TRIBUS File: NEWS.

6. Bud Selig of the Milwaukee Brewers, quoted in Bob Finnigan, "Selig: Small-Market Teams Need Help from Communities," *Seattle Times*, June 24, 1991.

7. "Sportsworld Revisited," *Journal of Sport and Social Issues* 1 (1976), 12.

8. Barbara Weiner of the Greater Houston Convention and Visitors Bureau, quoted in Mary Lou Fulton and Jean Davidson, "All-Star Game: Selling an Image," *Los Angeles Times*, July 9, 1989.

9. James F. Urbanski of the *Tampa Tribune*, quoted in Dudley Clendinen, "Wet, Happy Tampa Braces for the Game," *New York Times*, January 21, 1984.

10. Robert Payne, quoted in Armando Acuna, "San Diego Studies Today's Game

Plan as Practice for '88," *Los Angeles Times*, January 25, 1987. Payne was chairman of San Diego's host committee for the 1988 Super Bowl.

11. Mayor William Hudnut, quoted in David Morris, "Let Sports Fans Own Their Own Teams," *New York Times*, September 29, 1986.

12. Dick Darr, quoted in Kevin Sack, "Will Nashville Say No to N.F.L. Team? Maybe," *New York Times*, May 3, 1996.

13. Thomas W. Moses of the Indianapolis Water Company, quoted in Roger Piantadosi and Bart Barnes, "At Whose-ier Dome and Elsewhere, the Stakes Keep Getting Higher," *Washington Post*, July 11, 1983.

14. Xavier Hermosillo, quoted in Mark Arax, "Raiders Sign Pact to Build Stadium on Irwindale Site," *Los Angeles Times*, August 21, 1987.

15. Pat Williams, quoted in Barry Cooper, "Pro Sports Provide Boost," *Orlando Sentinel*, January 10, 1994.

16. Kevin Ross, quoted in Douglas A. Blackmon, "Are the Hawks Leaving or Just Bluffing?" *Atlanta Constitution*, November 6, 1994.

17. See the interview with Rankin Smith, owner of the Atlanta Falcons, in Ray Kennedy, "Who Are These Guys?" *Sports Illustrated*, January 31, 1977, 50–60.

18. Mayor Xavier Suarez, quoted in Ian Thomsen, "Miami Left under Cloud," *Boston Globe*, January 19, 1989.

19. Robert Lipsyte, *Sports World: An American Dreamland* (New York: Quadrangle, 1975), 23.

20. Gerry Yuen of the Northlands Coliseum, quoted in Joe Lapointe, "N.H.L.'s Northern Lights Starting to Dim," *New York Times*, February 21, 1993.

21. Harvey MacKay of the Minneapolis Chamber of Commerce, quoted in Amy Klobuchar, *Uncovering the Dome* (Prospect Heights, Ill.: Waveland Press, 1986), xvi.

22. *Ballpark: Camden Yards and the Building of an American Dream* (New York: Simon & Schuster, 1993), 65.

23. For a summary of economic benefit studies, see Hofmann and Greenberg, *Sport$biz*, 154–55 and Arthur T. Johnson, "The Sports Franchise Relocation Issue and Public Policy Responses," in Arthur T. Johnson and James H. Frey, eds., *Government and Sport: the Public Policy Issues* (Totowa, N.J.: Rowman & Allanheid, 1985), 223.

24. See Michael Dabney, "Penn Prof: Moving Teams Would Hurt Philadelphia Area," *United Press International*, March 5, 1990; the research was undertaken by Edward Shils for the Philadelphia Sports Consortium, a group formed by the four teams and concessionaires, and updated an earlier study by Shils for the Sports Consortium; see Edward Shils, "Report to the Philadelphia Professional Sports Consortium on Its Contribution to the Economy of Philadelphia" (Philadelphia, June 17, 1985).

25. See T. Keating Holland, "Field of Dreams," *Reason*, May 1990, 23.

26. Spurgeon Richardson, quoted in "World Series Games Are Economic Home Run for Atlanta," *Reuters*, October 21, 1991.

27. These estimates are from Hofmann and Greenberg, *Sport$biz*, 154.

28. Ty Stroh, quoted in Bob Webster, "Super Bowl to Kick $100 Million into Southern California," *United Press International*, January 21, 1987.

29. "Public Sports Policy: An Introduction," *American Behavioral Scientist* 21 (January/February 1978), 324.

30. "The Impact of Stadiums and Professional Sports on Metropolitan Area Development," *Growth and Change* 21 (Spring 1990), 6.

31. See Jack Broom, "What Are Sports Worth to City? It Depends," *Seattle Times*, April 20, 1990.

32. Mark S. Rosentraub and Samuel R. Nunn, "Suburban City Investment in Professional Sports: Estimating the Fiscal Returns of the Dallas Cowboys and Texas Rangers to Investor Communities," *American Behavioral Scientist* 21 (January/February 1978), 412–13.

33. Thomas Ferguson of the Beacon Council, quoted in David Whitford, *Playing Hardball: The High-Stakes Battle for Baseball's New Franchises* (New York: Doubleday, 1993), 31.

34. Donald Chipman, Randolph Campbell, and Robert Cavert, *The Dallas Cowboys and the NFL* (Norman: University of Oklahoma Press, 1970), 142.

35. Thomas Ferguson of the Beacon Council, quoted in John Helyar, "Big League Battle: Baseball's Expansion Is a High-Stakes Game of Money and Politics," *Wall Street Journal*, December 21, 1990.

36. Quoted in Whitford, *Playing Hardball*, 30.

37. "Field of Dreams," 25.

38. Louis DeMars, quoted in Klobuchar, *Uncovering the Dome*, 157–58.

39. Steven A. Riess, *City Games: The Evolution of American Urban Society and the Rise of Sports* (Urbana and Chicago: University of Illinois Press, 1989), 244.

40. "Sports from a Geographic Perspective," in Donald W. Ball and John W. Loy, eds., *Sport and Social Order: Contributions to the Sociology of Sport* (Reading, Mass.: Addison-Wesley, 1975), 112.

41. *City Games*, 245.

42. Bob Grant, quoted in "Two Stadium Winners: Busch, the Meadowlands," *Chicago Tribune*, November 10, 1985.

43. Riess, *City Games*, 242.

44. Klobuchar, *Uncovering the Dome*, 162–63.

45. Mark S. Rosentraub et al., "Sport and Downtown Development Strategy: If You Build It, Will Jobs Come?" *Journal of Urban Affairs* 16 (1994), 236.

46. Steve Kaplan, quoted in Whitford, *Playing Hardball*, 53.

47. Michael H. Ranzenhofer of the Erie County Legislature, quoted in Margaret Hammersley, "Gorski Urged to Hire Negotiator in Effort to Renew Stadium Lease," *Buffalo News*, March 22, 1995.

48. ABC News, *Nightline*, November 29, 1993 (Transcript #3266).

49. *Veeck—as in Wreck* (New York: G. P. Putnam's Sons, 1962), 120.

50. Lipsyte, "Sportsworld Revisited," 11.

51. Rick Dodge, quoted in Whitford, *Playing Hardball*, 175.

52. Representative Fortnoy H. Stark, U.S. Congress, Senate, Committee on the Judiciary, *Professional Sports Antitrust Immunity*, Hearings, 97th Cong., 2d sess. (Washington, D.C.: U.S. Government Printing Office, 1983), 23.

53. Mayor Diane Feinstein, ibid., 135.

54. *Sports Spectators* (New York: Columbia University Press, 1986), 182–83.

55. *American Sports: From the Age of Folk Games to the Age of Spectators* (Englewood, N.J.: Prentice-Hall, 1983), 293.

56. Chipman, Campbell, and Cavert, *The Dallas Cowboys and the NFL*, 139.

57. For an informative account of the violent aftermath of recent championships, see

William Oscar Johnson, "The Agony of Victory," *Sports Illustrated*, July 5, 1993, 31–37.

58. *To Every Thing a Season: Shibe Park and Urban Philadelphia 1909–1976* (Princeton: Princeton University Press, 1991), 145.

59. Herb Ross, quoted in Peter Golenbock, *Bums* (New York: Putnam, 1984), 433.

60. See Mark Starr, "Baseball's Black Problem," *Newsweek*, July 19, 1993, 56–57.

61. Peter Levine, *A. G. Spalding and the Rise of Baseball* (New York: Oxford University Press, 1985), 45.

62. See Steven A. Riess, *Touching Base: Professional Baseball and American Culture in the Progressive Era* (Westport, Conn.: Greenwood Press, 1980), 66–71.

63. Arthur Johnson, "The Uneasy Partnership of Cities and Professional Sports: Public Policy Considerations," in Nancy Theberge and Peter Donnelly, eds., *Sport and the Sociological Imagination* (Fort Worth: Texas Christian University Press, 1984), 218.

64. Bernard J. Frieden and Lynne B. Sagalyn, *Downtown, Inc.: How America Rebuilds Cities* (Cambridge: MIT Press, 1989), 281.

65. "The Uneasy Partnership of Cities and Professional Sports," 220.

66. Quoted in Isabel Wilkerson, "What Taxpayers and Their Teams Do for Each Other," *New York Times*, July 24, 1988.

67. Quoted in Neil J. Sullivan, *The Dodgers Move West* (New York: Oxford University Press, 1987), 174.

68. Quoted in Whitford, *Playing Hardball*, 52–53.

69. Charles Millard, quoted in Steven Lee Myers, "The $1 Billion Cure for Civic Insecurity," *New York Times*, April 14, 1996.

70. Quoted in Frank L. Hefner, "Using Economic Models to Measure the Impact of Sports on Local Economies," *Journal of Sport and Social Issues* 14 (Spring 1990), 2.

71. Baade and Dye, "The Impact of Stadiums and Professional Sports on Metropolitan Area Development," 13.

Chapter Eight
Competing for Teams

1. Rick Dodge of St. Petersburg, quoted in David Whitford, *Playing Hardball: The High-Stakes Battle for Baseball's New Franchises* (New York: Doubleday, 1993), 177.

2. Quoted in Neil J. Sullivan, *The Dodgers Move West* (New York: Oxford University Press), 99.

3. Ibid., 96.

4. *Playing the Field: Why Sports Teams Move and Cities Fight to Keep Them* (Baltimore: Johns Hopkins University Press, 1993), 107.

5. Quoted in Jane Leavy, "Colts' Twenty-Year Lease Approved Formally," *Washington Post*, April 1, 1984.

6. Mike Roos, "Stopping Sports Terrorism," letter to the editor, *Los Angeles Times*, October 23, 1987. Roos was a member of the California Assembly, where he served as speaker pro tem.

7. Randy Roberts and James Olson, *Winning Is the Only Thing: Sports in America Since 1945* (Baltimore: Johns Hopkins University Press, 1989), 148.

8. John Malmo, quoted in Roger Piantadosi and Bart Barnes, "At Whose-ier Dome and Elsewhere, the Stakes Keep Getting Higher," *Washington Post*, July 11, 1983.

9. Marcel Aubut, quoted in Helene Elliott, "These Towns Aren't Big Enough for NHL," *Los Angeles Times*, May 26, 1995.

10. Bud Selig of the Milwaukee Brewers, quoted in Bob Finnigan, "Selig: Small-Market Teams Need Help from Communities," *Seattle Times*, June 24, 1991.

11. Art Modell, quoted in Paul Attner, "For Many Cities, There's No Place Like a Dome," *Washington Post*, June 8, 1984.

12. Quoted by Don Benevento, *Gannett News Service*, June 10, 1991.

13. Quoted in Euchner, *Playing the Field*, 134.

14. Ibid., 175.

15. William A. Cunningham of the Oakland-Alameda County Coliseum, quoted in "Will the Raiders Be Ruled out of Bounds?" *Business Week*, March 31, 1980, 46.

16. Calvin Griffith, quoted in Michael Roberts, *Fans: How We Go Crazy over Sports* (Washington, D.C.: New Republic, 1976), 139.

17. Vince Naimoli, quoted in Ned Seaton et al., "Rays' Dome Negotiations Hit Snag," *St. Petersburg Times*, April 4, 1995.

18. Quoted in Whitford, *Playing Hardball*, 42.

19. James F. Hardy, quoted in "Will the Raiders Be Ruled out of Bounds?" 46.

20. *Pay Dirt: The Business of Professional Team Sports* (Princeton: Princeton University Press, 1992), 145.

21. President Bill White of the National League, quoted in Whitford, *Playing Hardball*, 130.

22. Tim Romani of the Illinois Sports Facilities Authority, quoted in Joni Balter, "How Other Cities Keep Baseball Teams," *Seattle Times*, October 6, 1991.

23. *Playing Hardball*, 38.

24. Quoted ibid., 42.

25. Quoted in Piantadosi and Barnes, "At Whose-ier Dome and Elsewhere, the Stakes Keep Getting Higher." Moses was president of the Indianapolis Water Company.

26. Rick Dodge, quoted in Whitford, *Playing Hardball*, 176–77.

27. Wellington Mara, quoted in Ronald Sullivan, "Football Giants to Leave City for Jersey after 1974 Season," *New York Times*, August 27, 1971.

28. Don Carter, quoted in Kim North, "Carter Helps Push Lewisville Tax Vote," *Dallas Morning News*, January 13, 1995.

29. Jim Blosser, quoted in Whitford, *Playing Hardball*, 163.

30. Donald Chipman, Randolph Campbell, and Robert Cavert, *The Dallas Cowboys and the NFL* (Norman: University of Oklahoma Press, 1970), 149.

31. Amy Klobuchar, *Uncovering the Dome* (Prospect Heights, Ill.: Waveland Press, 1986), 55.

32. Secretary Henry Cisneros, Department of Housing and Urban Development, quoted in Paul Barton, "HUD Chief: Save the Bengals," *Cincinnati Enquirer*, June 13, 1995.

33. *City of New York v. New York Jets Football Club, Inc.*, 90 Misc. 2d 311, 394 N.Y.S. 2d 799, 803 (N.Y. Sup. Ct. 1977).

34. *Sports Geography* (London: E. & F. N. Spon, 1989), 121.

35. John Cowles, Jr., Star-Tribune, quoted in Klobuchar, *Uncovering the Dome*, 52.

36. *Playing the Field*, 156.

37. See Whitford, *Playing Hardball*, 137.

38. Quoted in John McCarron and David Young, "White Sox Owners: It's Addison or Adios," *Chicago Tribune*, July 9, 1986.

39. Quoted by *United Press International*, January 6, 1987.

40. See "This Year's M.V.P.s (Most Valuable Plates)," advertisement, New York State Department of Motor Vehicles, *New York Times*, July 18, 1993. Tellingly, New York did not offer special plates for the other two teams located in the New Jersey portion of the New York metropolitan region, the New Jersey Devils and the New Jersey Nets.

41. Robert Nahas, quoted in Bowie Kuhn, *Hardball: The Education of a Baseball Commissioner* (New York: Times Books, 1987), 190.

42. Rick Dodge, quoted in Attner, "For Many Cities, There's No Place Like a Dome."

43. Commissioner Peter Ueberroth, quoted in Whitford, *Playing Hardball*, 41.

44. Twenty-four states and five provinces were represented in the four major leagues in 1996, compared with thirteen states and two provinces in 1950; the number of states will rise to twenty-five when the Oilers are moved to Tennessee.

45. See John P. Pelissero, Beth M. Henschen, and Edward I. Sidlow, "Urban Regimes, Sports Stadiums, and the Politics of Economic Development Agendas in Chicago," *Policy Studies Review* 10 (Spring/Summer 1991), 121; and Euchner, *Playing the Field*, 137–41.

Chapter Nine
Changing Places

1. The relocation of the Houston Oilers to Nashville was approved by the NFL in 1996, but was delayed by the team's lease obligations in Houston. All of the tabulations in this chapter count the Oilers as a relocated franchise.

2. "Discordant Notes from Musical Chairs," *New York Times*, September 24, 1971.

3. "Sport and Urban Life," *Journal of Sport and Social Issues* 14 (Fall 1990), 93.

4. "Self-Regulation in Baseball, 1909–71," in Roger G. Noll, ed., *Government and the Sports Business* (Washington, D.C.: Brookings Institution, 1974), 384.

5. *American Baseball*, vol. 3: *From Postwar Expansion to the Electronic Age* (University Park: Pennsylvania State University Press, 1983), xxiv.

6. *No Joy in Mudville: The Dilemma of Major League Baseball* (Cambridge, Mass.: Schenkman, 1965), 180.

7. Quoted by Larry Varnell, Denver Chamber of Commerce, in David Whitford, *Playing Hardball: The High-Stakes Battle for Baseball's New Franchises* (New York: Doubleday, 1993), 26.

8. David Harris, *The League: The Rise and Decline of the NFL* (New York: Bantam, 1986), 639.

9. "An Economic Analysis of Team Movements in Professional Sports," *Law and Contemporary Problems* 38 (Winter/Spring 1973), 52.

10. Bill Tuele of the Edmonton Oilers, quoted in Joe Lapointe, "N.H.L.'s Northern Lights Starting to Dim," *New York Times*, February 21, 1993.

11. See James Quirk and Rodney D. Fort, *Pay Dirt: The Business of Professional Team Sports* (Princeton: Princeton University Press, 1992), 264–65.

12. *The Diamond Revolution: The Prospects for Baseball after the Collapse of Its Ruling Class* (New York: St. Martin's Press, 1992), 48.

13. Quoted in Voigt, *American Baseball*, vol. 3: 130.

14. Calvin Griffith, quoted in Benjamin Rader, *In Its Own Image: How Television Has Transformed Professional Sports* (New York: Free Press, 1984), 52; Robert Short, quoted in Bowie Kuhn, *Hardball: The Education of a Baseball Commissioner* (New York: Times Books, 1987), 94.

15. *Sports for Sale: Television, Money, and the Fans* (New York: Oxford University Press, 1988), 120.

16. Quoted in Louis Effrat, "Braves Move to Milwaukee," *New York Times*, March 19, 1953.

17. The annual rate for the 1990s was 0.98 percent, compared with 2.05 percent in the 1950s.

18. See James Quirk and Mohamed El Hodiri, "The Economic Theory of a Professional Sports League," in Noll, *Government and the Sports Business*, 48.

19. *American Baseball*, vol. 3: xxv.

20. "A Tale of Many Cities," *Journal of the West* 17 (July 1978), 77.

21. Quoted in Harris, *The League*, 343; the quotation is from a letter from Rozelle to Kenneth Hahn, a Los Angeles County supervisor and member of the Los Angeles Memorial Coliseum Commission.

22. *Los Angeles Memorial Coliseum Commission v. National Football League*, 726 F.2d 1381, 1936 (9th Cir. 1984).

23. Quoted in Hal Bodley, "Baseball's Top Concern: Economics," *USA Today*, October 8, 1991.

24. A. B. (Happy) Chandler and John Underwood, "How I Jumped from Clean Politics into Dirty Baseball," *Sports Illustrated*, April 26, 1971, 76.

25. *San Francisco Seals, Ltd. v. National Hockey League*, 379 F. Supp. 966, 971 (C.D. Cal 1974).

26. Quoted in Harris, *The League*, 442.

27. *San Francisco Seals, Ltd. v. National Hockey League*, 970.

28. Quoted in Harris, *The League*, 431.

29. *Los Angeles Memorial Coliseum Commission v. National Football League*, 726 F.2d 1381, 1395 (9th Cir. 1984). See *Los Angeles Memorial Coliseum Commission v. National Football League*, 579 F. Supp. 58 (C.D. Cal. 1981), for the district court ruling.

30. The original jury award was $49.2 million; the NFL successfully appealed the award as excessive, leading to negotiations that produced the final figure of $18 million.

31. Paul J. Tagliabue, quoted in "The NFL Misses a Block and Gets Creamed," *Business Week*, May 2, 1983, 37. Tagliabue became commissioner of the still intact NFL in 1989.

32. Quoted in Harris, *The League*, 607.

33. Tex Schramm of the Dallas Cowboys, quoted in Rich Roberts, "State of the NFL," *Los Angeles Times*, January 31, 1988.

34. Alan Rothenberg, quoted in Kenneth Reich, "Extortion or Extinction?" *Los Angeles Times*, February 25, 1985.

35. See *National Basketball Association v. San Diego Clippers Basketball Club*, 815 F.2d 562 (9th Cir. 1987).

36. *Los Angeles Memorial Coliseum Commission v. National Football League*, 726 F.2d 1381, 1397 (9th Cir. 1984).

37. Quoted in Steve Berkowitz, "NL Nears Timetable for Adding 2 Teams," *Washington Post*, June 14, 1990.

Chapter Ten
Playing for Keeps

1. Quoted in Peter Richmond, *Ballpark: Camden Yards and the Building of an American Dream* (New York: Simon & Schuster, 1993), 58.

2. Quoted in Paul Hendrie, "Yo, Yanks: C'Mon Over," *New Jersey Reporter*, September 1993, 14.

3. Norman Green, quoted in "Canadian Developer Brought in as Majority Owner of Minnesota North Stars," *United Press International*, June 6, 1990.

4. Warren Giles, quoted in David Q. Voigt, *American Baseball*, vol. 3: *From Postwar Expansion to the Electronic Age* (University Park: Pennsylvania State University Press, 1983), 128.

5. Quoted in "Frick Supports Shift of Braves," *New York Times*, November 13, 1965.

6. Commissioner William Eckert, quoted in Randy Roberts and James Olson, *Winning Is the Only Thing: Sports in America Since 1945* (Baltimore: Johns Hopkins University Press, 1989), 135.

7. Quoted in Hal Bodley, "Switching Cities: Short-Sited Solution," *USA Today*, June 20, 1991.

8. Quoted in "N.B.A. Wants to Keep Team in Minneapolis," *New York Times*, February 12, 1994.

9. *Los Angeles Memorial Coliseum Commission v. National Football League*, 726 F.2d 1381, 1396 (9th Cir. 1984).

10. NFL statement, quoted in "N.F.L. Asks Court to Block Eagle Move," *New York Times*, December 15, 1984.

11. Quoted in Thomas George, "N.F.L. Owners Bask, but Tagliabue Has Warning," *New York Times,* March 12, 1996.

12. *Hardball: The Education of a Baseball Commissioner* (New York: Times Books, 1987), 95.

13. Art Modell of the Cleveland Browns and Gene Klein of the San Diego Chargers, quoted in David Harris, *The League: The Rise and Decline of the NFL* (New York: Bantam, 1986), 391–92.

14. Ralph Wilson, quoted in Michael Eisen, "NFL Owners Set to Tackle Issues," *Newark Star Ledger*, March 11, 1996.

15. Lee McPhail, quoted in Kuhn, *Hardball*, 193.

16. Pat Lynch, quoted in Kenneth Reich, "Extortion or Extinction?" *Los Angeles Times*, February 25, 1985.

17. Warren Giles, quoted in Joseph Durso, "Braves Put off Request to Move to Atlanta," *New York Times*, October 23, 1964.

18. Jeffrey E. Birren, quoted in Hal Lancaster, "Appeals Court, Backing NBA, Overturns Ruling on Sports Franchises," *Wall Street Journal*, April 22, 1987.

19. Quoted in Harris, *The League*, 371; see also Amy Klobuchar, *Uncovering the Dome* (Prospect Heights, Ill.: Waveland Press, 1986), 131–33.

20. Quoted in Thomas George, "N.F.L. Owners Approve Move to Nashville by the Oilers," *New York Times*, May 1, 1996.

21. Art Modell of the Cleveland Browns, quoted in Rich Roberts, "State of the NFL," *Los Angeles Times*, January 31, 1988.

22. Kuhn, *Hardball*, 95.

23. Quoted in Harris, *The League*, 480.

24. Commissioner Paul Tagliabue, quoted in Bob Glauber, "The NFL Is Going Forward, Commish? Get Outta Town," *Sporting News*, February 12, 1996.

25. Al Deisseroth, quoted in Eleanor Billmyer, "Nats Are Gone! Is Syracuse on the Way Down?" *Syracuse Post-Standard*, May 17, 1963. Deisseroth operated the Syracuse Chiefs (of baseball's International League).

26. Ron Fimrite, "Big George," *Sports Illustrated*, November 6, 1989, 128.

27. Hugh Brown of the *Philadelphia Bulletin*, quoted in Bruce Kuklick, *To Every Thing a Season: Shibe Park and Urban Philadelphia 1909–1976* (Princeton: Princeton University Press, 1991), 123.

28. *American Baseball*, vol. 2: *From the Commissioners to Continental Expansion* (University Park: Pennsylvania State University Press, 1983), 294.

29. "Sports' Integral Role with a Community," *New York Times*, February 2, 1986.

30. See *State v. Milwaukee Braves, Inc.*, Trade Reg. Rep. (1966 Trade Cas.) PP 71738 (Wis. Cir. Ct. April 13, 1966).

31. See *State v. Milwaukee Braves, Inc.*, 31 Wis.2d 699, 144 N.W.2d 1 (1966). See also "Constitutional Law—Commerce and Supremacy Clauses Exempt Professional Baseball from State Antitrust Statute," *Fordham Law Review* 35 (December 1966), 350; and James A. Thorpe, "Constitutional Law—Preemption—Baseball's Immunity from State Antitrust Law, *State v. Milwaukee Braves, Inc.*, 144 N.W. 2d 1 (1966)," *Wayne Law Review* 13 (1967), 417–25.

32. See *HMC Management Corp. v. New Orleans Basketball Club*, 375 So.2d 700 (La. 1979).

33. David Self, quoted in Robert Lindsey, "Oakland Cites Eminent Domain in Effort to Regain Football Team," *New York Times*, May 17, 1983.

34. See *City of Oakland v. Superior Court of Monterey County*, 150 Cal. App.3d 267, 179 Cal. Rptr. 729 (1983). Oakland's attempt to condemn the Raiders attracted considerable attention from legal scholars; see Eric Allen Mitnick, "Anticipating an Instant Replay: *City of Oakland v. Oakland Raiders* [646 P.2d 835 (Cal.)]," *U.C. Davis Law Review* 17 (Spring 1984), 963–1,007; Susan Crabtree, "Public Use in Eminent Domain: Are There Limits after *Oakland Raiders* and *Poletown*?" *California Western Law Review* 20 (Fall 1983), 82–108; Michael Schiano, "Eminent Domain Exercised— Stare Decisis or a Warning: *City of Oakland v. Oakland Raiders*," *Pace Law Review* 4 (Fall 1983), 169–93; Steven M. Crafton, "Taking the Oakland Raiders: A Theoretical Reconsideration of the Concepts of Public Use and Just Compensation," *Emory Law Journal* 32 (Summer 1983), 857; Stephen R. Barnett, "High Court Rulings Show Contrasting Attitudes," *California Lawyer* (October 1982), 58–61; Julius L. Sackman, "Public Use—Updated (City of Oakland v. Oakland Raiders)," *Proceedings of the Institute on Planning, Zoning and Eminent Domain* (1983), 203–35; and Scott R. Carpenter, "*City of Oakland v. Oakland Raiders*: Defining the Parameters of Limitless Power," *Utah Law Review* (1983), 397–414.

35. *City of Baltimore v. Baltimore Football Club*, 624 F. Supp. 278 (D.C. Md. 1985).

36. *Playing the Field: Why Sports Teams Move and Cities Fight to Keep Them* (Baltimore: Johns Hopkins University Press, 1993), 110–11.

37. Mayor Richard Caliguiri, quoted by John O'Brien, *United Press International*, April 27, 1981.

38. See *City of New York v. New York Jets Football Club, Inc.*, 90 Misc.2d 311, 394 N.Y.S.2d 799 (N.Y. Sup. Ct. 1977).

39. Michael Burke, New York Yankees, quoted in Joseph Durso, "Baseball Urged to Field Washington Club by '73," *New York Times*, December 2, 1971.

40. Senator Dennis DeConcini, quoted in Thomas Boswell, "Politics, Sports and the Law: An Unlikely Team to Stop Franchise Moves," *Washington Post*, February 9, 1985.

41. Richard L. Sinnott, "N.F.L. Antitrust Exemption Needed to Protect Cities," *New York Times*, March 6, 1983.

42. "Monopoly Sports Leagues," *Minnesota Law Review* 73 (February 1989), 654.

43. "The Sports Franchise Relocation Issue and Public Policy Responses," in Arthur T. Johnson and James H. Frey, eds., *Government and Sport: the Public Policy Issues* (Totowa, N.J.: Rowman & Allanheid, 1985), 233.

44. U.S. Congress, Senate, Committee on Commerce, Science, and Transportation, *Professional Sports Community Protection Act of 1985*, Hearings, 99th Cong., 1st sess. (Washington, D.C.: U.S. Government Printing Office, 1985), 115.

45. "Sports' Integral Role with a Community."

46. Quoted in Reich, "Extortion or Extinction?"

47. Eric M. Uslaner, "Halt NFL Moves by Creating New Political Footballs," *Wall Street Journal*, March 12, 1985.

48. Quoted in Sara Fritz, "Senators Unveil Legislation to Restrict Franchise Moves," *Los Angeles Times*, January 24, 1985.

49. Quoted in Kuhn, *Hardball*, 94.

50. "Better Red than Steinbrenner," *Washington Monthly* 18 (May 1986), 13.

51. *Hardball*, 228.

52. Quoted in Dave Disstel, "Padres for Sale but Will Stay in S.D.," *Los Angeles Times*, November 21, 1986.

53. *Hardball*, 96.

54. Paul Isaki, quoted in Joni Balter, "Mariners Pick a Bad Time to Foul off Stadium Pitch," *Seattle Times*, March 21, 1995.

55. *The Diamond Revolution: The Prospects for Baseball after the Collapse of Its Ruling Class* (New York: St. Martin's Press, 1992), 218.

56. Donnie Walsh, quoted in Mary Francis, "Pacers' Big Wins on the Court Can't Keep Them from Losing Money off It," *Indianapolis Star*, June 4, 1995.

57. Seymour Knox III, quoted in Jon R. Sorensen, "Knox Threatens to Move Three Franchises," *Buffalo News*, June 15, 1993.

58. Bob Flanagan, quoted in Richmond, *Ballpark*, 59.

Chapter Eleven
The Expanding Realm

1. These data include the two baseball expansion franchises that were granted in 1995, but would not field teams until the 1998 season: the Arizona Diamondbacks and the Tampa Bay Devil Rays.

2. Letter, *New York Times*, February 21, 1993.

3. The sixth team went to Minneapolis-St. Paul, which was the fifteenth-ranked metropolitan area in 1967.

4. James Quirk, "An Economic Analysis of Team Movements in Professional Sports," *Law and Contemporary Problems* 38 (Winter/Spring 1973), 47.

5. Jay H. Topkis, "Monopoly in Professional Sports," *Yale Law Journal* 58 (April 1949), 701.

6. Clarence Campbell, quoted in David Cruise and Alison Griffiths, *Net Worth: Exploding the Myths of Pro Hockey* (New York: Viking, 1991), 133.

7. Bill Giles of the Philadelphia Phillies, quoted in "Baseball's Future: What Can Fans Expect," *U.S. News & World Report*, April 12, 1982, 55.

8. Gordon Gund of the Cleveland Cavaliers, quoted in Roger Lowenstein, "Once-Ailing NBA Grows Selective as Expansion Plans Draw Investors," *Wall Street Journal*, January 15, 1986.

9. James D. Norris, quoted in Jack Olsen, "Private Game: No Admittance!" *Sports Illustrated*, April 12, 1965, 66.

10. Quoted in Hal Bodley, "Bonds Caught in Small-Market Vise," *USA Today*, January 31, 1991.

11. Quoted in "Monopoly Pays off in the Business of Sports," *Business Week*, October 13, 1980, 152.

12. *Hardball: The Education of a Baseball Commissioner* (New York: Times Books, 1987), 211.

13. Quoted in John Helyar, "Big League Battle: Baseball's Expansion Is a High-Stakes Game of Money and Politics," *Wall Street Journal*, December 21, 1990.

14. "Professional Basketball: Economic and Business Perspectives," in Paul D. Staudohar and James A. Mangan, eds., *The Business of Professional Sports* (Urbana and Chicago: University of Illinois Press, 1991), 35.

15. Quoted in William N. Wallace, "Tampa Gets N.F.L. Franchise; Seattle Next on Expansion List," *New York Times*, October 31, 1974.

16. President Bill White, quoted in David Whitford, *Playing Hardball: The High-Stakes Battle for Baseball's New Franchises* (New York: Doubleday, 1993), 123–24.

17. Bill Giles of the Philadelphia Phillies, quoted in Steve Berkowitz, "NL Nears Timetable for Adding Two Teams," *Washington Post*, June 14, 1990.

18. Norman Green of the Minnesota North Stars, quoted in Stephen Taub, "The Puck Stops Here," *Financial World*, July 9, 1991.

19. Rankin Smith of the Atlanta Falcons, quoted in Earl Gustkey, "Super Bowl XXI; The NFL Owners; The NFL West," *Los Angeles Times*, January 25, 1987. Smith was a member of Major Sports, Inc., the group that sought an AFL franchise.

20. The arrangement was also an alternative to relocating the North Stars to San Jose, but proved to be only a reprieve for Minneapolis-St. Paul since the team's new owner moved the franchise to Dallas after only two seasons in the Twin Cities.

21. *Pay Dirt: The Business of Professional Team Sports* (Princeton: Princeton University Press, 1992), 64–67.

22. Quoted in Attner, "The Big Bang and Its Effect," *Sporting News*, March 18, 1991.

23. Helyar, "Big League Battle."

24. Rankin Smith of the Atlanta Falcons, quoted in Chris Mortensen, "Let's Take a Swing at NFL Realignment," *Sporting News*, July 20, 1992.

25. Douglas Danforth, quoted in Murray Chass, "Owners Approve Realignment of Divisions," *New York Times*, September 10, 1993.

26. George Bush, quoted in Murray Chass, "Major Leagues Near Three-Division Format." *New York Times*, September 9, 1993.

27. The Tigers switched with the Cleveland Indians, whose management correctly figured that the team had a better chance to end its forty-year absence from postseason competition by moving to the weaker central division.

28. Commissioner David Stern, quoted in Sam Goldpaper, "Four New Franchises Awarded by NBA," *New York Times*, April 23, 1987.

Chapter Twelve
Making the Cut

1. Steve Katich of the Denver Baseball Commission, quoted in David Whitford, *Playing Hardball: The High-Stakes Battle for Baseball's New Franchises* (New York: Doubleday, 1993), 43.

2. Art Modell of the Cleveland Browns, quoted in Paul Attner, "Some NFL Owners Balk at Idea of Expanding in Current Climate," *Sporting News*, March 18, 1991.

3. Haywood Sullivan of the Boston Red Sox, quoted in Thomas Boswell, "Two Teams Could be Added by '86," *Washington Post*, December 9, 1983.

4. Quoted in Nancy Scannell, "Two-City Push for NL Seen," *Washington Post*, July 29, 1979.

5. Russell Granik, quoted in Paul Attner, "NBA's Expansion Provides Blueprint for Success," *Sporting News*, March 18, 1991.

6. Quoted in "Ueberroth Backs Expansion, Proposes Role for Colleges," *PR Newswire*, January 21, 1988.

7. Don Hinchley of the Denver Baseball Commission, quoted in Whitford, *Playing Hardball*, 32.

8. Mayor Dick Hackett, quoted in Jim Thomas, "NFL or Bust . . . No Guarantees in the Expansion Derby," *St. Louis Post-Dispatch*, September 22, 1991.

9. Quoted in Murray Chass, "Baseball Expands Roster with Miami and Denver," *New York Times*, June 11, 1991.

10. Pat Williams, quoted in *Gannett News Service*, August 13, 1990. Williams, the general manager of the Orlando Magic of the NBA led the effort to bring major league baseball to Orlando.

11. The emphasis was on the 4.2 million people in the Washington portion of the Washington-Baltimore consolidated metropolitan area, since Washington preferred to picture Washington and Baltimore as separate markets in order to deflect concerns about putting an expansion team in the same market as the Orioles.

12. Pat Williams, quoted in Whitford, *Playing Hardball*, 182.

13. Max Muhleman, quoted in Laura Zelenko, "Mid-Size Cities Blitz NFL for New Franchise," *American Demographics*, January 1992, 9.

14. William Melzer of D'Arcy Masius Benton & Bowles, quoted in John Wolfe, "Sites Air It out to Win NFL Nod," *Advertising Age*, August 5, 1991, 23, 27.

15. Greg Aiello, quoted in Jim Thomas, "Wooing the NFL: Four Cities Hope Exhibitions Made Impression," *St. Louis Post Dispatch*, August 31, 1991.

16. Robert Rich, Jr., quoted in Jeff Shain, "NL to Hear Expansion Presentations," *United Press International*, September 18, 1990. Rich owned the Buffalo Bisons of the

International League, led Buffalo's campaign for major league baseball, and was the
prospective owner if Buffalo was awarded a team.

17. Whitford, *Playing Hardball*, 128.

18. George R. Westfall, St. Louis County Executive, quoted in Jim Thomas, "The
Art of the Deal," *St. Louis Post-Dispatch*, January 22, 1995.

19. July 6, 1991.

20. Quoted in Steve Fainaru, "Pastime Far from Just a Game," *Boston Globe*, December 10, 1989.

21. Quoted in Chass, "Baseball Expands Roster with Miami and Denver."

22. Martin Stone, quoted by Greg Boeck and Mike Dodd, *Gannett News Service*,
August 13, 1990.

23. Quoted in Murray Chass, "National League Narrows Expansion Entries to 6,"
New York Times, December 19, 1990.

24. Rick Dodge of St. Petersburg, quoted in Whitford, *Playing Hardball*, 177.

25. Frank Litsky, "Hot (N.F.)L. Baltimore: N.F.L. Owners Have New Expansion
Favorite," *New York Times*, November 21, 1993; and Chris Mortensen, "The Expansion
Pick Won't End the Chaos," *Sporting News*, November 29, 1993. Despite suggestions
that Glazer and Weinglass carried the extra burden of being Jewish, Glazer later passed
muster when he bought the Tampa Bay Buccaneers.

26. Thomas Ferguson of the Beacon Council, quoted in Whitford, *Playing Hardball*,
172.

27. Quoted ibid., 60.

28. *Baseball and Billions: A Probing Look at Our National Pastime* (New York:
Basic Books, 1992), 142.

29. Quoted in Christy Wise, *States News Service*, August 2, 1989.

30. Quoted in Whitford, *Playing Hardball*, 66.

31. Quoted in Attner, "Some NFL Owners Balk at Idea of Expanding in Current
Climate."

32. Jack Adams, quoted in Jack Olsen, "Private Game: No Admittance!" *Sports
Illustrated*, April 12, 1965, 70. Adams was a former coach and general manager of the
Detroit Red Wings.

33. Jim Finks, New Orleans Saints, quoted in Paul Attner, "The Big Bang and Its
Effect," *Sporting News*, March 18, 1991.

34. Quoted ibid.

35. *Playing Hardball*, 76.

36. Quoted by *United Press International*, March 8, 1986.

37. Quoted in Michael Roberts, "The Separation of Sport and the State," *Skeptic* 21
(September/October 1977), 18. Long was chairman of the Senate Finance Committee
and Boggs was the majority leader in the House of Representatives.

38. Magnuson was chairman of the Senate Commerce Committee, which had jurisdiction over the television blackout legislation.

39. Quoted in David Harris, *The League: The Rise and Decline of the NFL* (New
York: Bantam, 1986), 516.

40. Quoted in Jeff Barker, "DeConcini: Hardball Lands Expansion Promise," *Arizona Republic*, June 29, 1994.

41. Quoted in David Dahl, "Anti-Trust Pressure Helped Secure Team," *St. Petersburg Times*, March 10, 1995.

42. The group unsuccessfully sued after the NBA rejected its bid to buy the Boston Celtics; see *Levin v. NBA*, 385 F. Supp. 149 (S.D.N.Y. 1974).

43. See *Mid-South Grizzlies v. National Football League*, 550 F. Supp. 558 (E.D. Pa. 1982); and *Mid-South Grizzlies v. National Football League*, 720 F.2d 712 (3d Cir. 1983).

44. See *Los Angeles Memorial Coliseum Commission v. National Football League*, 468 F. Supp. 154 (C.D. Cal. 1979).

45. Bowie Kuhn, *Hardball: The Education of a Baseball Commissioner* (New York: Times Books, 1987), 21. Kuhn was associated with Willkie Owen Farr Gallagher & Walton, the law firm that represented the National League in the Milwaukee litigation in 1966; he became baseball commissioner in 1969.

46. Lee McPhail, quoted in Hal Bodley, "Switching Cities: Short-Sited Solution," *USA Today*, June 20, 1991.

47. Walt MacPeek, "NHL 'Drafting' New Proposal that Would Share the Wealth," *Newark Star-Ledger*, January 3, 1993.

48. Sid Abel, quoted in David Cruise and Alison Griffiths, *Net Worth: Exploding the Myths of Pro Hockey* (New York: Viking, 1991), 140.

49. Norman Green of the Minnesota North Stars, quoted in Joe Lapointe, "Next N.H.L. Expansion Teams May Not Be So Lowly," *New York Times*, January 6, 1993.

50. Quoted in Paul Attner, "Baseball's Economic Future Hangs in the Balance as the National League Ponders Expansion Cities," *Washington Post*, March 25, 1991; see also Gerald W. Scully, *The Business of Professional Baseball* (Chicago: University of Chicago Press, 1989), 146.

51. None of the eleven expansion teams added to the major leagues between 1988 and 1993 had moved as of the end of 1995.

Chapter Thirteen
Back Door Play

1. J. David Molson of the Montreal Canadiens, quoted in Jack Olsen, "Private Game: No Admittance!" *Sports Illustrated*, April 12, 1965, 70.

2. Myles Tannenbaum of the Baltimore Stars, quoted in Sally Jenkins, "For USFL, an Uneasy Sigh of Relief," *Washington Post*, June 23, 1985.

3. Robert S. Carlson, "The Business of Professional Sports: A Reexamination in Progress," *New York Law Forum* 18 (Spring 1973), 916.

4. See *American Football League v. National Football League*, 205 F. Supp. 60, 69 (D.C. Md. 1962); and *American Football League v. National Football League*, 323 F.2d 124, 128 (4th Cir. 1963).

5. "Hawaii No Paradise for WFL Strangers," *New York Times*, August 10, 1974.

6. Quoted in Eugene Murdock, "The Tragedy of Ban Johnson," *Journal of Sport History* 1 (Spring 1974), 26.

7. Quoted in Mark Asher, "Federals Sale Clouded by Move to Fall," *Washington Post*, August 24, 1984.

8. George Preston Marshall of the Washington Redskins, quoted in Donald Chipman, Randolph Campbell, and Robert Cavert, *The Dallas Cowboys and the NFL* (Norman: University of Oklahoma Press, 1970), 29.

9. *American Football League v. National Football League*, 205 F. Supp. 60, 78 (D.C. Md. 1962).

10. See *United States Football League v. National Football League*, 842 F.2d 1335 (2d Cir. 1988).

11. See *Philadelphia World Hockey Club v. Philadelphia Hockey Club, Inc.*, 351 F. Supp. 462 (E.D. Pa. 1972).

12. Carlson, "The Business of Professional Sports," 916.

13. For a chronicle of the ABA's traveling road show, see Terry Pluto, *Loose Balls: The Short Wild Life of the American Basketball Association* (New York: Fireside, 1991).

14. Quoted in Bob Oates, "The NFL Owners: The AFC East," *Los Angeles Times*, January 25, 1987.

15. Resolution adopted at 1976 annual meeting, quoted in David Harris, *The League: The Rise and Decline of the NFL* (New York: Bantam, 1986), 229.

16. Quoted in William N. Wallace, "NFL Sings the Blues over Memphis Deal," *New York Times*, May 8, 1974.

17. North Carolina, Dallas, Louisville, Memphis, Miami, Norfolk, and Pittsburgh had teams in 1970–1971 and were either out of business or not included in the merger in 1976.

18. Birmingham, Cincinnati, Houston, and Indianapolis were included in the 1977 proposal, but left out of the merger in 1979.

19. Quoted in "Equitable Set-Up for Pros Promised," *New York Times*, December 13, 1949.

20. Quoted in David Harris, "New Troubles for the NFL," *New York Times Magazine*, September 7, 1986, 78.

21. The other relocating merger team was the Houston Oilers, whose move to Nashville was approved in 1996.

Chapter Fourteen
Ballpark Figures

1. *Sports in America* (New York: Random House, 1976), 338.

2. Bruce Kuklick, *To Every Thing a Season: Shibe Park and Urban Philadelphia 1909–1976* (Princeton: Princeton University Press, 1991), 28.

3. *Ballpark: Camden Yards and the Building of an American Dream* (New York: Simon & Schuster, 1993), 104.

4. Kuklick, *To Every Thing a Season*, 29.

5. Shibe Park was renamed Connie Mack Stadium in 1954; throughout, arenas and stadiums are referred to by their contemporary names.

6. See Benjamin Rader, *In Its Own Image: How Television Has Transformed Professional Sports* (New York: Free Press, 1984), 52.

7. Roger G. Noll, "Attendance and Price Setting," in Roger G. Noll, ed., *Government and the Sports Business* (Washington, D.C.: Brookings Institution, 1974), 128, 140.

8. Robert A. Baade and Laura J. Tiehen, "An Analysis of Major League Baseball Attendance, 1969–1987," *Journal of Sport and Social Issues* 14 (Spring 1990), 20.

9. See Robert Lipsyte, "There Goes the Street, There Goes the Team," *New York Times*, June 11, 1993.

10. *The Dodgers Move West* (New York: Oxford University Press, 1987), 40.

11. John Pastier, "Diamonds Aren't Forever," *Historic Preservation*, July/August 1993, 27.

12. William Haase, quoted in Walter Shapiro, "Remaking the Field of Dreams," *Time*, April 29, 1991, 81. The basic building dates to 1912, and was constructed on the site of Bennett Field, where the Tigers played between 1903 and 1911. Fenway Park was inaugurated at the same time as Navin Field.

13. See David Mills, "The Blue Line and the Bottom Line: Entrepreneurs and the Business of Hockey in Canada, 1927–90," in Paul D. Staudohar and James A. Mangan, eds., *The Business of Professional Sports* (Urbana and Chicago: University of Illinois Press, 1991), 181–82.

14. See Steven A. Riess, "Power Without Authority: Los Angeles' Elites and the Construction of the Coliseum," *Journal of Sport History* 8 (Spring 1981), 50–65.

15. See Benjamin A. Okner, "Subsidies of Stadiums and Arenas," in Noll, *Government and the Sports Business*, 325–47.

16. Quoted in Michael Roberts, *Fans: How We Go Crazy over Sports* (Washington, D.C.: New Republic, 1976), 137.

17. See *Meyer v. City of Cleveland*, 35 Ohio App. 20, 171 N.E. 606 (Ct. App. 1930).

18. *Bazell v. City of Cincinnati*, 13 Ohio St.2d 63, 68, 233 N.E.2d 864 (1968). For favorable rulings in other states, see *Martin v. City of Philadelphia*, 420 Pa. 14, 215 A.2d 894 (1966); *Conrad v. City of Pittsburgh*, 421 Pa. 492, 218 A.2d 906 (1966); and *New Jersey Sports & Exposition Authority v. McCrane*, 119 N.J. Super. 457, 292 A.2d 580 (App. Div. 1971).

19. See *Ginsberg v. City of Denver*, 164 Colo. 572, 436 P.2d 685 (1968).

20. The uncertainty arose from legislation introduced by Senator Daniel P. Moynihan of New York that would deny federal tax exemptions for purchasers of·state and local bonds used to finance professional sports facilities.

21. See Mark S. Rosentraub and Samuel R. Nunn, "Suburban City Investment in Professional Sports: Estimating the Fiscal Returns of the Dallas Cowboys and Texas Rangers to Investor Communities," *American Behavioral Scientist* 21 (January/February 1978), 396–97.

22. See *Pay Dirt: The Business of Professional Team Sports* (Princeton: Princeton University Press, 1992), 164–71.

23. See ibid., 145–55.

24. "Subsidies of Stadiums and Arenas," 331.

25. Ralph Wilson, quoted in Will McDonough, "Owners Seeing Red over Stadium Blues," *Boston Globe*, September 17, 1989.

26. *Hardball: The Education of a Baseball Commissioner* (New York: Times Books, 1987), 245.

27. Quoted in Dennis Hevesi, "A New Yankee Stadium Is Proposed in the Bronx," *New York Times*, January 25, 1990.

28. Rankin M. Smith, quoted in Earl Gustkey, "Super Bowl XXI; The NFL Owners; The NFL West," *Los Angeles Times*, January 25, 1987.

29. "The U.S. Team Sports Industry: An Introduction," in Noll, *Government and the Sports Business*, 13.

30. Bill Saporito, "The Owners' New Game Is Managing," *Fortune*, July 1, 1991, 86.

31. See *Pay Dirt*, 145–55.

32. Quoted in Ray Kennedy and Nancy Williamson, "Money: The Monster Threatening Sports," *Sports Illustrated*, July 17, 1978, 72.

33. Quoted in "Sonics Staying Put," *New York Times*, February 16, 1994.

Chapter Fifteen
Newer, Bigger, Better

1. Rankin M. Smith, quoted in Earl Gustkey, "Super Bowl XXI; The NFL Owners; The NFL West," *Los Angeles Times*, January 25, 1987.

2. Quoted in Jim Armstrong, "Stadium May Come via Rams," *Denver Post*, March 17, 1995.

3. See Jon E. Hilsenrath, "The Cost of Luxury Could Blow Sky High," *New York Times*, April 7, 1996.

4. Art Modell, quoted in David Harris, *The League: The Rise and Decline of the NFL* (New York: Bantam, 1986), 567.

5. Quoted in "Talking Sports," *New York Times*, October 5, 1985.

6. Paul Goldberger, "At Home in the City, Baseball's Newest Parks Succeed," *New York Times*, April 17, 1994.

7. Thomas W. Moses, quoted in Paul Attner, "For Many Cities, There's No Place Like a Dome," *Washington Post*, June 8, 1984.

8. See ibid.; and John Helyar, "More Cities Plan Domed Stadiums, but Returns May Prove Small," *Wall Street Journal*, May 17, 1984.

9. Billy Martin, quoted in Amy Klobuchar, *Uncovering the Dome* (Prospect Heights, Ill.: Waveland Press, 1986), 163.

10. See Paul Attner, "The Ringmaster," *Sporting News*, March 13, 1995.

11. Walter Shapiro, "Remaking the Field of Dreams," *Time*, April 29, 1991, 80.

12. See Hilsenrath, "The Cost of Luxury Could Blow Sky High."

13. Lou Lamoriello, quoted in Richard Sandomir, "Devils and New Jersey Call Truce," *New York Times*, July 14, 1995.

14. Warren N. Kellogg, Exeter, N.H., quoted in Ray Kennedy and Nancy Williamson, "The Fans: Are They up in Arms?" *Sports Illustrated*, July 31, 1978, 39.

15. "From Baseball and Apple Pie, to Greed and Sky Boxes," *New York Times*, October 31, 1993.

16. Quoted in Eric Bailey, "All-Star Game Sky-Boxes," *Los Angeles Times*, July 9, 1989.

17. Richard Gordon, quoted in Anthony Baldo, "Secrets of the Front Office," *Financial World*, July 9, 1991, 28.

18. Ed Snider, quoted in Joe Lapointe, "Help Us, Oh Help Us, We've Got Buildings," *New York Times*, October 5, 1994.

19. John Glennon of Lehman Brothers, quoted in Anthony Baldo, "Edifice Complex," *Financial World*, November 26, 1991, 36.

20. Quoted in Frank Litsky, "Money Is the Root of All Expansion Hopefuls," *New York Times*, September 26, 1993.

21. Tom Wilson, quoted in Baldo, "Secrets of the Front Office," 36.

22. Michael K. Ozanian, "What's Your Team Worth?" *Financial World*, July 9, 1991, 34.

23. Quoted in Neil J. Sullivan, *The Dodgers Move West* (New York: Oxford University Press, 1987), 195.

24. Dan Beyers, "Cooke Controls the Game," *Washington Post*, July 18, 1994.

25. "Wherever They Are, the Giants Don't Belong in a Dome," *New York Times*, August 16, 1992.

26. *The Diamond Revolution: The Prospects for Baseball after the Collapse of Its Ruling Class* (New York: St. Martin's Press, 1992), 78.

27. *The Dodgers Move West*, 215.

28. *The Diamond Revolution,* 80.

29. See Dean Baim, "Private Ownership Incentives in Professional Sports Facilities," in Calvin A. Kent, ed., *Entrepreneurship and the Privatizing of Government* (New York: Quorum Books, 1987), 110–17; see also Dean V. Baim, *The Sports Stadium as a Municipal Investment* (Westport, Conn.: Greenwood Press, 1994).

30. Baim, "Private Ownership Incentives in Professional Sports Facilities," 119.

31. Sullivan, *The Diamond Revolution*, 80–81.

32. Ibid., 92.

33. Pat Bowlen, quoted in Mike Monroe, "COMSAT's Arena Plans Won't Shortchange City," *Denver Post*, March 20, 1994.

34. James Busch Orthwein, quoted in Michael Madden and Ron Borges, "Orthwein Balks at Paying for Megaplex," *Boston Globe*, August 8, 1993.

35. See Thomas S. Hines, "Housing, Baseball, and Creeping Socialism: The Battle of Chavez Ravine, Los Angeles, 1949–1959," *Journal of Urban History* 8 (February 1982), 140–41; and Sullivan, *The Dodgers Move West*, 100.

36. David Q. Voigt, *American Baseball*, vol. 3: *From Postwar Expansion to the Electronic Age* (University Park: Pennsylvania State University Press, 1983), 130.

37. Quoted in Gary Mihoces, "Pulling Together Enough Money Has Become Whole New Ball Game," *USA Today*, March 31, 1987.

38. Quoted in Doug Bandow, "Sports Play in Fields of Government," *Washington Post*, December 27, 1987.

39. Tim Robbie, quoted in David Whitford, *Playing Hardball: The High-Stakes Battle for Baseball's New Franchises* (New York: Doubleday, 1993), 161.

40. "The Impact of Stadiums and Professional Sports on Metropolitan Area Development," *Growth and Change* 21 (Spring 1990), 3.

41. Sullivan, *The Diamond Revolution*, 94.

Chapter Sixteen
Political Players

1. *Uncovering the Dome* (Prospect Heights, Ill.: Waveland Press, 1986), 35.

2. *Lords of the Realm: The Real History of Baseball* (New York: Villiard, 1994), 448.

3. Neil J. Sullivan, *The Dodgers Move West* (New York: Oxford University Press, 1987), 216.

4. *The Diamond Revolution: The Prospects for Baseball after the Collapse of Its Ruling Class* (New York: St. Martin's Press, 1992), 74, 84.

5. John P. Pelissero, Beth M. Henschen, and Edward I. Sidlow, "Urban Regimes, Sports Stadiums, and the Politics of Economic Development Agendas in Chicago," *Policy Studies Review* 10 (Spring/Summer 1991), 125.

6. Sullivan, *The Dodgers Move West*, viii.

7. Peter Richmond, *Ballpark: Camden Yards and the Building of an American Dream* (New York: Simon & Schuster, 1993), 93.

8. *Playing the Field: Why Sports Teams Move and Cities Fight to Keep Them* (Baltimore: Johns Hopkins University Press, 1993), 104.

9. In addition to Philadelphia's four major league teams, the consortium included a concert tour and the concessionaires at the Spectrum and Veterans' Stadium; see Michael Dabney, "Penn Prof: Moving Teams Would Hurt Philadelphia Area," *United Press International*, March 5, 1990.

10. Euchner, *Playing the Field*, 107.

11. Quoted in Richard Sandomir, "N.F.L. Gives Modell a Ticket to Baltimore," *New York Times*, February 10, 1996.

12. Paul Attner, "Behring Straits," *Sporting News*, March 25, 1996.

13. *Hardball: The Education of a Baseball Commissioner* (New York: Times Books, 1987), 130.

14. Quoted in "Redskins Will Build Stadium Outside D.C.," *Newark Star-Ledger*, December 5, 1993.

15. Quoted ibid.

16. See Bob Andelman, *Stadium for Rent: Tampa Bay's Quest for Major League Baseball* (Jefferson, N.C.: McFarland, 1993), 47ff.

17. See David Foster, "Thomas G. Cousins: A Modern Master of the Land," *Business Atlanta* [on line], April 1987; available LEXIS Library: BUSATL file: NEWS.

18. Jeff Smulyan of the Seattle Mariners, quoted in Helyar, *Lords of the Realm*, 448.

19. Klobuchar, *Uncovering the Dome*, 80.

20. Norris Poulson, quoted in Sullivan, *The Dodgers Move West*, 96.

21. Quoted in Steven Lee Myers, "Recalling Dodgers' Flight, Mayor Makes His Pitch for New Stadium," *New York Times*, April 4, 1996.

22. *To Every Thing a Season: Shibe Park and Urban Philadelphia 1909–1976* (Princeton: Princeton University Press, 1991), 120.

23. Quoted in William Trombley, "Sacramento Told It Will Cost $172 Million to Get Raiders," *Los Angeles Times*, September 2, 1989.

24. Quoted in "N.J. Governor Says No-Go to 76ers' Arena," *Philadelphia Inquirer*, January 13, 1994.

25. Donald Poss of the Metropolitan Stadium Commission, quoted in Klobuchar, *Uncovering the Dome*, 95.

26. Bernard Landry, quoted in Herbert Bauch, "Tower Mad," *Montreal Gazette*, August 10, 1991.

27. Senator Jack Lapides, quoted in Richmond, *Ballpark*, 95.

28. William Trombley, "$50 Million for Raiders Okd by Sacramento," *Los Angeles Times*, September 14, 1989.

29. Ray Kennedy and Nancy Williamson, "The Fans: Are They up in Arms?" *Sports Illustrated*, July 31, 1978, 38; 38 percent favored use of tax dollars for sports facilities, 9 percent were unsure. The national poll, conducted for *Sports Illustrated* by Yankelovich, Skelly and White, surveyed 839 self-described sports fans.

30. See "Major League Team Sports," in Walter Adams, *The Structure of American Industry*, 5th ed. (New York: Macmillan, 1977), 375.

31. The Cincinnati survey involved 750 respondents and was conducted by Louis Harris and Associates for the *Cincinnati Enquirer*; see Richard Green, "City Poll Shows Most Opposed to New Stadium," *Cincinnati Enquirer*, April 27, 1995. For the New Jersey poll, 705 respondents in Bergen and Passaic County were surveyed by the

Record Poll; see Jeff Pillets and Stephen G. Hirsch, "Most Wouldn't Pay to Keep Devils," *Bergen Record*, July 2, 1995.

32. See Glenn Dickey, *Just Win, Baby: Al Davis & His Raiders* (New York: Harcourt Brace Jovanovich, 1991), 245.

Chapter Seventeen
Political Contests

1. Amy Klobuchar, *Uncovering the Dome* (Prospect Heights, Ill.: Waveland Press, 1986), 82.

2. See Bob Andelman, *Stadium for Rent: Tampa Bay's Quest for Major League Baseball* (Jefferson, N.C.: McFarland, 1993), 264.

3. *Playing the Field: Why Sports Teams Move and Cities Fight to Keep Them* (Baltimore: Johns Hopkins University Press, 1993), 14.

4. Steve Keefe, quoted in Klobuchar, *Uncovering the Dome*, xvii.

5. The court agreed with the state's argument that the legislation creating the sports authority was an appropriations bill that under state law could not be challenged in a referendum; see *Kelly v. Marylanders for Sports Sanity, Inc.*, 310 Md. 437, 530 A.2d 245 (1987).

6. Quoted in David Harris, *The League: The Rise and Decline of the NFL* (New York: Bantam, 1986), 609.

7. Quoted in John Helyar, *Lords of the Realm: The Real History of Baseball* (New York: Villiard, 1994), 451.

8. Knute F. Dobkins, Democratic party chair, Marion County, Indiana, quoted in James E. Ellis, "How the Boosters Plan to Rebuild Indianapolis," *Business Week* [on line], June 1, 1981. Available: LEXIS Library: BUSWK File: NEWS.

9. Rev. Rosendo Urrabazo, Communities Organized for Public Services, quoted in Lisa Belkin, "Vote Today in San Antonio Is about a Lot More than a Stadium," *New York Times*, January 21, 1987.

10. Howard Schneider, "Johnson Applauds Pollin Plan, Bows out of Arena Talks," *Washington Post*, January 5, 1995.

11. Mayor Ann Rudin, quoted in Dale Hofmann and Martin J. Greenberg, *Sport$biz: An Irreverent Look at Big Business in Pro Sports* (Champaign, Ill.: Leisure Press, 1989), 165.

12. Representative John Dunn, quoted in Isabel Wilkerson, "What Taxpayers and Their Teams Do for Each Other," *New York Times*, July 24, 1988.

13. Wendell Phillips of the Sacramento County Deputy Sheriffs Association, quoted in William Trombley, "$50 Million for Raiders Okd by Sacramento," *Los Angeles Times*, September 14, 1989.

14. Councilman John Draper on ABC News, *Nightline*, November 29, 1993 (Transcript #3266).

15. Eva Lash, quoted by William D. Murray, *United Press International*, November 10, 1990.

16. Quoted in Mark Horvit, "Anti-Trust Strategy Explored," *Houston Post*, September 12, 1994.

17. Quoted in Richard W. Larsen, "Proper Policy?—Public Money for Sports Arenas?" *Seattle Times*, April 1, 1990.

18. Gene Carey, quoted in Kim North, "Lewisville Voters Reject Sales Tax to Build Arena," *Dallas Morning News*, January 22, 1995.

19. Senator Jack Lapides, quoted in Peter Richmond, *Ballpark: Camden Yards and the Building of an American Dream* (New York: Simon & Schuster, 1993), 98–99.

20. John Antonucci, quoted in David Whitford, *Playing Hardball: The High-Stakes Battle for Baseball's New Franchises* (New York: Doubleday, 1993), 199. Antonucci was part of the original ownership group that sought an expansion franchise in Denver.

21. Andy Woods, quoted in Melvin Durslag, "Beware of Bidding for NFL Franchises," *Los Angeles Times*, March 7, 1990.

22. Bill Lyon, "Sixers Unlikely to Move the Fans," *Philadelphia Inquirer*, December 16, 1993.

23. Quoted in Charles G. Burck, "It's Promoters vs. Taxpayers in the Superstadium Game," *Fortune*, March 1973, 178.

24. See *Arata v. Louisiana Stadium and Exposition District*, 254 La. 579, 225 So.2d. 362 (1969).

25. Bill Robertson, quoted in Kenneth Reich, "Pro Teams: A Big Value for Small Cities," *Los Angeles Times*, December 3, 1989.

26. The new facilities were located next to J.F.K. Stadium, which seated over 100,000 and was used primarily for the Army-Navy football game.

27. Councilman James Kelly, quoted in Kevin Cullen, "Southie Warns It'll Have Its Say on Megaplex Plan," *Boston Globe*, June 26, 1995.

28. Brian Coyle of Minnesotans against the Downtown Dome, quoted in Lori Sturdevant, "These Folks Are Really Against the Stadium," *Minneapolis Tribune*, March 7, 1979.

29. *Playing the Field*, 120.

30. Mayor Patricia Ticer, quoted in "Va. Officials Balking at Skins Move," *Newark Star-ledger*, July 9, 1992.

31. Rick Dargis, quoted in Kim North, "Lewisville's Arena Proposal Criticized," *Dallas Morning News*, January 4, 1995.

32. "Urban Regimes, Sports Stadiums, and the Politics of Economic Development Agendas in Chicago," *Policy Studies Review* 10 (Spring/Summer 1991), 125.

33. Quoted in Rachel Alexander, "Pumping New Blood to Heart of a City," *Washington Post*, June 12, 1994.

Chapter Eighteen
Private Games and Public Stakes

1. "Stop Blaming Baseball," *New York Times Magazine*, April 4, 1993, 42.

2. "Alternatives in Sports Policy," in Roger G. Noll, ed., *Government and the Sports Business* (Washington, D.C.: Brookings Institution, 1974), 414.

3. "Municipal Administration and the Sports Franchise Relocation Issue," *Public Administration Review* 43 (November/December 1983), 524.

4. See *The Economics of Professional Team Sports* (Lexington, Mass.: Lexington Books, 1973), 91.

5. See "Alternatives in Sports Policy," 415.

6. "The Sports Franchise Relocation Issue and Public Policy Responses," in Arthur T. Johnson and James H. Frey, eds., *Government and Sport: the Public Policy Issues* (Totowa, N.J.: Rowman & Allanheid, 1985), 239.

7. See Arthur T. Johnson, "Public Sports Policy: An Introduction," *American Behavioral Scientist* 21 (January/February 1978), 338, and "Congress and Professional Sports: 1951–1978," *Annals of the American Academy of Political and Social Science*, 445 (September 1979), 111; and Phillip R. Hochberg, "Second and Goal to Go: The Legislative Attack in the 92nd Congress on Sports Broadcasting Practices," *New York Law Forum* 18 (Spring 1973), 876–79.

8. "The Separation of Sport and the State," *Skeptic* 21 (September/October 1977), 18.

9. "Secrets of the Front Office," *Financial World*, July 9, 1991, 28.

10. "The Economic Theory of a Professional Sports League," in Noll, *Government and the Sports Business*, 63.

11. "Professional Basketball: Economic and Business Perspectives," in Paul D. Staudohar and James A. Mangan, eds., *The Business of Professional Sports* (Urbana and Chicago: University of Illinois Press, 1991), 35.

12. *Class, Sports, and Social Development* (Amherst: University of Massachusetts Press, 1983), 124.

13. John Harrington of the Boston Red Sox, quoted in Claire Smith, "Padres' Small Step South Reflects Game's Growing Interest in Mexico," *New York Times*, March 29, 1996. Harrington was chair of the owners' expansion committee.

14. "Monopoly Sports Leagues," *Minnesota Law Review* 73 (February 1989), 646.

15. "Major League Team Sports," in Walter Adams, *The Structure of American Industry*, 5th ed. (New York: Macmillan, 1977), 398.

16. "Sports and the Law: An Overview," *New York Law Forum* 18 (Spring 1973), 835.

17. John Cairns, N. Jennett and Peter J. Sloane, "The Economics of Professional Team Sports: a Survey of Theory and Evidence," *Journal of Economic Studies* 13 (Spring 1986), 59.

18. "Break up the Sports League Monopolies," in Staudohar and Mangan, *The Business of Professional Sports*, 166–67.

19. Jerry Jones, quoted in Bob Glauber, "The NFL Is Going Forward, Commish? Get Outta Town," *Sporting News*, February 12, 1996.

20. "Let's Nationalize the National Pastime; Teams Should Be Owned by Hometown Fans," *Boston Globe*, March 18, 1990.

21. Henry Savelkoul of the Metropolitan Sports Facilities Commission, quoted in Jay Weiner and Dennis J. McGrath, "Officials Explore Purchase of Jets," *Minneapolis Star Tribune*, May 5, 1995.

22. "The Uneasy Partnership of Cities and Professional Sports: Public Policy Considerations," in Nancy Theberge and Peter Donnelly, eds. *Sport and the Sociological Imagination* (Fort Worth: Texas Christian University Press, 1984), 223.

23. Ibid.

24. *The Diamond Revolution: The Prospects for Baseball after the Collapse of Its Ruling Class* (New York: St. Martin's Press, 1992), 71.

25. "The Uneasy Partnership of Cities and Professional Sports," 223.

26. Allan H. Selig, acting commissioner of baseball, quoted in Robert Lipsyte, "The Urban Myth of Baseball as Savior," *New York Times*, April 28, 1996.

27. Jerry Gorman and Kirk Calhoun, *The Name of the Game: The Business of Sports* (New York: John Wiley & Sons, 1994), 251.

28. John McMullen, quoted in Bowie Kuhn, *Hardball: The Education of a Baseball Commissioner* (New York: Times Books, 1987), 235.

Note on Sources

WITHIN the vast literature on professional sports, a growing body of work deals with the nature of the sports business, its relationships with communities and government, and its place in a complex and dynamic urban society. Baseball has attracted by far the most attention from those who write about professional sports, whether journalists, academics, practitioners, or aficionados, which results in a great deal more material about the connections between places and professional baseball than the other three sports. The principal concerns of journalists and other writers understandably are games, players, teams, and leagues rather than economic, legal, historical, political, and sociological issues. Only a relatively small portion of the more serious literature of sports, however, has focused directly on the relations between places and professional teams and leagues, and even less on the interplay between urbanization and professional sports. Very little attention has been paid to the political aspects of the connections between places and professional sports, primarily in a handful of case studies that deal almost exclusively with baseball.

Among work dealing directly with cities and professional sports, Arthur T. Johnson's studies of sports politics, place issues, and public policy are indispensable to anyone interested in cities, home teams, and sports leagues. His research explores relations between cities, teams, and leagues in "The Uneasy Partnership of Cities and Professional Sports: Public Policy Considerations," in Nancy Theberge and Peter Donnelly, eds., *Sport and the Sociological Imagination* (Fort Worth: Texas Christian University Press, 1984), 210–27; city bargaining with teams in "Economic and Policy Implications of Hosting Sports Franchises: Lessons from Baltimore," *Urban Affairs Quarterly* 21 (March 1986), 411–33; franchise shifts in "Municipal Administration and the Sports Franchise Relocation Issue," *Public Administration Review* 43 (November/December 1983), 519–28 and "The Sports Franchise Relocation Issue and Public Policy Responses," in Arthur T. Johnson and James H. Frey, eds.,

Government and Sport: the Public Policy Issues (Totowa, N.J.: Rowman & Allanheid, 1985), 219–47; and congressional involvement in sports conflicts in "Congress and Professional Sports: 1951–1978," *Annals of the American Academy of Political and Social Science*, 445 (September 1979), 102–15. In *Government and Sport: the Public Policy Issues* (Totowa, N.J.: Rowman & Allanheid, 1985), Johnson and James H. Frey provide an excellent overview of the policy dilemmas raised by big league sports in framing a collection of first-rate essays that deal extensively with the relations between places and professional sports; also see Johnson's "Public Sports Policy: An Introduction," *American Behavioral Scientist* 21 (January/February 1978), 319–44.

Steven A. Riess provides the most detailed and informative historical treatment of the interplay of urban development, city politics, and professional sport, especially in the half century following the organization of the first baseball leagues, in *Touching Base: Professional Baseball and American Culture in the Progressive Era* (Westport, Conn.: Greenwood Press, 1979) and *City Games: The Evolution of American Urban Society and the Rise of Sports Century* (New York: Oxford University Press, 1980); see also his "The Baseball Magnate and Urban Politics in the Progressive Era," *Journal of Sport History* 1 (Spring 1974), 41–62 and "Baseball Myths, Baseball Realities, and the Social Functions of Baseball in the Progressive Era," *Stadion* 3 (1980), 273–311. Also of interest for the connections between urbanization and the development of sports are Melvin A. Adelman, *A Sporting Time: New York City and the Rise of Modern Athletics* (Urbana and Chicago: University of Illinois Press, 1986); and Stephen Hardy, *How Boston Played: Sport, Recreation, and Community, 1865–1915* (Boston: Northeastern University Press, 1982) and "The City and the Rise of American Sport: 1820–1920," *Exercise and Sports Sciences* 9 (1981), 183–219. Gunther Barth relates sports to other elements of development in the industrial city in *City People: The Rise of Modern City Culture in Nineteenth-Century America* (New York: Oxford University Press, 1980). Other useful works include Peter Levine's *A. G. Spalding and the Rise of Baseball* (New York: Oxford University Press, 1985) and Stephen Freedman, "The Baseball Fad in Chicago (1865–1870): An Exploration of the Role of Sport in the Nineteenth-Century City," *Journal of Sport History* 5 (Summer 1978), 42–64. The interplay of urbanization, technology, and sports is examined in John Rickards Betts, "The Technological Revolution and the Rise of Sport, 1850–1900," *Mississippi Valley Historical Review* 40 (September 1953), 231–56 and Peter R. Shergold, "The Growth of American Spectator Sport: A Technological Perspective," in Richard Cashman and Michael McKernan, *Sport in History: The Making of Modern Sporting History* (St. Lucia, Australia: University of Queensland Press, 1979), 21–42.

Of the more general historical treatments of professional sports, Benjamin Rader's *American Sports: From the Age of Folk Games to the Age of Spectators* (Englewood, N.J.: Prentice-Hall, 1983) is especially valuable because

Rader treats all four sports and gives considerable attention to place issues; see also Rader's *Baseball: A History of America's Game* (Urbana and Chicago: University of Illinois Press, 1992). Historians Randy Roberts and James Olson offer a biting critique of sports in *Winning Is the Only Thing: Sports in America Since 1945* (Baltimore: Johns Hopkins University Press, 1989) which touches on many important aspects of the relations between places and professional teams and leagues.

Cities are an important part of the story in David Q. Voigt's detailed history of *American Baseball*, vol. 2: *From the Commissioners to Continental Expansion* (University Park: Pennsylvania State University Press, 1983) and *American Baseball*, vol. 3: *From Postwar Expansion to the Electronic Age* (University Park: Pennsylvania State University Press, 1983). A good sense of the chaotic coming and going of cities in the first three decades of professional baseball is provided by Harold Seymour in *Baseball: The Early Years* (New York: Oxford University Press, 1960). Urban factors are a central element of the sweeping landscape of *Baseball: An Illustrated History* (New York: Alfred A. Knopf, 1994) by Geoffrey C. Ward and Ken Burns. And the interplay of a changing urban society with the national pastime is the subject of G. Edward White's excellent *Creating the National Pastime: Baseball Transforms Itself 1903–1953* (Princeton: Princeton University Press, 1996).

The urban aspects of the development of professional sports get less attention in histories of basketball, football, and hockey. The origins and the migration of pro football to the right places are examined in J. Thomas Jable, "The Birth of Professional Football: Pittsburgh Athletic Clubs Ring in Professionals in 1892," *Western Pennsylvania Historical Magazine* 62 (April 1979), 136–47; William Gudelunas and Stephen R. Couch, "The Stolen Championship of the Pottsville Maroons: A Case Study in the Emergence of Modern Professional Football," *Journal of Sport History* 9 (Spring 1982), 53–64; and Ernest L. Cuneo, "Present at the Creation: Professional Football in the Twenties," *American Scholar* 56 (Autumn 1987), 487–501. A sense of the early efforts by professional basketball to find suitable places to play is one of the concerns of Robert W. Peterson in *Cages to Jump Shots: Pro Basketball's Early Years* (New York: Oxford University Press, 1990).

Spatial and urban factors are in the forefront of treatments of sports by geographers. An excellent introduction to the geography of modern sports can be found in John Bale's *Sports Geography* (London: E. & F. N. Spon, 1989); Bale covers a wide range of sports from a comparative perspective, and has expanded his spatial analysis of sport in *Sport and Place* (London: Hurst, 1982) and *Landscapes of Modern Sport* (Leicester: Leicester University Press, 1994). John F. Rooney Jr. focuses on the United States in *A Geography of American Sport: From Cabin Creek to Anaheim* (Reading, Mass.: Addison-Wesley, 1974), but pays less attention to professional than college sports; more useful for the issues treated in this study is Rooney's "Sports from a

Geographic Perspective," in Donald W. Ball and John W. Loy, eds., *Sport and Social Order: Contributions to the Sociology of Sport* (Reading, Mass.: Addison-Wesley, 1975), 55–115. Geographic influences on the baseball business are discussed in Earl B. Shaw, "Geography and Baseball," *Journal of Geography* 62 (February 1963), 74–76; and Fred M. Shelley and Kevin F. Cartin, "The Geography of Baseball Fan Support in the United States," *North American Culture* 1 (1984), 77–95.

The distinctive place of professional sports in urban society has been illuminated by a number of writers. Allen Guttmann provides an excellent frame of reference for understanding the role of sports in *A Whole New Ball Game: An Interpretation of American Sports* (Chapel Hill: University of North Carolina Press, 1988); see also his *From Ritual to Record: The Nature of Modern Sport* (New York: Columbia University Press, 1978). Stephen Fox focuses specifically on the societal influence of professional sports in *Big Leagues: Professional Baseball, Football, and Basketball in National Memory* (New York: William Morrow and Company, 1994). Robert Lipsyte explores the special sphere of sports in *Sports World: An American Dreamland* (New York: Quadrangle, 1975) and "Sportsworld Revisited," *Journal of Sport and Social Issues* 1 (1976), 5–15. The pervasive role of sports in the United States is the subject of Richard Lipsky's *How We Play the Game: Why Sports Dominate American Life* (Boston: Beacon Press, 1981); Lipsky also seeks to unravel the mysteries of sports symbolism in "Toward a Theory of Sports Symbolism," *American Behavioral Scientist* 21 (January/February 1978), 345–60 and "Political Implications of Sports Team Symbolism," *Politics & Society* 9 (1979), 61–88.

The importance of professional sports in communal identification and cohesion is carefully examined by Gregory P. Stone in "Sport as a Community Representation" in Gunther R. F. Luschen and George H. Sage, eds., *Handbook of Social Science of Sport* (Champaign, Ill.: Stipes Publishing, 1981), 214–45; see also the detailed discussion of "Sport and Urban Life," *Journal of Sport and Social Issues* 14 (Fall 1990), 77–102, by David A. Karp and William C. Yoels. Peter Levine assesses the role of sports in the assimilation of immigrants in *Ellis Island to Ebbets Field: Sport and the American Jewish Experience* (New York: Oxford University Press, 1992). The complex bonds between fans and teams and cities are looked at systematically by Allan Guttmann in *Sports Spectators* (New York: Columbia University Press, 1986); and examined in a more popular vein in *Fans: How We Go Crazy over Sports* (Washington, D.C.: New Republic, 1976) by Michael Roberts. See also Gary J. Smith, B. Patterson, and J. Hogg, "A Profile of the Deeply Committed Sports Fan," *Arena Review* 5 (1981), 26–44; and Garry J. Smith, "The Noble Sports Fan," *Journal of Sport and Social Issues* 12 (Spring 1988), 54–65.

The impact of fans, familiar surroundings, and the other factors that lead most professional teams to play better at home than on the road have attracted a good deal of attention by social scientists. The most useful studies are by Barry Schwartz and Stephen F. Barsky, "The Home Advantage," *Social Forces* 55 (March 1977), 641–61 and Mark S. Mizruchi, "Local Sports Teams and Celebration of Community: A Comparative Analysis of the Home Advantage," *Sociological Quarterly* 26 (Winter 1985), 507–18. Other efforts to unravel the puzzle include John Edwards, "The Home Field Advantage," in Jeffrey H. Goldstein, ed., *Sports, Games, and Play: Social and Psychological Viewpoints* (Hillsdale, N.J.: Wiley, 1979); John E. Hocking, "Sports and Spectators: Intra-Audience Effects," *Journal of Communication* 32 (Winter 1982), 110–19; Roy F. Baumeister and Andrew Steinhilber, "Paradoxical Effects of Supportive Audiences on Performance under Pressure: The Home Field Disadvantage in Sports Championships," *Journal of Personality and Social Psychology* 47 (1984), 85–93; and William F. Gayton, Griffith R. Matthews, and C. Nickless, "The Home Field Disadvantage in Sports Championships: Does It Exist in Hockey?" *Journal of Sports Psychology* 9 (1987), 183–85.

The attachments of particular places to home teams are the subjects of countless books and articles, usually in the context of more general histories of a team. Within this literature, the Brooklyn Dodgers and their fans have attracted more attention than most. A real feel for the beloved Bums, their fans, and their intimate ballpark comes from Peter Golenbock's *Bums: An Oral History of the Brooklyn Dodgers* (New York: G.P. Putnam's Sons, 1984); a more scholarly and wide-ranging exploration is provided by Carl E. Prince in *Brooklyn's Dodgers: The Bums, the Borough, and the Best of Baseball* (New York: Oxford University Press, 1996). Terry Pluto's *The Curse of Rocky Colavito: A Loving Look at a Thirty-Year Slump* (New York: Simon & Schuster, 1994) captures the bittersweet love affair between the Cleveland Indians and their long-suffering fans. And for an intensely personal view of attachments to the home team, see *When the Colts Belonged to Baltimore* (New York: Ticknor & Fields, 1994), William Gildea's touching memoir of life with the Baltimore Colts.

The violent side of rooting for the home team is the subject of Janet Lever's fine study of *Soccer Madness* (Chicago: University of Chicago Press, 1983). An excellent look at the growing violence that has accompanied professional championships in the United States and Canada is provided by William O. Johnson in "The Agony of Victory," *Sports Illustrated*, July 5, 1993, 31–37. For an interesting examination of one of hockey's most notorious riots off the ice, see Jean R. Duperreault, "L'Affaire Richard: A Situational Analysis of the Montreal Hockey Riot of 1955," *Canadian Journal of History of Sport* 12 (May 1981), 66–83.

What Walter C. Neale terms "The Peculiar Economics of Professional Sports," *Quarterly Journal of Economics* 78 (February 1964), 1–14, has attracted the attention of economists interested in monopoly, labor markets, pricing practices, and other aspects of the big league business. Within this literature, relationships among sports, places, and government are a primary concern of Roger G. Noll, whose work commands the attention of any serious student of the economic and political world of professional sports. Noll's *Government and the Sports Business* (Washington, D.C.: Brookings Institution, 1974), a volume that he organized and edited for The Brookings Institution, remains indispensable for any serious student of the sports business, as do Noll's contributions to the volume on "The U.S. Team Sports Industry" (1–32), "Attendance and Price Setting," (115–57), and "Alternatives in Sports Policy" (412–28). Noll devotes considerable attention to place issues in "Professional Basketball: Economic and Business Perspectives," in Paul D. Staudohar and James A. Mangan, *The Business of Professional Sports* (Urbana and Chicago: University of Illinois Press, 1991), 18–47, which is particularly valuable because of the paucity of analytical work on basketball. For a useful overview of Noll's perspective on the economics of professional sports, see his "Major League Team Sports," in Walter Adams, ed., *The Structure of American Industry*, 5th ed. (New York: Macmillan, 1977), 365–400.

Considerable attention to place issues also is featured in the work of James Quirk. Of particular interest is "An Economic Analysis of Team Movements in Professional Sports," *Law and Contemporary Problems* 38 (Winter/Spring 1973), 42–66. A wealth of material on teams, leagues, relocation, expansion, and rival leagues has been examined clearly and thoughtfully by Quirk and Rodney D. Fort in *Pay Dirt: The Business of Professional Team Sports* (Princeton: Princeton University Press, 1992). A more technical analysis of the economics of sports leagues is presented by Quirk and Mohamed El Hodiri in "The Economic Theory of a Professional Sports League," in Noll, *Government and the Sports Business* (33–80); El Hodiri and Quirk also have examined "Stadium Capacities and Attendance in Professional Sports," in Shaul P. Ladany, ed., *Management Science Applications to Leisure-Time Operations* (Amsterdam: North Holland, 1975), 246–62.

Gerald W. Scully covers similar ground in *The Business of Professional Baseball* (Chicago: University of Chicago Press, 1989) and *The Market Structure of Sports* (Chicago: University of Chicago Press, 1995). A useful review of the sports economics literature and its findings is provided by John Cairns, N. Jennett, and Peter J. Sloane, "The Economics of Professional Team Sports: A Survey of Theory and Evidence," *Journal of Economic Studies* 13 (Spring 1986), 3–80. Of particular value to general readers is the treatment of sport economics by Henry G. Demmert in *The Economics of Professional Team Sports* (Lexington, Mass.: Lexington Books, 1973), which is accessible and clear headed. J. C. H. Jones provides a welcome focus on hockey in "The Economics of the National Hockey League," *Canadian Journal of Economics* 2 (February 1969), 1–20; and "Winners, Losers and Hosers: Demand and Survival in the National Hockey League," *Atlantic Economic Journal* 12 (September 1984), 54–63.

Andrew W. Zimbalist, an economist at Williams College who was involved with an aborted effort to launch a third baseball league in the mid-1990s, provides a critical look at baseball and its relations with places and the public in *Baseball and Billions: A Probing Look at Our National Pastime* (New York: Basic Books, 1992). Two other economists, Jesse Markham and Paul V. Teplitz, strongly defend the existing system of private government of professional sports in *Baseball Economics and Public Policy* (Lexington, Mass.: Lexington Books, 1981), a study that incorporates materials from interviews with a number of baseball officials. See also Kenneth M. Jennings, *Balls and Strike: The Money Game in Professional Baseball* (New York: Praeger, 1990).

Some economists have sought to untangle the complex issues of the economic benefits of professional sports to communities and the relative merits of private and public development of arenas and stadiums. Mark S. Rosentraub and various colleagues question the returns on investments in sports facilities and teams in the Dallas area in "Suburban City Investment in Professional Sports: Estimating the Fiscal Returns of the Dallas Cowboys and Texas Rangers to Investor Communities," *American Behavioral Scientist* 21 (January/February 1978), 393–414, and in Indianapolis in "Sport and Downtown Development Strategy: If You Build It, Will Jobs Come?" *Journal of Urban Affairs* 16 (1994), 221–39. Robert A. Baade, a persistent critic of the benefits of public expenditures on sports, presents his findings with Richard F. Dye in "The Impact of Stadiums and Professional Sports on Metropolitan Area Development," *Growth and Change* 21 (Spring 1990), 1–14. Benefits to Atlanta from the Falcons are calculated in William A. Schaffer and Lawrence S. Davidson, "The Economic Impact of Professional Football on Atlanta," in Shaul P. Ladany, *Management Science Applications to Leisure-Time Operations* (Amsterdam: North Holland, 1975), 276–96. Analytical techniques for the assessment of the costs and benefits of sports development are discussed in Frank L. Hefner, "Using Economic Models to Measure the Impact of Sports on Local Economies," *Journal of Sport and Social Issues* 14 (Spring 1990), 1–13.

Dean Baim presents the evidence for private development of stadiums and areas in "Private Ownership Incentives in Professional Sports Facilities," in Calvin A. Kent, ed., *Entrepreneurship and the Privatizing of Government* (New York: Quorum Books, 1987), 109–21, which summarizes the data and analysis later published in his *The Sports Stadium as a Municipal Investment* (Westport, Conn.: Greenwood Press, 1994). For an economic appraisal of the costs of public sports facilities, see Benjamin A. Okner, "Subsidies of Stadiums and Arenas" in Roger G. Noll, *Government and the Sports Business* (Washington, D.C.: Brookings Institution, 1974), 325–47. See also Stefan Kesenne and Paul Butzen. "Subsidizing Sports Facilities—the Shadow Price-Elasticities of Sports," *Applied Economics* (January 1987), 101–10.

Economists hardly have a monopoly on studies of the burgeoning professional sports industry. Work on the sports business from a variety of perspectives is brought together in a volume edited by Paul D. Staudohar and James A. Mangan, *The Business of Professional Sports* (Urbana and Chicago: University of Illinois Press, 1991). One of the most readable and entertaining treatments is *Sport$biz: An Irreverent Look at Big Business in Pro Sports* (Champaign, Ill.: Leisure Press, 1989) by Dale Hoffmann and Martin J. Greenberg; as promised, the book is irreverent, as well as full of informative tidbits about teams, leagues, and the connections between places and big league sports. One of the first and still an excellent general survey of the sports business is Joseph Durso's *The All-American Dollar: The Big Business of Sports* (Boston: Houghton Mifflin, 1971). Jerry Gorman and Kirk Calhoun, executives specializing in professional sports at Ernst & Young, provide an excellent overview in *The Name of the Game: The Business of Sports* (New York: John Wiley & Sons, 1994). Phil Schaaf, director of Pacific Sports Marketing, writes knowingly about a part of the business that increasingly shapes relations between professional sports and cities in *Sports Marketing: It's Not Just a Game Anymore* (Amherst, N.Y.: Prometheus Books, 1995). And Stephen Aris casts his net beyond the United States and Canada in *Sportsbiz: Inside the Sports Business* (London: Hutchinson, 1990).

Professional sports and related place issues are covered in increasing frequency and detail by a number of business publications, including *Bond Buyer, Business Week, Economist, Forbes, Fortune*, and the *Wall Street Journal*. See, for example, Charles G. Burck, "It's Promoters vs. Taxpayers in the Superstadium Game," *Fortune*, March 1973, 104–7, 178–82; and the work of John Merwin in *Forbes* and Hal Lancaster in the *Wall Street Journal*. Most valuable in recent years, however, has been the annual reports in *Financial World* on the revenues and values of major league franchises, which include detailed estimates of income, expenditures, and market values of every team annually, beginning in 1991. Along with the data, *Financial World* has devoted considerable attention to arenas and stadiums, public investments in facilities, and market size differences in articles like "Edifice Complex" by Anthony Baldo (November 26, 1991) and "Suite Deals" by Michael K. Ozanian (May 9, 1995).

League officials, owners, and other sports executives have left a meager paper trail, particularly in writing that deals with relations with host cities, relocation of teams, expansion of leagues, development of arenas and stadiums, and relations with governments. One that does is *Hardball: The Education of a Baseball Commissioner* (New York: Times Books, 1987), Bowie Kuhn's detailed history of his tenure as commissioner of baseball during a period of rapid change in the connections between places and big league sports, which is invaluable to anyone interested in relocation, expansion, and the interplay between owners, places, and leagues. Ford Frick, on the other hand, has remarkably little to say about any of these issues in *Games, Asterisks, People: Memoirs of a Lucky Fan* (New York: Crown, 1973), reflecting his passive approach to baseball's top job. Frick's successor, Happy Chandler, writes about baseball's first take on expansion and relocation in "How I Jumped from Clean Politics into Dirty Baseball" with John Underwood, *Sports Illustrated*, April 26, 1971, 72–86. One of the presidents of the ABA, Robert S. Carlson, provides some insights into the place-based strategies of a rival league in "The Business of Professional Sports: A Reexamination in Progress," *New York Law Forum* 18 (Spring 1973), 915–33.

Among owners who have told their tales, the most fascinating is Bill Veeck, the maverick owner of the Cleveland Indians, St. Louis Browns, and Chicago White Sox, who was in the middle of baseball's initial tussles over relocation and expansion, and provides his version in *Veeck—as in Wreck* (New York: G.P. Putnam's Sons, 1962) and *The Hustler's Handbook* (New York: G.P. Putnam's Sons, 1965), both with Ed Lynn. The early struggles of the NFL and professional football in the nation's second city are described by George Halas in *Halas by Halas: The Autobiography of George Halas*, with Gwen Morgan and Arthur Vesey (New York: McGraw-Hill, 1979). Paul Brown, who coached the Cleveland Browns in the AAFC and was an AFL owner at the time of the merger with the NFL, offers his version of the hardball negotiations over the AFL-NFL amalgamation in *PB: The Paul Brown Story*, with Jack Clary (New York: New American Library, 1981). Harold Parrott, a Dodgers executive during a tumultuous era, offers interesting insights in *The Lords of Baseball* (New York: Praeger, 1976). Another former Dodger executive who was deeply involved in expansion has his say in Buzzy Buvasi, *Off the Record* (Chicago: Contemporary Books, 1987) with John Strege.

Leagues and teams have come under detailed scrutiny in a handful of studies that proved valuable in this research. The best is David Harris' *The League: The Rise and Decline of the NFL* (New York: Bantam, 1986), an exhaustive critical history that illuminates relocation, expansion, stadium building, and other place issues, as well as the internal conflicts among owners and league officials. See also David Harris, "New Troubles for the NFL," *New York Times Magazine*, September 7, 1986, 30–38, 66–74. Although uneven, *Net Worth: Exploding the Myths of Pro Hockey* (New York: Viking, 1991) by David Cruise and Alison Griffiths is full of details and inside information, and is particularly useful given the terra incognita of hockey. The fate of Canada's game under the relentless assault of the bigger metropolitan markets and television dollars of the United States is a principal concern of Bruce Kidd and John McFarlane in *The Death of Hockey* (Toronto: New Press, 1972); see also Kidd's "Canada's National Sport," in Ian Lumsden, ed., *The Americanization of Canada* (Toronto: University of Toronto Press, 1970), 257–74.

The successful search of the NBA for the right places to play is part of the story in Leonard Koppett's informative *24 Seconds to Shoot; An Informal History of the National Basketball Association* (New York: Macmillan, 1968). Terry Pluto wonders whether the NBA can survive explosive growth in teams, markets, and revenue in *Falling from Grace: Can Pro Basketball Be Saved?* (New York: Simon and Schuster, 1995). Pluto also provides a window into the chaotic world of a new league and its ever-changing lineup of places to play in *Loose Balls: The Short Wild Life of the American Basketball Association* (New York: Fireside, 1991). Bob Curran discusses the shaky early years of the American Football League in *The $500,000 Quarterback; or The League That Came in from the Cold* (New York: Macmillan, 1965). David Pietrusza outlines the fate of the many leagues that have challenged the baseball establishment in *Major Leagues: The Formation, Sometimes Absorption and Mostly Inevitable Demise of 18 Professional Baseball Organizations, 1871 to Present* (Jefferson, N.C.: McFarland, 1991).

Change is the subject of a good deal of the popular literature on professional sports. Peter King examines the reasons why particular teams no longer seem to dominate their leagues despite growing market differences and the easing of restrictions on player movement in *The Season After: Are Sports Dynasties Dead?* (New York: Warner Books, 1989). John Helyar, who has written thoughtful pieces on expansion, stadium development, and other place issues in the *Wall Street Journal* promises more than he delivers in *Lords of the Realm: The Real History of Baseball* (New York: Villiard, 1994). A similar book by Jack Sands and Peter Gammons, *Coming apart at the Seams: How Baseball Owners, Players and Television Executives Have Led Our National Pastime to the Brink of Disaster* (New York: Macmillan, 1993), also does not shed much light on the connections between baseball and places, or clarify the nature of the disaster that is about to befall the national pastime.

Biographical studies are useful for understanding particular connections between professional sports and places. Few sports leaders better grasped the importance of market size and the forging of a network of cities than Ban Johnson, who successfully challenged the established major league with the creation of the American League, whose achievements are detailed in Eugene Murdock's *Ban Johnson: Czar of Baseball* (Westport, Conn.: Greenwood Press, 1982). Branch Rickey triumphed over market limitations as chief executive of the St. Louis Cardinals, then changed the face of professional sports by putting Jackie Robinson into the uniform of the Brooklyn Dodgers, and ended his remarkable career by organizing the Continental League, which forced baseball to expand in 1961–1962, all of which is captured by Murray Polner in *Branch Rickey: A Biography* (New York: Atheneum, 1982). One of the more creative baseball executives is the subject for Don Warfield in *The Roaring Redhead: Larry McPhail—Baseball's Great Innovator* (South Bend, Ind.: Diamond Communications, 1987). And Herbert Michelson chronicles *Charlie O: Charles Oscar Finley vs. the Baseball Establishment* (Indianapolis: Bobbs-Merrill, 1975); Finley's antics helped reshape baseball's map and redefine bad team-community relations.

Books and articles about teams usually pay scant attention to most of the concerns of this study. An interesting exception is *The Dallas Cowboys and the NFL* (Norman, Okla.: University of Oklahoma Press, 1970) by a trio of social scientists, Donald Chipman, Randolph Campbell, and Robert Cavert, who take a detailed look at the Cowboys from their beginnings, with insights into the connections between America's team and its hometown. Entrepreneurial histories of professional sports enterprises are few and far between, as Stephen Hardy emphasizes in "Entrepreneurs, Organizations, and the Sport Marketplace: Subjects in Search of Historians," *Journal of Sport History* 13 (Spring 1986), 14–33. The lack of such studies makes "The Blue Line and the Bottom Line: Entrepreneurs and the Business of Hockey in Canada, 1927–90" by David Mills in Paul D. Staudohar and James A. Mangan, *The Business of Professional Sports* (Urbana and Chicago: University of Illinois Press, 1991), 175–201, particularly valuable, and its concern with hockey in a Canadian city is an added bonus.

   The Baseball Business: Pursuing Pennants and Profits in Baltimore (Chapel Hill: University of North Carolina Press, 1990) by James Edward Miller details the business operations of the Baltimore Orioles, in the process underscoring the importance of place connections. Tensions in the relationship between a team and its community are explored by Harvey Araton and Filip Bondy in *The Selling of the Green: The Financial Rise and Moral Decline of the Boston Celtics* (New York: HarperCollins, 1992), which examines critically the Celtics' connections with fans, government, and blacks. Glenn Dickey's *Just Win, Baby: Al Davis & His Raiders* (New York: Harcourt Brace Jovanovich, 1991) is useful because Dickey covers the Raiders' odyssey from Oakland to Los Angeles and through the courts from the singular perspective of Al Davis. And Carson Van Lindt tells *The Seattle Pilots Story* (New York: Marabou Publishing, 1993), a sad story indeed of expansion gone awry, with a bad team playing in a pathetic excuse for a major league stadium, plagued by underfinanced owners and difficult relations with local officials, and lasting only one season in an undersized metropolitan market.

   Studies of communications, particularly of television, have become an increasingly important part of the literature of professional sports. For this research, Benjamin Rader's *In Its Own Image: How Television Has Transformed Professional Sports* (New York: Free Press, 1984) was most valuable because of Rader's concern with markets, relocation, expansion, and other place issues that have been significantly influenced by television. Other studies that deal with many of the implications of television for connections between places and professional sports are David A. Klatell and Norman Marcus, *Sports for Sale: Television, Money, and the Fans* (New York: Oxford University Press, 1988) and Joan M. Chandler, *Television and National Sport: The United States and Britain* (Urbana: University of Illinois Press, 1988). William O. Johnson's *Super Spectator and the Electric Lilliputians* (Boston: Little, Brown, 1971) provides a useful perspective on the impact of television on sports before 1970; see also his "Television Made It All a New Game," *Sports Illustrated*, December 22, 1969, 88. One of the architects of modern television sports,

Roone Arledge, explains why "It's Sports, It's Money ... It's TV," with Gilbert Rogan in *Sports Illustrated*, April 25, 1966, 92–106. Ron Powers covers similar ground in *Supertube: The Rise of Television Sports* (New York: Coward-McCann, 1984); see also Donald E. Parente, "The Interdependence of Sports and Television," *Journal of Communication* 27 (Summer 1977), 128–32. Much less has been written about the impact of newspapers and radio on the links between cities and big league sports; a useful study is John Rickards Betts' examination of the interplay of the development of cities, sports, and newspapers in "Sporting Journalism in Nineteenth-Century America," *American Quarterly* 5 (Spring 1953), 39–56.

One of television's most distinctive gifts to sports was Howard Cosell, a man of strong views pungently expressed. Cosell was disturbed by many of the changes in the relationships among teams, places, and fans, changes that were in part a product of the medium he rode to fame and fortune. His views on expansion, relocation, and public involvement in sports are scattered through *Cosell* (Chicago: Playboy Press, 1973), *I Never Played the Game* (New York: Morrow, 1985) with Peter Bonventre, and especially *What's Wrong with Sports* (New York: Simon & Schuster, 1991) with Shelby Whitfield.

Although somewhat dated, Ira Horowitz's work on various aspects of sports broadcasting and government regulation remains valuable in understanding the electronic links between professional sports and places; see "Sports Broadcasting" in Roger G. Noll, *Government and the Sports Business* (Washington, D.C.: Brookings Insitution, 1974), 275–323; "Sports Telecasts—Rights and Regulations," *Journal of Communication* 27 (Summer 1977), 160–68; and "Market Entrenchment and the Sports Broadcasting Act," *American Behavioral Scientist* 21 (January/February 1978), 415–30. For a critical perspective on regulation of blackouts and related issues concerning sports television, see Phillip R. Hochberg, "Second and Goal to Go: The Legislative Attack in the 92nd Congress on Sports Broadcasting Practices," *New York Law Forum* 18 (Spring 1973), 841–96 and "Congress Kicks a Field Goal: The Legislative Attack in the 93rd Congress on Sports Broadcasting Practices," *Federal Communications Bar Journal* 27 (1974), 27–79; see also Robert Alan Garrett and Philip R. Hochberg, "Sports Broadcasting and the Law," *Indiana Law Journal* 59 (Spring 1984), 155–93. On blackouts, Congress, and constituencies, see Harry M. Shooshan III, "Confrontation with Congress: Professional Sports and the Television Antiblackout Law," *Syracuse Law Review* 25 (Summer 1974), 713–45.

Professional team sports have attracted a great deal of attention among legal scholars, who have explored in detail many of the concerns of this study, including antitrust, league controls over owners and relocation, expansion procedures, rival leagues, public development of sports facilities, condemnation of sports teams, and the special treatment of professional sports under the U.S. tax code. The best general treatment of these and related legal matters is Robert

C. Berry and Glenn M. Wong, *Law and Business of the Sports Industries* (Dover, Mass.: Auburn House, 1986). See also John C. Weistart and Cym H. Lowell, *The Law of Sports* (Indianapolis: Bobbs-Merrill, 1979) and Raymond L. Yasser, *Sports Law: Cases and Materials* (Lanham, Md.: University Press of America, 1985). Lance Davis explains the legal underpinning of the private government of professional sports in "Self-Regulation in Baseball, 1909–71," in Roger G. Noll, *Government and the Sports Business* (Washington, D.C.: Brookings Institution, 1974), 349–86. For an early legal appraisal of the private government of sports, see John W. Stayton, "Baseball Jurisprudence," *American Law Review* 44 (May-June 1910), 374–93.

James A. Thorpe explains the legal catch-22 that apparently exempts baseball from both federal and state antitrust law in "Constitutional Law—Preemption—Baseball's Immunity from State Antitrust Law, *State v. Milwaukee Braves, Inc.*, 144 N.W.2d 1 (1966)," *Wayne Law Review* 13 (1967), 417–25. For a more general discussion, see Warren Freedman, *Professional Sports and Antitrust* (New York: Quorum Books, 1987); and Steven R. Rivkin, "Sports Leagues and the Federal Antitrust Laws," in Roger G. Noll, *Government and the Sports Business* (Washington, D.C.: Brookings Institution, 1974), 387–410; and Phillip J. Closius, "Professional Sports and Antitrust Law: The Ground Rules of Immunity, Exemption, and Liability," in Johnson and Frey, *Government and Sport: the Public Policy Issues* (Totowa, N.J: Rowman and Allanheid, 1985), 140–61. John Barnes' examination of *Sports and the Law in Canada* (Toronto: Butterworth's, 1983) is useful for understanding the differences in Canada's treatment of the legal status of professional sports. See also J. C. H. Jones and D. K. Davies, "Not Even Semi-Tough: Professional Sports and Canadian Antitrust," *Antitrust Bulletin* 23 (Winter 1978), 713–42.

The legal issues raised by franchise shifts have been addressed in a number of informative articles that both provide substantive details and examine public policy issues. See Jeffrey Glick, "Professional Sports Franchise Movements and the Sherman Act: When and Where Teams Should Be Able to Move," *Santa Clara Law Review* 23 (Winter 1983), 53–94; Lewis S. Kurlantzick, "Thoughts on Professional Sports and the Antitrust Laws: *Los Angeles Memorial Coliseum Commission v. National Football League*," *Connecticut Law Review* 15 (Winter 1983), 183–208; D. E. Lazaroff, "The Antitrust Implications of Franchise Relocation Restrictions in Professional Sports," *Fordham Law Review* 53 (November 1984), 157–220; and Glenn M. Wong, "Of Franchise Relocation, Expansion and Competition in Professional Team Sports: The Ultimate Political Football," *Seton Hall Legislative Journal* 9 (1985), 7–79.

Stephen F. Ross makes a spirited case for the benefits to places, fans, and the public that would result from breaking up monopoly sports leagues in "Monopoly Sports Leagues," *Minnesota Law Review* 73 (1989), 643–761, and summarizes his arguments in "Break up the Sports League Monopolies," in

Paul D. Staudohar and James A. Mangan, *The Business of Professional Sports* (Urbana and Chicago: University of Illinois Press, 1991), 152–74. The legal defense of sport leagues is offered by Gary R. Roberts, "Professional Sports and the Antitrust Laws," in Staudohar and Mangan, *The Business of Professional Sports*, 135–51. See also Myron C. Grauer, "Recognition of the National Football League as a Single Entity under Section 1 of the Sherman Act: Implications of the Consumer Welfare Model," *Michigan Law Review* 82 (October 1983), 1–59.

Legal scholars have expended considerable energy on the issue of condemnation of sports teams, especially in the wake of the Raiders' decisions; see Eric Allen Mitnick, "Anticipating an Instant Replay: *City of Oakland v. Oakland Raiders* [646 P.2d 835 (Cal.)]" *U.C. Davis Law Review* 17 (Spring 1984), 963–1,007; Susan Crabtree, "Public Use in Eminent Domain: Are There Limits after *Oakland Raiders* and *Poletown*?" *California Western Law Review* 20 (Fall 1983), 82–108; Michael Schiano, "Eminent Domain Exercised—Stare Decisis or a Warning: *City of Oakland v. Oakland Raiders*," *Pace Law Review* 4 (Fall 1983), 169–93; Steven M. Crafton, "Taking the Oakland Raiders: A Theoretical Reconsideration of the Concepts of Public Use and Just Compensation," *Emory Law Journal* 32 (Summer 1983), 857; Stephen R. Barnett, "High Court Rulings Show Contrasting Attitudes," *California Lawyer* (October 1982), 58–61; Julius L. Sackman, "Public Use—Updated (City of Oakland v. Oakland Raiders)," *Proceedings of the Institute on Planning, Zoning and Eminent Domain* (1983), 203–35; and Scott R. Carpenter, "*City of Oakland v. Oakland Raiders*: Defining the Parameters of Limitless Power," *Utah Law Review* (1983), 397–414.

Tax questions affect who owns professional sports teams, and thus their relations with places. The effect of federal taxes in the United States on sports teams are examined in a number of legal studies, including Michael L. Lewis, "Professional Sports Franchising and the IRS," *Washburn Law Review* 14 (Spring 1975), 321–29; Valerie Nelson Strandell, "The Impact of the 1976 Tax Reform Act on the Owners of Professional Sports Teams," *Journal of Contemporary Law* 4 (Spring 1978), 219–32; and Howard Zaritsky, "Taxation of Professional Sports Teams after 1976: A Whole New Ball Game," *William & Mary Law Review* 18 (Summer 1977), 679–702.

A growing body of academic literature, primarily in the sociology of sport, underscores the critical role of capitalism and economic power in the development of professional sports in the United States and Canada. A critical overview of this work is provided by William J. Morgan in *Leftist Theories of Sport: A Critique and Reconstruction* (Urbana and Chicago: University of Illinois Press, 1994). Particularly useful in this research has been work in the sociology of sport that is attentive to place issues, notably Richard Gruneau's *Class, Sports, and Social Development* (Amherst: University of Massachusetts Press, 1983); "The Political Economy of Professional Sport" by Rob Beamish in Jean Harvey and Hart Cantelon, eds., *Not Just a Game: Essays in Canadian Sport Sociology* (Ottawa: Ottawa University Press, 1988), 141–57; and Alan G. Ingham, Jeremy W. Howell, and Todd S. Schilperoort, "Professional Sports and Community: A Review and Exegesis," *Exercise and Sports Sciences Review* 15 (1987), 427–65. See also Richard Gruneau, "Elites, Class, and Corporate Power in Canadian Sport: Some Preliminary Findings," in F. Landry and W. A. K. Orba, eds., *Sociology and Legal Aspects of Sports and Leisure* (Miami: Symposia Specialists, 1978), 201–42; Alan Ingham and Stephen Hardy, "Sport, Structuration, Subjugation and Hegemony," *Theory, Culture and Society* 2 (1984), 85–103; and Terry R. Furst, "Social Change and the Commercialization of Professional Sports," *International Review of Sports Sociology* 6 (1971), 153–70.

The dominant role of business elites in professional sports is the subject of a number of studies, including Paul Hoch, *Rip off the Big Game: The Exploitation of Sports by the Power Elite* (Garden City, N.Y.: Doubleday, 1972); Don Kowett, *The Rich Who Own Sports* (New York: Random House, 1977), and J. Brower, "Professional Sports Team Ownership: Fun, Profit, and Ideology of the Power Elite," *Journal of Sport and Social Issues* 1 (1976), 16–51. Of particular interest is George Lipsitz's "Sports Stadia and Urban Development: A Tale of Three Cities," *Journal of Sport and Social Issues* 8 (Summer/Fall 1984), 1–18, which focuses on the role of economic elites in securing professional sports facilities in Houston, Los Angeles, and St. Louis.

Good case studies dealing with the connections between professional sports and cities are in short supply. Among the most useful are a trio by journalists that offer a wealth of details and insights into stadium building, expansion, relocation, and relations among baseball teams, leagues, and places. The best of this bunch is David Whitford's *Playing Hardball: The High-Stakes Battle for Baseball's New Franchises* (New York: Doubleday, 1993); Whitford's treatment of baseball's 1995 expansion is comprehensive, informed, and amusing, with a nuanced understanding of the dynamics of the expansion game and power relationships. In *Ballpark: Camden Yards and the Building of the American Dream* (New York: Simon & Schuster, 1993), Peter Richmond dissects Baltimore's stadium politics, the complex relationships between the Orioles and public officials, and the process that produced Orioles Park at Camden Yards and a new era in ballpark development. *Stadium for Rent: Tampa Bay's Quest for Major League Baseball* (Jefferson, N.C.: McFarland, 1993) by Bob Andelman is the bizarre saga of St. Petersburg's quest to win a place in major league baseball.

A handful of academic case studies also explore the linkages between places and professional sports. Bruce Kuklick's masterful examination of the rise and fall of Shibe Park and its Philadelphia neighborhood, *To Every Thing a Season: Shibe Park and Urban Philadelphia 1909–1976* (Princeton: Princeton University Press, 1991) captures the essence of the interplay between urban change, home teams, and the sports business. In *The Dodgers Move West* (Oxford University Press, 1987), Neil J. Sullivan has dissected the move of the Dodgers to Los Angeles in a detailed appraisal that treats many of the urban, economic, and political questions addressed here. Sullivan offers additional thoughts on the connections between places and major league baseball in *The Diamond Revolution: The Prospects for Baseball after the Collapse of Its Ruling Class* (New York: St. Martin's Press, 1992). The move of the Dodgers and the transfer of city land at Chavez Ravine for Walter O'Malley's stadium also are examined by Lee Elihu Lowenfish, "A Tale of Many Cities," *Journal of the West* 17 (July 1978), 71–82; Cary Henderson in "Los Angeles and the Dodger War, 1957–1962," *Southern California Quarterly* 62 (Fall 1980), 261–89; and Thomas S. Hines, "Housing, Baseball, and Creeping Socialism: The Battle of Chavez Ravine, Los Angeles, 1949–1959," *Journal of Urban History* 8 (February 1982), 123–43.

Charles C. Euchner explores critical aspects of the relationship between places and teams in the context of case studies of Baltimore and Camden Yards, Chicago and the White Sox, and Los Angeles and the Raiders in *Playing the Field: Why Sports Teams Move and Cities Fight to Keep Them* (Baltimore: Johns Hopkins University Press, 1993). Euchner's work has the added virtue for a political scientist of being framed by systematic concerns about political analysis. Both Euchner and Sullivan emphasize that the interplay between places and professional sports must be understood in the context of particular political systems and complex political economies. A particularly nuanced appreciation of these complexities is found in the case study of stadium politics in Chicago by John P. Pelissero, Beth M. Henschen, and Edward I. Sidlow, "Urban Regimes, Sports Stadiums, and the Politics of Economic Development Agendas in Chicago," *Policy Studies Review* 10 (Spring/Summer 1991), 117–29. Efforts to lure and keep teams in the Baltimore, Indianapolis, Philadelphia, San Francisco-Oakland, and Washington areas are examined in Kenneth L. Shropshire's *The Sports Franchise Game: Cities in Pursuit of Sports Franchises, Events, Stadiums, and Arenas* (Philadelphia: University of Pennsylvania Press, 1995).

Mention should also be made of Amy Klobuchar's *Uncovering the Dome* (Prospect Heights, Ill.: Waveland Press, 1986), a lively account of sports politics in the Twin Cities. Klobuchar's study was her senior essay at Yale; this author, having advised scores of undergraduate theses at Princeton, has not read a better senior research paper on urban politics. Another undergraduate effort, the report of the task force directed by the author at Princeton University in 1992, examines a number of the connections between places, teams, and leagues; see *Cities and Major League Sports*, Final Report, Spring 1992 Policy Task Force, Undergraduate Program, Woodrow Wilson School of Public and International Affairs, Princeton University (Princeton: Center of Comparative and Domestic Policy Studies, Princeton University, 1993).

Ballparks get almost all the attention in the scholarly and journalistic literature about sports facilities. A happy exception is Steven A. Riess' article on the development of the Los Angeles Coliseum, one of the earliest municipal stadiums in the United States, in "Power without Authority: Los Angeles' Elites and the Construction of the Coliseum," *Journal of Sport History* 8 (Spring 1981), 50–65. A nice sense of the evolution of arena development is provided by the text and photos in Joseph Durso, *Madison Square Garden: 100 Years of History* (New York: Simon and Schuster, 1979). David C. Petersen summarizes general design and siting approaches and a number of specific projects in *Convention Centers, Stadiums, and Arenas* (Washington, D.C.: Urban Land Institute, 1989). A great deal of useful information about contemporary arenas and stadiums can be found in Tom Dyja, ed., *The Complete Four Sport Stadium Guide* (New York: Balliett & Fitzgerald, 1994). Anyone interested in field research will enjoy *Major League Stadiums: A Vacation Planning Reference* (Jefferson, N.C.: McFarland, 1991) by Dan Dickinson and Kieran Dickinson, but their book is rapidly becoming dated as new ballparks replace more and more of the stadiums whose location, seating, prices, food, and amenities are discussed in this volume.

Michael Gershman's *Diamonds: The Evolution of the Ballpark* (Boston: Houghton Mifflin, 1993) is a magnificent history of the ballpark, with copious photos, drawings, and diagrams, played out against the changing context of the American city and metropolis. How ballparks and stadiums have evolved and their place in cities are discussed in Robert F. Bluthardt, "Fenway Park and the Golden Age of the Baseball Park," *Journal of Popular Culture* 21 (Summer 1987), 43–52; Michael V. Oriard, "Sports and Space," *Landscape* 21:1 (1976), 32–40, and Brian James Nelson, "Dialogue with the City: The Evolution of Baseball Parks," *Landscape* 29:1 (1986), 39–47. John Pastier makes a case for preserving old ballparks in "Diamonds Aren't Forever," *Historic Preservation* (July/August 1993), 26–33, 84–85. Ballparks are located, described, and discussed in Philip J. Lowry, *Green Cathedrals: The Ultimate Celebration of All 271 Major League and Negro League Ballparks Past and Present* (Reading, Mass.: Addison-Wesley, 1992); Michael Benson, *Ballparks of North America* (Jefferson, N.C.: McFarland, 1989); and Lowell Reidenbaugh, *Take Me out to the Ball Park* (St. Louis: Sporting News Publishing Company, 1983).

Court decisions provide detailed information about relocation, expansion, rival leagues, and other aspects of professional sports that affect connections with places. Among the more useful are the following decisions grouped by topic: antitrust and the merger of leagues: *Federal Baseball Club of Baltimore v. National League*, 259 U.S. 200 (1922); league controls over relocation: *State v. Milwaukee Braves, Inc.*, Trade Reg. Rep. (1966 Trade Cas.) PP 71738 (Wis. Cir. Ct. April 13, 1966); *Wisconsin v. Milwaukee Braves, Inc.*, 31 Wis.2d 699, 144 N.W.2d 1 (1966); *Washington v. American League*, 460 F.2d 654 (9th Cir. 1972); *San Francisco Seals, Ltd. v. National Hockey League*, 379 F.

Supp. 966 (C.D. Cal 1974); *HMC Management Corp. v. New Orleans Basketball Club*, 375 So.2d 700 (La. 1979); *Los Angeles Memorial Coliseum Commission v. National Football League*, 468 F. Supp. 154 (C.D. Cal. 1979); *Los Angeles Memorial Coliseum Commission v. National Football League*, 579 F. Supp. 58 (C.D. Cal. 1981); and *Los Angeles Memorial Coliseum Commission v. National Football League*, 726 F.2d 1381 (9th Cir. 1984); relocation and condemnation: *City of Oakland v. Oakland Raiders*, 123 Cal. App.3d 422 (1981); *City of Oakland v. Oakland Raiders*, 32 Cal. 3d 60, 646 P.2d 835, 183 Cal.Rptr. 673 (1982); *City of Oakland v. Superior Court of Monterey County*, 150 Cal. App.3d 267, 179 Cal.Rptr. 729 (1983); and *City of Baltimore v. Baltimore Football Club*, 624 F. Supp. 278 (D.C. Md. 1985); intrametropolitan relocation and lease obligations: *City of New York v. New York Jets Football Club, Inc.*, 90 Misc.2d 311, 394 N.Y.S.2d 799 (N.Y. Sup. Ct. 1977); league controls over expansion: *Mid-South Grizzlies v. National Football League*, 550 F. Supp. 558 (E.D. Pa. 1982); *Mid-South Grizzlies v. National Football League*, 720 F.2d 712 (3d Cir. 1983); and *National Basketball Association v. San Diego Clippers Basketball Club*, 815 F.2d 562 (9th Cir. 1987); disputes with rival leagues: *American Football League v. National Football League*, 205 F. Supp. 60 (D.C. Md. 1962); *American Football League v. National Football League*, 323 F.2d 124 (4th Cir. 1963); *Philadelphia World Hockey Club v. Philadelphia Hockey Club, Inc.*, 351 F. Supp. 462 (E.D. Pa. 1972); and *United States Football League v. National Football League*, 842 F.2d 1335 (2d Cir. 1988); league controls over ownership: *Levin v. NBA*, 385 F. Supp. 149 (S.D.N.Y. 1974); conflicts with other sports: *North American Soccer League v. National Football League*, 505 F. Supp. 659 (S.D. N.Y. 1980); and *North American Soccer League v. National Football League*, 670 F.2d 1249 (2d Cir. 1982); government authority to build sports facilities: *Martin v. City of Philadelphia*, 420 Pa. 14, 215 A.2d 894 (1966); *Bazell v. City of Cincinnati*, 13 Ohio St.2d 63, 233 N.E.2d 864 (1968); *Ginsberg v. City of Denver*, 164 Colo. 572, 436 P.2d 685 (1968); *New Jersey Sports & Exposition Authority v. McCrane*, 119 N.J. Super. 457, 292 A.2d 580 (App. Div. 1971); and *Alan v. County of Wayne*, 388 Mich. 210, 200 N.W.2d 628 (1972); use of public sports facilities by rival leagues: *Hecht v. Pro-Football, Inc.*, 444 F.2d 931 (D.C. Cir. 1971) and *Hecht v. Pro-Football, Inc.*, 570 F.2d 982 (D.C. Cir. 1977); stadium referendums: *Kelly v. Marylanders for Sports Sanity, Inc.*, 310 Md. 437, 530 A.2d 245 (1987); league television contracts: *United States v. National Football League*, 116 F. Supp. 319, 327 (E.D. Pa. 1953); and *United States v. National Football League*, 196 F. Supp. 445 (E.D. Pa. 1961); league and local television rights: *Chicago Professional Sports L.P. v. National Basketball Association*, 754 F. Supp. 1336 (N.D. Ill. 1991); and team rights to local broadcasts: *Pittsburgh Athletic Co. v. KQV Broadcasting Co.*, 24 F. Supp. 490 (W.D. Pa. 1938).

Congressional hearings also offer a valuable source of information on relocation, expansion, merger of leagues, sports facility development, television arrangements, and other elements of the relations between teams, leagues, government, places, and the public. The following hearings in the House of Representatives (all published by Washington, D.C.: U.S. Government Printing Office) on the organization of professional sports were particularly useful in the preparation of this study: *Study of Monopoly Power: Organized Baseball*, 82d Cong., 1st sess. (1952); *Organized Professional Team Sports*, 85th Cong., 1st sess. (1957); *Organized Team Sports*, 86th Cong., 1st sess. (1959); *Inquiry into Professional Sports*, 94th Cong., 2d sess. (1976); *Antitrust Policy and Professional Sports*, 97th Cong., 1st and 2d sess. (1984); *Professional Sports*, 99th Cong., 1st sess. (1985); *Baseball's Antitrust Exemption*, 103d Cong., 1st sess. (1994); and *Baseball's Antitrust Exemption*, 103d Cong., 2d sess. (1995).

Hearings on the same general subjects in the Senate include: *Subjecting Professional Baseball Clubs to Antitrust Laws*, 83d Cong., 2d sess. (1956); *Organized Professional Team Sports*, 85th Cong., 2d sess. (1958); *Organized Professional Team Sports*, 86th Cong., 1st sess. (1959); *Organized Professional Team Sports*, 86th Cong., 2d sess. (1960); *Professional Sports Antitrust Bill—1964*, 88th Cong., 2d sess. (1964); *Professional Sports Antitrust Bill—1965*, 89th Cong., 1st sess. (1965); *Professional Sports Antitrust Immunity*, 97th Cong., 2d sess. (1983); *Professional Sports Antitrust Immunity*, 99th Cong., 1st sess. (1986); *Baseball's Antitrust Immunity*, 102d Cong., 2d sess. (1993); and *Professional Baseball Teams and the Antitrust Laws*, 103d Cong., 2d sess. (1995).

On league mergers, the House hearings include *Professional Football League Merger*, 89th Congress, 2d sess. (1966) and *The Antitrust Laws and Organized Professional Team Sports Including Consideration of the Proposed Merger of the American and National Basketball Associations*, 92d Cong., 2d sess. (1972); and in the Senate, *Professional Basketball*, 92d Cong., 1st sess. (1972). Hearings on relocation in the House considered the *Professional Sports Team Community Protection Act*, 98th Cong., 2d sess. (1985); and in the Senate, *Professional Sports Community Protection Act of 1985*, 99th Cong., 1st sess. (1985) and *Professional Sports Team Community Protection Act*, 98th Cong., 2d sess. (1984). See also the Senate hearings on the *Federal Sports Act of 1972*, 92d Cong., 2d sess. (1972) and the House hearing on *Tax Issues Involved in the Sale or Transfer of Professional Sports Franchises*, 97th Cong., 1st sess. (1981).

Congressional hearings on broadcasting have covered a wide range of place issues, including territorial rights, blackouts, and local and network contract arrangements. House hearings include *Telecasting of Professional Sports Contests*, 85th Congress, 2d sess. (1958); *Telecasting of Professional Sports Contests*, 87th Cong., 1st sess. (1961); *Professional Sports Blackouts*, 93d Cong., 1st sess. (1973); *Sports Broadcasting Act of 1975*, 94th Cong., 1st sess. (1975); *Network Sports Practices*, 95th Cong., 1st sess. (1977); and *Sports Anti-Blackout Legislation—Oversight*, 95th Cong., 2d sess. (1978). In the

Senate, hearings have dealt with *Broadcasting and Telecasting Baseball Games*, 83d Cong., 1st sess. (1953); *Antitrust Implications of the Recent NFL Television Contract*, 100th Cong., 1st sess. (1987); *Blackout of Sporting Events on TV*, 92d Cong., 2nd sess. (1973); *Blackout of Sporting Events on TV*, 93d Cong., 1st sess. (1974); *TV Blackout of Sporting Events*, 94th Cong., 1st sess. (1976); and *Sports Programming and Cable Television*, 101st Cong., 1st sess. (1991).

No listing of useful sources for this kind of research would be complete without an acknowledgment of the wealth of information and insights provided by the hundreds of people who write about major league sports for newspapers and magazines. Through the wonders of electronic data bases, more and more of the products of these endeavors are widely available, certainly to the enrichment of this particular study. The more newspapers one has access to, however, the more one appreciates the *New York Times*. No newspaper in the United States or Canada comes close to the *Times* in the range and depth of its coverage of sports issues of the kind that concern this volume. Nor does any other publication have anywhere near the number of journalists dealing regularly with the complex questions raised by the interconnections between places and big league sports. Among the *Times* writers past and present whose work has been particularly valuable are Harvey Araton, Murray Chass, Arthur Daley, Joseph Durso, Gerald Eskanazi, Clyde Farnsworth, Thomas George, Sam Goldpaper, Thomas C. Hayes, Leonard Koppett, Joe Lapointe, Frank Litsky, Steven Lee Myers, Richard Sandomir, Calvin Sims, Claire Smith, and William N. Wallace.

The *Washington Post* provides solid coverage of general sports questions like relocation and stadium development, as well as excellent coverage of the complex local efforts to lure a baseball team, build a stadium for the Redskins, develop a new arena for the area's basketball and hockey team, and unravel the interconnected fates of Baltimore and Washington in the quest for baseball and football teams. Most helpful has been the work of Mark Asher, Paul Attner, Steve Berkowitz, and Thomas Boswell. The *Los Angeles Times* is also a first-rate source of information about sports issues, and has been especially strong in providing extensive coverage of the relocation issues, stadium problems and intercity competitions that have plagued the area and state. *USA Today* provides extensive coverage of sports, with timely work on issues like market size and relocation by Hal Bodley. The best of the rest of the press, primarily for their treatment of local sports controversies, were the *Atlanta Constitution, Boston Globe, Buffalo News, Chicago Tribune, Cincinnati Enquirer, Dallas Morning News, Denver Post, Houston Chronicle, Minneapolis Star, Montreal Gazette, Newark Star-Ledger, St. Louis Post Dispatch, Seattle Times*, and *Toronto Star*.

Two sports publications deserve special mention. *Sports Illustrated* changed many aspects of sports journalism; not the least was its attention to the business and political aspects of sports, realities that the traditional "good times" approach of the sports page usually ignored. Among the many writers whose work in *Sports Illustrated* has been most helpful in puzzling through the intricacies of the web of cities and professional sports have been Michael Farber, Ron Fimrite, Richard Hoffer, William Oscar Johnson, Tex Maule, and the team of Ray Kennedy and Nancy Williamson. The *Sporting News* has slowly transformed itself from "baseball's bible" to covering all four team sports with frequent attention to the concerns of this study. Among the contributors whose work has been most useful are Bob Glauber, Chris Mortensen, and Jack Olsen.

A few other sources should be mentioned. The *1996 Information Please Sports Almanac* (New York: Houghton Mifflin, 1996), which appears annually, provides a wealth of information about professional team sports; it is more detailed than a similar volume published by *Sports Illustrated*. Any research on major league sports benefits from use of the galaxy of reference books published annually by the *Sporting News*—the *Baseball Guide* and *Baseball Register*, the *Official NBA Guide*, the *Pro Football Guide*, and the *Complete Hockey Book*. For baseball, listings for all the places with major league teams are provided by Donald Dewey and Nicholas Acocella, *Encyclopedia of Major League Baseball Teams* (New York: HarperCollins, 1994); Peter Filichia has catalogued *Professional Baseball Franchises: From the Abbeville Athletics to the Zanesville Indians* (New York: Facts On File, 1993). Harvey Frommer has compiled *Sports Roots: How Nicknamers, Trophies, Competitions, and Expressions in the World of Sports Came to Be* (New York: Atheneum, 1979). And Rand McNally suggests the best hometowns for sports in *Sports Places Rated: Ranking America's Best Places to Enjoy Sports* (Chicago: Rand McNally, 1986).

Index

THE INDEX includes places, people, teams, organizations, and sports facilities. Cities and metropolitan areas are combined in a single entry, with the exception of San Francisco-Oakland-San Jose, Tampa-St. Petersburg, and Washington-Baltimore, which have separate entries for each, as well as a reference to the metropolitan area. The New York and New Jersey components of the New York-New Jersey area have separate entries. Relocations of a team from a city, i.e., the move of the Boston Braves from Boston, are indexed under the team; moves and threatened moves of a team to a place, i.e., the relocation of the Braves to Milwaukee, are indexed under the place.

ABOUT THE AUTHOR

Michael N. Danielson is B. C. Forbes Professor of Public Affairs and Professor of Politics and Public Affairs at Princeton University, where he directs the Center for Domestic and Comparative Policy Studies. He is the author of *The Politics of Exclusion* and *Profits and Politics in Paradise: The Development of Hilton Head Island.*